KS2 Success SATs

Level 4

Maths

LEARN AND PRACTISE

Paul Broadbent

Contents

Using and applying mathematics

Word problems 4
Problems and puzzles 6
Rules and patterns 8

Counting and understanding numbers

Decimals 10
Ordering and rounding decimals 12
Fractions 14
Fractions, decimals, percentages 16

Knowing and using number facts

Number facts 18
Multiples and factors 20

Calculating

Mental addition 22
Mental subtraction 24
Written addition 26
Written subtraction 28
Multiplication 30
Division 32
Fractions of quantities 34
Percentages of quantities 36

Understanding shape

Symmetry 38

2D shapes 40

3D shapes 42

Coordinates 44

Angles 46

Measuring

Measures 48

Perimeter and area 50

Reading the time 52

Handling data

Handling data 54

Glossary

Glossary 56

Answers

Answer booklet (detach from centre of book) 1–4

3

Word problems

Answering problems

If you have a word problem to solve, it may help to follow these four stages.

Four tickets for a concert cost £58 altogether. What is the cost for three tickets?

1. Read the problem.
Try to picture the problem and imagine going through it in real life.

2. Sort out the calculations.
58 ÷ 4 will give the price of one ticket, then multiply the answer by 3 to find the cost of three tickets.

3. Answer the calculations.
58 ÷ 4 = 14.5
14.5 × 3 = 43.5

4. Answer the problem.
Look back at the question – what is it asking?
The cost for three tickets is £43.50.

 Top Tip *When you divide with money, you need a decimal answer rather than a remainder.*

Multi-step problems

Word problems can have different numbers of calculations to answer before you reach the final answer.

There are 26 boxes of light bulbs in a storeroom. There are 15 light bulbs in each box. How many light bulbs are there in total?

```
      26
×     15
     130
     260
=    390
```

There are 390 light bulbs altogether.

A square room has sides 8m long. A carpet costs £20 per square metre. What is the cost to carpet the whole room?

Step 1
Area of room is 8 × 8 = 64m².

Step 2
64 × 20 = 1280

Step 3
The carpet costs £1280.

 Key words   remainder   area

4

Answering problems

1. A chef makes 340 sandwiches for a wedding. He has made 4 sandwiches per person. How many people are expected at the wedding?

2. It is 291km from Norwich to York. A bus travels there and back every day for 5 days. How far does the bus travel in total for these 5 days? _____ km

3. A garden shed costs £487.35. It costs an extra £94.80 to have it delivered and put up. What will the total cost be? £ _____

4. Ali wants to raise £200 sponsorship by cleaning cars. He charges £6 to clean a car. What is the fewest number of cars he needs to clean to raise £200?

5. The cost of a holiday is £489 in March and £945 in August. What is the difference in cost between the two months? £ _____

6. Rebecca needs another 373 badges to have 2000 in her collection. How many badges does she have?

6

Multi-step problems

1. In an office store there are 28 boxes of folders. Each box holds 36 folders, but one of the boxes has had 19 folders removed. How many folders are there in total?

2. A shirt costs £28 and a jumper costs £31. There is a 10% sale on these items. What will the total cost be in the sale?

3. Josh uses 75g of flour, 40g of sugar and 53g of butter to make cookies. He divides the mixture equally to make 8 cookies. What is the weight of the mixture for each cookie?

4. For 38 weeks of the year, a gardener works 8 hours a day for 5 days of the week. How many hours does he work in total for a year?

5. A pack of six cartons of drink contains 942ml of drink in total. An individual can holds 168ml. Which holds more, a can or a carton?

5

TOTAL MARKS 11

Problems and puzzles

Reasoning

If you need to think carefully about a way to solve a problem, you are likely to be using reasoning skills to make sense of it. Some maths questions look simple but involve a lot of thought. It may help to explain the problem to someone else, describing the way you could try to solve it.

I'm thinking of a number.

If I **double** it, the answer is 14 less than 40.

What is my number?

To answer this, work backwards through the problem.

14 less than 40 is 26. This is double the mystery number, so find half of 26.

The mystery number is 13.

Finding all possibilities

Some types of problems often have lots of different choices of answer and the skill is finding the correct one. You need to work systematically, making lists of all the possible answers to find the right one.

Robert's parcel cost £2.00 to post. He put 6 stamps on the parcel and each stamp was either 30p or 40p in value. How many of each stamp did he stick on his parcel?

Draw a table to help you answer this:

Number of stamps	30p stamps	40p stamps
1	30p	40p
2	60p	**80p**
3	90p	120p
4	**120p**	160p
5	150p	200p
6	180p	240p
7	210p	280p

Look for 6 stamps that total £2.00.

4 × 30p stamps and 2 × 40p stamps total £2.00.

USING AND APPLYING MATHEMATICS — LEARN

 Key words — double

6

Reasoning

1. I'm thinking of a number. If I halve the number and then add 8, the answer is 20. What number am I thinking of?

2. Sam bought three different coloured T-shirts. The white and black T-shirts cost a total of £14. The black and green T-shirts cost a total of £17. The white and green T-shirts cost a total of £15. What is the cost of each T-shirt?

   Black T-shirt £ ☐   White T-shirt £ ☐   Green T-shirt £ ☐

3. Ben's father was 33 when Ben was born. 8 years ago Ben's father was twice as old as Ben is now. How old is Ben?

4. These are the bills for three meals at a cafe.

1 cake	2 cakes	1 tea
1 coffee	2 teas	2 coffees
Total: £1.70	Total: £3.20	Total: £2.30

   What is the cost of each item?

   1 cake = ☐ p   1 coffee = ☐ p   1 tea = ☐ p

Finding all possibilities

1. Which two square numbers total 100? _____

2. Ryan has some 20p and 10p coins. He has two more 10p coins than 20p coins and altogether he has £2.90. How many of each coin does he have? _____

3. **A** and **B** are two different whole numbers. A + B = 121   A is 35 greater than B.

   What are the numbers **A** and **B**?   A = _____   B = _____

4. Parveen buys some ice-creams and some lollies. Ice-creams cost £1.20 each and lollies cost 90p each. She buys three more ice-creams than lollies and spends exactly £12. How many of each does she buy?

   _____ ice-creams   _____ lollies

TOTAL MARKS 8

Rules and patterns

Number sequences

A **sequence** is a list of numbers which usually have a pattern. You can often find the pattern or rule in a sequence by looking at the **difference** between the numbers.

What is the next number in this sequence?

39   35   31   27   _____

Each number is 4 less than the previous one, so the next number is 23.

Formulae and equations

A **formula** (plural is formulae) uses letters or words to give a rule.

Each table in a hall has 6 chairs around it.

How many chairs are needed for 8 tables? $6 \times 8 = 48$ chairs

How many chairs are needed for n tables? $6n$ chairs

Equations have symbols or letters instead of numbers in a calculation.

$\Delta + 2 = 15$

$? - 5 = 9$

$2y = 14$

You need to work out what the symbol or letter stands for. Use the numbers to help you and say it as a sentence. For example, What added to 2 makes 15?

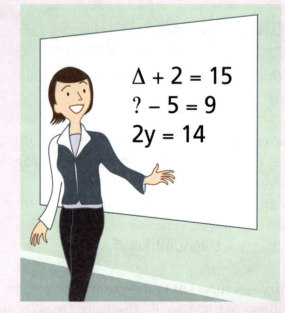

Top Tip: $2y$ means y multiplied by 2. The × sign for multiplication isn't used in equations because it might look like a letter.

Key words: sequence   difference   formula   equation

Number sequences

Write the missing numbers in these sequences.

1 [ ]   38   46   54   62   [ ]

2 95   [ ]   [ ]   50   35   20

3 425   450   [ ]   500   [ ]   550

4 79   [ ]   71   [ ]   63   59

In these sequences each number is double the previous number. Write the missing numbers. You will need to use decimals for some sequences.

5 [ ]   [ ]   8   16   32   [ ]   [ ]

6 [ ]   [ ]   44   88   176   [ ]   [ ]

7 [ ]   [ ]   10   20   40   [ ]   [ ]

8 [ ]   [ ]   30   60   120   [ ]   [ ]

[ ] 8

Formulae and equations

Write the value of each symbol or letter.

1 $16 + \triangle = 23$ $\triangle =$ [ ]   5 $y + 22 = 38$ $y =$ [ ]

2 $? - 8 = 7$ $? =$ [ ]   6 $40 - b = 15$ $b =$ [ ]

3 $9\blacklozenge = 36$ $\blacklozenge =$ [ ]   7 $7n = 35$ $n =$ [ ]

4 $? \div 6 = 3$ $? =$ [ ]   8 $27 \div t = 3$ $t =$ [ ]

Top Tip If you're finding it difficult to work out the value of a letter, write it out again using a box instead of the letter. You can then try different numbers in the box to see if the equation works.

[ ] 8

TOTAL MARKS [ ] 16

PRACTISE USING AND APPLYING MATHEMATICS

Decimals

Decimal numbers

Decimal numbers are whole numbers divided into tenths, hundredths and thousandths. A decimal point is used to separate whole numbers from decimals.

Look at these number lines.

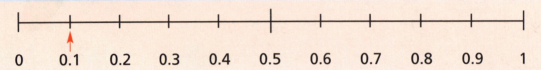

This shows tenths. 0.1 is the same as $\frac{1}{10}$.

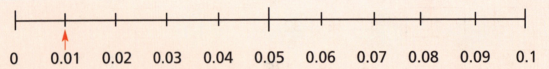

This shows hundredths. 0.01 is the same as $\frac{1}{100}$.

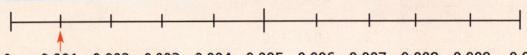

This shows thousandths. 0.001 is the same as $\frac{1}{1000}$.

Multiplying and dividing by 10 and 100

To multiply by 10:
Move the digits one place to the left and fill the space with zero if needed.

$17.4 \times 10 = 174$
$238 \times 10 = 2380$

To multiply by 100:
Move the digits two places to the left and fill the spaces with zeros if needed.

$38.9 \times 100 = 3890$
$0.08 \times 100 = 8$

To divide by 10:
Move the digits one place to the right.

$17.8 \div 10 = 1.78$
$206 \div 10 = 20.6$

To divide by 100:
Move the digits two places to the right.

$49 \div 100 = 0.49$
$385 \div 100 = 3.85$

Decimal numbers

Circle the fraction that is the same as each decimal number.

1 0.8   8   8/10   8/100   8/1000

2 0.007   7   7/10   7/100   7/1000

3 0.02   2   2/10   2/100   2/1000

4 0.63   63   63/10   63/100   63/1000

5 0.5   1/5   1/4   1/2   3/4

6 0.75   1/5   1/4   1/2   3/4

6

Multiplying and dividing by 10 and 100

Write the answers to these.

1 0.9 × 10 =

2 1.67 × 10 =

3 5.02 × 100 =

4 38.4 × 100 =

5 13 ÷ 10 =

6 9.7 ÷ 10 =

7 405 ÷ 100 =

8 28 ÷ 100 =

9 21.5 × 100 =

10 21.5 ÷ 100 =

 Top Tip Putting a zero on the end of a decimal doesn't change the number. 1.2 is the same as 1.20 and 1.200.

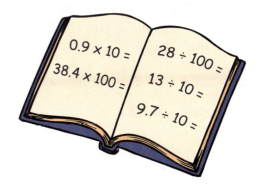

10

TOTAL MARKS 16

PRACTISE

COUNTING AND UNDERSTANDING NUMBERS

11

Ordering and rounding decimals

Ordering decimals

Putting decimals in order is just like putting whole numbers in order – you need to look carefully at the value of each **digit**.

35.2cm   34.85cm   45.16cm   44.78cm   45.08cm   34.8cm

Write these flowers in order of size, starting with the tallest.

Write them out one under the other, lining up the **decimal points**.	Compare the digits from left to right and re-order the numbers.
35.2cm 34.85cm 45.16cm 44.78cm 45.08cm 34.8cm	45.16cm 45.08cm 44.78cm 35.2cm 34.85cm 34.8cm

Rounding decimals

Decimals are usually rounded to the nearest whole number or nearest tenth.

Rounding to the nearest whole number:	**Rounding to the nearest tenth:**
Look at the tenths digit. If it is 5 or more, round up to the next whole number. If it is less than 5, the units digit stays the same. 8.5 rounds up to 9. 3.46 rounds down to 3.	Look at the hundredths digit. If it is 5 or more, round up to the next tenth. If it is less than 5, the tenth digit stays the same. 6.76 rounds up to 6.8. 4.347 rounds down to 4.3.

 Key words   digit   decimal point

Ordering decimals

Write each set of decimals in order in the boxes to make these correct.

1 4.7   7.4   7.7   4.4   ☐ < ☐ < ☐ < ☐

2 29.1 12.9 19.2 9.2   ☐ > ☐ > ☐ > ☐

3 3.58 5.83 5.38 8.35   ☐ > ☐ > ☐ > ☐

4 2.46 19.23 2.09 19.18   ☐ < ☐ < ☐ < ☐

5 6.06 60.6 60.66 60.06   ☐ < ☐ < ☐ < ☐

6 5.1   15.51 15.5 5.15   ☐ > ☐ > ☐ > ☐

Top Tip: < and > are symbols used to compare numbers.
< means *is less than*. For example: 9.57 < 9.75
> means *is greater than*. For example: 0.9 > 0.78

6

Rounding decimals

Round each amount to the nearest whole number.

1 27.6cm → ☐ cm   4 20.5g → ☐ g

2 5.92ml → ☐ ml   5 11.08km → ☐ km

3 £83.49 → £ ☐

Round each amount to the nearest tenth.

6 £7.07 → £ ☐

7 5.364 litres → ☐ litres

8 15.51m → ☐ m

9 9.828kg → ☐ kg

10 42.339km → ☐ km

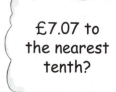

£7.07 to the nearest tenth?

10

TOTAL MARKS 16

13

Fractions

Types of fractions

Look at these three types of fractions.

1. A **proper fraction**, such as $\frac{2}{5}$, which is less than 1.

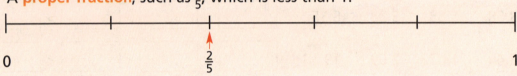

2. An **improper fraction**, such as $\frac{11}{4}$, which is greater than 1.

   These oranges show 11 quarters, or $\frac{11}{4}$, which is the same as $2\frac{3}{4}$.

3. A **mixed number**, such as $3\frac{1}{5}$, which has whole numbers and fractions.

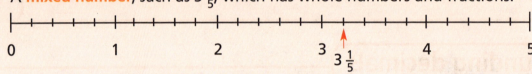

Improper fractions can be converted to mixed numbers:

$\frac{14}{3}$ is the same as $4\frac{2}{3}$. Divide 14 by 3, which is 4, remainder 2. In this example, the remainder is $\frac{2}{3}$ of a whole number.

 Top Tip The **denominator** (bottom number) shows the number of equal parts in total. The **numerator** (top number) shows how many equal parts are taken.

Equivalent fractions

Equivalent fractions have different numerators and denominators but have the same value.

$\frac{2}{3} = \frac{4}{6}$

A fraction can be changed into its equivalent by multiplying the numerator and denominator by the same amount.

$\frac{3 \times 4}{4 \times 4} = \frac{12}{16}$

You can reduce a fraction to an equivalent fraction by dividing the top and bottom by the same number.

$\frac{40 \div 10}{50 \div 10} = \frac{4}{5}$

Key words: proper fraction   improper fraction   mixed number   denominator   numerator   equivalent fractions

Types of fractions

Match each improper fraction to the mixed number which has the same value. One has been done for you.

1. $\frac{21}{5}$
2. $\frac{7}{3}$
3. $\frac{9}{5}$
4. $\frac{7}{4}$
5. $\frac{8}{3}$
6. $\frac{11}{3}$
7. $\frac{13}{5}$
8. $\frac{5}{2}$

$\frac{9}{2}$ —— $4\frac{1}{2}$

$1\frac{4}{5}$ $4\frac{1}{5}$ $1\frac{3}{4}$ $2\frac{2}{3}$ $2\frac{1}{3}$ $2\frac{1}{2}$ $2\frac{3}{5}$ $3\frac{2}{3}$

8

Equivalent fractions

Complete these equivalent fractions.

1. $\frac{1}{2} = \frac{12}{\Box}$

2. $\frac{2}{16} = \frac{\Box}{8}$

3. $\frac{\Box}{10} = \frac{30}{100}$

4. $\frac{6}{18} = \frac{1}{\Box}$

5. $\frac{2}{3} = \frac{\Box}{15}$

6. $\frac{20}{25} = \frac{\Box}{5}$

7. $\frac{3}{\Box} = \frac{12}{16}$

8. $\frac{2}{5} = \frac{6}{\Box}$

8

TOTAL MARKS 16

Fractions, decimals, percentages

Percentages and fractions

Percentages are simply fractions out of 100. That's what per cent means: out of 100. % is the percentage sign.

In a tile pattern of 100 square tiles, 40 are coloured red.

40% of the tiles are red.

Another tile pattern of 20 square tiles has 8 red tiles.

This also means 40% of the tiles are red.

To change fractions to percentages, make them out of 100. This means you need to find an equivalent fraction with the denominator 100.

$\frac{2}{5}$ is equivalent to $\frac{40}{100}$.

$\frac{2}{5}$ = 40%

To change per cent to fraction, write the percentage as a fraction out of 100 and then simplify.

25% is $\frac{25}{100}$, which is the same as $\frac{1}{4}$.

Equivalent values

Decimals	0.1	0.2	0.3	0.4	0.5	0.6	0.7	0.8	0.9	0.25	0.75
Fractions	$\frac{1}{10}$	$\frac{1}{5}$	$\frac{3}{10}$	$\frac{2}{5}$	$\frac{1}{2}$	$\frac{3}{5}$	$\frac{7}{10}$	$\frac{4}{5}$	$\frac{9}{10}$	$\frac{1}{4}$	$\frac{3}{4}$
Per cent	10%	20%	30%	40%	50%	60%	70%	80%	90%	25%	75%

Percentages and decimals

Converting between percentages and decimals is easy.

Per cent to decimal:

Divide the percentage by 100.

60% is the same as 0.6.

35% is the same as 0.35.

Decimal to per cent:

Multiply the decimal by 100.

0.7 is the same as 70%.

0.25 is the same as 25%.

 Key words — percentage

Percentages and fractions

Change these maths test scores to percentages.

1 Leah $\frac{7}{10}$ →   ☐ %

2 Ryan $\frac{15}{20}$ →   ☐ %

3 Josh $\frac{4}{5}$ →   ☐ %

4 Gita $\frac{33}{50}$ →   ☐ %

5 Beth $\frac{15}{25}$ →   ☐ %

6 Which child has the highest percentage score? _____

 Top Tip *If you find it easier, write the fraction as a decimal and then multiply by 100. $\frac{3}{4}$ is 0.75, which is the same as 75%.*

 6

Equivalent values

Read and answer these questions.

1 What is nought point eight as a percentage?   ☐ %

2 Write twenty per cent as a decimal.   ☐

3 What is three quarters as a decimal?   ☐

4 What is half as a percentage?   ☐ %

4

Percentages and decimals

Write the missing percentage or decimal to complete this table.

0.3		0.94	0.05		
	60%			1%	26%

 6

TOTAL MARKS ☐ 16

17

Number facts

Multiplication and division facts

Here are all the multiplication and division facts to 100. Cover up different numbers in the grid and say the hidden numbers as quickly as possible.

×	1	2	3	4	5	6	7	8	9	10
1	1	2	3	4	5	6	7	8	9	10
2	2	4	6	8	10	12	14	16	18	20
3	3	6	9	12	15	18	21	24	27	30
4	4	8	12	16	20	24	28	32	36	40
5	5	10	15	20	25	30	35	40	45	50
6	6	12	18	24	30	36	42	48	54	60
7	7	14	21	28	35	42	49	56	63	70
8	8	16	24	32	40	48	56	64	72	80
9	9	18	27	36	45	54	63	72	81	90
10	10	20	30	40	50	60	70	80	90	100

$9 \times 3 = 27$ $27 \div 3 = 9$
$3 \times 9 = 27$ $27 \div 9 = 3$

Top Tip Remember that 3 × 8 gives the same answer as 8 × 3, so you only have to learn half the facts.

These are the facts that cause the most problems:

3 × 8   4 × 7   4 × 8   4 × 9   6 × 7
6 × 8   7 × 8   9 × 6   7 × 9   8 × 9

Learn one fact a day – it will only take 10 days! Try this: every time you go through a doorway at home, say the fact out loud. You'll soon know it off by heart.

Square numbers

The numbers in the green squares above are square numbers.

1 × 1 = 1   2 × 2 = 4   3 × 3 = 9   4 × 4 = 16   5 × 5 = 25
6 × 6 = 36   7 × 7 = 49   8 × 8 = 64   9 × 9 = 81   10 × 10 = 100

Learn these special numbers. Why do you think they are called square numbers?

 Key words — square number

Multiplication and division facts

1 9 × 7 = ☐

2 15 ÷ 3 = ☐

3 7 × 6 = ☐

4 36 ÷ 9 = ☐

5 8 × 4 = ☐

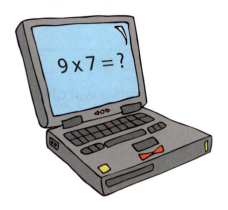

6 Divide twenty-eight by seven. ☐

7 What is eight multiplied by three? ☐

8 What is fifty-six divided by eight? ☐

9 Multiply six by nine. ☐

10 What number multiplied by five equals forty-five? ☐

10

Square numbers

Answer these questions.

1 9 × 9 = _____

2 7 × 7 = _____

3 Here are some number cards. 7 4 8 6 2

Use two of the cards as digits to make a square number. _____

4 Write the next square number after four. _____

5 Explain why 100 is a square number. _____

_____

6 Circle all the numbers that are square numbers.

22   24   16   15   25   14

6

TOTAL MARKS ☐ 16

19

Multiples and factors

Factors

Factors are numbers that will divide exactly into other numbers. It is useful to put factors of numbers into pairs.

Factors of 21 → (1, 21), (3, 7)   21 has 4 factors.

Factors of 18 → (1, 18), (2, 9), (3, 6)   18 has 6 factors.

Did you know that numbers always have an even number of factors, unless it is a square number? Try it – how many factors has 16 or 25 got?

Top Tip: A *prime number* only has two factors, 1 and itself. For example, 23 is a prime number as it can only be divided exactly by 1 and 23.

Multiples

A **multiple** is a number made by multiplying together two other numbers. So the multiples of:

2 are 2, 4, 6, 8, 10 … and so on.   3 are 3, 6, 9, 12, 15 … and so on.

Rules of divisibility

These are rules to test whether a number is a multiple of 2, 3, 4, 5, 6, 8, 9 and 10. A whole number can be divided by:

2, if the last digit is even. — 56, 204, 4350

3, if the sum of its digits can be divided by 3. — 435 (4 + 3 + 5 = 12), 3840 (3 + 8 + 4 + 0 = 15)

4, if the last two digits can be divided by 4. — 184, 740, 2364

5, if the last digit is 0 or 5. — 920, 175, 6085

6, if it is even and divisible by 3. — 828, 504, 126

8, if half of the number is divisible by 4. — 240, 112, 328, 488

9, if the sum of its digits is divisible by 9. — 495, 108, 585, 270

10, if the last digit is 0. — 760, 980, 370, 160

 Key words   factor   prime number   multiple

Factors

1 Circle the numbers that are **not** factors of 24.

1   2   3   4   5   6   7   8   9

2 Write the missing factors for 32.

(1, 32) (☐ , ☐) (☐ , ☐)

3 Write a factor of 30 that is greater than 12. ☐

4 Write the factors for 49 in order, starting with the smallest.

_____

4

Multiples

Write each of these four numbers in the correct place on this Venn diagram.

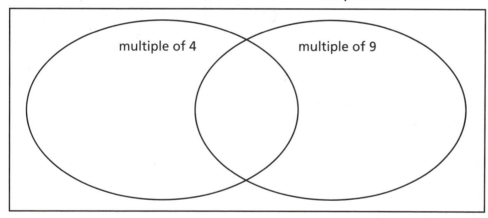

48
36
27
64

4

Rules of divisibility

1 Can 435 be divided exactly by 9? _____

2 Jo says, "Only numbers ending in 5 are divisible by 5."
   Is he correct? Write YES or NO. _____

3 Explain how you know. _____

4 What is the smallest whole number that is divisible
   by three and four? _____

4

TOTAL MARKS 12

Mental addition

Mental methods for addition

When you add numbers in your head, the first thing you should do is look at the numbers to help you choose the best method to find the answer. These are a few possible methods, but choose the one that works for you.

Use patterns:

6 + 7 = 13

86 + 7 = 93

60 + 70 = 130

0.6 + 0.7 = 1.3

Use rounding:

37 + 9 ➜ 37 + 10 − 1 = 46

23 + 19 ➜ 23 + 20 − 1 = 42

2.5 + 3.9 ➜ 2.5 + 4 − 0.1 = 6.4

Use near doubles:

18 + 19 = 18 + 18 + 1 = 37

25 + 26 = 25 + 25 + 1 = 51

1.6 + 1.7 = 1.6 + 1.6 + 0.1 = 3.3

Adding 2-digit numbers

If you need to add two big numbers in your head, it helps to break the numbers up and add the tens, then the ones.

85 + 57 Use these three steps:

1. Hold the bigger number in your head: 85.
2. Break 57 into 50 + 7. Add the tens: 85 + 50 = 135.
3. Add the ones: 135 + 7 = 142.

Adding decimals

To add decimals in your head, you may find it easier to add the whole numbers, then add the tenths. If the tenths total more than 1, you just add 1 more to the whole number total.

What is the **sum** of 4.6 and 3.8?

4 + 3 = 7   0.6 + 0.8 = 1.4   So, 7 + 1.4 = 8.4

 Key words — sum

22

Mental methods for addition

Choose a mental method and write the answers to these.

1 What number is nineteen more than fifty-seven?

2 In Year 5 there are two classes. One has 28 pupils, the other has 27. How many children are there in the year in total?

3 Add together sixty and ninety.

4 A bus has 34 passengers and another 17 get on the bus. How many passengers are there altogether on the bus now?

5 What is the total weight of two cakes weighing 2.5kg and 2.6kg? kg

5

Adding 2-digit numbers

Join five pairs of numbers that total 124. One pair has been completed for you.

28   33   87   96   62
     62
  37   91   89
79   45   35

5

Adding decimals

Answer these.

1 Add three point seven to six point five.

2 5.9 + 3.6 =

3 What is one point eight plus four point four?

4 2.1 + 7.9 =

5 What is double four point six?

6 5.7 + 2.8 =

6

TOTAL MARKS 16

Mental subtraction

Mental methods for subtraction

When you subtract numbers in your head, look at the numbers to help you choose the best method to find the answer. Here are some possible methods, but choose the one that works for you.

Use patterns:	Use rounding:	Use inverses:
13 − 8 = 5	24 − 9 → 24 − 10 + 1 = 15	25 − ☐ = 18
53 − 8 = 45	35 − 19 → 35 − 20 + 1 = 16	18 + 7 = 25
130 − 80 = 50	6.5 − 3.9 → 6.5 − 4 + 0.1 = 2.6	So 25 − 7 = 18
1.3 − 0.8 = 0.5		

Counting on

A really good method for a take-away or subtraction is to find the difference between the numbers by counting on.

What is the difference between 38 and 64?

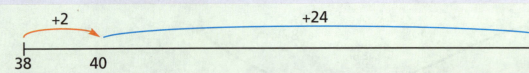

This number line shows exactly what goes on in your head.

Count on from 38 to 40. Hold the 2 in your head.

40 to 64 is 24.   24 + 2 is 26.   So 64 − 38 = 26

Top Tip: If it helps, draw a quick number line and show the steps. Remember to put the smallest number on the left and the largest on the right.

Subtracting decimals

To subtract decimals in your head, try counting on from the smaller decimal to the next whole number and then counting on to the larger decimal.

Subtract 3.8 from 7.4. → 3.8 on to 4 is 0.2 (hold that in your head).
→ 4 on to 7.4 is 3.4. → 3.4 added to 0.2 is 3.6.

7.4 − 3.8 = 3.6

Mental methods for subtraction

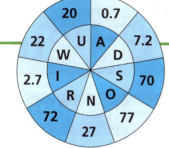

Use a mental method to answer these subtractions and write the matching letters to find the code words. You will get one mark per letter.

1. 150 – 80 = ☐ → ☐
    110 – 90 = ☐ → ☐
    34 – 7 = ☐ → ☐

2. 81 – 9 = ☐ → ☐
    1.4 – 0.7 = ☐ → ☐
    6.6 – 3.9 = ☐ → ☐
    46 – 19 = ☐ → ☐

3. 77 – 55 = ☐ → ☐
    5.4 – 2.7 = ☐ → ☐
    58 – 31 = ☐ → ☐
    9.1 – 1.9 = ☐ → ☐

4. 120 – 50 = ☐ → ☐
    100 – 73 = ☐ → ☐
    96 – 19 = ☐ → ☐
    51 – 29 = ☐ → ☐

☐ 15

Counting on

Write the five missing numbers on this difference grid.

	53	17	84
25		8	
96	43		12
60		43	

☐ 5

Subtracting decimals

Use these numbers to answer the following: 8.3   2.4   4.9   7.5   5.6

1. Which two numbers have a difference of 3.2? ☐ ☐

2. Which number is 4.6 less than 9.5? ☐

3. Which two numbers have a difference of 0.8? ☐ ☐

4. What is the answer if you subtract the smallest number from the greatest number? ☐

☐ 4

TOTAL MARKS ☐ 24

Written addition

Written addition

When you add numbers using this written method, make sure you line up the **columns** carefully.

What is 3492 added to 2631?

Step 1
2 + 1 = 3

```
   3492
+  2631
   ────
      3
```

Step 2
90 + 30 = 120

```
   3492
+  2631
   ────
     23
    1
```

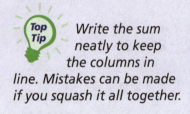 *Top Tip: Write the sum neatly to keep the columns in line. Mistakes can be made if you squash it all together.*

Step 3
100 + 400 + 600 = 1100

```
   3492
+  2631
   ────
    123
   1 1
```

Step 4
1000 + 3000 + 2000 = 6000

```
   3492
+  2631
   ────
   6123
   1 1
```

Adding decimals

When you add decimals, remember to line up the **decimal points**. The method is the same as with whole numbers.

What is the total of 17.9, 3.8 and 8.64?

1. Write them in a column, lining up the decimal points.
2. Start by adding from the right-hand column.
3. Keep going left until all the columns have been added.

```
    1 7 . 9
        3 . 8
+       8 . 6 4
    ─────────
    3 0 . 3 4
     2 2
```

 Key words column   decimal point

Written addition

Write in the missing numbers to complete these additions.

```
1      4 6 1 ▢         3      1 8 4 9
     + 3 ▢ 4 8              + 3 6 6 ▢
       ─────                  ───────
       8 2 6 7                  5 5 ▢ 3

2      2 1 ▢ 5         4      4 ▢ 9 4
     + 5 4 1 ▢              + 3 7 ▢ 6
       ─────                  ───────
       7 5 3 1                8 0 8 0
```

Calculate these additions.

5   2399 + 2600 = ▢   7   4067 + 1188 = ▢

6   2787 + 4251 = ▢   8   5536 + 3546 = ▢

Adding decimals

Complete these additions.

```
1    8.3        2   27.8       3    5.7       4    1.1
    19.4            9.2            30.9            2.8
+    6.5        + 13.6         +   4.4        + 26.5
   ─────          ─────           ─────          ─────
```

Write the total weight for each group of parcels.

5   4.7kg, 9.5kg, 12.3kg   = ▢ kg

6   15.4kg, 11.8kg, 3.9kg   = ▢ kg

7   10.1kg, 6.6kg, 8.8kg   = ▢ kg

8   4.2kg, 24.1kg, 14.2kg   = ▢ kg

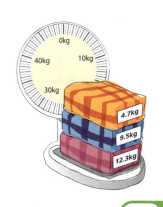

TOTAL MARKS   16

Written subtraction

Written subtraction

If you can't work out a subtraction in your head, this is one method you can try.

What is 3674 subtract 1738?

Step 1

Rename 70 + 4 as 60 + 14.

14 − 8 = 6

```
  3 6 ⁶7 ¹4
−  1 7 3 8
_____
           6
```

Step 2

60 − 30 = 30.

```
  3 6 ⁶7 ¹4
−  1 7 3 8
_____
         3 6
```

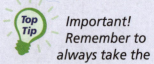

Important! Remember to always take the bottom number away from the top number.

Step 3

Rename 3000 + 600 as 2000 + 1600

1600 − 700 = 900.

```
  ²3 ¹6 ⁶7 ¹4
−    1 7 3 8
_____
       9 3 6
```

Step 4

2000 − 1000 = 1000.

```
  ²3 ¹6 ⁶7 ¹4
−    1 7 3 8
_____
     1 9 3 6
```

Number line method

Another written method to try uses a number line to find the difference between the numbers by counting on.

What is the difference between 126.8 and 173?

1. Draw a blank number line from 126.8 to 173.

2. Count on to 127, then to 130 and then to 173 to find the difference:

   +0.2   +3   +43

   126.8 127   130   173

3. Add up all the jumps.   0.2 + 3 + 43 = 46.2

   So the difference between 126.8 and 173 is 46.2.

Written subtraction

Complete these subtractions.

1) 8391
  − 7157
  _____

2) 5106
  − 3872
  _____

3) 6732
  − 5378
  _____

4) 8544
  − 7298
  _____

Calculate the answers to these subtractions.

5) What is 8391 subtract 3719?

6) What is the difference between 3846 and 7203?

7) Which number is 2948 less than 6149?

8) What is 4006 minus 1557?

8

Number line method

Use a number line to find the difference between each pair of numbers.

1) 56.9 ——————————— 94

2) 119.5 ——————————— 182

3) 35.3 ——————————— 77.6

4) 143.9 ——————————— 162.7

Calculate these subtractions.

5) 185 − 126.4 =

6) 374 − 309.8 =

7) 96.2 − 55.9 =

8) 171.5 − 139.7 =

374 − 309.8 = ?

8

TOTAL MARKS 16

29

Multiplication

Mental calculations

Use times tables to help to multiply 2-digit numbers by a single digit in your head.

What is 53 multiplied by 4?

Use these three steps:

1. Multiply the tens: 50 × 4 = 200.
2. Multiply the units: 3 × 4 = 12.
3. Add the two parts: 200 + 12 = 212.

Column method

This is a written method for multiplying 2-digit numbers.

Top Tip: With all multiplications, always *estimate* an *approximate* answer first. 47 × 23 is approximately 50 × 20, so the answer should be close to 1000.

What is 47 multiplied by 23?

```
    47            →   leading to   →        47
 ×  23                                   ×  23
   800   (40 × 20)                         940   (47 × 20)
   140   (7 × 20)                          141   (47 × 3)
   120   (40 × 3)                         1081
    21   (7 × 3)
  1081
```

Grid method

For this method, the numbers are broken up into tens and units and written in a grid. Multiply each pair of numbers to complete the grid and add up each row to find the total.

×	40	7		
20	800	140	→	940
3	120	21	→	141

Total: 1081

Key words estimate approximate

Answers

PAGE 5
Answering problems
1	85	4	34
2	2910km	5	£456
3	£582.15	6	1627

Multi-step problems
1	989	4	1520
2	£53.10	5	a can
3	21g		

PAGE 7
Reasoning
1 24
2 Black T-shirt ➜ £8   White T-shirt ➜ £6
   Green T-shirt ➜ £9
3 25 years old
4 1 cake = 90p   1 coffee = 80p
   1 tea = 70p

Finding all possibilities
1 36 and 64
2 nine 20p coins and eleven 10p coins
3 A = 78   B = 43
4 7 ice-creams   4 lollies

PAGE 9
Number sequences
1 **30** 38 46 54 62 **70**
2 95 **80** **65** 50 35 20
3 425 450 **475** 500 **525** 550
4 79 **75** 71 **67** 63 59
5 2 4 8 16 32 **64** **128**
6 **11** **22** 44 88 176 **352** **704**
7 2.5 5 10 20 40 **80** **160**
8 7.5 **15** 30 60 120 **240** **480**

Formulae and equations
1	$\triangle = 7$	5	$y = 16$
2	$? = 15$	6	$b = 25$
3	$\blacklozenge = 4$	7	$n = 5$
4	$? = 18$	8	$t = 9$

PAGE 11
Decimal numbers
1	$\frac{8}{10}$	4	$\frac{63}{100}$
2	$\frac{7}{1000}$	5	$\frac{1}{2}$
3	$\frac{2}{100}$	6	$\frac{3}{4}$

Multiplying and dividing by 10 and 100
1	9	6	0.97
2	16.7	7	4.05
3	502	8	0.28
4	3840	9	2150
5	1.3	10	0.215

PAGE 13
Ordering decimals
1	4.4	<	4.7	<	7.4	<	7.7
2	29.1	>	19.2	>	12.9	>	9.2
3	8.35	>	5.83	>	5.38	>	3.58
4	2.09	<	2.46	<	19.18	<	19.23
5	6.06	<	60.06	<	60.6	<	60.66
6	15.51	>	15.5	>	5.15	>	5.1

Rounding decimals
1	28cm	6	£7.10
2	6ml	7	5.4 litres
3	£83.00	8	15.5m
4	21g	9	9.8kg
5	11km	10	42.3km

PAGE 15
Types of fractions
1	$\frac{21}{5}$	➜	$4\frac{1}{5}$	5	$\frac{8}{3}$	➜	$2\frac{2}{3}$
2	$\frac{7}{3}$	➜	$2\frac{1}{3}$	6	$\frac{11}{3}$	➜	$3\frac{2}{3}$
3	$\frac{9}{5}$	➜	$1\frac{4}{5}$	7	$\frac{13}{5}$	➜	$2\frac{3}{5}$
4	$\frac{7}{4}$	➜	$1\frac{3}{4}$	8	$\frac{5}{2}$	➜	$2\frac{1}{2}$

Equivalent fractions
1	$\frac{1}{2} = \frac{12}{24}$	5	$\frac{2}{3} = \frac{10}{15}$
2	$\frac{2}{16} = \frac{1}{8}$	6	$\frac{20}{25} = \frac{4}{5}$
3	$\frac{3}{10} = \frac{30}{100}$	7	$\frac{3}{4} = \frac{12}{16}$
4	$\frac{6}{18} = \frac{1}{3}$	8	$\frac{2}{5} = \frac{6}{15}$

PAGE 17
Percentages and fractions
1	70%	4	66%
2	75%	5	60%
3	80%	6	Josh

Equivalent values
1	80%	3	0.75
2	0.2	4	50%

Percentages and decimals
0.3	**0.6**	0.94	0.05	**0.01**	**0.26**
30%	60%	**94%**	5%	1%	26%

PAGE 19
Multiplication and division facts
1	63	6	4
2	5	7	24
3	42	8	7
4	4	9	54
5	32	10	9

MATHS LEVEL 4

Square numbers
1. 81
2. 49
3. 64
4. 9
5. 10 multiplied by itself is 100.
6. 16, 25

PAGE 21
Factors
1. 5, 7, 9
2. (1, 32) (2, 16) (4, 8)
3. 15 or 30
4. 1, 7, 49

Multiples

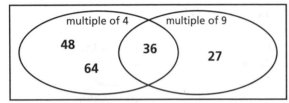

Rules of divisibility
1. No
2. No
3. 10, 20 and other numbers ending with zero can also be divided by 5.
4. 12

PAGE 23
Mental methods for addition
1. 76
2. 55
3. 150
4. 51
5. 5.1kg

Adding 2-digit numbers
33 → 91
62 → 62
79 → 45
37 → 87
89 → 35

Adding decimals
1. 10.2
2. 9.5
3. 6.2
4. 10
5. 9.2
6. 8.5

PAGE 25
Mental methods for subtraction
1. 70 → S
   20 → U
   27 → N
2. 72 → R
   0.7 → A
   2.7 → I
   27 → N
3. 22 → W
   2.7 → I
   27 → N
   7.2 → D
4. 70 → S
   27 → N
   77 → O
   22 → W

Counting on

	53	17	84
25	28	8	59
96	43	79	12
60	7	43	24

Subtracting decimals
1. 2.4 and 5.6
2. 4.9
3. 8.3 and 7.5
4. 5.9

PAGE 27
Written addition
1.   4 6 1 9
   + 3 6 4 8
     8 2 6 7
2.   2 1 1 5
   + 5 4 1 6
     7 5 3 1
3.   1 8 4 9
   + 3 6 6 4
     5 5 1 3
4.   4 2 9 4
   + 3 7 8 6
     8 0 8 0
5. 4999
6. 7038
7. 5255
8. 9082

Adding decimals
1. 34.2
2. 50.6
3. 41
4. 30.4
5. 26.5kg
6. 31.1kg
7. 25.5kg
8. 42.5kg

PAGE 29
Written subtraction
1. 1234
2. 1234
3. 1354
4. 1246
5. 4672
6. 3357
7. 3201
8. 2449

Number line method
1. 37.1
2. 62.5
3. 42.3
4. 18.8
5. 58.6
6. 64.2
7. 40.3
8. 31.8

PAGE 31
Mental calculations

1. 1		2. 3	3	3. 5		4. 2
5. 1	9	0		6. 1	8	4
4		7. 8	3	0		5

Column method
Check the method and each answer.
1. 910
2. 1596
3. 2736
4. 2116

Grid method
Check the method and each answer.
1. 1426
2. 2862

PAGE 33
Written methods
Check the method and each answer.
1. 162
2. 65 r 2
3. 276 r 1
4. 52 r 3
5. 51 r 3
6. 292
7. 88 r 4
8. 230

2

Remainder problems
1. 7 packs
2. 8 bunches
3. 2 packs
4. 14 panels
5. 9 weeks
6. 14 full egg boxes
7. 7 packs
8. 17 2kg bags

PAGE 35
Fractions and division
1. 20
2. 15
3. 4
4. 60
5. 12
6. 30

Numerator greater than 1
1. 6, 12
2. 4, 12
3. 3, 6
4. 2, 10
5. £9
6. 16 girls
7. 80 metres
8. 30
9. 20

PAGE 37
Percentages of a quantity

	10%	20%	5%	50%	25%
£20	£2	£4	£1	£10	£5
£60	£6	£12	£3	£30	£15
£50	£5	£10	£2.50	£25	£12.50

Discounts and sale prices
1. £36
2. £81
3. £27
4. £63
5. £72
6. £9

PAGE 39
Lines of symmetry

1.
1 line of symmetry

2.
0 lines of symmetry

3.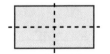
2 lines of symmetry

4.
1 line of symmetry

5.
3 lines of symmetry

6.
4 lines of symmetry

7.
5 lines of symmetry

8.
6 lines of symmetry

Reflections

1.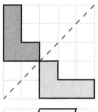
2.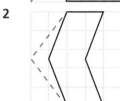
3.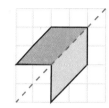
4.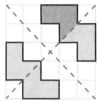

PAGE 41
Triangles

1.
2.
3.
4.

5. 60°
6. Yes

Quadrilaterals
1. rectangle
2. kite
3. square
4. True
5. False
6. True

PAGE 43
Properties of 3D shapes

Shape	Number of flat faces	Number of vertices	Number of edges
Sphere	0	0	0
Cuboid	6	8	12
Triangular prism	5	6	9
Tetrahedron	4	4	6
Cylinder	2	0	2
Square-based pyramid	5	5	8

Nets of solids
1.
2. Any one of the following squares shaded.

MATHS LEVEL 4

3 and 4

red   blue

PAGE 45
Positions on a grid
1. gate
2. bridge
3. stables
4. tree
5. (1,5)
6. (8,2)
7. (3,8)
8. (6,4)

Shapes and coordinates
1. (4,4)
2. (6,9)
3. (5,10)
4. (0,5)

PAGE 47
Types of angles

Number of:	right angles	obtuse angles	acute angles	reflex angles
Shape A	2	1	1	0
Shape B	1	2	1	0
Shape C	0	0	3	0
Shape D	0	0	3	1

Measuring angles
1. 130°
2. 105°
3. 30°
4. 280°

Angles and shapes
1. 50°
2. 60°
3. 75°
4. 20°

PAGE 49
Units of measure
1. 80ml, 180ml, 1.8 litres, 18 litres
2. 3.5mm, 30mm, 3.5cm, 350cm
3. 50g, 250g, $\frac{1}{2}$ kg, 1.2kg
4. 600ml, 6 litres, 6600ml, 60 litres

Converting units
1. 400ml or 0.4l
2. 1.75m, 175cm, or 1m 75cm
3. 10 jugs
4. 95cm or 0.95m

Reading scales
1. Jug A
2. 850ml
3. 1.2kg
4. Check that arrow is pointing to 1.2kg.

PAGE 51
Perimeter of rectangles
1. 29cm
2. 44cm
3. 36m
4. 176m

Finding areas
1. 2 squares
2. 10 squares
3. 6 squares
4. 5.5 squares

Area of rectangles
1. 127.5m^2 2. 400cm^2 3. 14cm

PAGE 53
24-hour time

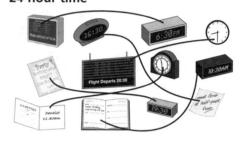

Calculating times
1. 10.10am
2. 19.55
3. 50 minutes
4. 4.13

Appleby	09.35	11.50	**14.02**	16.38
Berrytown	09.58	12.13	14.25	**17.01**
Limewich	**11.00**	13.15	15.27	**18.03**
Pearham	11.39	**13.54**	**16.06**	18.42

PAGE 55
Bar charts
1. 16
2. sparrow
3. 9
4. pigeons
5. 10
6. finches
7. 94

Frequency charts and grouped data
1. under 2km
2. 9
3. 9
4. 4–6km
5. 18

Letts Educational
4 Grosvenor Place, London SW1X 7DL
School enquiries: 015395 64911/65921
Parent & student enquiries: 015395 64913
E-mail: mail@lettsandlonsdale.co.uk

Website: www.letts-educational.com

First published 2008

Editorial and design: 2ibooks [publishing solutions] Cambridge
Author: Paul Broadbent
Book concept and development: Helen Jacobs, Publishing Director
Editorial: Sophie London, Senior Commissioning Editor
    Katy Knight, Editorial Assistant
Illustrators: Andy Roberts and Phillip Burrows
Cover design: Angela English

Letts & Lonsdale make every effort to ensure all paper used in our books is made from wood pulp obtained from sustainable and well-managed forests. Every effort has been made to trace copyright holders and obtain their permission for the use of copyright material. The authors and publishers will gladly receive information enabling them to rectify any error or omission in subsequent editions. All facts are correct at time of going to press.

All our Rights Reserved. No part of the publication may be produced, stored in a retrieval system, or transmitted, in any form or by any means, electronic, mechanical, photocopying, recording or otherwise, without the prior permission of Letts Educational.

British Library Cataloging in Publication Data. A CIP record of this book is available from the British Library.

ISBN 9781843158813

Text, design and illustration © Letts Educational Limited 2008

Printed in Italy

Mental calculations

Answer these multiplications and complete the number puzzle.

1.		2.		3.		4.
5.				6.		
		7.				

Across
2 67 x 5
5 95 x 2
6 46 x 4
7 83 x 10

Down
1 38 x 3
2 77 x 4
3 85 x 6
4 49 x 5

8

Column method

Complete these multiplications. Show your method.

1   26
    × 35
   ____

2   84
    × 19
   ____

3   48
    × 57
   ____

4   23
    × 92
   ____

4

Grid method

Complete these multiplications. Show your method.

1 31 × 46

2 54 × 53

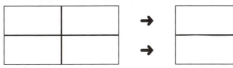

Total: _____

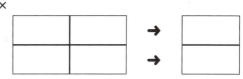

Total: _____

2

TOTAL MARKS 14

Division

Written methods

Before you start on a written division, work out an approximate answer first.

What is 789 divided by 4?

789 ÷ 4 is approximately 800 ÷ 4, so the answer will be less than 200.

```
       1 9 7 r 1
   4 ) 7 8 9
     − 4 0 0      (4 × 100)
       3 8 9
     − 3 6 0      (4 × 90)
         2 9
     −   2 8      (4 × 7)
           1
```

789 ÷ 4 = 197 remainder 1

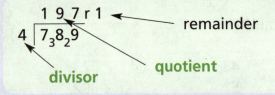

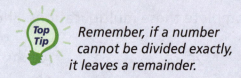

Remember, if a number cannot be divided exactly, it leaves a remainder.

Remainder problems

When you have a division problem with a remainder, you need to decide what to do with the remainder. Should you round up the answer or round down?

Round up

54 people attend a dinner. The room has tables in it, with 4 people seated at each table. How many tables are needed in total?

54 ÷ 4 is 13 remainder 2, so 14 tables are needed.

Round down

I have £54. How many £4 posters could I buy for that amount?

54 ÷ 4 is 13 remainder 2, so 13 posters could be bought.

Key words   divisor   quotient

Written methods

Calculate the answer for each of these divisions. Show your method. You may need to use a separate piece of paper.

1. 4) 648
2. 3) 197
3. 2) 553
4. 4) 211

5. 6) 309
6. 3) 876
7. 5) 444
8. 4) 920

 Division is the inverse or opposite of multiplication. So if you know your tables, it will really help you to divide numbers. What is 63 divided by 9? 9 × 7 = 63   63 ÷ 9 = 7

Remainder problems

Answer these questions.

1. The school breakfast club needs 53 sausages. There are 8 sausages in a pack. How many packs are needed so that there are enough sausages?

2. Flowers are sold in bunches of 9. How many complete bunches can be made from 74 flowers?

3. A dog eats three chews a day. There are 12 chews in a pack. How many packs are needed for a week?

4. Fence panels are 3m wide. The distance round a garden is 40m. How many fence panels will be needed to put a fence the whole way round the garden?

5. Mr Jones wants to save £7 a week to buy a new garden chair at £59. How many weeks will it be before he can buy the chair?

6. A farmer collects 85 eggs in one day. How many egg boxes can he fill if each box holds 6 eggs?

7. Liam has a £15 gift voucher. How many £2 packs of stickers can he buy?

8. How many 2kg bags can be filled from a 35kg sack of rice?

Fractions of quantities

Fractions and division

Finding fractions of quantities is very similar to dividing amounts.

Look at these examples. What is…

$\frac{1}{3}$ of 15?

$\frac{1}{4}$ of 20?

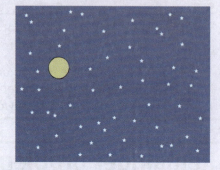

These have 1 as a numerator, so simply divide by the denominator.

$\frac{1}{3}$ of 15 is 15 ÷ 3 = 5.

$\frac{1}{4}$ of 20 is 20 ÷ 4 = 5.

Numerator greater than 1

$\frac{1}{3}$ of 15 = 5.

This is easy, because we just divide by the denominator and count one of the groups.

$\frac{2}{3}$ of 15 = 10.

Now the numerator is 2, it means we count two of the groups.

If the numerator is more than 1, divide by the denominator and then multiply by the numerator. Look at these examples.

$\frac{2}{3}$ of 12 is 12 ÷ 3 = 4, then × 2 = 8.

$\frac{3}{5}$ of 25 is 25 ÷ 5 = 5, then × 3 = 15.

$\frac{3}{4}$ of 24 is 24 ÷ 4 = 6, then × 3 = 18.

Fractions and division

Write the missing numbers to make each of these correct.

1. $\frac{1}{2}$ of 10 = $\frac{1}{4}$ of ☐
2. $\frac{1}{4}$ of 12 = $\frac{1}{5}$ of ☐
3. $\frac{1}{10}$ of 20 = $\frac{1}{2}$ of ☐
4. $\frac{1}{3}$ of 18 = $\frac{1}{10}$ of ☐
5. $\frac{1}{6}$ of 24 = $\frac{1}{3}$ of ☐
6. $\frac{1}{5}$ of 25 = $\frac{1}{6}$ of ☐

Numerator greater than 1

Complete these sums.

1. ★★★★★★ ★★★★★★ ★★★★★★
   $\frac{1}{3}$ of 18 is ☐ $\frac{2}{3}$ of 18 is ☐

2. ★★★★ ★★★★ ★★★★ ★★★★
   $\frac{1}{4}$ of 16 is ☐ $\frac{3}{4}$ of 16 is ☐

3. ★★★ ★★★ ★★★ ★★★ ★★★
   $\frac{1}{5}$ of 15 is ☐ $\frac{2}{5}$ of 15 is ☐

4. ★★ ★★ ★★ ★★ ★★ ★★
   $\frac{1}{6}$ of 12 is ☐ $\frac{5}{6}$ of 12 is ☐

Answer these questions.

5. What is three-quarters of twelve pounds? £

6. There are twenty-four children in a class and two-thirds are girls. How many are girls?

7. What is four-fifths of one hundred metres? m

8. One third of a number is ten. What is the number?

9. Three-quarters of a number is fifteen. What is the number? ☐

Percentages of quantities

Percentages of a quantity

What is 20% of £30?

There are several methods you could use to solve this type of **percentage** question.

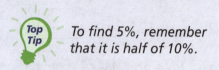 To find 5%, remember that it is half of 10%.

Method 1
Change to a fraction and work it out.

20% = $\frac{20}{100}$ = $\frac{1}{5}$

$\frac{1}{5}$ of £30 = £30 ÷ 5 = £6

Method 2
Use 10% to work it out – just divide the number by 10.

10% of £30 is £3.

So, 20% of £30 is double that: £6.

Method 3
If you are allowed, use a calculator to work it out.

Key in
20 ÷ 100 × 30 = ____

Discounts and sale prices

If you know how to work out percentages of amounts, you can work out sale prices.

A tennis racket costs £40. If there is 10% off, what is the sale price?

There are 2 steps to remember:

Step 1
Work out the percentage:

10% of £40 is £4.

Step 2
Take away this amount from the price:

£40 − £4 = £36

So the sale price is £36.

 Key words   percentage

Percentages of a quantity

Fill in the ten missing amounts to complete this table, by working out the percentages of the amounts on the left.

	10%	20%	5%	50%	25%
£20			£1	£10	
£60	£6				
£50		£10			£12.50

10

Discounts and sale prices

In a sale everything is reduced by 10%. Write the cost of each item.

1 WAS £40   now 10% off
   Sale Price: £ ____

2 £90   LESS 10%
   Sale Price: £ ____

3 WAS £30   10% discount today
   Sale Price: £ ____

4 £70   SPECIAL OFFER 10% OFF
   Sale Price: £ ____

5 WAS £80   now reduced by 10%
   Sale Price: £ ____

6 £10   Bargain – SAVE 10% NOW
   Sale Price: £ ____

6

TOTAL MARKS 16

Symmetry

Lines of symmetry

Some shapes are **symmetrical** – they have lines of symmetry, or reflective symmetry. Look at this shape.

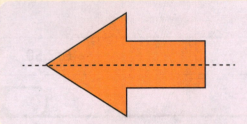

If you imagine it folded down the middle, the two sides would look exactly the same. That fold line is the line of symmetry and shows if a shape or pattern is symmetrical.

Some shapes have more than one line of symmetry or no lines of symmetry:

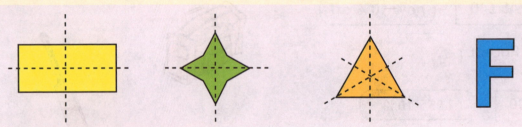

Reflections

You may be asked to draw the reflection of a picture or pattern, so that it is symmetrical. The mirror line is always drawn to help you, and the shapes are usually drawn on a grid. Use the squares on the grid to help you work out the position of each corner of the shape.

Draw the reflection of this shape.

Imagine the line is a mirror. Draw dots on each corner and count the squares across so that each point is reflected.

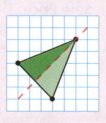

 When a mirror is put on the line of symmetry, the half shape and its reflection show the whole shape. Practise using a small mirror to help you find symmetrical shapes.

Key words | symmetrical

Lines of symmetry

Draw all the lines of symmetry on these shapes and write the number of lines of symmetry.

1  ☐ line(s) of symmetry

2 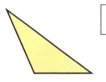 ☐ line(s) of symmetry

3 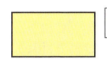 ☐ line(s) of symmetry

4 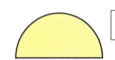 ☐ line(s) of symmetry

5 ☐ line(s) of symmetry

6 ☐ line(s) of symmetry

7 ☐ line(s) of symmetry

8 ☐ line(s) of symmetry

☐ 8

Reflections

Complete these questions.

1 Shade more squares to make a reflection on the mirror line.

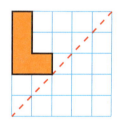

2 Here is part of a shape. Draw two more lines to make a shape with a line of symmetry. Use a ruler.

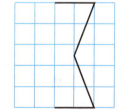

3 Draw a reflection of this shape. Use a ruler.

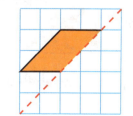

4 Shade more squares so that the design is symmetrical in both mirror lines.

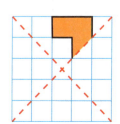

☐ 4

TOTAL MARKS ☐ 12

2D shapes

Triangles

Look at the properties of these different triangles.

Equilateral
3 equal sides.
3 equal angles.

Isosceles
2 equal sides.
2 equal angles.

Right-angled
One angle is a
right angle.

Scalene
No equal sides.
No equal angles.

Quadrilaterals

These are some special four-sided shapes.

Square
4 equal sides.
4 equal angles.

Rectangle
2 pairs of equal sides.
4 right angles.

Rhombus
4 equal sides.
Opposite angles equal.
Opposite sides parallel.

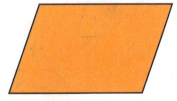 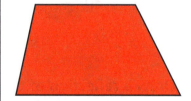

Parallelogram
Opposite sides are equal
and parallel.

Kite
Two pairs of adjacent
sides are equal.

Trapezium
One pair of parallel sides.

Key words   parallel   adjacent

Triangles

Here are four regular hexagons.
Join three dots to make each of these triangles inside them. Use a ruler.

1 isosceles triangle
2 equilateral triangle
3 scalene triangle
4 right-angled triangle

Answer these questions.

5 What is the size of each angle in an equilateral triangle?   °

6 Can an isosceles triangle also be a right-angled triangle?
   Circle the answer.   Yes   No

Quadrilaterals

These diagrams show the diagonals of three quadrilaterals. Write the name of each quadrilateral.

1 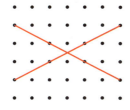   2 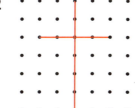   3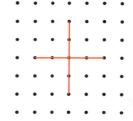

_____   _____   _____

For each statement tick (✔) True or False.   True   False

4 A trapezium always has a pair of parallel lines.

5 A rectangle always has 4 equal sides and 4 right angles.

6 A kite sometimes has a right angle.

3D shapes

Properties of 3D shapes

Solid shapes are 3-dimensional. Learn the names and properties of these 3D shapes.

cube

cuboid

cylinder

tetrahedron

cone

triangular prism

sphere

square-based pyramid

3D shapes are made up of **faces**, **edges** and **vertices**, or corners.

5 faces, 8 edges, 5 vertices.

Some shapes have flat faces and some are curved.

2 flat faces, 1 curved face, 2 curved edges, 0 vertices.

Nets of solids

The **net** of a shape is what it looks like when it is opened out flat. If you carefully pull open a cereal box so that it is one large piece of cardboard – this is the net of the box.

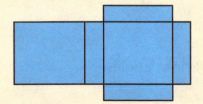

Net of a cuboid

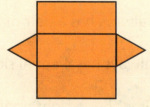

Net of a triangular prism

Key words   face   edge   vertex/vertices   net

Properties of 3D shapes

Write in the properties of each shape to complete this table.

Shape		Number of flat faces	Number of vertices	Number of edges
Sphere				0
Cuboid		6		
Triangular prism			6	
Tetrahedron		4		
Cylinder				2
Square-based pyramid			5	

Nets of solids

Here is a net of a cube with no top.

1. Put a tick (✔) on the square which is its base.

2. Shade an extra square to make the net of a cube that does have a top.

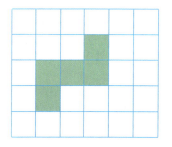

Look at these nets of 3D shapes.

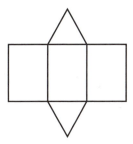 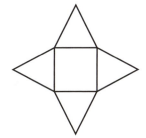 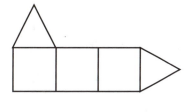

3. Colour red the net that will make a triangular prism.

4. Colour blue the net that will make a square-based pyramid.

Coordinates

Positions on a grid

Coordinates are used to show an exact position of a point on a grid.

Two numbers, one from the x **axis** and one from the y axis, show the position.

> The coordinates of A are (2,5).
>
> The coordinates of B are (4,3).

Coordinates are always written in brackets and separated by a comma.

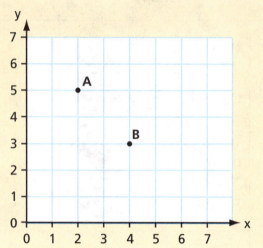

The number on the **horizontal** x axis is written first, then the number on the **vertical** y axis. You can remember this in two ways:
- because x comes before y in the alphabet
- x is 'a cross': across!

Shapes and coordinates

Coordinates are very useful for plotting the vertices of shapes.

> The grid below shows two sides of a square.
>
> What are the coordinates of the three vertices?
>
> Mark the missing coordinates for the fourth vertex and complete the square.

Remember to read the numbers across and then up for each position.

Draw in the missing lines, using a ruler to make it as accurate as possible.

The missing coordinates for the fourth vertex are (3,5).

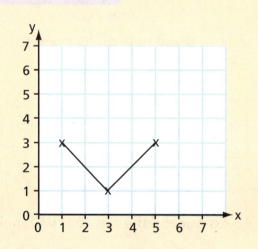

Key words: **axis**   **horizontal**   **vertical**

Positions on a grid

The tractor has coordinates (7,6).
Answer these questions.

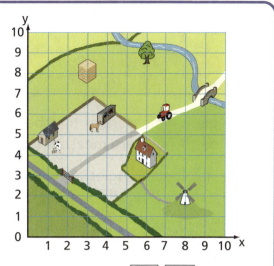

1   What is at (2,3)? _____

2   What is at (9,7)? _____

3   What is at (4,6)? _____

4   What is at (6,9)? _____

5   What are the coordinates of the cowshed? (,)

6   What are the coordinates of the windmill? (,)

7   What are the coordinates of the haystack? (,)

8   What are the coordinates of the farmhouse? (,)

8

Shapes and coordinates

1   A, B and C are corners of a rectangle. What are the coordinates of the fourth corner?

   (,)

2   K, L and M are corners of a parallelogram. What are the coordinates of the fourth corner?

   (,)

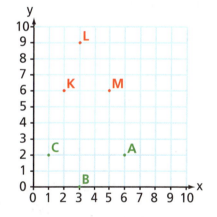

This diagram shows two identical squares. C is at (5,5).

3   What are the coordinates of A?   (,)

4   What are the coordinates of B?   (,)

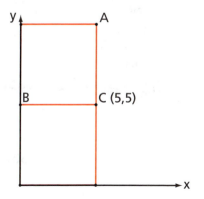

4

TOTAL MARKS 12

45

Angles

Types of angles

An angle is a measure of turn between two lines. Angles are measured in degrees (°).

There are 360° in a full circle.

These are special angles to remember:

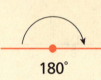
180°
(straight line)

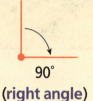
90°
(right angle)

acute angle
(less than a right angle)

obtuse angle
(between 90° and 180°)

reflex angle
(between 180° and 360°)

Measuring angles

A protractor is used to measure the size of an angle. It is a good idea to estimate the angle first and then measure it.

Read from the 0° on the scale.

Place the cross at the point of the angle you are measuring.

This angle is 45°.

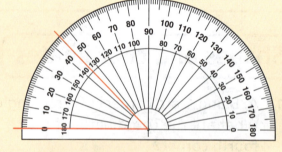

 Make sure you put the 0° at the start position and read from the correct scale. If you estimate the angle first, it will give you a good idea of the scale you should be reading.

Angles and shapes

All the angles of a triangle add up to 180°.

a + b + c = 180°

All the angles of a quadrilateral add up to 360°.

a + b + c + d = 360°

To find the value of a missing angle on a triangle, find the total of the angles given and take it away from 180°.

35° + 90° = 125°   180° − 125° = 55°

The missing angle is 55°.

 Key words   right angle   acute angle   obtuse angle   reflex angle

46

The shapes below relate to all questions on this page.

A 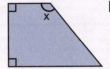   B   C    D

Types of angles

Write in how many of each angle these shapes have to complete the chart.

Number of:	right angles	obtuse angles	acute angles	reflex angles
Shape A				
Shape B				
Shape C				
Shape D				

4

Measuring angles

Use a protractor and measure the angle marked x in each of the shapes above.

1 Shape A   angle x = ____°   3 Shape C   angle x = ____°

2 Shape B   angle x = ____°   4 Shape D   angle x = ____°

4

Angles and shapes

Without using a calculator, look at Shapes A–D and answer these. You have already measured angle x on each shape.

1 What is the size of the smallest angle on shape A?   ____°

2 What is the size of the smallest angle on shape B?   ____°

3 Shape C is an isosceles triangle. Calculate the size of one of the two equal angles.   ____°

4 Each of the two equal angles on Shape D is 30°. Calculate the size of the smallest angle.   ____°

4

TOTAL MARKS   12

47

Measures

Units of measure

Length, weight (or mass) and capacity are all measured using different units.

Length	Weight
1 centimetre (cm) = 10 millimetres (mm)	1 kilogram (kg) = 1000 grams (g)
1 metre (m) = 100 centimetres (cm)	**Capacity**
1 kilometre (km) = 1000 metres (m)	1 litre (l) = 1000 millilitres (ml)

It is important to write the units in your answers. For example, there is a big difference between 100g and 100kg!

Converting units

Once you know these *equivalent* measures, then you can convert from one unit to another. This always means multiplying or dividing by 10, 100 or 1000, depending on what you are converting.

This bookcase is 1.35m or 135cm high.

This bottle holds 2.25 litres or 2250 millilitres.

This pumpkin weighs 6.84kg or 6840g.

Reading scales

A scale is the marking of lines to help us measure, e.g. up the side of a jug, on weighing scales or on a ruler. You need to read scales carefully, using these steps:

1. Look at the unit – is it ml, cm, mm, g ..?
2. If it is level with a number, read off that number.
3. If it is between numbers, work out what each mark means and count on or back.
4. Remember to include cm, mm, g or whatever in the answer.

 Key words   equivalent

LEARN — **MEASURING**

48

Units of measure

Write each set of measures in size order, starting with the smallest.

1 1.8 litres   180ml   18 litres   80ml   _____

2 30mm   3.5cm   3.5mm   350cm   _____

3 $\frac{1}{2}$ kg   250g   50g   1.2kg   _____

4 60 litres   6600ml   600ml   6 litres   _____

4

Converting units

1 A recipe for soup needs 1 litre of water. 600ml is poured in. How much more is needed?   _____

2 A 2m length of wood is too long by 25cm. What is the exact length of wood that is needed?   _____

3 A jug holds $\frac{1}{2}$ litre of water. How many full jugs will it take to fill a 5-litre bucket?   _____

4 Noel is 1.35m. His younger brother David is 40cm shorter than Noel. What height is David?   _____

4

Reading scales

1 Which jug contains more water, Jug **A** or Jug **B**?   _____

2 All the water in these two containers is to be poured into an empty jug. How much water will there be altogether?   _____

3 What is the weight of the flour on Scale **A**?   _____

4 Scale **B** contains exactly the same amount of flour as Scale **A**. Draw an arrow on Scale **B** to the same weight as Scale **A**.

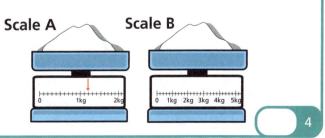

4

TOTAL MARKS 12

Perimeter and area

Perimeter of rectangles

The **perimeter** of a shape is simply the distance all the way around the edge.

The perimeter of rectangles can be found by totalling the length and width and then multiplying this by 2. Here is a formula for this:

2(length + width) or 2(l+w)

Perimeter = 2 (6.5 + 5) = 2 × 11.5 = 23cm

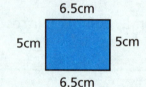

Finding areas

The **area** of a shape is the amount of surface that it covers. You can often measure the area of shapes by counting squares.

These shapes both have an area of 8 squares.

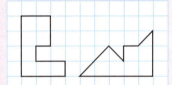

If the shape is not made up from whole squares, count all the squares that are bigger than a half.

This shape has an area of approximately 12 squares.

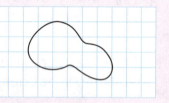

Area of rectangles

Finding the area of a rectangle is easy if you know the length and width.

The area is length x width.

Area = 3cm x 5cm = 15cm^2

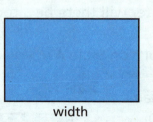

Top Tip: Area is usually measured in square centimetres or square metres, written as cm^2 and m^2. Always remember to write this at the end of the measurement.

Key words   perimeter   area

Perimeter of rectangles

Use the formula 2(l+w) to calculate the perimeter of these rectangles.

1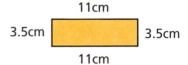

2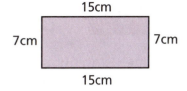

3 What is the perimeter of a rectangle twelve metres long and six metres wide? ☐ m

4 A farmer puts a length of electric wire around a 28m × 60m field to keep in his cows. What length of electric wire did he use? ☐ m

4

Finding areas

Calculate the area of each shape.

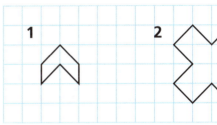

1 _____ squares   2 _____ squares   3 _____ squares   4 _____ squares

4

Area of rectangles

1 What is the area of a rectangular swimming pool 8.5m by 15m? ☐ m²

2 What is the area of a square tile with a 20cm side? ☐ cm²

3 The area of a rectangle is 12cm². One of the sides is 3cm. What is the perimeter of the rectangle? ☐ cm

3

TOTAL MARKS ☐ 11

PRACTISE MEASURING

51

Reading the time

24-hour time

We read the time using an **analogue clock** (circular) or **digital clock** (time in numbers). Digital clocks can be 12-hour or 24-hour clocks.

Timetables and digital watches often use the 24-hour clock.

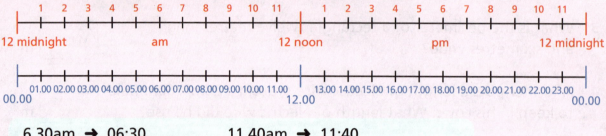

6.30am → 06:30   11.40am → 11:40

6.30pm → 18:30   11.40pm → 23:40

Morning (am) times look the same when you use 24-hour time.

For afternoon and evening (pm) times, you add 12 hours to find the 24-hour time.

You always use 4 numbers when you write the 24-hour clock, even for morning times. So 9.45am is 09:45.

Top Tip: **am** stands for **ante meridiem** and means before midday – from 12 midnight to 12 noon.
pm stands for **post meridiem** and means after midday – from 12 noon to 12 midnight.

Calculating times

To work out how long an event lasts, try counting on from the start to the finish.

A film starts at 6.40pm and finishes at 8.15pm.
How long does the film last?

Use a time line and count on.

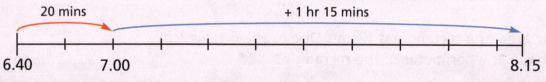

20 mins + 1 hr 15 mins is 1 hour 35 minutes.

 Key words   analogue clock   digital clock
ante meridiem (am)   post meridiem (pm)

24-hour time

Draw a line to join six pairs of matching times.

6

Calculating times

Calculate the time for each of these.

1   A bus should arrive at 9.55am but it is 15 minutes late.
    At what time will the bus arrive now? _____

2   A film starts at 18:25 and lasts an hour and a half.
    What time will the film end? _____

3   A school lunchtime is from twenty past twelve until
    ten past one. How long is this school lunchtime? _____

4   My watch shows three minutes past four and is five
    minutes slow. My alarm clock is five minutes fast. What
    time will be shown on my alarm clock at this moment? _____

5   Write in the six missing times on this train timetable. Each train starts in Appleby
    and takes exactly the same amount of time to travel between each station.

Appleby	09:35	11:50		16:38
Berrytown	09:58	12:13	14:25	
Limewich		13:15	15:27	
Pearham	11:39			18:42

10

TOTAL MARKS 16

53

Handling data

Bar charts

Bar charts are a useful way of showing information. To understand bar charts and other types of graph, look carefully at the different parts of the graph.

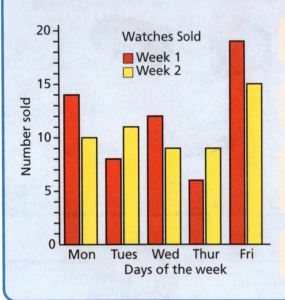

1. Read the title – what is it all about? Is there any other information given?

2. Look at the **axis** labels – these should explain the lines that go up and across.

3. Work out the scale – look carefully at the numbers – do they go up in 1s, 5s, 10s ..?

4. Compare the bars – read them across to work out the amounts.

Frequency charts and grouped data

The word frequency means 'how many', so a frequency chart is a record of how many there are in a group.

A teacher wanted to compare the number of laps of the playing field walked by a class of children on a sponsored walk. Here is the table of results.

Laps completed	6–10	11–15	16–20	21–25	26–30
Number of children	2	7	17	18	25

This group data can then be shown on a graph:

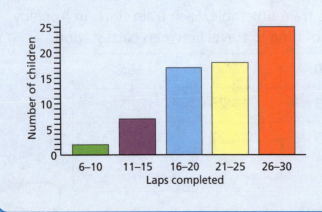

Key words   axis

Bar charts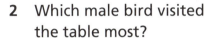

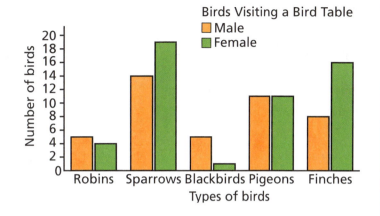

1. How many female finches visited the bird table?

   _____

2. Which male bird visited the table most?

   _____

3. How many male and female robins visited the bird table in total? _____

4. Which type of bird had the same number of male and female visitors to the bird table? _____

5. How many more female pigeons visited the bird table than female blackbirds? _____

6. Which type of bird had double the number of females than males visit the bird table? _____

7. How many birds visited the bird table in total? _____

7

Frequency charts and grouped data

Distance	Under 2km	2–4km	4–6km	6–8km	8–10km	Over 10km
Number of children	18	12	12	9	6	3

1. Which distance did the largest number of children travel? _____

2. How many children travelled a distance of 6–8km to school? _____

3. Half of the children travelling under 2km walk to school. How many children walk to school? _____

4. Kate travels 4.5km to school. Which distance group would she be included in? _____

5. How many children in total travel over 6km to school? _____

5

TOTAL MARKS 12

Glossary

acute angle an angle smaller than a right angle

adjacent near or next to something

analogue clock a round clock face with hands

ante meridiem (am) – past midnight and before midday

approximate a 'rough' answer – near to the real answer

area the area of a shape is the amount of surface that it covers

axis (plural is axes) the horizontal or vertical line on a graph

column a vertical arrangement of numbers, words or objects going up or down

decimal point a point that separates whole numbers from decimal fractions

denominator the bottom number of a fraction, the number of parts it is divided into. Example: $\frac{2}{3}$

difference the difference between two numbers is the amount that one number is greater than the other. The difference between 18 and 21 is 3

digit there are 10 digits, 0 1 2 3 4 5 6 7 8 and 9, that are used to make all the numbers we use

digital clock a clock with no hands that uses just numbers to show the time

divisor a divisor is a number that another number is divided by. Example: For 32 ÷ 4 = 8, the divisor is 4

double make something twice as big, or multiply by 2

edge where two faces of a solid shape meet

equation where symbols or letters are used instead of numbers. Example: 3y = 12, so y = 4

equivalent two numbers or measures are equivalent if they are the same or equal

equivalent fractions these are equal fractions. Example: $\frac{1}{2} = \frac{2}{4} = \frac{3}{6}$

estimate a good guess

face the flat sides of a solid shape

factor a number that will divide exactly into other numbers. Example: 5 is a factor of 20

formula a formula (plural is formulae) uses letters or words to give a rule

horizontal a horizontal line is a straight level line across, in the same direction as the horizon

improper fraction any fraction which is greater than 1, such as $\frac{5}{3}$, $\frac{8}{5}$ or $\frac{6}{2}$

mixed number any whole number and fraction written together, such as $2\frac{1}{2}$, $4\frac{3}{5}$ or $1\frac{3}{10}$

multiple a multiple is a number made by multiplying together two other numbers

net the net of a 3D shape is what it looks like when it is opened out flat

numerator the top number of a fraction. Example: $\frac{3}{5}$

obtuse angle an angle less than 180° (a straight line) but greater than 90° (a right angle)

parallel lines that are parallel always stay the same distance apart and never meet

percentage this is a fraction out of 100, shown with a % sign

perimeter the distance all the way around the edge of a shape or object

post meridiem (pm) – after midday or after noon

prime number only has two factors, 1 and itself. For example, 23 is a prime number as it can only be divided exactly by 1 and 23

proper fraction any fraction which is less than 1, such as $\frac{2}{3}$, $\frac{3}{5}$ or $\frac{1}{10}$

quotient this is the number of times that one number will divide into another number. Example: When you divide 18 by 3, the quotient is 6

reflex angle an angle between 180° (a straight line) and 360°

remainder if a number cannot be divided exactly by another number, then there is a whole number answer with an amount left over, called a remainder

right angle a quarter turn. The corner of a square is a right angle

sequence a list of numbers which usually have a pattern. They are often numbers written in order

square number numbers multiplied by themselves make square numbers. Example: 4 x 4 = 16. The first five square numbers are 1, 4, 9, 16 and 25

sum the sum of two or more numbers is the answer you get when you add them together

symmetrical when two halves of a shape or pattern are identical

vertical a line that is straight up or down, at right angles to a horizontal line

vertices (single is vertex) these are the corners of 3D shapes, where edges meet

Notes

NOTES

NOTES

NOTES

NOTES

OS MISÉRABLES
Volume II

Por Victor Hugo

Direitos de Autor © 2024 por Autri Books

Todos os direitos reservados. Nenhuma parte desta publicação pode ser reproduzida, por fotocópia, gravação ou outros métodos electrónicos ou mecânicos, sem a autorização prévia por escrito do editor, exceto no caso de breves citações incluídas em recensões críticas e outras utilizações não comerciais permitidas pela lei dos direitos de autor.

Esta edição faz parte da "Autri Books Classic Literature Collection" e inclui traduções, conteúdo editorial e elementos de design que são originais desta publicação e estão protegidos pela lei dos direitos de autor. O texto subjacente é do domínio público e não está sujeito a direitos de autor, mas todos os aditamentos e modificações estão protegidos por direitos de autor da Autri Books.

As publicações da Autri Books podem ser adquiridas para uso educativo, comercial ou promocional.

Para mais informações, contactar:

autribooks.com | support@autribooks.com

ISBN: 979-8-3485-2506-4
Primeira edição publicada pela Autri Books em 2024.

Índice

VOLUME II" COSETTE

LIVRO UM —WATERLOO

CAPÍTULO I" O QUE SE ENCONTRA NO CAMINHO DE NIVELLES

CAPÍTULO II—HOUGOMONT

CAPÍTULO III" DEZOITO DE JUNHO DE 1815

CAPÍTULO IV—A

CAPÍTULO V" O QUID OBSCURUM DAS BATALHAS

CAPÍTULO VI" QUATRO HORAS DA TARDE

CAPÍTULO VII" NAPOLEÃO DE BOM HUMOR

CAPÍTULO VIII" O IMPERADOR FAZ UMA PERGUNTA AO GUIA LACOSTE

CAPÍTULO IX" O INESPERADO

CAPÍTULO X" O PLANALTO DO MONTE SAINT-JEAN

CAPÍTULO XI" UM MAU GUIA PARA NAPOLEÃO; UM BOM GUIA PARA BÜLOW

CAPÍTULO XII" A GUARDA

CAPÍTULO XIII" A CATÁSTROFE

CAPÍTULO XIV" O ÚLTIMO QUADRADO

CAPÍTULO XV" CAMBRONNE

CAPÍTULO XVI" CITAÇÃO LIBRAS EM DUCE?

CAPÍTULO XVII" WATERLOO DEVE SER CONSIDERADO
BOM?

CAPÍTULO XVIII" UM RECRUDESCIMENTO DO DIREITO
DIVINO

CAPÍTULO XIX" O CAMPO DE BATALHA À NOITE

LIVRO DOIS — O NAVIO ORION

CAPÍTULO I" O NÚMERO 24.601 PASSA A SER O NÚMERO
9.430

CAPÍTULO II" EM QUE O LEITOR EXAMINARÁ DOIS
VERSOS, QUE SÃO DA COMPOSIÇÃO DO DIABO,
POSSIVELMENTE

CAPÍTULO III" A CORRENTE DO TORNOZELO DEVE TER
SOFRIDO UMA CERTA MANIPULAÇÃO PREPARATÓRIA
PARA SER QUEBRADA COM UM GOLPE DE MARTELO

**LIVRO TRÊS — CUMPRIMENTO DA PROMESSA FEITA À
MULHER MORTA**

CAPÍTULO I" A QUESTÃO DA ÁGUA EM MONTFERMEIL

CAPÍTULO II" DOIS RETRATOS COMPLETOS

CAPÍTULO III" OS HOMENS DEVEM TER VINHO E OS
CAVALOS DEVEM TER ÁGUA

CAPÍTULO IV" ENTRADA EM CENA DE UM BONECO

CAPÍTULO V" O PEQUENO SOZINHO

CAPÍTULO VI" O QUE POSSIVELMENTE PROVA A INTELIGÊNCIA DE BOULATRUELLE

CAPÍTULO VII" COSETTE LADO A LADO COM O ESTRANHO NO ESCURO

CAPÍTULO VIII" O DESAGRADO DE RECEBER EM CASA UM POBRE QUE PODE SER UM HOMEM RICO

CAPÍTULO IX" THÉNARDIER E AS SUAS MANOBRAS

CAPÍTULO X" AQUELE QUE PROCURA MELHORAR A SI MESMO PODE PIORAR A SUA SITUAÇÃO

CAPÍTULO XI - O NÚMERO 9.430 REAPARECE E COSETTE GANHA NA LOTERIA

LIVRO QUATRO — O CASEBRE DE GORBEAU

CAPÍTULO I" MESTRE GORBEAU

CAPÍTULO II—UM NINHO PARA CORUJA E UMA TOUTINEGRA

CAPÍTULO III" DOIS INFORTÚNIOS FAZEM UM PEDAÇO DE BOA SORTE

CAPÍTULO IV" AS OBSERVAÇÕES DO INQUILINO PRINCIPAL

CAPÍTULO V" UMA PEÇA DE CINCO FRANCOS CAI NO CHÃO E PRODUZ UM TUMULTO

LIVRO CINCO — PARA UMA CAÇA NEGRA, UM PACOTE MUDO

CAPÍTULO I" OS ZIGUEZAGUES DA ESTRATÉGIA

CAPÍTULO II" É UMA SORTE QUE A PONT D'AUSTERLITZ TENHA CARRUAGENS

CAPÍTULO III" A SABER, O PLANO DE PARIS EM 1727

CAPÍTULO IV" AS TATEADAS DO VOO

CAPÍTULO V" O QUE SERIA IMPOSSÍVEL COM LANTERNAS A GÁS

CAPÍTULO VI" O INÍCIO DE UM ENIGMA

CAPÍTULO VII" CONTINUAÇÃO DO ENIGMA

CAPÍTULO VIII" O ENIGMA TORNA-SE DUPLAMENTE MISTERIOSO

CAPÍTULO IX" O HOMEM DO SINO

CAPÍTULO X" QUE EXPLICA COMO JAVERT ENTROU NO CHEIRO

LIVRO SEIS — PETIT-PICPUS

CAPÍTULO I" NÚMERO 62 RUE PETIT-PICPUS

CAPÍTULO II" A OBEDIÊNCIA DE MARTIN VERGA

CAPÍTULO III" AUSTERIDADES

CAPÍTULO IV" GAYETIES

CAPÍTULO V" DISTRAÇÕES

CAPÍTULO VI" O PEQUENO CONVENTO

CAPÍTULO VII" ALGUMAS SILHUETAS DESTA
ESCURIDÃO

CAPÍTULO VIII" PÓS CORDA LAPIDES

CAPÍTULO IX" UM SÉCULO SOB UM GUIMPE

CAPÍTULO X" ORIGEM DA ADORAÇÃO PERPÉTUA

CAPÍTULO XI" FIM DO PETIT-PICPUS

LIVRO SETE — PARÊNTESIS

CAPÍTULO I" O CONVENTO COMO IDEIA ABSTRATA

CAPÍTULO II" O CONVENTO COMO FACTO HISTÓRICO

CAPÍTULO III" EM QUE CONDIÇÕES SE PODE RESPEITAR
O PASSADO

CAPÍTULO IV" O CONVENTO DO PONTO DE VISTA DOS
PRINCÍPIOS

CAPÍTULO V" ORAÇÃO

CAPÍTULO VI" A BONDADE ABSOLUTA DA ORAÇÃO

CAPÍTULO VII" PRECAUÇÕES A OBSERVAR EM CASO DE
CULPA

CAPÍTULO VIII" FÉ, LEI

LIVRO OITO — OS CEMITÉRIOS TOMAM O QUE LHES É COMPROMETIDO

CAPÍTULO I" QUE TRATA DO MODO DE ENTRAR NUM CONVENTO

CAPÍTULO II" FAUCHELEVENT NA PRESENÇA DE UMA DIFICULDADE

CAPÍTULO III" MÃE INOCENTE

CAPÍTULO IV" EM QUE JEAN VALJEAN TEM BASTANTE AR DE TER LIDO AUSTIN CASTILLEJO

CAPÍTULO V – NÃO É NECESSÁRIO ESTAR BÊBADO PARA SER IMORTAL

CAPÍTULO VI" ENTRE QUATRO TÁBUAS

CAPÍTULO VII" NO QUAL SE ENCONTRARÁ A ORIGEM DO DITADO: NÃO PERCAM A CARTA

CAPÍTULO VIII" UM INTERROGATÓRIO BEM-SUCEDIDO

CAPÍTULO IX" CLAUSURA

VOLUME II
COSETTE

LIVRO UM

WATERLOO

CAPÍTULO I

O QUE SE ENCONTRA NO CAMINHO DE NIVELLES

No ano passado (1861), numa bela manhã de maio, um viajante, a pessoa que está contando esta história, estava vindo de Nivelles, e dirigindo seu curso para La Hulpe. Ele estava a pé. Ele estava perseguindo uma ampla estrada pavimentada, que ondulava entre duas fileiras de árvores, sobre as colinas que se sucedem, levantam a estrada e a deixam cair novamente, e produzem algo na natureza de ondas enormes.

Ele tinha passado Lillois e Bois-Seigneur-Isaac. No oeste, ele percebeu a torre de ardósia de Braine-l'Alleud, que tem a forma de um vaso invertido. Ele tinha acabado de deixar para trás uma madeira sobre uma eminência; e no ângulo da encruzilhada, ao lado de uma espécie de gibbet mofado com a inscrição *Antiga Barreira nº 4,* uma casa pública, tendo na sua frente este sinal: *Nos Quatro Ventos* (Aux Quatre Vents). *Échabeau, Café privado.*

Um quarto de légua mais adiante, chegou ao fundo de um pequeno vale, onde há água que passa por baixo de um arco feito através do aterro da estrada. O amontoado de árvores escassamente plantadas, mas muito verdes, que enche o vale de um lado da estrada, está disperso sobre os prados do outro, e desaparece graciosamente e como em ordem na direção de Braine-l'Alleud.

À direita, perto da estrada, havia uma pousada, com um carrinho de quatro rodas à porta, um grande feixe de postes de lúpulo, um arado, um monte de madeira seca perto de uma sebe florescente, fumando cal em um buraco quadrado e uma escada suspensa ao longo de uma antiga cobertura com divisórias de palha. Uma jovem estava a capinar num campo, onde um enorme cartaz amarelo, provavelmente de algum espetáculo exterior, como uma festa paroquial, tremulava ao vento. Em um canto da pousada, ao lado de uma piscina na qual navegava uma flotilha de patos, um caminho mal pavimentado mergulhou nos arbustos. O viajante acertou nisso.

Depois de percorrer uma centena de passos, contornando uma muralha do século XV, encimada por uma empena pontiaguda, com tijolos postos em contraste, encontrou-se diante de uma grande porta de pedra arqueada, com um impostor retilíneo, no estilo sombrio de Luís XIV., ladeada por dois medalhões planos. Uma fachada severa ergueu-se acima desta porta; uma parede, perpendicular à fachada, quase tocou a porta, e flanqueou-a com um ângulo reto abrupto. No prado diante da porta jaziam três grades, através das quais, em desordem, cresciam todas as flores de maio. A porta estava fechada. As duas folhas decrépitas que o barravam estavam ornamentadas com um velho batedor enferrujado.

O sol era encantador; os ramos tinham aquele suave arrepio de maio, que parece proceder mais dos ninhos do que do vento. Um passarinho corajoso, provavelmente um amante, estava se enrolando distraído em uma grande árvore.

O viajante inclinou-se e examinou uma escavação circular bastante grande, semelhante ao oco de uma esfera, na pedra à esquerda, ao pé do cais da porta.

Neste momento, as folhas da porta se separaram e uma camponesa surgiu.

Ela viu o viajante e percebeu o que ele estava olhando.

"Foi uma bola de canhão francesa que fez isso", disse-lhe. E acrescentou: —

"O que você vê ali, mais acima na porta, perto de um prego, é o buraco de uma grande bala de ferro do tamanho de um ovo. A bala não perfurou a madeira".

"Qual é o nome deste lugar"?, perguntou o viajante.

"Hougomont" disse a camponesa.

O viajante endireitou-se. Ele andou em alguns passos e saiu para olhar por cima das sebes. No horizonte através das árvores, ele percebeu uma espécie de pequena elevação, e nessa elevação algo que àquela distância se assemelhava a um leão.

Ele estava no campo de batalha de Waterloo.

CAPÍTULO II

HOUGOMONT

Hougomont, este foi um local fúnebre, o início do obstáculo, a primeira resistência, que aquele grande lenhador da Europa, chamado Napoleão, encontrou em Waterloo, o primeiro nó sob os golpes de seu machado.

Era um castelo, já não é mais nada além de uma fazenda. Para o antiquário, Hougomont é *Hugomons*. Esta mansão foi construída por Hugo, Sire de Somerel, o mesmo que dotou a sexta capelania da Abadia de Villiers.

O viajante abriu a porta, deu uma cotovelada numa antiga calash sob o alpendre e entrou no pátio.

A primeira coisa que o impressionou neste paddock foi uma porta do século XVI, que aqui simula uma arcada, tudo o resto tendo caído prostrado à sua volta. Um aspeto monumental muitas vezes tem seu nascimento em ruína. Numa parede junto à arcada abre-se outra porta arqueada, do tempo de Henrique IV., permitindo vislumbrar as árvores de um pomar; ao lado desta porta, um buraco de estrume, algumas picaretas, algumas pás, algumas carroças, um poço velho, com a sua laje e o seu carretel de ferro, uma galinha a saltar, e um peru a estender a cauda, uma capela encimada por uma pequena torre sineira, uma pereira em flor treinada em espalier contra a parede da capela – eis a corte, cuja conquista era um dos sonhos de Napoleão. Este canto da terra, se não o tivesse aproveitado, talvez lhe tivesse dado o mundo da mesma forma. As galinhas estão espalhando sua poeira para o exterior com seus bicos. Um rosnado é audível; é um cão enorme, que mostra os dentes e substitui os ingleses.

Os ingleses se comportaram de forma admirável lá. As quatro companhias de guardas de Cooke resistiram durante sete horas contra a fúria de um exército.

Hougomont visto no mapa, como um plano geométrico, compreendendo edifícios e recintos, apresenta uma espécie de retângulo irregular, um ângulo do qual é cortado. É este ângulo que contém a porta sul, guardada por esta parede, que a comanda a apenas um comprimento de canhão de distância. Hougomont tem duas portas: a porta sul, a do castelo; e a porta norte, pertencente à quinta. Napoleão enviou seu irmão Jérôme contra Hougomont; as divisões de Foy, Guilleminot e Bachelu lançaram-se contra ele; quase todo o corpo de Reille foi empregado contra ele, e abortou; As bolas de Kellermann estavam esgotadas nesta secção heroica da parede. A brigada de Bauduin não era forte o suficiente para forçar Hougomont no norte, e a brigada de Soye não podia fazer mais do que efetuar o início de uma brecha no sul, mas sem tomá-la.

Os edifícios da quinta fazem fronteira com o pátio a sul. Um pouco da porta norte, quebrada pelos franceses, está suspensa na parede. Consiste em quatro tábuas pregadas em duas vigas transversais, nas quais as cicatrizes do ataque são visíveis.

A porta norte, que foi batida pelos franceses, e que lhe foi aplicada uma peça para substituir o painel suspenso na parede, está entreaberta na parte inferior do paddock; é cortado diretamente na parede, construída de pedra abaixo, de tijolo acima do qual se fecha no pátio ao norte. É uma porta simples para carroças, como existe em todas as quintas, com as duas grandes folhas feitas de tábuas rústicas: para lá estão os prados. A disputa por essa entrada foi furiosa. Durante muito tempo, todos os tipos de marcas de mãos ensanguentadas foram visíveis nas ombreiras das portas. Foi lá que Bauduin foi morto.

A tempestade do combate ainda permanece neste pátio; o seu horror é visível ali; a confusão da briga foi petrificada ali; vive e morre lá; foi ainda ontem. As paredes estão na agonia da morte, as pedras caem; as brechas gritam em voz alta; os buracos são feridas; as árvores caídas e trêmulas parecem estar fazendo um esforço para fugir.

Este pátio foi mais construído em 1815 do que é hoje. Edifícios que desde então foram derrubados formaram redans e ângulos.

Os ingleses barricaram-se ali; os franceses entraram, mas não conseguiram resistir. Ao lado da capela, uma ala do castelo, a única ruína que resta agora do solar de Hougomont, ergue-se em estado de ruína, desencarnada, pode-se dizer. O castelo servia para uma masmorra, a capela para uma casa de blocos. Lá os homens se exterminaram. Os franceses, disparados de todos os pontos", de trás das paredes, dos cumes das guarnições, das profundezas das caves, através de todos os casements, através de todos os orifícios de ar, através de cada fenda nas pedras", buscavam bichas e incendiavam paredes e homens; A resposta ao tiro de uva foi uma conflagração.

Na ala arruinada, através de janelas guarnecidas com barras de ferro, são visíveis as câmaras desmontadas do edifício principal de tijolo; os guardas ingleses estavam em emboscada nessas salas; A espiral da escada, rachada do piso térreo até o próprio telhado, parece o interior de uma concha quebrada. A escadaria tem dois andares; os ingleses, sitiados na escadaria, e amontoados nos seus degraus superiores, tinham cortado os degraus inferiores. Estes consistiam em grandes lajes de pedra azul, que formam uma pilha entre as urtigas. Meia dúzia de degraus ainda se agarra à parede; no primeiro é cortada a figura de um tridente. Esses passos inacessíveis são sólidos em seus nichos. Todo o resto se assemelha a uma mandíbula que foi desnudada de seus dentes. Há duas árvores antigas lá: uma está morta; o outro é ferido em sua base, e é vestido com verdure em abril. Desde 1815 que passou a crescer através da escadaria.

Um massacre ocorreu na capela. O interior, que recuperou a calma, é singular. A missa não é dita lá desde a carnificina. No entanto, o altar foi deixado lá - um altar de madeira não polida, colocado sobre um fundo de pedra áspera. Quatro paredes caiadas de branco, uma porta em frente ao altar, duas pequenas janelas arqueadas; sobre a porta um grande crucifixo de madeira, abaixo do crucifixo um buraco de ar quadrado parou com um feixe de feno; No chão, num canto, uma velha moldura de janela com o vidro todo partido em pedaços – tal é a capela. Perto do altar está pregada uma estátua de madeira de Santa Ana, do século XV; a cabeça do menino Jesus foi levada por uma grande bola. Os franceses, que foram mestres da capela por um momento, e depois foram desalojados, incendiaram-na. As chamas encheram este edifício; era um forno perfeito; a porta foi queimada, o chão foi queimado, o Cristo de madeira não foi queimado. O fogo predava-lhe os pés, dos quais só se vêem agora os tocos enegrecidos; depois parou, um milagre, segundo a afirmação das pessoas do bairro. O menino Jesus, decapitado, teve menos sorte do que o Cristo.

As paredes estão cobertas de inscrições. Perto dos pés de Cristo deve ler-se este nome: *Henquinez*. Depois estes outros: *Conde de Rio Maior Marques y Marquesa de Almagro (Habana)*. Há nomes franceses com pontos de exclamação, um sinal de ira. A parede foi recentemente caiada de branco em 1849. As nações insultaram-se mutuamente lá.

Foi à porta desta capela que foi recolhido o cadáver que segurava um machado na mão; este cadáver era do Subtenente Legros.

Ao emergir da capela, um poço é visível à esquerda. Há dois neste pátio. Pergunta-se: Por que não há balde e polia para isso? É porque a água já não é atraída para lá. Porque é que a água não é captada para lá? Porque está cheio de esqueletos.

A última pessoa que tirou água do poço chamou-se Guillaume van Kylsom. Ele era um camponês que vivia em Hougomont, e era jardineiro lá. No dia 18 de junho de 1815, sua família fugiu e se escondeu na mata.

A floresta ao redor da Abadia de Villiers abrigou essas pessoas infelizes que haviam sido espalhadas no exterior, por muitos dias e noites. Há hoje certos vestígios reconhecíveis, como velhos bolos de árvores queimadas, que marcam o local destes pobres bivouacs a tremer nas profundezas dos matagais.

Guillaume van Kylsom permaneceu em Hougomont, "para guardar o castelo", e escondeu-se na adega. Os ingleses descobriram-no lá. Arrancaram-no do seu esconderijo, e os combatentes forçaram este homem assustado a servi-los, desferindo golpes com as espadas. Tinham sede; este Guillaume trouxe-lhes água. Foi deste poço que a tirou. Muitos beberam lá o seu último chope. Este poço onde bebiam tantos mortos estava destinado a morrer ele mesmo.

Após o noivado, eles se apressaram para enterrar os cadáveres. A morte tem uma moda de assediar a vitória, e ela faz com que a praga siga a glória.

O tifo é concomitante ao triunfo. Este poço era profundo e transformou-se num sepulcro. Trezentos cadáveres foram lançados nela. Talvez com demasiada pressa. Estavam todos mortos? A lenda diz que não. Parece que, na noite seguinte ao enterro, vozes fracas foram ouvidas chamando do poço.

Este poço está isolado no meio do pátio. Três paredes, parte pedra, parte tijolo, e simulando uma pequena torre quadrada, e dobrada como as folhas de uma tela, rodeiam-na por todos os lados. O quarto lado está aberto. Foi lá que a água foi tirada. A parede na parte inferior tem uma espécie de brecha sem forma, possivelmente o buraco feito por uma concha. Esta pequena torre tinha uma plataforma, da qual restam apenas as vigas. Os suportes de ferro do poço à direita formam uma cruz. Ao inclinar-se, o olho perde-se num cilindro profundo de tijolo que é preenchido com uma massa amontoada de sombras. A base das paredes ao redor do poço está escondida em um crescimento de urtigas.

Este poço não tem à sua frente aquela grande laje azul que forma a mesa para todos os poços na Bélgica. A laje foi aqui substituída por uma viga transversal, contra a qual se inclinam cinco ou seis fragmentos disformes de madeira nodosa e petrificada que se assemelham a ossos enormes. Não há mais pail, corrente ou polia; mas ainda há a bacia de pedra que serviu o transbordamento. A água da chuva se acumula lá e, de vez em quando, um pássaro das florestas vizinhas vem beber e depois voa para longe. Uma casa nesta ruína, a quinta, ainda é habitada. A porta desta casa abre-se no pátio. Sobre esta porta, ao lado de uma bonita fechadura gótica, há um cabo de ferro com trevos colocados inclinados. No momento em que o tenente hanoveriano, Wilda, agarrou este cabo para se refugiar na fazenda, um sapador francês arrancou sua mão com um machado.

A família que ocupava a casa tinha para o avô Guillaume van Kylsom, o velho jardineiro, morto há muito tempo. Uma mulher de cabelos grisalhos disse-nos: "Eu estava lá. Eu tinha três anos. Minha irmã, que era mais velha, ficou apavorada e chorou. Eles nos levaram para a floresta. Fui lá nos braços da minha mãe. Colámos os ouvidos à terra para ouvir. Eu imitei o canhão, e fui *boum"!*

Uma porta que se abria do pátio à esquerda levava ao pomar, então nos disseram. O pomar é terrível.

Divide-se em três partes; Pode-se quase dizer, em três atos. A primeira parte é um jardim, a segunda é um pomar, a terceira é uma madeira. Estas três partes têm um recinto comum: do lado da entrada, os edifícios do castelo e da quinta; à esquerda, uma sebe; à direita, um muro; e, no final, um muro. A parede à direita é de tijolo, a parede na parte inferior é de pedra. Entra-se primeiro no jardim. Inclina-se para baixo, está plantada com arbustos de groselha, sufocada com um crescimento selvagem de vegetação, e terminada por um monumental terraço de pedra cortada, com balaustrada com uma curva dupla.

Foi um jardim seignorial no primeiro estilo francês que precedeu Le Nôtre; hoje em dia são ruínas e briares. As pilastras são encimadas por globos que se assemelham a balas de canhão de pedra. Quarenta e três balaústres ainda podem ser contados em suas tomadas; o resto jaz prostrado na relva. Quase todos ostentam arranhões de balas. Um balaustrado quebrado é colocado no frontão como uma perna fraturada.

Foi neste jardim, mais abaixo do pomar, que seis homens de infantaria ligeira do 1º, tendo feito o seu caminho e não conseguindo escapar, caçaram e apanharam como ursos nas suas tocas, aceitaram o combate com duas companhias hanoverianas, uma das quais estava armada com carabinas. Os hanoverianos forraram esta balaustrada e dispararam de cima. Os homens de infantaria, respondendo de baixo, seis contra duzentos, intrépidos e sem abrigo a não ser os arbustos de groselha, demoraram um quarto de hora a morrer.

Monta-se alguns degraus e passa-se do jardim para o pomar, propriamente dito. Ali, dentro dos limites daquelas poucas braças quadradas, mil e quinhentos homens caíram em menos de uma hora. O muro parece pronto para renovar o combate. Trinta e oito lacunas, perfuradas pelos ingleses em alturas irregulares, ainda existem. Em frente à sexta são colocados dois túmulos ingleses de granito. Há brechas apenas na parede sul, já que o ataque principal veio daquele bairro. A parede está escondida no exterior por uma sebe alta; os franceses subiram, pensando que tinham de lidar apenas com uma sebe, atravessaram-na, e encontraram o muro tanto um obstáculo como uma ambuscada, com os guardas ingleses atrás dele, as trinta e oito brechas disparando de uma só vez uma chuva de tiros de uva e bolas, e a brigada de Soye foi quebrada contra ele. Assim começou Waterloo.

No entanto, o pomar foi levado. Como não tinham escadas, os franceses escalaram-na com as unhas. Eles lutaram corpo a corpo em meio às árvores. Toda esta relva foi embebida em sangue. Um batalhão de Nassau, setecentos fortes, foi dominado lá. O exterior da parede, contra o qual as duas baterias de Kellermann foram treinadas, é roído por tiros de uva.

Este pomar é senciente, como outros, no mês de maio. Tem as suas borboletas e as suas margaridas; a grama é alta lá; os carroças navegam por lá; cordões de cabelo, sobre os quais o linho está a secar, atravessam os espaços entre as árvores e obrigam o transeunte a dobrar a cabeça; caminha-se sobre esta terra inculta, e o pé mergulha em buracos. No meio da relva observa-se uma árvore-bolo arrancada que ali jaz toda verdejante. O major Blackmann encostou-se nela para morrer. Debaixo de uma grande árvore no bairro caiu o general alemão, Duplat, descendente de uma família francesa que fugiu com a revogação do Édito de Nantes. Uma macieira envelhecida e em queda inclina-se para um lado, a sua ferida vestida com uma ligadura de palha e de loam argiloso. Quase todas as macieiras estão caindo com a idade. Não há um que não tenha tido a sua bala ou o seu biscaia.6 Os esqueletos de árvores mortas abundam neste pomar. Corvos voam através de seus ramos, e no final dele é uma madeira cheia de violetas.

Bauduin morto, Foy ferido, conflagração, massacre, carnificina, uma rivuleta formada de sangue inglês, sangue francês, sangue alemão misturado em fúria, um poço abarrotado de cadáveres, o regimento de Nassau e o regimento de Brunswick destruídos, Duplat morto, Blackmann morto, os guardas ingleses mutilados, vinte batalhões franceses, além dos quarenta do corpo de Reille, dizimados, três mil homens naquele casebre de Hougomont só cortados, cortados em pedaços, fuzilados, queimados, com a garganta cortada, e tudo isto para que um camponês possa dizer hoje ao viajante: *Monsieur, dá-me três francos e, se quiseres, explicar-te-ei o caso de Waterloo!*

CAPÍTULO III

DEZOITO DE JUNHO DE 1815

Voltemos atrás, esse é um dos direitos do contador de histórias, e nos coloquemos mais uma vez no ano de 1815, e até um pouco antes da época em que ocorreu a ação narrada na primeira parte deste livro.

Se não tivesse chovido na noite entre 17 e 18 de junho de 1815, o destino da Europa teria sido diferente. Algumas gotas de água, mais ou menos, decidiram a queda de Napoleão. Tudo o que a Providência exigia para fazer de Waterloo o fim de Austerlitz era um pouco mais de chuva, e uma nuvem atravessando o céu fora de época era suficiente para fazer um mundo desmoronar.

A batalha de Waterloo não pôde ser iniciada até as onze e meia da tarde, e isso deu tempo para Blücher subir. Porquê? Porque o chão estava molhado. A artilharia teve que esperar até ficar um pouco mais firme antes de poder manobrar.

Napoleão era oficial de artilharia e sentiu os efeitos disso. A fundação deste maravilhoso capitão foi o homem que, no relatório ao Diretório sobre Aboukir, disse: *Tal uma das nossas bolas matou seis homens.* Todos os seus planos de batalha foram arranjados para projéteis. A chave para sua vitória foi fazer a artilharia convergir em um ponto. Ele tratou a estratégia do general hostil como uma cidadela, e fez uma brecha nela. Ele dominou o ponto fraco com tiro de uva; Juntou-se e dissolveu batalhas com canhões. Havia algo do atirador em sua genialidade. Bater em praças, pulverizar regimentos, quebrar linhas, esmagar e dispersar massas – para ele tudo estava nisto, atacar, atacar, atacar incessantemente – e confiou essa tarefa à bola de canhão. Um método irrefutável e que, unido ao génio, tornou invencível este sombrio atleta do pugilismo da guerra no espaço de quinze anos.

Em 18 de junho de 1815, ele confiou ainda mais em sua artilharia, porque tinha números ao seu lado. Wellington tinha apenas cento e cinquenta e nove bocas de fogo; Napoleão tinha duzentos e quarenta.

Suponhamos que o solo seco e a artilharia capaz de se mover, a ação teria começado às seis horas da manhã. A batalha teria sido vencida e terminado às duas horas, três horas antes da mudança de sorte a favor dos prussianos. Que culpa atribui a Napoleão pela perda desta batalha? O naufrágio deve-se ao piloto?

Foi o evidente declínio físico de Napoleão que complicou esta época por uma diminuição interior da força? Teriam os vinte anos de guerra desgastado a lâmina como tinha usado a bainha, a alma e o corpo? Será que o veterano se fez sentir desastrosamente no líder? Numa palavra, este génio, como muitos historiadores notáveis pensaram, estava a sofrer de um eclipse? Será que ele entrou em um frenesi para disfarçar seus poderes enfraquecidos de si mesmo? Será que ele começou a vacilar sob o delírio de um sopro de aventura? Tornara-se" um assunto grave em geral" inconsciente do perigo? Existe uma época, nesta classe de grandes homens materiais, que podem ser chamados de gigantes da ação, em que o gênio se torna míope? A velhice não se apodera dos génios do ideal; para os Dantes e Miguel Ângelo envelhecer é crescer em grandeza; é crescer menos para os Aníbales e os Bonapartes? Napoleão perdera o sentido direto da vitória? Teria ele chegado a um ponto em que já não podia reconhecer o recife, não poderia mais adivinhar a armadilha, não poderia mais discernir a beira do abismo? Teria ele perdido o poder de perfumar catástrofes? Aquele que outrora conhecera todos os caminhos para triunfar, e que, do cume da sua carruagem de relâmpagos, os apontava com um dedo soberano, chegara agora àquele estado de sinistro espanto quando podia levar as suas tumultuosas legiões agarradas a ele, ao precipício? Foi tomado aos quarenta e seis anos de idade por uma suprema loucura? Será que aquele cocheiro titânico do destino já não passava de um imenso diabo atrevido?

Pensamos que não.

O seu plano de batalha era, pela confissão de todos, uma obra-prima. Ir direto para o centro da linha dos Aliados, fazer uma brecha no inimigo, cortá-los em dois, empurrar a metade britânica de volta para Hal, e a metade prussiana para Tongres, fazer dois fragmentos estilhaçados de Wellington e Blücher, carregar Mont-Saint-Jean, tomar Bruxelas, lançar o alemão no Reno, e o inglês para o mar. Tudo isso estava contido naquela batalha, segundo Napoleão. Depois as pessoas viam.

É claro que não temos aqui a pretensão de fornecer uma história da batalha de Waterloo, uma das cenas da fundação da história que estamos relatando está ligada a essa batalha, mas essa história não é o nosso assunto, essa história, aliás, foi terminada, e terminada de maneira magistral, de um ponto de vista por Napoleão, e de outro ponto de vista por toda uma plêiade de historiadores.[7]

Quanto a nós, deixamos os historiadores em desacordo; somos apenas uma testemunha distante, um transeunte na planície, um buscador curvando-se sobre aquele solo todo feito de carne humana, tomando aparências para realidades, por acaso; não temos o direito de nos opor, em nome da ciência, a um conjunto de factos que contêm ilusões, sem dúvida; não possuímos nem prática militar nem capacidade estratégica que autorizem um sistema; na nossa opinião, uma cadeia de acidentes dominou os dois líderes em Waterloo; e quando se torna uma questão de destino, esse misterioso culpado, julgamos como aquele juiz engenhoso, a população.

CAPÍTULO IV

Um

As pessoas que desejam ter uma ideia clara da batalha de Waterloo têm apenas de colocar, mentalmente, no terreno, um A maiúsculo. O membro esquerdo do A é a estrada para Nivelles, o membro direito é a estrada para Genappe, a gravata do A é a estrada oca para Ohain de Braine-l'Alleud. O topo do A é Mont-Saint-Jean, onde está Wellington; a ponta inferior esquerda é Hougomont, onde Reille está estacionado com Jérôme Bonaparte; a ponta direita é a Belle-Alliance, onde Napoleão estava. No centro deste acorde está o ponto preciso onde a palavra final da batalha foi pronunciada. Foi lá que o leão foi colocado, o símbolo involuntário do heroísmo supremo da Guarda Imperial.

O triângulo incluído no topo do A, entre os dois membros e a gravata, é o planalto de Mont-Saint-Jean. A disputa por esse planalto constituiu toda a batalha. As alas dos dois exércitos se estendiam à direita e à esquerda das duas estradas até Genappe e Nivelles; d'Erlon de frente para Picton, Reille de frente para Hill.

Atrás da ponta do A, atrás do planalto de Mont-Saint-Jean, está a floresta de Soignes.

Quanto à planície em si, que o leitor imagine para si mesmo uma vasta ondulação de terreno; cada subida comanda a próxima subida, e todas as ondulações se montam em direção ao Monte Saint-Jean, e lá terminam na floresta.

Duas tropas hostis em um campo de batalha são dois lutadores. É uma questão de agarrar o adversário pela cintura. Um procura tropeçar no outro. Agarram-se a tudo: um arbusto é um ponto de apoio; um ângulo da parede oferece-lhes um descanso ao ombro; pela falta de um casebre sob cuja cobertura possam elaborar, um regimento cede o seu terreno; Um desnível no terreno, uma viragem fortuita na paisagem, um caminho cruzado encontrado no momento certo, um bosque, uma ravina, podem ficar no calcanhar daquele colosso que se chama exército, e impedir o seu recuo. Quem abandona o campo é espancado; daí a necessidade de recair sobre o líder responsável, de examinar o mais insignificante amontoado de árvores e de estudar profundamente o menor relevo no solo.

Os dois generais estudaram atentamente a planície de Mont-Saint-Jean, agora chamada de planície de Waterloo. No ano anterior, Wellington, com a sagacidade da clarividência, examinou-a como a possível sede de uma grande batalha. Neste local, e para este duelo, no dia 18 de junho, Wellington teve o bom poste, Napoleão o mau poste. O exército inglês estava estacionado acima, o exército francês abaixo.

É quase supérfluo aqui esboçar a aparição de Napoleão a cavalo, de vidro na mão, nas alturas de Rossomme, ao amanhecer, em 18 de junho de 1815. Todo o mundo o viu antes que possamos mostrá-lo. Aquele perfil calmo sob o pequeno chapéu de três cantos da escola de Brienne, aquele uniforme verde, os reversos brancos escondendo a estrela da Legião de Honra, seu grande casaco escondendo seus epaulets, o canto da fita vermelha espreitando por baixo de seu colete, suas calças de couro, o cavalo branco com o pano de sela de veludo roxo ostentando nos cantos coroados N e águias, Botas hessianas sobre meias de seda, esporas de prata, a espada de Marengo", toda aquela figura do último dos Cæsars está presente em todas as imaginações, saudada com aclamações por uns, severamente considerada por outros.

Essa figura permaneceu por muito tempo totalmente na luz; isto surgiu de uma certa penumbra lendária desenvolvida pela maioria dos heróis, e que sempre esconde a verdade por mais ou menos tempo; Mas a história e a luz do dia chegaram.

Essa luz chamada história é impiedosa; possui esta qualidade peculiar e divina, que, pura luz como é, e precisamente porque é inteiramente luz, muitas vezes projeta uma sombra em lugares onde as pessoas até então tinham visto raios; do mesmo homem constrói dois fantasmas diferentes, e um ataca o outro e executa a justiça sobre ele, e as sombras do déspota lutam com o brilhantismo do líder. Daí surge uma medida mais verdadeira nos juízos definitivos das nações. Babilônia violada diminui Alexandre, Roma acorrentada diminui César, Jerusalém assassinada diminui Tito, tirania segue o tirano. É uma desgraça para um homem deixar para trás a noite que tem a sua forma.

CAPÍTULO V

O QUID OBSCURUM DAS BATALHAS

Todos conhecem a primeira fase desta batalha; um início conturbado, incerto, hesitante, ameaçador para ambos os exércitos, mas ainda mais para os ingleses do que para os franceses.

Choveu a noite toda, a terra foi cortada pela chuva, a água acumulou-se aqui e ali nos ocos da planície como se estivesse em barris; em alguns pontos a engrenagem das carruagens de artilharia foi enterrada até os eixos, os circingles dos cavalos estavam pingando com lama líquida. Se o trigo e o centeio pisoteados por esta coorte de transportes na marcha não tivessem preenchido os trilhos e espalhado uma ninhada sob as rodas, todo o movimento, particularmente nos vales, na direção de Papelotte teria sido impossível.

O caso começou tarde. Napoleão, como já explicamos, tinha o hábito de manter toda a sua artilharia bem na mão, como uma pistola, apontando-a ora para um ponto, ora para outro, da batalha; e era seu desejo esperar até que as baterias do cavalo pudessem se mover e galopar livremente. Para isso, era necessário que o sol saísse e secasse o solo. Mas o sol não apareceu. Já não era o encontro de Austerlitz. Quando o primeiro canhão foi disparado, o general inglês, Colville, olhou para o seu relógio e notou que passavam trinta e cinco minutos das onze.

A ação foi iniciada furiosamente, com mais fúria, talvez, do que o imperador desejaria, pela ala esquerda dos franceses apoiada em Hougomont. Ao mesmo tempo, Napoleão atacou o centro lançando a brigada de Quiot sobre La Haie-Sainte, e Ney empurrou a ala direita dos franceses contra a ala esquerda dos ingleses, que repousava sobre Papelotte.

O ataque a Hougomont foi uma espécie de finta; o plano era puxar Wellington e fazê-lo desviar para a esquerda. Este plano teria sido bem sucedido se as quatro companhias da guarda inglesa e os bravos belgas da divisão de Perponcher não tivessem mantido a posição de forma sólida, e Wellington, em vez de concentrar as suas tropas lá, pudesse limitar-se a enviar mais três, como reforços, apenas mais quatro companhias de guardas e um batalhão de Brunswick.

O ataque da ala direita dos franceses a Papelotte foi calculado, na verdade, para derrubar a esquerda inglesa, para cortar a estrada para Bruxelas, para barrar a passagem contra possíveis prussianos, para forçar Mont-Saint-Jean, para virar Wellington de volta em Hougomont, daí em Braine-l'Alleud, daí em Hal; nada mais fácil. Com exceção de alguns incidentes, este ataque foi bem-sucedido. Papelotte foi levado; La Haie-Sainte foi transportada.

Um detalhe a ser observado. Havia na infantaria inglesa, particularmente na brigada de Kempt, muitos recrutas brutos. Estes jovens soldados foram valentes na presença da nossa infantaria duvidosa; a sua inexperiência extirpou-os intrépidamente do dilema; eles prestaram um serviço particularmente excelente como escaramuças: o soldado escaramuçador, deixado um pouco para si mesmo, torna-se, por assim dizer, seu próprio general. Estes recrutas exibiam alguma da engenhosidade e fúria francesas. Este noviço de infantaria tinha traço. Isso desagradou Wellington.

Após a tomada de La Haie-Sainte, a batalha vacilou.

Há neste dia um intervalo obscuro, do meio-dia às quatro horas; A parte intermediária desta batalha é quase indistinta e participa da sombria do conflito corpo-a-corpo. Crepúsculo reina sobre ele. Percebemos grandes flutuações naquele nevoeiro, uma miragem vertiginosa, parafernália de guerra quase desconhecida nos dias de hoje, colbacks pendentes, sabre-taches flutuantes, cintos cruzados, caixas de cartuchos para granadas, dolmans hussar, botas vermelhas com mil rugas, shakos pesados guarnecidos de torsades, a infantaria quase negra de Brunswick misturada com a infantaria escarlate da Inglaterra, os soldados ingleses com grandes almofadas circulares brancas nas encostas dos ombros para epaulets, o cavalo-luz hanoveriano com as suas cascos oblongas de couro, com mãos de latão e rabos de cavalo vermelhos, o escocês com os seus joelhos nus e plaids, as grandes polainas brancas dos nossos granadeiros; imagens, não linhas estratégicas – o que Salvator Rosa exige, não o que é adequado às necessidades de Gribeauval.

Uma certa tempestade é sempre misturada com uma batalha. *Quid obscurum, quid divinum.* Cada historiador traça, em certa medida, a particularidade que lhe agrada no meio deste pell-mell. Quaisquer que sejam as combinações dos generais, o choque das massas armadas tem um refluxo incalculável. Durante a ação, os planos dos dois líderes entram um no outro e tornam-se mutuamente fora de forma. Tal ponto do campo de batalha devora mais combatentes do que outro, assim como solos mais ou menos esponjosos absorvem mais ou menos rapidamente a água que é derramada sobre eles. Torna-se necessário despejar mais soldados do que se gostaria; uma série de despesas que são imprevistas. A linha de batalha ondula e ondula como um fio, os rastros de sangue jorram ilogicamente, as frentes dos exércitos vacilam, os regimentos formam capas e golfos à medida que entram e se retiram; Todos esses recifes estão continuamente se movendo na frente uns dos outros. Onde estava a infantaria a artilharia chega, a cavalaria corre onde a artilharia estava, os batalhões são como fumaça. Havia algo ali; buscá-lo. Desapareceu; os pontos abertos mudam de lugar, as dobras sombrias avançam e recuam, uma espécie de vento do sepulcro empurra para a frente, lança para trás, distende e dispersa essas multidões trágicas. O que é uma briga? uma oscilação? A imobilidade de um plano matemático expressa um minuto, não um dia. Para retratar uma batalha, é necessário um daqueles pintores poderosos que têm o caos em seus pincéis. Rembrandt é melhor que Vandermeulen; Vandermeulen, exatamente ao meio-dia, fica às três horas. A geometria é enganosa; só o furacão é confiável. É isso que confere a Folard o direito de contradizer Políbio. Acrescentemos que há um certo instante em que a batalha degenera em combate, se especializa e se dispersa em inúmeros feitos detalhados, que, para usar a expressão do próprio Napoleão, "pertencem mais à biografia dos regimentos do que à história do exército". O historiador tem, neste caso, o direito evidente de resumir o todo. Ele não pode fazer mais do que aproveitar os principais contornos da luta, e não é dado a nenhum narrador, por mais consciente que seja, consertar, absolutamente, a forma dessa nuvem horrível que se chama batalha.

Isto, que é verdade para todos os grandes encontros armados, é particularmente aplicável a Waterloo.

No entanto, em determinado momento da tarde, a batalha chegou a um ponto.

CAPÍTULO VI

QUATRO HORAS DA TARDE

Por volta das quatro horas, o estado do exército inglês era grave. O Príncipe de Orange estava no comando do centro, Hill da ala direita, Picton da ala esquerda. O príncipe de Orange, desesperado e intrépido, gritou aos holandeses-belgas: "Nassau! Brunswick! Nunca recue"! Hill, enfraquecido, tinha vindo a apoiar Wellington; Picton estava morto. No exato momento em que os ingleses haviam capturado dos franceses a bandeira do 105º da linha, os franceses mataram o general inglês, Picton, com uma bala na cabeça. A batalha teve, para Wellington, duas bases de ação, Hougomont e La Haie-Sainte; Hougomont ainda resistiu, mas estava em chamas; La Haie-Sainte foi levada. Do batalhão alemão que o defendeu, apenas quarenta e dois homens sobreviveram; todos os oficiais, exceto cinco, foram mortos ou capturados. Três mil combatentes tinham sido massacrados naquele celeiro. Um sargento da Guarda Inglesa, o principal boxeador da Inglaterra, reputado invulnerável por seus companheiros, havia sido morto ali por um pequeno baterista francês. Baring tinha sido deslocado, Alten posto à espada. Muitas bandeiras haviam sido perdidas, uma da divisão de Alten e outra do batalhão de Lunenburg, carregadas por um príncipe da casa de Deux-Ponts. Os Scotch Grays já não existiam; Os grandes dragões de Ponsonby tinham sido cortados em pedaços. Aquela cavalaria valente curvara-se sob os lanceiros de Bro e sob os cuirassiers de Travers; de mil e duzentos cavalos, restaram seiscentos; dos três tenentes-coronéis, dois jaziam na terra", Hamilton ferido, Mater morto. Ponsonby tinha caído, crivado por sete lances. Gordon estava morto. Marsh estava morto. Duas divisões, a quinta e a sexta, foram aniquiladas.

Hougomont ferido, La Haie-Sainte tomada, agora existia apenas um ponto de concentração, o centro. Esse ponto manteve-se firme. Wellington reforçou. Ele convocou Thither Hill, que estava em Merle-Braine; ele convocou Chassé, que estava em Braine-l'Alleud.

O centro do exército inglês, bastante côncavo, muito denso e muito compacto, foi fortemente posicionado. Ocupava o planalto de Mont-Saint-Jean, tendo atrás de si a aldeia, e à sua frente a encosta, então toleravelmente íngreme. Repousava sobre aquela robusta habitação de pedra que na altura pertencia ao domínio de Nivelles, e que marca o cruzamento das estradas – uma pilha do século XVI, e tão robusta que as balas de canhão se retiraram dela sem a ferir. Em todo o planalto, os ingleses cortaram as sebes aqui e ali, fizeram abraços nos espinheiros, empurraram a garganta de um canhão entre dois ramos, afrontaram os arbustos. Lá, a artilharia foi emboscada no mato. Este trabalho punitivo, incontestavelmente autorizado pela guerra, que permite armadilhas, foi tão bem feito, que Haxo, que fora despachado pelo imperador às nove horas da manhã para reconhecer as baterias do inimigo, não descobriu nada disso, e voltou e relatou a Napoleão que não havia obstáculos, exceto as duas barricadas que barravam a estrada para Nivelles e para Genappe. Foi na época em que o grão é alto; à beira do planalto, um batalhão da brigada de Kempt, o 95°, armado com carabinas, estava escondido no trigo alto.

Assim assegurado e reforçado, o centro do exército anglo-holandês estava bem posicionado. O perigo desta posição estava na floresta de Soignes, então adjacente ao campo de batalha, e cortada pelas lagoas de Groenendael e Boitsfort. Um exército não podia recuar sem se dissolver; os regimentos teriam se desfeito imediatamente ali. A artilharia ter-se-ia perdido entre os meandros. O recuo, segundo muitos versados na arte, embora seja contestado por outros, teria sido um voo desorganizado.

A este centro, Wellington acrescentou uma das brigadas de Chassé tiradas da ala direita, e uma das brigadas de Wincke tiradas da ala esquerda, mais a divisão de Clinton. Aos seus ingleses, aos regimentos de Halkett, às brigadas de Mitchell, aos guardas de Maitland, deu como reforços e ajudas, a infantaria de Brunswick, o contingente de Nassau, os hanoverianos de Kielmansegg e os alemães de Ompteda. Isto colocou vinte e seis batalhões sob a sua mão. *A ala direita*, como diz Charras, *foi jogada de volta ao centro*. Uma enorme bateria foi mascarada por sacos de terra no local onde agora está o que é chamado de "Museu de Waterloo". Além disso, Wellington tinha, por trás de uma subida no chão, os Guardas Dragões de Somerset, catorze cavalos fortes. Era a metade restante da justamente celebrada cavalaria inglesa. Ponsonby destruído, Somerset permaneceu.

A bateria, que, se concluída, teria sido quase um reduto, estava atrás de um muro de jardim muito baixo, apoiado por um revestimento de sacos de areia e uma grande encosta de terra. Este trabalho não estava concluído; não houve tempo para fazer uma paliçada para ele.

Wellington, inquieto mas impassível, estava a cavalo, e lá permaneceu o dia inteiro na mesma atitude, um pouco antes do velho moinho de Mont-Saint-Jean, que ainda existe, debaixo de um ulmeiro, que um inglês, um vândalo entusiasta, comprou mais tarde por duzentos francos, cortou e levou. Wellington foi friamente heroico. As balas choviam sobre ele. Seu ajudante de campo, Gordon, caiu ao seu lado. Lord Hill, apontando para uma concha que tinha rebentado, disse-lhe: "Meu senhor, quais são as tuas ordens para o caso de seres morto"? "Para fazer como eu", respondeu Wellington. A Clinton disse laconicamente: "Para manter este lugar até ao último homem". O dia estava evidentemente a passar mal. Wellington gritou aos seus velhos companheiros de Talavera, de Vittoria, de Salamanca: "Meninos, pode-se pensar em retirar? Pense na velha Inglaterra"!

Por volta das quatro horas, a linha inglesa recuou. De repente, nada era visível na crista do planalto, exceto a artilharia e os atiradores; o resto tinha desaparecido: os regimentos, desalojados pelos projéteis e pelas balas francesas, recuaram para o fundo, agora entrecortado pela estrada secundária da fazenda de Mont-Saint-Jean; houve um movimento retrógrado, a frente inglesa escondeu-se, Wellington recuou. "O início do retiro"!, gritou Napoleão.

CAPÍTULO VII

NAPOLEÃO DE BOM HUMOR

O Imperador, embora doente e incomodado a cavalo por um problema local, nunca tinha estado com melhor humor do que naquele dia. Sua impenetrabilidade sorria desde a manhã. No dia 18 de junho, aquela alma profunda mascarada de mármore irradiava cegamente. O homem que tinha sido sombrio em Austerlitz era gay em Waterloo. Os maiores favoritos do destino cometem erros. Nossas alegrias são compostas de sombra. O sorriso supremo é só de Deus.

Ridet Cæsar, Pompeius flebit, disse os legionários da Legião Fulmineira. Pompeu não estava destinado a chorar naquela ocasião, mas é certo que César riu. Enquanto explorava a cavalo à uma hora da noite anterior, em tempestade e chuva, em companhia de Bertrand, as comunas do bairro de Rossomme, satisfeitas com a visão da longa fila de fogueiras inglesas iluminando todo o horizonte, de Frischemont a Braine-l'Alleud, pareceu-lhe esse destino, a quem atribuira um dia no campo de Waterloo, foi exato para a consulta; parou o cavalo e permaneceu por algum tempo imóvel, olhando para o relâmpago e ouvindo o trovão; e ouviu-se este fatalista lançar nas trevas este misterioso ditado: "Estamos de acordo". Napoleão estava enganado. Já não estavam de acordo.

Ele não teve um momento para dormir; Cada instante daquela noite foi marcado por uma alegria para ele. Atravessou a linha dos principais postos avançados, parando aqui e ali para falar com as sentinelas. Às duas e meia, perto do bosque de Hougomont, ouviu o pisar de uma coluna em marcha; pensou no momento que se tratava de um recuo por parte de Wellington. Ele disse: "É a retaguarda dos ingleses que está começando com o propósito de descampar. Vou fazer prisioneiros os seis mil ingleses que acabam de chegar a Ostend". Conversou expansivamente; recuperou a animação que mostrara no seu desembarque no dia primeiro de março, quando apontou ao Grão-Marechal o entusiasmado camponês do Golfo Juan, e gritou: "Bem, Bertrand, aqui já está um reforço"! Na noite de 17 para 18 de junho, reuniu Wellington. "Esse pequeno inglês precisa de uma lição", disse Napoleão. A chuva redobrou em violência; o trovão rolou enquanto o imperador falava.

Às três e meia da manhã, perdeu uma ilusão; Os oficiais que tinham sido enviados para o Reconnoitre anunciaram-lhe que o inimigo não estava a fazer qualquer movimento. Nada mexia; nem um bivouac-fire tinha sido extinto; o exército inglês estava dormindo. O silêncio na terra era profundo; o único barulho estava nos céus. Às quatro horas, um camponês foi trazido até ele pelos escoteiros; este camponês tinha servido de guia para uma brigada de cavalaria inglesa, provavelmente a brigada de Vivian, que estava a caminho de assumir uma posição na aldeia de Ohain, na extrema esquerda. Às cinco horas, dois desertores belgas informaram-lhe que tinham acabado de abandonar o seu regimento e que o exército inglês estava pronto para a batalha. "Tanto melhor"!, exclamou Napoleão. "Prefiro derrubá-los a expulsá-los".

De manhã, desmontou-se na lama da encosta que forma um ângulo com a estrada de Plancenoit, mandou trazer da quinta de Rossomme uma mesa de cozinha e uma cadeira de camponês, sentou-se, com uma treliça de palha para um tapete, e estendeu sobre a mesa a carta do campo de batalha, dizendo a Soult enquanto o fazia: "Um belo tabuleiro de xadrez".

Em consequência das chuvas da noite, os transportes de mantimentos, encravados nas estradas suaves, não tinham conseguido chegar pela manhã, os soldados não tinham dormido, estavam molhados e em jejum. Isso não impediu Napoleão de exclamar alegremente a Ney: "Temos noventa chances em cem". Às oito horas, o café da manhã do imperador foi trazido até ele. Ele convidou muitos generais para isso. Durante o pequeno-almoço, dizia-se que Wellington tinha ido a um baile duas noites antes, em Bruxelas, na Duquesa de Richmond; e Soult, um homem rude de guerra, com rosto de arcebispo, disse: "A bola acontece hoje". O Imperador brincou com Ney, que disse: "Wellington não será tão simples a ponto de esperar por Vossa Majestade". No entanto, esse foi o seu caminho. "Ele gostava de gozar", diz Fleury de Chaboulon. "Um humor alegre estava na base de seu personagem", diz Gourgaud. "Ele abundava em prazeres, que eram mais peculiares do que espirituosos", diz Benjamin Constant. Estas gayeties de um gigante são dignas de insistência. Foi ele quem chamou seus granadeiros de "seus resmungões"; apertou-lhes as orelhas; puxou-lhes os bigodes. "O imperador não fez nada além de brincar com a gente", é a observação de um deles. Durante a misteriosa viagem da ilha de Elba para França, no dia 27 de fevereiro, em alto mar, o brigue de guerra francês, *Le Zéphyr*, tendo encontrado o brigue *L'Inconstant*, no qual Napoleão estava escondido, e tendo pedido a notícia de Napoleão a *L'Inconstant*, o Imperador, que ainda usava no chapéu a cacau branca e amarantina semeada com abelhas, que ele tinha adotado na ilha de Elba, agarrou rindo a trombeta falante, e respondeu por si mesmo: "O imperador está bem". Um homem que ri assim está familiarizado com os acontecimentos. Napoleão entregou-se a muitos ataques desta gargalhada durante o pequeno-almoço em Waterloo. Após o café da manhã, ele meditou por um quarto de hora; depois dois generais sentaram-se sobre a treliça de palha, de caneta na mão e papel de joelhos, e o imperador lhes ditou a ordem de batalha.

Às nove horas, no instante em que o exército francês, escalonado em escalões e posto em marcha em cinco colunas, se tinha mobilizado" as divisões em duas linhas, a artilharia entre as brigadas, a música à cabeça; enquanto batiam a marcha, com rolos nos tambores e as explosões de trombetas, poderosas, vastas, alegres, um mar de cascos, de sabres e de baionetas no horizonte, o imperador foi tocado e exclamou duas vezes: "Magnífico! Magnífico"!

Entre as nove e as dez e meia da tarde, todo o exército, por incrível que pareça, tomou posição e dividiu-se em seis linhas, formando, para repetir a expressão do Imperador, "a figura dos seis V's". Poucos instantes depois da formação do conjunto de batalhas, no meio daquele profundo silêncio, como aquele que anuncia o início de uma tempestade, que antecede os combates, o imperador bateu no ombro de Haxo, enquanto contemplava as três baterias de doze libras, separadas por suas ordens do corpo de Erlon, Reille e Lobau, e destinadas a iniciar a ação tomando Mont-Saint-Jean, que estava situado no cruzamento das estradas Nivelles e Genappe, e disse-lhe: "Há quatro e vinte belas empregadas, General".

Seguro da questão, encorajou com um sorriso, enquanto passavam à sua frente, a companhia de sapadores do primeiro corpo, que ele designara para barricar Mont-Saint-Jean assim que a aldeia fosse transportada. Toda esta serenidade tinha sido atravessada por apenas uma única palavra de altiva piedade; Percebendo à sua esquerda, num local onde agora se ergue um grande túmulo, aqueles admiráveis Scotch Grays, com os seus soberbos cavalos, amontoando-se, disse: "É uma pena".

Em seguida, montou seu cavalo, avançou além de Rossomme e selecionou para seu posto de observação uma elevação contraída de grama à direita da estrada de Genappe para Bruxelas, que foi sua segunda estação durante a batalha. A terceira estação, a adotada às sete da noite, entre La Belle-Alliance e La Haie-Sainte, é formidável; é um nó bastante elevado, que ainda existe, e atrás do qual a guarda estava concentrada numa encosta da planície. Em torno deste knoll as bolas repercutiram das calçadas da estrada, até o próprio Napoleão. Como em Brienne, tinha sobre a cabeça o grito das balas e da artilharia pesada. Bolas de canhão mofadas e velhas espadas e projéteis disformes, devorados pela ferrugem, foram apanhados no local onde estavam os pés de seu cavalo. *Scabra rubigine.* Há alguns anos, um projétil de sessenta quilos, ainda carregado, e com o fusível quebrado nivelado com a bomba, foi desenterrado. Foi neste último posto que o imperador disse ao seu guia, Lacoste, um camponês hostil e aterrorizado, que estava preso à sela de um hussar, e que se virava a cada descarga de lata e tentava esconder-se atrás de Napoleão: "Bobo, é vergonhoso! Você vai se matar com uma bola nas costas". Aquele que escreve estas linhas encontrou, ele próprio, no solo friável deste nó, ao virar a areia, os restos do pescoço de uma bomba, desintegrados, pela oxidação de seis e quarenta anos, e velhos fragmentos de ferro que se partiam como galhos de ancião entre os dedos.

Todos sabem que as ondulações das planícies, onde ocorreu o confronto entre Napoleão e Wellington, já não são o que eram em 18 de junho de 1815. Ao retirar deste campo triste os meios para fazer um monumento a ele, o seu verdadeiro relevo foi retirado, e a história, desconcertada, já não encontra ali o seu rumo. Foi desfigurado para o glorificar. Wellington, quando viu Waterloo mais uma vez, dois anos depois, exclamou: "Eles alteraram meu campo de batalha"! Onde hoje se ergue a grande pirâmide de terra, encimada pelo leão, havia uma colina que descia numa encosta fácil em direção à estrada de Nivelles, mas que era quase uma escarpa à beira da estrada para Genappe. A elevação desta escarpa pode ainda ser medida pela altura dos dois knolls dos dois grandes sepulcros que circundam a estrada de Genappe a Bruxelas: um, o túmulo inglês, está à esquerda; o outro, o túmulo alemão, está à direita. Não há túmulo francês. Toda aquela planície é um sepulcro para a França. Graças aos milhares e milhares de carruagens de terra empregadas na colina de cento e cinquenta metros de altura e meia milha de circunferência, o planalto de Mont-Saint-Jean é agora acessível por uma encosta fácil. No dia da batalha, particularmente do lado de La Haie-Sainte, foi abrupto e difícil de abordar. A encosta ali é tão íngreme que o canhão inglês não conseguia ver a fazenda, situada no fundo do vale, que era o centro do combate. No dia 18 de junho de 1815, as chuvas ainda tinham aumentado mais essa aclividade, a lama complicou o problema da subida, e os homens não só escorregaram para trás, como se prenderam rapidamente no pântano. Ao longo da crista do planalto corria uma espécie de trincheira cuja presença era impossível para o observador distante divinar.

O que era essa trincheira? Vamos explicar. Braine-l'Alleud é uma aldeia belga; Ohain é outro. Estas aldeias, ambas escondidas em curvas da paisagem, estão ligadas por uma estrada com cerca de légua e meia de comprimento, que atravessa a planície ao longo do seu nível ondulado, e muitas vezes entra e enterra-se nas colinas como um sulco, que faz uma ravina desta estrada em alguns lugares. Em 1815, como nos dias atuais, esta estrada cortava a crista do planalto de Mont-Saint-Jean entre as duas rodovias de Genappe e Nivelles; só que agora está em um nível com a planície; era então um caminho oco. Suas duas encostas foram apropriadas para a colina monumental. Esta estrada foi, e ainda é, uma trincheira durante a maior parte do seu percurso; uma trincheira oca, às vezes com uma dúzia de metros de profundidade, e cujas margens, sendo muito íngremes, desmoronaram aqui e ali, particularmente no inverno, sob fortes chuvas. Acidentes aconteceram aqui. A estrada era tão estreita na entrada de Braine-l'Alleud que um transeunte foi esmagado por uma carroça, como é provado por uma cruz de pedra que fica perto do cemitério, e que dá o nome dos mortos, *Monsieur Bernard Debrye, Mercador de Bruxelas*, e a data do acidente, fevereiro de *1637*. Era tão profundo no terreno da mesa de Mont-Saint-Jean que um camponês, Mathieu Nicaise, foi esmagado lá, em 1783, por um deslizamento da encosta, como se afirma em outra cruz de pedra, cujo topo desapareceu no processo de limpeza do terreno, mas cujo pedestal virado ainda é visível na encosta gramada à esquerda da estrada entre La Haie-Sainte e a fazenda de Mont-Saint-Jean.

No dia da batalha, esta estrada oca, cuja existência não era de modo algum indicada, margeando a crista do Mont-Saint-Jean, uma trincheira no cume da escarpa, uma ruela escondida no solo, era invisível; ou seja, terrível.

CAPÍTULO VIII

O IMPERADOR COLOCA UMA PERGUNTA AO GUIA LACOSTE

Assim, na manhã de Waterloo, Napoleão estava contente.

Ele tinha razão; O plano de batalha concebido por ele era, como vimos, realmente admirável.

A batalha uma vez começou, suas várias mudanças, - a resistência de Hougomont; a tenacidade de La Haie-Sainte; o assassinato de Bauduin; a incapacitação de Foy; o muro inesperado contra o qual a brigada de Soye foi quebrada; a fatal negligência de Guilleminot quando não tinha nem petardo nem sacos de pólvora; o atolamento das baterias; as quinze peças sem escolta esmagadas de forma oca por Uxbridge; o pequeno efeito das bombas caindo nas linhas inglesas, e lá se embutindo no solo encharcado de chuva, e só conseguindo produzir vulcões de lama, de modo que o botijão foi transformado em um respingo; a inutilidade da demonstração de Piré sobre Braine-l'Alleud; toda aquela cavalaria, quinze esquadras, quase exterminada; a ala direita dos ingleses muito alarmada, a ala esquerda mal cortada; o estranho erro de Ney em massa, em vez de escalonar as quatro divisões do primeiro corpo; homens entregues a tiro de uva, dispostos em fileiras de vinte e sete de profundidade e com uma fachada de duzentos; os buracos assustadores feitos nessas massas pelas bolas de canhão; atacar colunas desorganizadas; a bateria lateral subitamente desmascarada no flanco; Bourgeois, Donzelot e Durutte comprometeram-se; Quiot repeliu; o tenente Vieux, que Hércules formou na Escola Politécnica, ferido no momento em que batia com um machado na porta de La Haie-Sainte sob o fogo da barricada inglesa que barrava o ângulo da estrada de Genappe a Bruxelas; A divisão de Marcognet presa entre a infantaria e a cavalaria, abatida no focinho das armas em meio ao grão por

Best e Pack, posta à espada por Ponsonby; sua bateria de sete peças cravou; o Príncipe de Saxe-Weimar segurando e guardando, apesar do Conde d'Erlon, tanto Frischemont como Smohain; a bandeira da 105ª tomada, a bandeira da 45ª capturada; aquele hussar negro prussiano parado por corredores da coluna voadora de trezentas cavalarias ligeiras no batedor entre Wavre e Plancenoit; as coisas alarmantes que tinham sido ditas pelos prisioneiros; o atraso de Grouchy; mil e quinhentos homens mortos no pomar de Hougomont em menos de uma hora; Oitocentos homens derrubados em um tempo ainda mais curto sobre La Haie-Sainte, todos esses incidentes tempestuosos que passavam como as nuvens da batalha diante de Napoleão, mal tinham perturbado seu olhar e não tinham ofuscado aquela face da certeza imperial. Napoleão estava habituado a olhar fixamente para a guerra; ele nunca somou os detalhes comoventes, cifrado por cifra; as cifras pouco importavam para ele, desde que fornecessem o total" vitória; não se assustava se os primórdios se desviassem, pois julgava-se senhor e possuidor no fim; soube esperar, supondo-se fora de questão, e tratou o destino como seu igual: parecia dizer ao destino: Não ousarás.

Composto metade de luz e metade de sombra, Napoleão julgava-se protegido no bem e tolerado no mal. Tinha, ou pensava ter, uma conivência, quase se poderia dizer uma cumplicidade, de acontecimentos a seu favor, que equivalia à invulnerabilidade da antiguidade.

No entanto, quando se tem Bérésina, Leipzig e Fontainebleau atrás de um, parece que se pode desconfiar de Waterloo. Uma carranca misteriosa torna-se percetível nas profundezas dos céus.

No momento em que Wellington recuou, Napoleão estremeceu. De repente, viu a mesa do Monte Saint-Jean limpa, e a carrinha do exército inglês desaparecer. Era um rali, mas escondendo-se. O Imperador levantou-se meio em seus estribos. O relâmpago da vitória brilhou de seus olhos.

Wellington, empurrado para um canto na floresta de Soignes e destruído - que foi a conquista definitiva da Inglaterra pela França; foi Crécy, Poitiers, Malplaquet e Ramillies vingados. O homem de Marengo dizimava Agincourt.

Assim, o Imperador, meditando sobre esta terrível viragem da sorte, varreu o seu copo pela última vez sobre todos os pontos do campo de batalha. Seu guarda, de pé atrás dele com os braços aterrados, o observava de baixo com uma espécie de religião. Ele ponderou; examinou as encostas, observou as declividades, examinou os aglomerados de árvores, o quadrado de centeio, o caminho; ele parecia estar contando cada arbusto. Ele olhou com alguma intenção para as barricadas inglesas das duas rodovias, - dois grandes abatis de árvores, que na estrada para Genappe acima de La Haie-Sainte, armados com dois canhões, os únicos de toda a artilharia inglesa que comandava a extremidade do campo de batalha, e que na estrada para Nivelles onde brilhavam as baionetas holandesas da brigada de Chassé. Perto desta barricada, observou a antiga capela de São Nicolau, pintada de branco, que fica no ângulo do cruzamento perto de Braine-l'Alleud; inclinou-se e falou em voz baixa ao guia Lacoste. O guia fez um sinal negativo com a cabeça, que provavelmente era pérfido.

O Imperador endireitou-se e caiu a pensar.

Wellington recuou.

Tudo o que restava fazer era completar este retiro esmagando-o.

Napoleão virando-se abruptamente, enviou um expresso a toda velocidade para Paris para anunciar que a batalha estava ganha.

Napoleão era um daqueles gênios de quem o trovão lança.

Acabara de encontrar o seu trovão.

Ele deu ordens aos cuirassiers de Milhaud para carregar a mesa-terra de Mont-Saint-Jean.

CAPÍTULO IX

O INESPERADO

Eram três mil e quinhentos. Eles formaram uma frente de um quarto de légua em extensão. Eram homens gigantes, em cavalos colossais. Havia seis e vinte esquadrões deles; e tinham atrás de si para apoiá-los a divisão de Lefebvre-Desnouettes, os cento e seis gendarmes escolhidos, a cavalaria ligeira da Guarda, onze cento e noventa e sete homens, e os lanceiros da guarda de oitocentas e oitenta lanças. Usavam cascos sem rabo de cavalo e cuirasses de ferro batido, com pistolas de cavalo nos coldres e longas espadas de sabre. Naquela manhã, todo o exército os admirara, quando, às nove horas, com o bradar das trombetas e toda a música tocando "Observemos a Segurança do Império", eles vieram em uma coluna sólida, com uma de suas baterias no flanco, outra no centro, e posicionados em duas fileiras entre as estradas para Genappe e Frischemont, e tomaram a sua posição para a batalha naquela poderosa segunda linha, tão habilmente organizada por Napoleão, que, tendo na sua extrema esquerda os cuirassiers de Kellermann e na sua extrema-direita os cuirassiers de Milhaud, tinham, por assim dizer, duas asas de ferro.

O ajudante de campo Bernardo levou-lhes as ordens do Imperador. Ney sacou sua espada e se colocou na cabeça deles. Os enormes esquadrões foram postos em movimento.

Em seguida, um espetáculo formidável foi visto.

Toda a sua cavalaria, com espadas erguidas, estandartes e trombetas lançadas à brisa, formada em colunas por divisões, desceu, por um movimento simultâneo e como um só homem, com a precisão de um aríete descarado que está a efetuar uma rutura, a colina de La Belle Alliance, mergulhou nas terríveis profundezas em que tantos homens já tinham caído, desapareceram ali na fumaça, emergindo então daquela sombra, reapareceram do outro lado do vale, ainda compactos e em fileiras estreitas, montando-se a todo o trote, através de uma tempestade de tiro de uva que irrompeu sobre eles, a terrível encosta lamacenta da mesa-terra de Mont-Saint-Jean. Ascenderam, graves, ameaçadores, imperturbáveis; Nos intervalos entre a mosquetaria e a artilharia, o seu pisoteio colossal era audível. Sendo duas divisões, havia duas colunas delas; A divisão de Wathier mantinha a direita, a divisão de Delort estava à esquerda. Parecia que dois imensos acrescentadores de aço se viam rastejando em direção à crista da mesa-terra. Atravessou a batalha como um prodígio.

Nada como tinha sido visto desde a tomada do grande reduto de Muskowa pela cavalaria pesada; Faltava Murat, mas Ney estava novamente presente. Parecia que aquela massa se tornara um monstro e tinha apenas uma alma. Cada coluna ondulava e inchava como o anel de um pólipo. Eles podiam ser vistos através de uma vasta nuvem de fumaça que estava alugada aqui e ali. Uma confusão de capacetes, de gritos, de sabres, um amontoado tempestuoso de cavalos entre os canhões e o florescimento de trombetas, um tumulto terrível e disciplinado; Acima de tudo, os cuirasses gostam das escamas na hidra.

Essas narrações pareciam pertencer a outra época. Algo paralelo a essa visão apareceu, sem dúvida, nos antigos épicos órficos, que falavam dos centauros, dos velhos hippanthropes, daqueles titãs com cabeças humanas e peitos equestres que escalavam o Olimpo a galope, horríveis, invulneráveis, sublimes – deuses e bestas.

Estranha coincidência numérica: vinte e seis batalhões montaram para encontrar vinte e seis batalhões. Atrás da crista do planalto, à sombra da bateria mascarada, a infantaria inglesa, formada em treze quadrados, dois batalhões à praça, em duas linhas, com sete na primeira linha, seis na segunda, os estoques de suas armas aos ombros, mirando o que estava prestes a aparecer, esperou, calmo, mudo, imóvel. Eles não viram os cuirassiers, e os cuirassiers não os viram. Eles ouviram o surgimento dessa enxurrada de homens. Ouviram o barulho inchado de três mil cavalos, o alternado e simétrico dos cascos a todo vapor, o jingle dos cuirasses, o barulho dos sabres e uma espécie de respiração grandiosa e selvagem. Seguiu-se um silêncio terrível; então, de uma só vez, um longo arquivo de braços erguidos, brandindo sabres, apareceu acima da crista, e cascos, trombetas e padrões, e três mil cabeças com bigodes cinzas, gritando: "Vive l'Empereur"! Toda esta cavalaria debochava no planalto, e era como o aparecimento de um terramoto.

De uma só vez, um trágico incidente; à esquerda inglesa, à nossa direita, a cabeça da coluna de cuirassiers erguia-se com um clamor assustador. Ao chegarem ao ponto culminante da crista, ingovernável, totalmente entregue à fúria e ao seu curso de extermínio das praças e dos canhões, os cuirassiers tinham acabado de avistar uma trincheira, uma trincheira entre eles e os ingleses. Era a estrada oca de Ohain.

Foi um momento terrível. O barranco estava ali, inesperado, bocejando, diretamente sob os pés dos cavalos, duas braças profundas entre suas encostas duplas; o segundo arquivo empurrou o primeiro para dentro dele, e o terceiro empurrou o segundo; os cavalos se levantaram e caíram para trás, pousaram em suas assombrações, deslizaram, todos com quatro pés no ar, esmagando e sobrecarregando os cavaleiros; e não havendo meios de recuar", toda a coluna já não passava de um projétil —, a força adquirida para esmagar os ingleses esmagou os franceses; o barranco inexorável só podia ceder quando cheio; Cavalos e cavaleiros rolavam ali pell-mell, moendo uns aos outros, formando apenas uma massa de carne neste golfo: quando esta trincheira estava cheia de homens vivos, o resto marchava sobre eles e passava adiante. Quase um terço da brigada de Dubois caiu nesse abismo.

Começou assim a perda da batalha.

Uma tradição local, que evidentemente exagera as coisas, diz que dois mil cavalos e mil e quinhentos homens foram enterrados na estrada oca de Ohain. Esta figura provavelmente compreende todos os outros cadáveres que foram lançados nesta ravina no dia seguinte ao combate.

Note-se, de passagem, que foi a brigada de Dubois que, uma hora antes, fazendo uma carga para um lado, tinha capturado a bandeira do batalhão de Lunenburg.

Napoleão, antes de dar a ordem para esta carga dos cuirassiers de Milhaud, tinha examinado o chão, mas não tinha sido capaz de ver aquela estrada oca, que nem sequer formava uma ruga na superfície do planalto. Avisado, no entanto, e colocado em alerta pela pequena capela branca que marca o seu ângulo de junção com a estrada de Nivelles, ele provavelmente tinha colocado uma questão sobre a possibilidade de um obstáculo, ao guia Lacoste. O guia tinha respondido que não. Podemos quase afirmar que a catástrofe de Napoleão teve origem naquele sinal da cabeça de um camponês.

Outras mortes estavam destinadas a surgir.

Era possível que Napoleão tivesse vencido essa batalha? Respondemos que não. Porquê? Por causa de Wellington? Por causa da Blücher? Não. Por causa de Deus.

Bonaparte victor em Waterloo; Isso não se enquadra na lei do século XIX. Outra série de fatos estava em preparação, na qual não havia mais espaço para Napoleão. A má vontade dos acontecimentos tinha-se declarado muito antes.

Estava na hora de este vasto homem cair.

O peso excessivo deste homem no destino humano perturbou o equilíbrio. Este indivíduo sozinho contava para mais do que um grupo universal. Estas infinidades de toda a vitalidade humana concentravam-se numa única cabeça; o mundo montado no cérebro de um homem, isso seria mortal para a civilização se durasse. Chegara o momento de a incorruptível e suprema equidade alterar o seu plano. Provavelmente os princípios e os elementos, dos quais dependem as gravitações regulares da moral, como do mundo material, se queixaram. Fumar sangue, cemitérios superlotados, mães em lágrimas, são líderes formidáveis. Quando a terra sofre de um fardo demasiado pesado, há misteriosos gemidos das sombras, aos quais o abismo dá ouvidos.

Napoleão tinha sido denunciado no infinito e a sua queda tinha sido decidida.

Ele envergonhou a Deus.

Waterloo não é uma batalha; é uma mudança de frente por parte do Universo.

CAPÍTULO X

O PLANALTO DO MONTE SAINT-JEAN

A bateria foi desmascarada no mesmo momento com o barranco.

Sessenta canhões e os treze quadrados atreveram à queima-roupa os cuirassiers. O intrépido general Delort fez a saudação militar à bateria inglesa.

Toda a artilharia voadora dos ingleses tinha reentrado nas praças a galope. Os cuirassiers não tiveram sequer tempo para parar. O desastre da estrada oca dizimou-os, mas não os desencorajou. Pertenciam àquela classe de homens que, quando diminuídos em número, aumentam de coragem.

Só a coluna de Wathier tinha sofrido no desastre; A coluna de Delort, que Ney desviara para a esquerda, como se tivesse um pressentimento de emboscada, chegara inteira.

Os cuirassiers atiraram-se sobre as praças inglesas.

A toda velocidade, com freios soltos, espadas nos dentes, pistolas no punho, tal foi o ataque.

Há momentos em batalhas em que a alma endurece o homem até que o soldado é transformado em estátua, e quando toda essa carne se transforma em granito. Os batalhões ingleses, desesperadamente assaltados, não se agitaram.

Então foi terrível.

Todos os rostos das praças inglesas foram atacados de uma só vez. Um turbilhão frenético os envolveu. Aquela infantaria fria permanecia impassível. O primeiro escalão ajoelhou-se e recebeu os cuirassiers nas suas baionetas, o segundo escalão abateu-os; Atrás do segundo escalão os canhões carregaram suas armas, a frente da praça se separou, permitiu a passagem de uma erupção de tiro de uva, e fechou novamente. Os cuirassiers responderam esmagando-os. Os seus grandes cavalos criaram, atravessaram as fileiras, saltaram sobre as baionetas e caíram, gigantescos, no meio destes quatro poços vivos. As bolas de canhão lavravam sulcos nestes cuirassiers; Os cuirassiers faziam brechas nas praças. Arquivos de homens desapareceram, moídos em pó sob os cavalos. As baionetas mergulharam na barriga desses centauros; daí uma hediondez de feridas que provavelmente nunca foi vista em nenhum outro lugar. As praças, desperdiçadas por esta cavalaria louca, fecharam as suas fileiras sem vacilar. Inesgotáveis em matéria de tiro de uva, criaram explosões no meio dos seus assaltantes. A forma deste combate era monstruosa. Estas praças já não eram batalhões, eram crateras; aqueles cuirassiers já não eram cavalaria, eram uma tempestade. Cada praça era um vulcão atacado por uma nuvem; A lava enfrentou um raio.

A praça da extrema-direita, a mais exposta de todas, estando no ar, quase foi aniquilada logo no primeiro choque. It foi formado do 75° regimento de Highlanders. O gaiteiro de foles no centro deixou cair os olhos melancólicos, cheios dos reflexos das florestas e dos lagos, em profunda desatenção, enquanto os homens eram exterminados à sua volta, e sentado num tambor, com o pibroch debaixo do braço, tocava os ares das Terras Altas. Estes escoceses morreram pensando em Ben Lothian, assim como os gregos lembrando Argos. A espada de um cuirassier, que desceu a gaita de foles e o braço que a suportava, pôs fim à canção matando o cantor.

Os cuirassiers, relativamente poucos em número, e ainda mais diminuídos pela catástrofe do barranco, tinham quase todo o exército inglês contra eles, mas eles se multiplicaram de modo que cada homem deles era igual a dez. No entanto, alguns batalhões hanoverianos cederam. Wellington percebeu e pensou em sua cavalaria. Se Napoleão tivesse pensado nesse mesmo momento na sua infantaria, teria vencido a batalha. Este esquecimento foi o seu grande e fatal erro.

De repente, os cuirassiers, que tinham sido os assaltantes, viram-se assaltados. A cavalaria inglesa estava às suas costas. Diante deles dois quadrados, atrás deles Somerset; Somerset significava catorze dragões da guarda. À direita, Somerset tinha Dornberg com o cavalo ligeiro alemão e, à esquerda, Trip com os mosquetões belgas; Os cuirassiers atacaram no flanco e na frente, antes e na retaguarda, por infantaria e cavalaria, tiveram que enfrentar todos os lados. O que importava para eles? Eram um turbilhão. O seu valor era algo indescritível.

Além disso, tinham atrás de si a bateria, que ainda trovejava. Era necessário que assim fosse, ou nunca poderiam ter sido feridos nas costas. Um de seus cuirasses, perfurado no ombro por uma bola de um biscaia,9 está na coleção do Museu de Waterloo.

Para tais franceses era necessário nada menos do que tais ingleses. Já não era um conflito corpo-a-corpo; era uma sombra, uma fúria, um transporte vertiginoso de almas e coragem, um furacão de espadas relâmpago. Num instante, os catorze guardas dragões eram apenas oitocentos. Fuller, seu tenente-coronel, caiu morto. Ney correu com os lanceiros e o cavalo de luz de Lefebvre-Desnouettes. O planalto de Mont-Saint-Jean foi capturado, recapturado, capturado novamente. Os cuirassiers abandonaram a cavalaria para voltar à infantaria; ou, para dizer mais exatamente, toda aquela formidável goleada se colava sem soltar a outra. As praças mantiveram-se firmes.

Houve uma dezena de assaltos. Ney mandou matar quatro cavalos. Metade dos cuirassiers permaneceu no planalto. Este conflito durou duas horas.

O exército inglês ficou profundamente abalado. Não há dúvida de que, se não tivessem sido enfraquecidos no primeiro choque pelo desastre da estrada oca, os cuirassiers teriam dominado o centro e decidido a vitória. Esta cavalaria extraordinária petrificou Clinton, que tinha visto Talavera e Badajoz. Wellington, três quartos vencidos, admirado heroicamente. Ele disse em tom de desabafo: "Sublime"!

Os cuirassiers aniquilaram sete praças de treze, levaram ou cravaram sessenta peças de artilharia, e capturaram dos regimentos ingleses seis bandeiras, que três cuirassiers e três chasseurs da Guarda levaram ao Imperador, em frente à fazenda de La Belle Alliance.

A situação de Wellington tinha piorado. Esta estranha batalha foi como um duelo entre dois homens furiosos e feridos, cada um dos quais, ainda lutando e ainda resistindo, está gastando todo o seu sangue.

Qual dos dois será o primeiro a cair?

O conflito no planalto continuou.

O que tinha acontecido aos cuirassiers? Ninguém poderia ter contado. Uma coisa é certa, que no dia seguinte à batalha, um cuirassier e seu cavalo foram encontrados mortos entre a marcenaria das balanças para veículos em Mont-Saint-Jean, no exato ponto onde as quatro estradas de Nivelles, Genappe, La Hulpe e Bruxelas se encontram e se cruzam. Este cavaleiro tinha furado as linhas inglesas. Um dos homens que recolheu o corpo ainda vive em Mont-Saint-Jean. Seu nome é Dehaze. Tinha dezoito anos na altura.

Wellington sentiu que estava cedendo. A crise estava próxima.

Os cuirassiers não conseguiram, uma vez que o centro não foi quebrado. Como todos estavam na posse do planalto, ninguém o detinha, e de facto ficou, em grande medida, com os ingleses. Wellington detinha a aldeia e a planície culminante; Ney tinha apenas a crista e a inclinação. Pareciam enraizados naquele solo fatal de ambos os lados.

Mas o enfraquecimento dos ingleses parecia irremediável. A sangria daquele exército foi horrível. Kempt, na ala esquerda, exigiu reforços. "Não há", respondeu Wellington; "Deve deixar-se matar"! Quase nesse mesmo momento, uma singular coincidência que pinta a exaustão dos dois exércitos, Ney exigiu infantaria de Napoleão, e Napoleão exclamou: "Infantaria! Onde ele espera que eu o obtenha? Será que ele acha que eu consigo"?

No entanto, o exército inglês estava no pior dos dois. Os furiosos ataques daquelas grandes esquadras com cuirasses de ferro e peitos de aço não tinham levado a infantaria a nada. Alguns homens agrupados em torno de uma bandeira marcavam o posto de um regimento; tal e tal batalhão era comandado apenas por um capitão ou um tenente; A divisão de Alten, já tão grosseiramente tratada em La Haie-Sainte, foi quase destruída; os intrépidos belgas da brigada de Van Kluze espalharam os campos de centeio ao longo da estrada de Nivelles; quase nada sobrou daqueles granadeiros holandeses que, misturados com espanhóis em nossas fileiras em 1811, lutaram contra Wellington; e que, em 1815, aderiu ao padrão inglês, lutou contra Napoleão. A perda de oficiais foi considerável. Lord Uxbridge, que teve a perna enterrada no dia seguinte, teve o joelho quebrado. Se, do lado francês, naquela briga dos cuirassiers, Delort, l'Héritier, Colbert, Dnop, Travers e Blancard foram incapacitados, do lado dos ingleses houve Alten ferido, Barne ferido, Delancey morto, Van Meeren morto, Ompteda morto, todo o pessoal de Wellington dizimado, e a Inglaterra teve o pior naquela escala sangrenta. O segundo regimento de guardas a pé tinha perdido cinco tenentes-coronéis, quatro capitães e três alferes; o primeiro batalhão da 30ª infantaria tinha perdido 24 oficiais e 1.200 soldados; o 79º Highlanders perdeu 24 oficiais feridos, 18 oficiais mortos, 450 soldados mortos. Os hussardos hanoverianos de Cumberland, um regimento inteiro, com o coronel Hacke à cabeça, que estava destinado a ser julgado mais tarde e descartado, viraram freio na presença da briga, e fugiram para a floresta de Soignes, semeando a derrota até Bruxelas. Os transportes, os vagões de munição, os vagões de bagagem, os vagões cheios de feridos, ao perceberem que os franceses estavam ganhando terreno e se aproximando da floresta, correram de cabeça para baixo. Os holandeses, abatidos pela cavalaria francesa, gritaram: "Alarme"! De Vert-Coucou a Groenendael, por uma distância de quase duas léguas em direção a Bruxelas, de acordo com o depoimento de testemunhas oculares que ainda estão vivas, as estradas estavam cheias de fugitivos. Este pânico foi tal que atacou o príncipe de Condé em Mechlin, e Luís XVIII. em Ghent. Com exceção da débil reserva montada atrás da ambulância estabelecida na fazenda de Mont-Saint-Jean, e das brigadas de Vivian e Vandeleur, que ladeavam a ala esquerda, Wellington não tinha mais cavalaria. Várias baterias estavam desmontadas. Estes factos são atestados por Siborne; e Pringle, exagerando o desastre, chega a dizer que o exército anglo-holandês foi reduzido a trinta e quatro mil homens. O Duque de Ferro manteve-se calmo, mas os lábios branquearam. Vicente, o comissário austríaco, Alava, o comissário espanhol, que estavam presentes na batalha no cajado inglês, pensou que o duque perdeu. Às cinco horas, Wellington sacou o relógio e ouviu-se murmurar estas palavras sinistras: "Blücher, ou noite"!

Foi mais ou menos nesse momento que uma linha distante de baionetas brilhou nas alturas na direção de Frischemont.

Aí vem a mudança de cara neste drama gigante.

CAPÍTULO XI

UM MAU GUIA PARA NAPOLEÃO; UM BOM GUIA PARA BÜLOW

A dolorosa surpresa de Napoleão é bem conhecida. Grouchy esperava, Blücher chegando. Morte em vez de vida.

O destino tem estas voltas; esperava-se o trono do mundo; foi Santa Helena que se viu.

Se o pastorinho que serviu de guia a Bülow, tenente de Blücher, o tivesse aconselhado a debouch da floresta acima de Frischemont, em vez de abaixo de Plancenoit, a forma do século XIX poderia, talvez, ter sido diferente. Napoleão teria vencido a batalha de Waterloo. Por qualquer outra rota que não a abaixo de Plancenoit, o exército prussiano teria saído em uma ravina intransponível para artilharia, e Bülow não teria chegado.

Agora, o general prussiano, Muffling, declara que uma hora de atraso, e Blücher não teria encontrado Wellington de pé. "A batalha estava perdida".

Estava na hora de Bülow chegar, como se verá. Além disso, tinha sido muito atrasado. Ele tinha bivouacked em Dion-le-Mont, e tinha partido ao amanhecer; mas as estradas estavam intransitáveis, e suas divisões ficavam firmes no pântano. As rotas subiam até os cubos dos canhões. Além disso, ele tinha sido obrigado a passar o Dyle na ponte estreita de Wavre; a rua que levava à ponte tinha sido disparada pelos franceses, de modo que os caissons e vagões de munição não podiam passar entre duas fileiras de casas em chamas, e tinham sido obrigados a esperar até que a conflagração fosse extinta. Era meio-dia antes que a vanguarda de Bülow conseguisse chegar a Chapelle-Saint-Lambert.

Se a ação tivesse começado duas horas antes, teria terminado às quatro horas, e Blücher teria caído na batalha vencida por Napoleão. Tais são esses imensos riscos proporcionais a um infinito que não podemos compreender.

O Imperador fora o primeiro, já ao meio-dia, a descer com o seu copo de campo, no horizonte extremo, algo que lhe tinha atraído a atenção. Ele disse: "Vejo uma nuvem, que me parece ser tropas". Então ele perguntou ao Duque de Dalmácia: "Soult, o que você vê na direção de Chapelle-Saint-Lambert"? O marechal, nivelando o copo, respondeu: "Quatro ou cinco mil homens, Senhor; evidentemente Grouchy". Mas permaneceu imóvel na névoa. Todos os óculos do cajado haviam estudado "a nuvem" apontada pelo Imperador. Alguns disseram: "São árvores". A verdade é que a nuvem não se moveu. O imperador destacou a divisão de cavalaria ligeira de Domon para o reconhecimento naquele quartel.

Bülow não se mexeu, de fato. Sua vanguarda era muito fraca e não conseguia realizar nada. Ele foi obrigado a esperar pelo corpo do corpo do exército, e ele tinha recebido ordens para concentrar suas forças antes de entrar na linha; mas às cinco horas, percebendo o perigo de Wellington, Blücher ordenou que Bülow atacasse, e proferiu estas palavras notáveis: "Devemos dar ar ao exército inglês".

Um pouco mais tarde, as divisões de Losthin, Hiller, Hacke e Ryssel se posicionaram diante do corpo de Lobau, a cavalaria do príncipe Guilherme da Prússia debouched da floresta de Paris, Plancenoit estava em chamas, e as bolas de canhão prussianas começaram a chover mesmo sobre as fileiras da guarda na reserva atrás de Napoleão.

CAPÍTULO XII

A GUARDA

Cada um sabe o resto: a irrupção de um terceiro exército; a batalha despedaçada; oitenta e seis bocas de fogo trovejando simultaneamente; Pirch o primeiro a surgir com Bülow; A cavalaria de Zieten liderada por Blücher em pessoa, os franceses recuaram; Marcognet varreu do planalto de Ohain; Durutte desalojado de Papelotte; Donzelot e Quiot recuando; Lobau apanhado no flanco; uma nova batalha precipitando-se sobre os nossos regimentos desmantelados ao cair da noite; toda a linha inglesa retomando a ofensiva e avançando; a gigantesca brecha feita no exército francês; o shot de uva inglês e o shot de uva prussiano ajudando-se mutuamente; o extermínio; desastre na frente; desastre no flanco; a Guarda entrando na linha no meio desse terrível desmoronamento de todas as coisas.

Conscientes de que estavam prestes a morrer, gritaram: "Vive l'Empereur"! A história não registra nada mais comovente do que aquela agonia que irrompe em aclamações.

O céu estava nublado durante todo o dia. De repente, naquele exato momento, eram oito horas da noite, as nuvens no horizonte se separaram e permitiram que o brilho grandioso e sinistro do sol poente passasse, frustrando os ulmeiros na estrada de Nivelles. Tinham-na visto crescer em Austerlitz.

Cada batalhão da Guarda foi comandado por um general para esta catástrofe final. Friant, Michel, Roguet, Harlet, Mallet, Poret de Morvan, estavam lá. Quando apareceram os altos gorros dos granadeiros da Guarda, com as suas grandes placas com a águia, simétricos, em linha, tranquilos, no meio daquele combate, o inimigo sentiu um respeito pela França; pensavam ter visto vinte vitórias entrando no campo de batalha, com asas abertas, e aqueles que eram os conquistadores, acreditando estar vencidos, recuaram; mas Wellington gritou: "Levanta-te, guarda, e mira direito"! O regimento vermelho de guardas ingleses, deitado atrás das sebes, brotou, uma nuvem de tiro de uva crivava a bandeira tricolor e assobiava em torno de nossas águias; todos se atiraram para a frente, e a carnificina final começou. Na escuridão, a Guarda Imperial sentiu o exército perder terreno à sua volta e, no grande choque da derrota, ouviu a fuga desesperada que tomara o lugar do "Vive l'Empereur"! e, com a fuga atrás dele, continuou a avançar, mais esmagada, perdendo mais homens a cada passo que dava. Não havia ninguém que hesitasse, nenhum homem tímido em suas fileiras. O soldado daquela tropa era tão herói quanto o general. Nenhum homem estava desaparecido naquele suicídio.

Ney, desnorteado, grande com toda a grandeza da morte aceita, ofereceu-se a todos os golpes naquela tempestade. Ele teve seu quinto cavalo morto sob ele lá. Transpirando, os olhos em chamas, espumando na boca, com uniforme desabotoado, um de seus epaulets meio cortado por um golpe de espada de um guarda de cavalos, sua placa com a grande águia amassada por uma bala; sangrando, triste, magnífico, com uma espada quebrada na mão, disse: "Venha ver como morre um marechal da França no campo de batalha"! Mas em vão; ele não morreu. Ele estava maltrapilho e zangado. Em Drouet d'Erlon, ele lançou esta pergunta: "Você não vai se matar"? No meio de toda aquela artilharia empenhada em esmagar um punhado de homens, gritou: "Então não há nada para mim! Ah! Gostaria que todas estas balas inglesas entrassem nas minhas entranhas"! Homem infeliz, estás reservado às balas francesas!

CAPÍTULO XIII

A CATÁSTROFE

A goleada atrás da Guarda foi melancólica.

O exército cedeu subitamente por todos os lados ao mesmo tempo: Hougomont, La Haie-Sainte, Papelotte, Plancenoit. O grito "Traição"! foi seguido por um grito de "Salvem-se quem puder"! Um exército que está a dissolver-se é como um degelo. Todos os rendimentos, rachaduras, rachaduras, flutuadores, rolos, quedas, solavancos, pressas, são precipitados. A desintegração não tem precedentes. Ney pega um cavalo emprestado, salta sobre ele e, sem chapéu, cravat ou espada, coloca-se do outro lado da estrada de Bruxelas, parando tanto o inglês como o francês. Esforça-se por deter o exército, recorda-o ao seu dever, insulta-o, agarra-se à derrota. Ele está sobrecarregado. Os soldados voam dele, gritando: "Viva o Marechal Ney"! Dois dos regimentos de Durutte vão e vêm em aflição como se jogados de um lado para o outro entre as espadas dos Uhlans e a fusilada das brigadas de Kempt, Best, Pack e Rylandt; O pior dos conflitos corpo a corpo é a derrota; os amigos matam-se uns aos outros para escapar; Esquadrões e batalhões quebram e se dispersam uns contra os outros, como a tremenda espuma da batalha. Lobau numa extremidade, e Reille na outra, são arrastados para a maré. Em vão Napoleão ergue muros do que lhe resta da sua Guarda; em vão gasta num último esforço os seus últimos esquadrões úteis. Quiot retira-se antes de Vivian, Kellermann antes de Vandeleur, Lobau antes de Bülow, Morand antes de Pirch, Domon e Subervic antes do príncipe Guilherme da Prússia; Guyot, que liderou os esquadrões do imperador até a carga, cai sob os pés dos dragões ingleses. Napoleão galopa para além da linha dos fugitivos, arenga, insiste, ameaça, seduzi-os. Todas as bocas que pela manhã gritaram: "Viva o Imperador"! permanecem escancaradas; dificilmente o reconhecem. A cavalaria prussiana, recém-chegada, avança, voa, corta, mata, extermina. Os cavalos atacam, os canhões fogem; os soldados do trem de artilharia desaproveitam os caissons e usam os cavalos para fazer sua fuga; Transportes capotados, com as quatro rodas no ar, entopem a estrada e ocasionam massacres. Os homens são esmagados, pisoteados, outros caminham sobre os mortos e os vivos. Perdem-se os braços. Uma multidão vertiginosa enche as estradas, os caminhos, as pontes, as planícies, as colinas, os vales, os bosques, onerados por esta invasão de quarenta mil homens. Gritos de desespero, mochilas e armas arremessadas entre o centeio, passagens forçadas na ponta da espada, não mais camaradas, não mais oficiais, não mais generais, um terror inexprimível. Zieten põe a França à espada à vontade. Leões convertidos em cabras. Tal foi o voo.

Em Genappe, fez-se um esforço para rodar, para apresentar uma frente de batalha, para traçar em linha. Lobau reuniu trezentos homens. A entrada da aldeia foi barricada, mas na primeira rajada de lata prussiana, todos levantaram voo novamente, e Lobau foi levado. Essa saraivada de tiros de uva pode ser vista hoje impressa na antiga empena de um edifício de tijolos à direita da estrada, a poucos minutos de distância antes de entrar em Genappe. Os prussianos lançaram-se em Genappe, furiosos, sem dúvida, por não serem mais inteiramente os conquistadores. A perseguição foi estupenda. Blücher ordenou o extermínio. Roguet tinha dado o exemplo lúgubre de ameaçar de morte qualquer granadeiro francês que lhe trouxesse um prisioneiro prussiano. Blücher superou Roguet. Duhesme, o general da Jovem Guarda, cercado à porta de uma pousada em Genappe, entregou sua espada a um huzzar da morte, que pegou a espada e matou o prisioneiro. A vitória foi completada pelo assassinato dos vencidos. Inflijamos castigo, já que somos história: o velho Blücher desgraçava-se. Esta ferocidade deu o toque final ao desastre. A rota desesperada atravessou Genappe, atravessou Quatre-Bras, atravessou Gosselies, atravessou Frasnes, atravessou Charleroi, atravessou Thuin e só parou na fronteira. Infelizmente! e quem, então, fugia daquela maneira? O Grande Exército.

Esta vertigem, este terror, esta queda em ruína da mais elevada bravura que alguma vez assombrou a história, isso não tem causa? Não. A sombra de uma enorme direita projeta-se sobre Waterloo. É o dia do destino. A força que é mais poderosa do que o homem produziu naquele dia. Daí a rugas aterrorizadas daquelas sobrancelhas; daí todas aquelas grandes almas entregando suas espadas. Aqueles que tinham conquistado a Europa caíram de bruços sobre a terra, sem nada mais para dizer nem fazer, sentindo a sombra presente de uma presença terrível. *Hoc erat in fatis*. Naquele dia, a perspetiva da raça humana sofreu uma mudança. Waterloo é a dobradiça do século XIX. O desaparecimento do grande homem foi necessário para o advento do grande século. Alguém, uma pessoa a quem não se responde, assumiu a responsabilidade sobre si mesmo. O pânico dos heróis pode ser explicado. Na batalha de Waterloo há algo mais do que uma nuvem, há algo do meteoro. Deus passou.

Ao cair da noite, num prado perto de Genappe, Bernard e Bertrand agarraram-se à saia do casaco e detiveram um homem, maltrapilho, pensativo, sinistro, sombrio, que, arrastado até aquele ponto pela corrente da rout, acabara de desmontar, passara o freio do cavalo sobre o braço, e com olhos selvagens regressava sozinho a Waterloo. Era Napoleão, o imenso sonâmbulo desse sonho que se desmoronara, ensaiando mais uma vez avançar.

CAPÍTULO XIV

O ÚLTIMO QUADRADO

Várias praças da Guarda, imóveis no meio desta corrente da derrota, como pedras em água corrente, mantiveram-se até à noite. Chegou a noite, a morte também; Esperavam aquela dupla sombra e, invencíveis, deixavam-se envolver nela. Cada regimento, isolado dos demais, e sem vínculo com o exército, agora despedaçado em todas as partes, morreu sozinho. Eles haviam tomado posição para esta ação final, alguns nas alturas de Rossomme, outros na planície de Mont-Saint-Jean. Ali, abandonadas, vencidas, terríveis, aquelas praças sombrias suportaram os seus estertores de morte de forma formidável. Ulm, Wagram, Jena, Friedland, morreram com eles.

Ao crepúsculo, por volta das nove horas da noite, um deles foi deixado aos pés do planalto de Mont-Saint-Jean. Naquele vale fatal, ao pé daquela declividade que os cuirassiers tinham subido, agora inundada pelas massas dos ingleses, sob os fogos convergentes da cavalaria hostil vitoriosa, sob uma densidade assustadora de projéteis, esta praça lutou. Foi comandado por um oficial obscuro chamado Cambronne. A cada descarga, o quadrado diminuía e respondia. Respondeu ao tiro de uva com uma fusilada, contraindo continuamente as suas quatro paredes. Os fugitivos, parando sem fôlego por um momento ao longe, ouviram na escuridão aquele trovão sombrio e cada vez menor.

Quando esta legião tinha sido reduzida a um punhado, quando nada restava da sua bandeira senão um pano, quando as suas armas, as balas todas sumiam, já não passavam de paus, quando o amontoado de cadáveres era maior do que o grupo de sobreviventes, reinava entre os conquistadores, em torno daqueles homens que morriam tão sublimemente, uma espécie de terror sagrado, e a artilharia inglesa, respirando, calou-se. Isso proporcionou uma espécie de trégua. Estes combatentes tinham à sua volta algo na natureza de um enxame de espectros, silhuetas de homens a cavalo, os perfis negros de canhão, o céu branco visto através de rodas e carruagens de armas, a colossal cabeça da morte, que os heróis viam constantemente através do fumo, nas profundezas da batalha, avançavam sobre eles e olhavam para eles. Através das sombras do crepúsculo podiam ouvir as peças a serem carregadas; os fósforos todos iluminados, como os olhos dos tigres à noite, formavam um círculo em torno de suas cabeças; todos os fiapos das baterias inglesas aproximaram-se dos canhões e, em seguida, emocionado, segurando o momento supremo suspenso sobre esses homens, um general inglês, Colville segundo alguns, Maitland segundo outros, gritou-lhes: "Rendam-se, bravos franceses"! Cambronne respondeu: "—".

{COMENTÁRIO DO EDITOR: Outra edição deste livro tem a palavra "Merde"! no lugar do —"acima.}

CAPÍTULO XV

CAMBRONNE

Se algum leitor francês se opuser a que as suas suscetibilidades sejam ofendidas, terá de se abster de repetir na sua presença aquela que é talvez a melhor resposta que um francês alguma vez fez. Isso nos obrigaria a não consignar algo sublime à História.

Por nossa conta e risco, violemos esta injunção.

Agora, então, entre esses gigantes, havia um Titã: Cambronne.

Para dar essa resposta e depois perecer, o que poderia ser maior? Porque estar disposto a morrer é o mesmo que morrer; e não foi culpa deste homem se ele sobreviveu depois de ser baleado.

O vencedor da batalha de Waterloo não foi Napoleão, que foi posto em fuga; nem Wellington, cedendo às quatro horas, em desespero às cinco; nem Blücher, que não participou do noivado. O vencedor de Waterloo foi Cambronne.

Trovejar tal resposta no relâmpago que te mata é conquistar!

Assim, para responder à Catástrofe, para falar ao Destino, para dar este pedestal ao futuro leão, para lançar tal desafio à tempestade da meia-noite, ao muro traiçoeiro de Hougomont, à estrada submersa de Ohain, ao atraso de Grouchy, à chegada de Blücher, para ser a própria Ironia no túmulo, para agir de modo a ficar de pé embora caído, afogar em duas sílabas a coligação europeia, oferecer aos reis as privações que os Césares conheciam, fazer da mais baixa das palavras a mais sublime, entrelaçando com ela a glória da França, terminar insolentemente Waterloo com Mardigras, terminar Leônidas com Rabellais, coroar esta vitória por uma palavra impossível de falar, perder o campo e preservar a história, ter o riso do seu lado depois de uma carnificina dessas, isso é imenso!

Foi um insulto como uma nuvem de trovão pode lançar! Atinge a grandeza de Ésquilo!

A resposta de Cambronne produz o efeito de uma rutura violenta. "É como a quebra de um coração sob um peso de desprezo. "É o transbordamento da agonia irrompendo. Quem venceu? Wellington? Não! Não fosse Blücher, ele estava perdido. Foi Blücher? Não! Se Wellington não tivesse começado, Blücher não poderia ter terminado. Este Cambronne, este homem que passa a sua última hora, este soldado desconhecido, este infinitesimal de guerra, percebe que aqui está uma falsidade, uma falsidade numa catástrofe, e tão duplamente agonizante; e no momento em que a sua fúria irrompe por causa dela, é-lhe oferecida esta zombaria:" a vida! Como ele poderia se conter? Yonder são todos os reis da Europa, o general ruborizado de vitória, os raios atrevidos de Júpiter; eles têm cem mil soldados vitoriosos, e de volta dos cem mil um milhão; seus canhões ficam com bocas bocejando, o fósforo é aceso; trituram sob seus calcanhares os guardas imperiais e o grande exército; eles acabaram de esmagar Napoleão, e só resta Cambronne – só resta esta minhoca para protestar. Ele vai protestar. Então ele procura a palavra apropriada como se procura uma espada. Sua boca espuma, e a espuma é a palavra. Perante esta vitória mesquinha e poderosa, perante esta vitória que não conta com nenhum vitorioso, este soldado desesperado mantém-se ereto. Concede a sua imensidão avassaladora, mas estabelece a sua trivialidade; e ele faz mais do que cuspir nela. Suportado pelos números, pela força superior, pela matéria bruta, encontra na alma uma expressão: *«Excrément!»* Repetimos: usar essa palavra, fazer assim, inventar tal expressão, é ser o conquistador!

O espírito dos dias poderosos naquele momento portentoso fez sua descida sobre aquele homem desconhecido. Cambronne inventa a palavra para Waterloo como Rouget inventa a "Marselhesa", sob a visitação de um sopro do alto. Uma emanação do redemoinho divino salta e vem varrendo esses homens, e eles tremem, e um deles canta o cântico supremo, e o outro profere o grito assustador.

Este desafio de desprezo titânico que Cambronne lança não só contra a Europa em nome do Império, como seria uma ninharia: lança-o contra o passado em nome da Revolução. Ouve-se, e Cambronne é reconhecida como possuída pelo antigo espírito dos Titãs. Danton parece estar falando! Kléber parece estar de folga!

Perante essa palavra de Cambronne, a voz inglesa respondeu: "Fogo"! As baterias arderam, a colina tremeu, de todas aquelas bocas descaradas arrotou um último jorro terrível de tiro de uva; Um grande volume de fumaça, vagamente branco à luz da lua nascente, rolou e, quando a fumaça se dispersou, não havia mais nada lá. Esse formidável remanescente fora aniquilado; a Guarda estava morta. As quatro paredes do reduto vivo estavam propensas, e dificilmente se discernia, aqui e ali, sequer uma aljava nos corpos; foi assim que as legiões francesas, maiores que as legiões romanas, expiraram em Mont-Saint-Jean, no solo regado de chuva e sangue, em meio ao grão sombrio, no local onde hoje José, que dirige a carroça de Nivelles, passa assobiando, e alegremente chicoteando seu cavalo às quatro horas da manhã.

CAPÍTULO XVI

CITAÇÃO LIBRAS EM DUCE?

A batalha de Waterloo é um enigma. É tão obscuro para aqueles que o ganharam como para aqueles que o perderam. Para Napoleão foi um pânico; Blücher não vê nada nele além de fogo; Wellington não entende nada em relação a isso. Veja os relatórios. Os boletins são confusos, os comentários envolvidos. Uns gaguejam, outros gaguejam. Jomini divide a batalha de Waterloo em quatro momentos; O abafamento corta-o em três mudanças; Só Charras, embora tenhamos outro juízo que o seu em alguns pontos, captou com o seu olhar altivo os contornos característicos daquela catástrofe do génio humano em conflito com o acaso divino. Todos os outros historiadores sofrem por estarem um pouco deslumbrados e, neste estado de deslumbramento, atrapalham-se. Foi um dia de brilho relâmpago; na verdade, um desmoronamento da monarquia militar que, para a vasta estupefação dos reis, atraiu todos os reinos depois dela – a queda da força, a derrota da guerra.

Neste caso, carimbado com uma necessidade sobre-humana, o papel desempenhado pelos homens não equivale a nada.

Se tomarmos Waterloo de Wellington e Blücher, estaremos assim a privar a Inglaterra e a Alemanha de alguma coisa? Não. Nem aquela ilustre Inglaterra nem aquela augusta Alemanha entram no problema de Waterloo. Graças a Deus, as nações são grandes, independentemente dos feitos lúgubres da espada. Nem a Inglaterra, nem a Alemanha, nem a França estão contidas numa bainha. Nesta época em que Waterloo é apenas um embate de espadas, acima de Blücher, a Alemanha tem Schiller; acima de Wellington, a Inglaterra tem Byron. Uma vasta aurora de ideias é a peculiaridade do nosso século, e nessa aurora a Inglaterra e a Alemanha têm um brilho magnífico. São majestosos porque pensam. A elevação de nível que contribuem para a civilização é intrínseca a eles; procede de si mesmo e não de um acidente. O engrandecimento que trouxeram ao século XIX não tem Waterloo como fonte. Só os povos bárbaros é que sofrem um rápido crescimento após uma vitória. Essa é a vaidade temporária de torrentes inchadas por uma tempestade. As pessoas civilizadas, especialmente nos nossos dias, não são elevadas nem humilhadas pela boa ou má sorte de um capitão. A sua gravidade específica na espécie humana resulta de algo mais do que um combate. Sua honra, graças a Deus! A sua dignidade, a sua inteligência, o seu génio, não são números que esses jogadores, heróis e conquistadores, possam colocar na lotaria das batalhas. Muitas vezes perde-se uma batalha e conquista-se o progresso. Há menos glória e mais liberdade. O tambor mantém a sua paz; a razão leva a palavra. É um jogo em que ganha quem perde. Falemos, pois, friamente de Waterloo de ambos os lados. Façamos ao acaso o que é devido ao acaso, e a Deus o que é devido a Deus. Qual é Waterloo? Uma vitória? Não. O número vencedor na loteria.

A quina ganha pela Europa, paga pela França.

Não valia a pena colocar um leão lá.

Waterloo, aliás, é o encontro mais estranho da história. Napoleão e Wellington. Não são inimigos; são opostos. Nunca Deus, que gosta de antíteses, fez um contraste mais marcante, uma comparação mais extraordinária. De um lado, a precisão, a clarividência, a geometria, a prudência, o recuo assegurado, as reservas poupadas, com uma frieza obstinada, um método imperturbável, a estratégia, que aproveita o terreno, as táticas, que preservam o equilíbrio dos batalhões, a carnificina, executada segundo a regra, a guerra regulada, o relógio na mão, nada voluntariamente deixado ao acaso, a antiga coragem clássica, a regularidade absoluta; por outro, a intuição, a adivinhação, a estranheza militar, o instinto sobre-humano, um olhar flamejante, uma coisa indescritível que olha como uma águia, e que atinge como o relâmpago, uma arte prodigiosa em impetuosidade desdenhosa, todos os mistérios de uma alma profunda, associada ao destino; o riacho, a planície, a floresta, o monte, convocados e, de certa forma, forçados a obedecer, o déspota chegando ao ponto de tiranizar o campo de batalha; a fé numa estrela misturava-se com a ciência estratégica, elevando-a, mas perturbando-a. Wellington era o Barême da guerra; Napoleão era o seu Miguel Ângelo; e, nesta ocasião, o génio foi vencido pelo cálculo. De ambos os lados esperava-se um. Foi a calculadora exata que conseguiu. Napoleão estava à espera de Grouchy; ele não veio. Wellington esperava Blücher; ele veio.

Wellington é clássico da guerra vingando-se. Bonaparte, ao amanhecer, encontrou-o em Itália e bateu-lhe soberbamente. A velha coruja fugira diante do jovem abutre. As velhas táticas tinham sido não só atingidas como por um raio, mas desonradas. Quem era aquele corso de seis e vinte? O que significou aquele esplêndido ignorante, que, com tudo contra ele, nada a seu favor, sem provisões, sem munição, sem canhão, sem sapatos, quase sem exército, com um mero punhado de homens contra massas, lançou-se sobre a Europa combinada, e absurdamente obteve vitórias no impossível? De onde tinha emitido aquele condenado fulminante, que quase sem respirar, e com o mesmo conjunto de combatentes na mão, pulverizou, um após o outro, os cinco exércitos do imperador da Alemanha, perturbando Beaulieu em Alvinzi, Wurmser em Beaulieu, Mélas em Wurmser, Mack em Mélas? Quem era esse novato em guerra com o descaramento de um luminar? A escola militar académica excomungou-o, e como perdeu o pé; daí o rancor implacável do velho cesarismo contra o novo; da espada regular contra a espada flamejante; e do erário contra o génio. Em 18 de junho de 1815, esse rancor teve a última palavra, e abaixo de Lodi, Montebello, Montenotte, Mântua, Arcola, escreveu: Waterloo. Um triunfo dos medíocres que é doce para a maioria. O destino consentiu com esta ironia. Em seu declínio, Napoleão encontrou Wurmser, o mais jovem, novamente à sua frente.

Na verdade, para obter Wurmser, bastava branquear o cabelo de Wellington.

Waterloo é uma batalha de primeira ordem, vencida por um capitão da segunda.

O que deve ser admirado na batalha de Waterloo, é a Inglaterra; a firmeza inglesa, a resolução inglesa, o sangue inglês; a coisa soberba sobre a Inglaterra lá, nenhuma ofensa a ela, era ela mesma. Não era o seu capitão; era o seu exército.

Wellington, estranhamente ingrato, declara em uma carta a Lord Bathurst, que seu exército, o exército que lutou em 18 de junho de 1815, era um "exército detestável". O que pensa dessa sombria mistura de ossos enterrados sob os sulcos de Waterloo?

A Inglaterra tem sido demasiado modesta na questão de Wellington. Tornar Wellington tão grande é menosprezar a Inglaterra. Wellington não passa de um herói como muitos outros. Aqueles Scotch Grays, aqueles Guardas de Cavalos, aqueles regimentos de Maitland e de Mitchell, aquela infantaria de Pack e Kempt, aquela cavalaria de Ponsonby e Somerset, aqueles Highlanders jogando o pibroch sob a chuva de tiro de uva, aqueles batalhões de Rylandt, aqueles recrutas totalmente crus, que mal sabiam como manusear um mosquete que se segurava contra as antigas tropas de Essling e Rivoli",isso é que era grandioso. Wellington foi tenaz; nisso reside o seu mérito, e não estamos a tentar diminuí-lo: mas o menor dos seus soldados e da sua cavalaria teria sido tão sólido como ele. O soldado de ferro vale tanto quanto o Duque de Ferro. Quanto a nós, toda a nossa glorificação vai para o soldado inglês, para o exército inglês, para o povo inglês. Se houver troféu, é à Inglaterra que o troféu é devido. A coluna de Waterloo seria mais justa, se, em vez da figura de um homem, levasse no alto a estátua de um povo.

Mas esta grande Inglaterra ficará zangada com o que estamos a dizer aqui. Ela ainda acalenta, depois do seu próprio 1688 e do nosso 1789, a ilusão feudal. Ela acredita na hereditariedade e na hierarquia. Este povo, superado por ninguém em poder e glória, considera-se como uma nação, e não como um povo. E como povo, subordina-se voluntariamente e toma um senhor como cabeça. Como operário, deixa-se desprezar; como soldado, deixa-se açoitar.

Recorde-se que, na batalha de Inkermann, um sargento que, ao que parece, salvou o exército, não podia ser mencionado por Lord Paglan, pois a hierarquia militar inglesa não permite que qualquer herói abaixo do grau de oficial seja mencionado nos relatórios.

O que admiramos acima de tudo, num encontro com a natureza de Waterloo, é a maravilhosa esperteza do acaso. Uma chuva noturna, o muro de Hougomont, a estrada oca de Ohain, Grouchy surdo ao canhão, o guia de Napoleão enganando-o, o guia de Bülow esclarecendo-o, todo este cataclismo é maravilhosamente conduzido.

De um modo geral, digamos claramente, foi mais um massacre do que uma batalha em Waterloo.

De todas as batalhas campais, Waterloo é a que tem a menor frente para um número tão grande de combatentes. Napoleão três quartos de légua; Wellington, meia légua; setenta e dois mil combatentes de cada lado. Desta densidade surgiu a carnificina.

Foi feito o seguinte cálculo, e estabelecida a seguinte proporção: Perda de homens: em Austerlitz, francês, catorze por cento; russos, trinta por cento; Austríacos, quarenta e quatro por cento. Em Wagram, francês, treze por cento; Austríacos, catorze. No Moskowa, francês, trinta e sete por cento; Russos, quarenta e quatro. Em Bautzen, na França, treze por cento; Russos e prussianos, catorze. Em Waterloo, França, cinquenta e seis por cento; os Aliados, trinta e um. Total para Waterloo, quarenta e um por cento; cento e quarenta e quatro mil combatentes; sessenta mil mortos.

Hoje o campo de Waterloo tem a calma que pertence à terra, o suporte impassível do homem, e se assemelha a todas as planícies.

À noite, além disso, dela surge uma espécie de névoa visionária; e se um viajante passeia por lá, se ouve, se assiste, se sonha como Virgílio nas planícies fatais de Filipos, a alucinação da catástrofe toma conta dele. O assustador 18 de junho vive de novo; a falsa colina monumental desaparece, o leão desaparece no ar, o campo de batalha retoma a sua realidade, linhas de infantaria ondulam sobre a planície, galopes furiosos atravessam o horizonte; o sonhador assustado contempla o clarão de sabres, o brilho das baionetas, o clarão das bombas, o tremendo intercâmbio de trovões; ouve, por assim dizer, o chocalho da morte nas profundezas de um túmulo, o vago clamor do fantasma da batalha; essas sombras são granadeiros, essas luzes são cuirassiers; esse esqueleto Napoleão, esse outro esqueleto é Wellington; tudo isto já não existe e, no entanto, choca-se e combate ainda; e as ravinas estão roxas, e as árvores tremem, e há fúria mesmo nas nuvens e nas sombras; todas essas alturas terríveis, Hougomont, Mont-Saint-Jean,

Frischemont, Papelotte, Plancenoit, parecem confusamente coroadas com redemoinhos de espectros empenhados em exterminar uns aos outros.

CAPÍTULO XVII

WATERLOO DEVE SER CONSIDERADO BOM?

Existe uma escola liberal muito respeitável que não odeia Waterloo. Não lhe pertencemos. Para nós, Waterloo é apenas a data estupefacta da liberdade. Que tal águia saia de tal ovo é certamente inesperado.

Se nos colocarmos no ponto de vista culminante da questão, Waterloo é intencionalmente uma vitória contrarrevolucionária. É a Europa contra a França; é Petersburgo, Berlim e Viena contra Paris; é o *statu quo* contra a iniciativa; é o 14 de julho de 1789, atacado até 20 de março de 1815; são as monarquias limpando os baralhos em oposição ao indomável motim francês. A extinção definitiva daquele vasto povo que estava em erupção há vinte e seis anos – tal era o sonho. A solidariedade dos Brunswicks, dos Nassaus, dos Romanoffs, dos Hohenzollerns, dos Habsburgos com os Bourbons. Waterloo tem direito divino em sua crupper. É verdade, que o Império tendo sido despótico, o reino pela reação natural das coisas, foi forçado a ser liberal, e que uma ordem constitucional foi o resultado involuntário de Waterloo, para grande pesar dos conquistadores. É porque a revolução não pode ser realmente conquistada, e sendo providencial e absolutamente fatal, ela está sempre surgindo de novo: antes de Waterloo, em Bonaparte derrubar os antigos tronos; depois de Waterloo, em Luís XVIII. concessão e conformidade com a carta. Bonaparte coloca um postilion no trono de Nápoles, e um sargento no trono da Suécia, empregando a desigualdade para demonstrar igualdade; Luís XVIII. em Saint-Ouen contra-assina a declaração dos direitos do homem. Se você quiser ter uma ideia do que é a revolução, chame-a de Progresso; e se você deseja adquirir uma ideia da natureza do progresso, chame-o de To-morrow. To-morrow cumpre o seu trabalho irresistivelmente, e já o está a cumprir hoje. Atinge sempre o seu objetivo de forma estranha. Emprega

Wellington para fazer de Foy, que era apenas um soldado, um orador. Foy cai em Hougomont e ressurge na tribuna. Assim, o progresso prossegue. Não existe uma ferramenta ruim para esse trabalhador. Não se desconcerta, mas ajusta-se à sua obra divina o homem que venceu os Alpes e o bom e velho inválido do Padre Eliseu. Faz uso do homem gotoso, bem como do conquistador; do conquistador fora, do homem gotoso dentro. Waterloo, ao interromper a demolição dos tronos europeus pela espada, não teve outro efeito senão fazer com que o trabalho revolucionário continuasse em outra direção. Os slashers acabaram; foi a vez dos pensadores. O século que Waterloo pretendia prender prosseguiu a sua marcha. Essa vitória sinistra foi vencida pela liberdade.

Em suma, e incontestavelmente, o que triunfou em Waterloo, o que sorriu na retaguarda de Wellington, o que lhe trouxe todos os quadros de marechais da Europa, incluindo, diz-se, o pessoal de um marechal de França, o que alegremente trunfou os carrinhos cheios de ossos para erguer o nó do leão, o que inscreveu triunfantemente naquele pedestal a data "*junho* 18, 1815"; o que encorajou Blücher, ao pôr o exército voador à espada; aquilo que, do alto do planalto de Mont-Saint-Jean, pairava sobre a França como sobre a sua presa, era a contrarrevolução. Foi a contrarrevolução que murmurou aquela infame palavra "desmembramento". Ao chegar a Paris, viu a cratera próxima; sentiu aquelas cinzas que lhe queimaram os pés, e mudou de opinião; voltou ao gaguejar de uma carta.

Vejamos em Waterloo apenas o que está em Waterloo. De liberdade intencional não há. A contrarrevolução foi involuntariamente liberal, da mesma forma que, por um fenômeno correspondente, Napoleão foi involuntariamente revolucionário. No dia 18 de junho de 1815, o montado Robespierre foi arremessado de sua sela.

CAPÍTULO XVIII

UM RECRUDESCIMENTO DO DIREITO DIVINO

Fim da ditadura. Todo um sistema europeu se desmoronou.

O Império afundou-se numa escuridão que se assemelhava à do mundo romano quando expirou. Mais uma vez contemplamos o abismo, como nos dias dos bárbaros; apenas a barbárie de 1815, que deve ser chamada pelo seu nome de estimação de contrarrevolução, não tardou a respirar, logo caiu ofegante e parou. O Império foi varrido" reconheçamos o fato" e tomado por olhos heroicos. Se a glória está na espada convertida em cetro, o Império tinha sido glória em pessoa. Difundiu sobre a terra toda a luz que a tirania pode dar" uma luz sombria. Diremos mais; uma luz obscura. Em comparação com a verdadeira luz do dia, é noite. Este desaparecimento da noite produz o efeito de um eclipse.

Luís XVIII. reentrou em Paris. As danças circulares do 8 de julho apagaram os entusiasmos do 20 de março. O corso tornou-se a antítese do urso. A bandeira na cúpula das Tulherias era branca. O exílio reinou. A mesa de pinheiros de Hartwell tomou o seu lugar em frente ao trono de flor-de-lise de Luís XIV. Bouvines e Fontenoy foram mencionados como se tivessem ocorrido no dia anterior, tendo Austerlitz se tornado antiquado. O altar e o trono confraternizaram majestosamente. Uma das formas mais indiscutíveis de saúde da sociedade no século XIX foi estabelecida sobre a França e sobre o continente. A Europa adotou o cacau branco. Trestaillon foi celebrado. O dispositivo *non pluribus impar* reapareceu nos raios de pedra que representam um sol na frente do quartel no Quai d'Orsay. Onde havia uma Guarda Imperial, agora havia uma casa vermelha. O Arco do Carrossel, todo carregado de vitórias mal suportadas, atirado do seu elemento entre estas novidades, um pouco envergonhado, talvez seja, de

Marengo e Arcola, desvencilhou-se da sua situação com a estátua do Duque d'Angoulême. O cemitério da Madeleine, uma terrível sepultura de indigentes em 1793, estava coberto de jaspe e mármore, já que os ossos de Luís XVI e Maria Antonieta jaziam naquele pó.

No fosso de Vincennes, um poço sepulcral brotou da terra, lembrando o fato de que o Duque d'Enghien havia morrido no mesmo mês em que Napoleão foi coroado. O Papa Pio VII., que tinha realizado a coroação muito perto desta morte, concedeu tranqüilamente a sua bênção à queda, tal como a tinha concedido à elevação. Em Schoenbrunn havia uma pequena sombra, de quatro anos, a quem era sedicioso chamar de Rei de Roma. E estas coisas aconteceram, e os reis retomaram seus tronos, e o mestre da Europa foi colocado em uma jaula, e o antigo regime tornou-se o novo regime, e todas as sombras e toda a luz da terra mudaram de lugar, porque, na tarde de um certo dia de verão, um pastor disse a um prussiano na floresta: "Vá por este caminho, e não por isso"!

Este 1815 foi uma espécie de abril lúgubre. Antigas realidades insalubres e venenosas foram cobertas de novas aparências. Uma mentira casada em 1789; o direito divino foi mascarado sob uma carta; as ficções tornaram-se constitucionais; preconceitos, superstições e reservas mentais, com o artigo 14 no coração, foram envernizados com o liberalismo. Foi a mudança de pele da serpente.

O homem tornara-se maior e menor por Napoleão. Sob este reinado de matéria esplêndida, o ideal recebera o estranho nome de ideologia! É uma grave imprudência de um grande homem transformar o futuro em escárnio. A população, no entanto, aquele alimento para canhão que tanto gosta do canhão, procurou-o com o seu olhar. Onde é que ele está? O que é que ele está a fazer? "Napoleão está morto", disse um transeunte a um veterano de Marengo e Waterloo. "Ele morreu"!, gritou o soldado; "Você não o conhece". A imaginação desconfiava deste homem, mesmo quando derrubado. As profundezas da Europa estavam cheias de escuridão depois de Waterloo. Algo enorme permaneceu muito tempo vazio com o desaparecimento de Napoleão.

Os reis colocaram-se neste vazio. A Europa antiga aproveitou para empreender reformas. Havia uma Santa Aliança; *Belle-Alliance*, Beautiful Alliance, o campo fatal de Waterloo tinha dito antecipadamente.

Na presença e face àquela Europa antiga reconstruída, esboçaram-se as características de uma nova França. O futuro, que o imperador havia mobilizado, fez a sua entrada. Na testa trazia a estrela, Liberty. Os olhos brilhantes de todas as novas gerações estavam voltados para ele. Fato singular! as pessoas eram, ao mesmo tempo, apaixonadas pelo futuro, pela Liberdade, e pelo passado, Napoleão. A derrota tornara os vencidos maiores. Bonaparte caído parecia mais elevado do que Napoleão ereto. Aqueles que haviam triunfado ficaram alarmados. A Inglaterra mandou-o vigiar por Hudson Lowe, e a França mandou-o vigiar Montchenu. Seus braços cruzados tornaram-se uma fonte de inquietação para os tronos. Alexandre chamou-lhe "a minha insónia". Este terror foi o resultado da quantidade de revolução que estava contida nele. É isso que explica e desculpa o liberalismo bonapartista. Este fantasma fez tremer o velho mundo. Os reis reinavam, mas mal à vontade, com a rocha de Santa Helena no horizonte.

Enquanto Napoleão passava pela luta da morte em Longwood, os sessenta mil homens que haviam caído no campo de Waterloo estavam apodrecendo silenciosamente, e algo de sua paz foi derramada no exterior em todo o mundo. O Congresso de Viena fez os tratados em 1815, e a Europa chamou isso de Restauração.

Foi isso que Waterloo foi.

Mas o que importa para o Infinito? toda aquela tempestade, toda aquela nuvem, aquela guerra, depois aquela paz? Toda aquela escuridão não perturbou por um momento a luz daquele imenso Olho diante do qual um arranque saltando de uma lâmina de grama para outra equivale à águia voando de campanário em campanário nas torres de Notre Dame.

CAPÍTULO XIX

O CAMPO DE BATALHA À NOITE

Voltemos – é uma necessidade neste livro – àquele campo de batalha fatal.

No dia 18 de junho a lua estava cheia. Sua luz favoreceu a perseguição feroz de Blücher, traiu os vestígios dos fugitivos, entregou aquela massa desastrosa à ansiosa cavalaria prussiana e ajudou no massacre. Tais favores trágicos da noite ocorrem às vezes durante catástrofes.

Após o último tiro de canhão ter sido disparado, a planície de Mont-Saint-Jean permaneceu deserta.

Os ingleses ocuparam o acampamento dos franceses; É o habitual sinal de vitória dormir na cama dos vencidos. Eles estabeleceram seu bivouac além de Rossomme. Os prussianos, soltos na derrota recuada, avançaram. Wellington foi à aldeia de Waterloo para elaborar seu relatório para Lord Bathurst.

Se alguma vez o *sic vos non vobis* foi aplicável, foi certamente àquela aldeia de Waterloo. Waterloo não participou e ficou a meia légua do local da ação. Mont-Saint-Jean foi canhão, Hougomont foi queimado, La Haie-Sainte foi tomada de assalto, Papelotte foi queimada, Plancenoit foi queimada, La Belle-Alliance viu o abraço dos dois conquistadores; esses nomes são pouco conhecidos, e Waterloo, que não trabalhou na batalha, carrega toda a honra.

Não somos do número dos que bajulam a guerra; Quando a ocasião se apresenta, dizemos a verdade sobre ela. A guerra tem belezas terríveis que não escondemos; tem também, reconhecemos, algumas características hediondas. Um dos mais surpreendentes é o rápido despojamento dos corpos dos mortos após a vitória. O amanhecer que se segue a uma batalha ergue-se sempre sobre cadáveres nus.

Quem faz isso? Quem assim suja o triunfo? Que mão hedionda e furtiva é aquela que escorrega para o bolso da vitória? Que carteiristas são esses que exercem o seu ofício na retaguarda da glória? Alguns filósofos – Voltaire entre os vários – afirmam que foram precisamente essas pessoas que fizeram a glória. São os mesmos homens, dizem; não existe um corpo de socorro; os que estão eretos saqueiam os que estão propenso na terra. O herói do dia é o vampiro da noite. Afinal de contas, tem-se seguramente o direito de despir um pouco um cadáver quando se é o autor desse cadáver. Pela nossa parte, pensamos que não; Parece-nos impossível que a mesma mão arranque louros e arranque os sapatos de um morto.

Uma coisa é certa, ou seja, que geralmente depois os conquistadores seguem os ladrões. Mas deixemos o soldado, especialmente o soldado contemporâneo, fora de questão.

Cada exército tem uma retaguarda, e é ela que deve ser responsabilizada. criaturas semelhantes a morcegos, meio bandidos e lacaios; todos os tipos de vespertillos que aquele crepúsculo chamado guerra gera; os portadores de uniformes, que não participam dos combates; fingidos inválidos; manceiros formidáveis; sutlers entrelaçados, trotando em pequenos carrinhos, às vezes acompanhados por suas esposas, e roubando coisas que eles vendem novamente; mendigos oferecendo-se como guias aos oficiais; servos de soldados; saqueadores; Exércitos em marcha em tempos passados – não estamos falando do presente – arrastaram tudo isso para trás, de modo que, na linguagem especial, são chamados de "retardatários". Nenhum exército, nenhuma nação, foi responsável por esses seres; falavam italiano e seguiam os alemães, depois falavam francês e seguiam os ingleses. Foi por um desses desgraçados, um retardatário espanhol que falava francês, que o Marquês de Fervacques, enganado pelo seu jargão Picard, e tomando-o por um dos nossos homens, foi traitoriamente morto e roubado no próprio campo de batalha, no decurso da noite que se seguiu à vitória de Cerisoles. O malandro brotou desse saque. A máxima detestável, *Viva no inimigo!* produziu esta lepra, que só uma disciplina rigorosa poderia curar. Há reputações que são enganosas; Nem sempre se sabe por que certos generais, grandes em outras direções, têm sido tão populares. Turenne era adorado por seus soldados porque tolerava a pilhagem; o mal permitido constitui parte do bem. Turenne era tão bom que permitiu que o Palatinado fosse entregue ao fogo e ao sangue. Os saqueadores no trem de um exército eram mais ou menos em número, de acordo com o chefe era mais ou menos severo. Hoche e Marceau não tinham retardatários; Wellington tinha poucos, e fazemos-lhe a justiça de o mencionar.

No entanto, na noite de 18 para 19 de junho, os mortos foram roubados. Wellington era rígido; deu ordens para que qualquer pessoa apanhada em flagrante fosse baleada; Mas Rapine é tenaz. Os saqueadores roubaram em um canto do campo de batalha, enquanto outros estavam sendo baleados em outro.

A lua era sinistra sobre esta planície.

Por volta da meia-noite, um homem rondava, ou melhor, subia na direção da estrada oca de Ohain. Ao que tudo indica, ele foi um daqueles que acabamos de descrever, nem inglês nem francês, nem camponês nem soldado, menos um homem do que um ghoul atraído pelo cheiro dos cadáveres que roubaram para sua vitória, e vieram fuzilar Waterloo. Ele estava vestido com uma blusa que era algo como um grande casaco; era inquieto e audacioso; andou para a frente e olhou para trás. Quem era esse homem? A noite provavelmente sabia mais dele do que o dia. Não tinha saco, mas evidentemente tinha grandes bolsos debaixo do casaco. De vez em quando parava, escrutinava a planície à sua volta como se fosse observado, curvava-se abruptamente, perturbava algo silencioso e imóvel no chão, depois levantava-se e fugia. O seu movimento deslizante, as suas atitudes, os seus gestos misteriosos e rápidos, fizeram-no assemelhar-se àquelas larvas crepusculares que assombram ruínas, e que as antigas lendas normandas chamam de Alleurs.

Certas aves noturnas produzem estas silhuetas entre os pântanos.

Um olhar capaz de perfurar profundamente toda aquela névoa teria percebido a certa distância uma espécie de carroça de pequeno sutler com um capuz de vime canelado, agarrado a um nag faminto que cortava a grama em toda a sua parte enquanto parava, escondido, por assim dizer, atrás do casebre que contíguo à estrada para Nivelles, no ângulo da estrada de Mont-Saint-Jean a Braine l'Alleud; e na carroça, uma espécie de mulher sentada nos cofres e nos pacotes. Talvez houvesse alguma ligação entre aquele vagão e aquele ronco.

A escuridão era serena. Não uma nuvem no zênite. O que importa se a terra for vermelha! a lua permanece branca; Estas são as indiferenças do céu. Nos campos, ramos de árvores quebradas por tiros de uva, mas não caídos, sustentados pela casca, balançavam suavemente na brisa da noite. Uma respiração, quase uma respiração, movia o arbusto. Quivers que se assemelhavam à partida das almas corriam pela grama.

Ao longe, o ir e vir das patrulhas e as rondas gerais do acampamento inglês eram audíveis.

Hougomont e La Haie-Sainte continuaram a arder, formando, uma a oeste, outra a leste, duas grandes chamas às quais se juntou o cordão de fogos bivouac dos ingleses, como um colar de rubis com dois carbúnculos nas extremidades, enquanto se estendiam num imenso semicírculo sobre as colinas ao longo do horizonte.

Descrevemos a catástrofe da estrada de Ohain. O coração fica apavorado ao pensar no que aquela morte deve ter sido para tantos homens corajosos.

Se há algo de terrível, se existe uma realidade que ultrapassa os sonhos, é esta: viver, ver o sol; estar em plena posse da força viril; possuir saúde e alegria; rir bravamente; correr para uma glória que se vê deslumbrante à sua frente; sentir no peito pulmões que respiram, um coração que bate, uma vontade que raciocina; falar, pensar, esperar, amar; ter mãe, ter esposa, ter filhos; ter a luz – e de uma só vez, no espaço de um grito, em menos de um minuto, afundar-se num abismo; cair, rolar, esmagar, esmagar; ver espigas de trigo, flores, folhas, ramos; não conseguir agarrar nada; sentir a espada inútil, homens debaixo de um, cavalos em cima de um; lutar em vão, já que os ossos foram quebrados por algum chute na escuridão; sentir um calcanhar que faz com que os olhos partam das suas órbitas; morder os sapatos dos cavalos com raiva; sufocar, gritar, contorcer-se; estar por baixo e dizer a si mesmo: "Mas há pouco tempo eu era um homem vivo"!

Ali, onde aquele lamentável desastre tinha proferido o seu chocalho de morte, tudo era silêncio agora. As bordas da estrada oca estavam sobrecarregadas de cavalos e cavaleiros, inextricavelmente amontoados.

Emaranhamento terrível! Já não havia declive, pois os cadáveres tinham nivelado a estrada com a planície, e chegado à borda como um alqueire bem cheio de cevada. Um monte de cadáveres na parte superior, um rio de sangue na parte inferior – tal era aquela estrada na noite de 18 de junho de 1815. O sangue correu até à autoestrada de Nivelles, e lá transbordou numa grande piscina em frente aos abates de árvores que barravam o caminho, num local que ainda está apontado.

Recorde-se que foi no ponto oposto, em direção à estrada de Genappe, que se verificou a destruição dos cuirassiers. A espessura da camada de corpos foi proporcional à profundidade da estrada oca. Para o meio, no ponto em que se tornou nivelado, por onde a divisão de Delort tinha passado, a camada de cadáveres era mais fina.

O ronco noturno que acabamos de mostrar ao leitor estava indo nessa direção. Ele estava procurando aquele vasto túmulo. Ele olhou em volta. Ele passou os mortos em algum tipo de revisão horrível. Andava com os pés no sangue.

De repente, fez uma pausa.

Alguns passos à sua frente, na estrada oca, no ponto em que a pilha de mortos chegava ao fim, uma mão aberta, iluminada pela lua, projetada por baixo daquele monte de homens. Essa mão tinha no dedo algo cintilante, que era um anel de ouro.

O homem inclinou-se, permaneceu agachado por um momento, e quando se levantou já não havia um anel na mão.

Ele não se levantou precisamente; Permaneceu em atitude inclinada e assustada, de costas voltadas para o monte de mortos, perscrutando o horizonte de joelhos, com toda a parte superior do corpo apoiada nos dois dedos indicadores, que repousavam sobre a terra, e a cabeça espreitando acima da borda da estrada oca. As quatro patas do chacal se adequam a algumas ações.

Então, chegando a uma decisão, ele se levantou.

Naquele momento, ele deu um péssimo começo. Sentiu alguém agarrá-lo por trás.

Ele rodou em volta; era a mão aberta, que se fechara, e agarrara a saia do casaco.

Um homem honesto teria ficado aterrorizado; Este homem caiu na gargalhada.

"Venha", disse ele, "é apenas um cadáver. Prefiro um susto a um gendarme".

Mas a mão enfraqueceu-o e libertou-o. O esforço esgota-se rapidamente na sepultura.

"Bem, agora", disse o prowler, "esse sujeito morto está vivo? Vamos ver".

Inclinou-se novamente, atrapalhou-se entre o monte, afastou tudo o que estava em seu caminho, agarrou a mão, segurou o braço, libertou a cabeça, puxou o corpo para fora e, alguns instantes depois, estava arrastando o homem sem vida, ou pelo menos inconsciente, pelas sombras da estrada oca. Ele era um cuirassier, um oficial e até mesmo um oficial de patente considerável; uma grande epaulette dourada espreitava por baixo da cuiras; Este oficial já não possuía capacete. Um furioso corte de espada tinha marcado seu rosto, onde nada era discernível além de sangue.

No entanto, ele não parecia ter nenhum membro quebrado e, por algum feliz acaso, se essa palavra é permitida aqui, os mortos foram abobadados acima dele de modo a preservá-lo de ser esmagado. Seus olhos ainda estavam fechados.

Na sua cuirass usava a cruz de prata da Legião de Honra.

O ronco arrancou esta cruz, que desapareceu num dos abismos que tinha debaixo do seu grande casaco.

Em seguida, ele sentiu o barulho do policial, descobriu um relógio e tomou posse dele. Em seguida, ele vasculhou seu colete, encontrou uma bolsa e a embolsou.

Quando chegou a esta fase de socorro que estava a administrar a este moribundo, o oficial abriu os olhos.

"Obrigado", disse ele fracamente.

A abruptidade dos movimentos do homem que o manipulava, a frescura da noite, o ar que podia inalar livremente, tinham-no despertado da sua letargia.

O ronqueiro não respondeu. Ele levantou a cabeça. Um som de passos era audível na planície; Alguma patrulha provavelmente estava se aproximando.

O oficial murmurou, pois a agonia da morte ainda estava em sua voz:

"Quem ganhou a batalha"?

"Os ingleses", respondeu o prowler.

O oficial prosseguiu:

"Olhe nos meus bolsos; Você vai encontrar um relógio e uma bolsa. Leve-os".

Já estava feito.

O prowler executou a finta necessária e disse:

"Não há nada lá".

"Fui roubado", disse o policial; "Lamento por isso. Você deveria tê-los tido".

Os passos da patrulha tornaram-se cada vez mais distintos.

"Alguém está vindo" disse o prowler, com o movimento de um homem que está indo embora.

O oficial levantou o braço fracamente e o deteve.

"Você salvou minha vida. Quem é você"?

O prowler respondeu rapidamente, e em voz baixa:

"Como você, eu pertencia ao exército francês. Devo deixar-vos. Se me pegassem, atirariam em mim. Salvei a sua vida. Agora saia do arranhão você mesmo".

"Qual é a sua posição"?

"Sargento".

"Qual é o seu nome"?

"Thenardier".

"Não esquecerei esse nome" disse o oficial; "E você se lembra do meu. Meu nome é Pontmercy".

LIVRO DOIS

O NAVIO ORION

CAPÍTULO I

O NÚMERO 24.601 PASSA A SER O NÚMERO 9.430

Jean Valjean tinha sido recapturado.

O leitor agradecer-nos-á se passarmos rapidamente por cima dos tristes pormenores. Limitar-nos-emos a transcrever dois parágrafos publicados pelas revistas da época, poucos meses depois dos surpreendentes acontecimentos ocorridos em M. sur M.

Estes artigos são bastante resumidos. Recorde-se que, nessa época, a *Gazette des Tribunaux* ainda não existia.

Nós pegamos emprestado o primeiro do *Drapeau Blanc*. Tem a data de 25 de julho de 1823.

Um arrondissement do Pas de Calais acaba de ser o palco de um evento fora do normal. Um homem, que era um estranho no Departamento, e que levava o nome de M. Madeleine, tinha, graças aos novos métodos, ressuscitado há alguns anos uma antiga indústria local, a fabricação de jato e de bugigangas de vidro preto. Tinha feito fortuna no negócio, e também no arrondissement, admitemos. Ele havia sido nomeado prefeito, em reconhecimento aos seus serviços. A polícia descobriu que M. Madeleine não era outro senão um ex-presidiário que havia quebrado sua proibição, condenado em 1796 por roubo, e chamado Jean Valjean. Jean Valjean voltou a ser preso. Verifica-se que, antes da sua detenção, tinha conseguido retirar das mãos de M. Laffitte uma quantia superior a meio milhão que aí tinha depositado e que, além disso, e por meios perfeitamente legítimos, tinha adquirido na sua empresa. Ninguém conseguiu descobrir onde Jean Valjean escondeu esse dinheiro desde o seu regresso à prisão em Toulon.

O segundo artigo, que entra um pouco mais em detalhes, é um extrato do *Journal de Paris*, da mesma data.

Um ex-condenado, que tinha sido libertado, chamado Jean Valjean, acaba de comparecer perante o Tribunal de Assizes do Var, em circunstâncias calculadas para atrair a atenção. Este desgraçado conseguira escapar à vigilância da polícia, mudara de nome e conseguira ser nomeado presidente da câmara de uma das nossas pequenas cidades do norte; nesta cidade tinha estabelecido um comércio considerável. Foi finalmente desmascarado e preso, graças ao zelo incansável do Ministério Público. Ele tinha como concubina uma mulher da cidade, que morreu de choque no momento de sua prisão. Este, dotado de força hercúlea, encontrou meios de escapar; mas, três ou quatro dias depois da sua fuga, a polícia voltou a pôr-lhe as mãos, em Paris, no preciso momento em que entrava num daqueles pequenos veículos que circulam entre a capital e a aldeia de Montfermeil (Seine-et-Oise). Diz-se que ele lucrou com este intervalo de três ou quatro dias de liberdade, para sacar uma quantia considerável depositada por ele em um dos nossos principais banqueiros. Este montante foi estimado em seiscentos ou setecentos mil francos. Se a acusação é confiável, ele a escondeu em algum lugar conhecido apenas por si mesmo, e não foi possível impô-la as mãos. Seja como for, o dito Jean Valjean acaba de ser levado perante os Assizes do Departamento do Var como acusado de roubo de estrada acompanhado de violência, há cerca de oito anos, na pessoa de uma daquelas crianças honestas que, como disse o patriarca de Ferney, em verso imortal,

> "... Chegam de Saboia todos os anos, e que, com mãos suaves, limpam aqueles longos canais sufocados com fuligem".

Este bandido recusou-se a defender-se. Ficou provado pelo hábil e eloquente representante do Ministério Público, que o furto foi cometido em cumplicidade com outros, e que Jean Valjean era membro de um bando de assaltantes no sul. Jean Valjean foi declarado culpado e, consequentemente, condenado à pena de morte. Este criminoso recusou-se a interpor recurso. O rei, na sua inesgotável clemência, dignou-se comutar a sua pena para a de servidão penal vitalícia. Jean Valjean foi imediatamente levado para a prisão de Toulon.

O leitor não esqueceu que Jean Valjean tinha hábitos religiosos em M. sur M. Alguns artigos, entre outros o *Constitucional,* apresentavam essa comutação como um triunfo do partido sacerdotal.

Jean Valjean mudou de número nas galés. Ele foi chamado 9.430.

No entanto, e vamos mencioná-lo imediatamente para que não sejamos obrigados a voltar ao assunto, a prosperidade de M. sur M. desapareceu com M. Madeleine, tudo o que ele havia previsto durante sua noite de febre e hesitação foi realizado, faltando-lhe realmente *uma alma.* Depois desta queda, teve lugar em M. sur M. aquela divisão egoísta das grandes existências que caíram, aquele desmembramento fatal das coisas florescentes que se realiza todos os dias, obscuramente, na comunidade humana, e que a história só observou uma vez, porque ocorreu depois da morte de Alexandre. Os tenentes são reis coroados; os superintendentes improvisam os fabricantes a partir de si mesmos. Surgiram rivalidades invejosas. As vastas oficinas de M. Madeleine foram fechadas; os seus edifícios caíram em ruínas, os seus operários dispersos. Alguns deles abandonaram o país, outros abandonaram o comércio. A partir daí, tudo foi feito em pequena escala, em vez de em grande escala; para lucrar em vez do bem geral. Já não havia um centro; em todos os lugares havia competição e animosidade. M. Madeleine reinou sobre todos e dirigiu todos. Assim que ele caiu, cada um puxou as coisas para si; o espírito de combate sucedeu ao espírito de organização, a amargura à cordialidade, o ódio uns aos outros à benevolência do fundador para com todos; os fios que M. Madeleine tinha colocado estavam emaranhados e quebrados, os métodos foram adulterados, os produtos foram aviltados, a confiança foi morta; o mercado diminuiu, por falta de encomendas; os salários foram reduzidos, as oficinas pararam, a falência chegou. E depois não havia mais nada para os pobres. Todos tinham desaparecido.

O próprio Estado percebeu que alguém tinha sido esmagado em algum lugar. Menos de quatro anos após o acórdão do Tribunal de Assizes que determinou a identidade de Jean Valjean e M. Madeleine, em benefício das galés, o custo da cobrança de impostos tinha duplicado no arrondissement de M. sur M.; e M. de Villèle chamou a atenção para o fato na tribuna, no mês de fevereiro de 1827.

CAPÍTULO II

EM QUE O LEITOR EXAMINARÁ DOIS VERSOS, QUE SÃO DA COMPOSIÇÃO DO DIABO, POSSIVELMENTE

Antes de prosseguir, caberá narrar com algum detalhe, uma ocorrência singular que ocorreu mais ou menos na mesma época, em Montfermeil, e à qual não falta coincidência com certas conjeturas da acusação.

Existe na região de Montfermeil uma superstição muito antiga, que é ainda mais curiosa e ainda mais preciosa, porque uma superstição popular nas proximidades de Paris é como um aloé na Sibéria. Estamos entre aqueles que respeitam tudo o que é da natureza de uma planta rara. Eis, então, a superstição de Montfermeil: pensa-se que o diabo, desde tempos imemoriais, escolheu a floresta como esconderijo para os seus tesouros. Goodwives afirmam que não é raridade encontrar ao cair da noite, em recantos isolados da floresta, um homem negro com ar de carpinteiro ou cortador de madeira, usando sapatos de madeira, vestido com calças e uma blusa de linho, e reconhecível pelo fato de que, em vez de um boné ou chapéu, ele tem dois chifres imensos na cabeça. Isso deveria, de fato, torná-lo reconhecível. Este homem está habitualmente empenhado em cavar um buraco. Há três formas de lucrar com esse encontro. A primeira é aproximar-se do homem e falar com ele. Então vê-se que o homem é simplesmente um camponês, que ele parece negro porque é anoitecer; que ele não está cavando nenhum buraco, mas está cortando grama para suas vacas, e que o que foi levado para chifres não passa de um garfo de esterco que ele está carregando nas costas, e cujos dentes, graças à perspetiva da noite, pareciam brotar de sua cabeça. O homem volta para casa e morre dentro da semana. A segunda maneira é observá-lo, esperar até que ele tenha cavado seu buraco, até que ele o tenha preenchido e ido embora;

depois correr com grande velocidade para a trincheira, abri-la mais uma vez e apoderar-se do "tesouro" que o negro ali necessariamente colocou. Neste caso, morre-se dentro de um mês. Finalmente, o último método é não falar com o negro, não olhar para ele e fugir na melhor velocidade das pernas. Um morre dentro de um ano.

Como todos os três métodos são atendidos com seus inconvenientes especiais, o segundo, que em todos os casos, apresenta algumas vantagens, entre outras a de possuir um tesouro, mesmo que apenas por um mês, é o mais geralmente adotado. Assim, homens ousados, tentados por todos os acasos, abriram com bastante frequência, como estamos certos, os buracos escavados pelo negro e tentaram roubar o diabo. O sucesso da operação parece ser moderado. Pelo menos, se acreditarmos na tradição e, em particular, nas duas linhas enigmáticas em latim bárbaro, que um monge normando malvado, um pouco feiticeiro, chamado Tryphon deixou sobre este assunto. Este Tryphon está enterrado na Abadia de Saint-Georges de Bocherville, perto de Rouen, e sapos desovam em seu túmulo.

Por conseguinte, são envidados enormes esforços. Tais trincheiras são normalmente extremamente profundas; um homem sua, cava, labuta a noite toda, pois isso deve ser feito à noite; molha a camisa, queima a vela, quebra o colchão e, quando chega ao fundo do buraco, quando põe a mão no "tesouro", o que encontra? Qual é o tesouro do diabo? Um sou, às vezes uma coroa, uma pedra, um esqueleto, um corpo sangrando, às vezes um espectro dobrado em quatro como uma folha de papel em um portfólio, às vezes nada. É o que os versos de Tryphon parecem anunciar aos indiscretos e curiosos:

> "Fodit, et in fossa thesauros condit opaca,As, nummas,
> lapides, cadáver, simulacra, nihilque".

Parece que em nossos dias às vezes se encontra um chifre de pólvora com balas, às vezes um velho pacote de cartas gordurosas e gastas, que evidentemente serviu ao diabo. Tryphon não registra esses dois achados, uma vez que Tryphon viveu no século XII, e desde que o diabo não parece ter tido a sagacidade de inventar pó antes do tempo de Roger Bacon, e cartas antes do tempo de Carlos VI.

Além disso, se jogarmos às cartas, com certeza perderemos tudo o que possuímos! e quanto ao pó no chifre, ele possui a propriedade de fazer sua arma estourar em seu rosto.

Ora, muito pouco tempo depois da época em que parecia ao procurador que o condenado libertado Jean Valjean, durante a sua fuga de vários dias, rondava Montfermeil, notou-se naquela aldeia que um certo velho trabalhador rodoviário, chamado Boulatruelle, tinha "maneiras peculiares" na floresta. As pessoas pensavam que sabiam que esta Boulatruelle tinha estado nas galés. Foi sujeito a uma certa supervisão policial e, como não conseguia encontrar trabalho em lado nenhum, a administração empregou-o a taxas reduzidas como ajudante de estrada na encruzilhada de Gagny a Lagny.

Este Boulatruelle era um homem que era visto com desagrado pelos habitantes do distrito como demasiado respeitoso, demasiado humilde, demasiado rápido a retirar o boné a todos, e trêmulo e sorridente na presença dos gendarmes, provavelmente filiados a bandos de ladrões, diziam; suspeito de deitar em emboscada à beira dos polícias ao cair da noite. A única coisa a seu favor era que ele era um bêbado.

Isto é o que as pessoas pensavam ter notado:

Ultimamente, Boulatruelle abandonara a sua tarefa de quebrar pedras e cuidar da estrada muito cedo, e a dirigir-se para a floresta com a sua picareta. Encontrou-se à noite nas clareiras mais desertas, nos matagais mais selvagens; e ele tinha a aparência de estar em busca de algo, e às vezes ele estava cavando buracos. As boas esposas que passaram levaram-no, a princípio, para Belzebu; depois reconheceram Boulatruelle, e não ficaram minimamente tranquilos com isso. Estes encontros pareciam causar a Boulatruelle um vivo desagrado. Era evidente que ele procurava esconder-se e que havia algum mistério no que estava a fazer.

Dizia-se na aldeia: "É claro que o diabo apareceu. Boulatruelle viu-o e está à procura. Em calmaria, ele é astuto o suficiente para embolsar o tesouro de Lúcifer".

Os voltairianos acrescentaram: "Boulatruelle vai pegar o diabo, ou o diabo vai pegar Boulatruelle"? As velhinhas fizeram muitos sinais da cruz.

Entretanto, cessaram as manobras de Boulatruelle na floresta; e retomou a sua ocupação regular de reparação de estradas; e as pessoas fofocavam de outra coisa.

Algumas pessoas, no entanto, ainda estavam curiosas, supondo que em tudo isso provavelmente não havia um tesouro fabuloso das lendas, mas algum belo lucro de um tipo mais sério e palpável do que as contas bancárias do diabo, e que o homem da estrada tinha descoberto metade do segredo. Os mais "perplexos" eram o mestre e Thénardier, o proprietário da taberna, que era amigo de todos e não desdenhava aliar-se a Boulatruelle.

"Ele esteve nas galés", disse Thénardier. "Eh! Oh meu Deus! ninguém sabe quem esteve lá ou estará lá".

Uma noite, o mestre afirmou que, em tempos passados, a lei teria instaurado um inquérito sobre o que Boulatruelle fez na floresta, e que este teria sido forçado a falar, e que ele teria sido submetido à tortura em caso de necessidade, e que Boulatruelle não teria resistido ao teste da água, Por exemplo. "Vamos testá-lo ao vinho", disse Thénardier.

Fizeram um esforço e levaram o velho homem da estrada a beber. Boulatruelle bebeu muito, mas disse muito pouco. Combinava com admirável arte, e em proporções magistrais, a sede de um gormandizer com a discrição de um juiz. No entanto, ao voltar à carga e ao comparar e juntar as poucas palavras obscuras que ele permitiu escapar-lhe, foi isso que Thénardier e o mestre imaginaram que tinham feito:

Certa manhã, quando Boulatruelle estava a caminho do seu trabalho, ao amanhecer, surpreendeu-se ao ver, num recanto da floresta na vegetação rasteira, uma pá e uma picareta, *escondidas, como se poderia dizer.*

No entanto, ele poderia ter suposto que eles eram provavelmente a pá e a picareta do Pai Six-Fours, o portador de água, e não teria pensado mais nisso. Mas, na noite desse dia, viu, sem ser visto, escondido por uma grande árvore, "uma pessoa que não pertencia àquelas partes e que ele, Boulatruelle, conhecia bem", dirigindo os seus passos para a parte mais densa da madeira. Tradução de Thénardier: *Um camarada das galés.* Boulatruelle recusou-se obstinadamente a revelar o seu nome. Essa pessoa carregava um pacote" algo quadrado, como uma caixa grande ou um pequeno porta-malas. Surpresa por parte de Boulatruelle. No entanto, só depois de decorridos sete ou oito minutos é que lhe ocorreu a ideia de seguir aquela "pessoa". Mas era tarde demais; a pessoa já estava no matagal, a noite tinha descido e Boulatruelle não conseguira alcançá-lo. Então ele adotou o curso de observá-lo à beira da floresta. "Era luar". Duas ou três horas depois, Boulatruelle tinha visto essa pessoa emergir do mato, carregando não mais o cofre, mas uma pá e uma picareta. Boulatruelle deixara a pessoa passar, e não sonhara em abordá-la, porque disse a si mesmo que o outro homem era três vezes mais forte do que ele, e armado com uma picareta, e que provavelmente o derrubaria na cabeça ao reconhecê-lo e ao perceber que ele era reconhecido. Efusão comovente de dois velhos camaradas ao reencontrarem-se. Mas a pá e a picareta tinham servido de raio de luz a Boulatruelle; apressara-se para o matagal de manhã e não encontrara pá nem picareta. A partir disso, ele tirou a inferência de que essa pessoa, uma vez na floresta, havia cavado um buraco com sua picareta, enterrado o cofre e fechado novamente o buraco com sua pá. Ora, o cofre era demasiado pequeno para conter um corpo; portanto, continha dinheiro. Daí suas pesquisas. Boulatruelle tinha explorado, sondado, vasculhado toda a floresta e o matagal, e cavado onde quer que a terra lhe parecesse ter sido recentemente encontrada. Em vão.

Ele não tinha "encaminhado" nada. Ninguém em Montfermeil pensou mais nisso. Havia apenas alguns fofoqueiros corajosos, que disseram: "Você pode estar certo de que o mender na estrada Gagny não tomou todo esse problema por nada; tinha a certeza de que o diabo tinha vindo".

CAPÍTULO III

A CORRENTE DO TORNOZELO DEVE TER SOFRIDO UMA CERTA MANIPULAÇÃO PREPARATÓRIA PARA SER ASSIM QUEBRADA COM UM GOLPE DE UM MARTELO

No final de outubro, nesse mesmo ano de 1823, os habitantes de Toulon viram a entrada no seu porto, após mau tempo, e com o objetivo de reparar alguns danos, do navio *Orion*, que mais tarde foi empregado em Brest como navio-escola, e que então fazia parte da esquadra mediterrânica.

Esta embarcação, fustigada como estava, pois o mar a manuseara grosseiramente, produzia um belo efeito quando entrava nas estradas. Voou algumas cores que lhe proporcionaram a saudação regulamentar de onze armas, que devolveu, disparadas a tiro; total, vinte e dois. Calcula-se que o que com salvos, politenesses reais e militares, trocas cortês de alvoroço, sinais de etiqueta, formalidades de estradas e cidadelas, nasceres e pores-do-sol, saudados todos os dias por todas as fortalezas e todos os navios de guerra, aberturas e fechamentos de portos, etc., o mundo civilizado, descarregado por toda a terra, no decurso de quatro e vinte horas, cento e cinquenta mil tiros inúteis. A seis francos o tiro, que chega a novecentos mil francos por dia, trezentos milhões por ano, que desaparecem em fumaça. Trata-se de um mero pormenor. Durante todo este tempo, os pobres morriam de fome.

O ano de 1823 foi o que a Restauração chamou de "época da guerra espanhola".

Esta guerra continha muitos eventos em um só, e uma quantidade de peculiaridades. Um grande caso de família para a casa de Bourbon; o ramo da França socorrendo e protegendo o ramo de Madrid, isto é, praticando um ato que incumbe ao ancião; um aparente regresso às nossas tradições nacionais, complicado pela servidão e pela sujeição aos gabinetes do Norte; M. le Duc d'Angoulême, apelido pelos lençóis liberais *de herói de Andujar*, comprimindo numa atitude triunfal um tanto contrariada pelo seu ar pacífico, o antigo e muito poderoso terrorismo do Santo Ofício em desacordo com o terrorismo quimérico dos liberais, os *sansculottes* ressuscitados, para grande terror das viúvas, sob o nome de *descamisados*; monarquia que se opõe a um obstáculo ao progresso descrito como anarquia; as teorias de 89 interrompidas grosseiramente na seiva; uma paragem europeia, chamada à ideia francesa, que fazia a volta ao mundo; ao lado do filho da França como generalíssimo, o príncipe de Carignan, depois Carlos Alberto, inscrevendo-se naquela cruzada de reis contra o povo como voluntário, com epaulets de granadeiros de vermelho worsted; os soldados do Império iniciando uma nova campanha, mas envelhecidos, entristecidos, depois de oito anos de repouso, e sob o calcanhar branco; o estandarte tricolor acenado no exterior por um punhado heroico de franceses, como o padrão branco havia sido trinta anos antes em Coblentz; monges misturavam-se com as nossas tropas; o espírito de liberdade e de novidade trazido aos seus sentidos pelas baionetas; princípios abatidos por canhões; A França desfazendo pelos braços o que fizera pela mente; além disso, líderes hostis vendidos, soldados hesitando, cidades sitiadas por milhões; sem perigos militares, e ainda possíveis explosões, como em todas as minas que são surpreendidas e invadidas; mas pouco derramamento de sangue, pouca honra conquistada, vergonha para alguns, glória para ninguém. Tal foi esta guerra, feita pelos príncipes descendentes de Luís XIV., e conduzida por generais que tinham estado sob Napoleão. O seu triste destino não foi recordar nem a grande guerra nem a grande política.

Alguns feitos de armas foram graves, a tomada do Trocadéro, entre outros, foi uma bela ação militar, mas afinal, repetimos, as trombetas desta guerra devolvem um som rachado, todo o efeito foi suspeito, a história aprova a França por ter dificuldade em aceitar esse falso triunfo. Parecia evidente que certos oficiais espanhóis encarregados da resistência cediam com demasiada facilidade; a ideia de corrupção estava ligada à vitória; Parece que generais e não batalhas foram vencidas, e o soldado conquistador voltou humilhado. Uma guerra aviltante, em suma, em que o *Banco de França* podia ser lido nas dobras da bandeira.

Os soldados da guerra de 1808, sobre os quais Saragoça tinha caído em formidável ruína, franziram a testa em 1823 com a fácil rendição das cidadelas, e começaram a lamentar Palafox. É da natureza da França preferir ter Rostopchine em vez de Ballesteros à sua frente.

De um ponto de vista ainda mais grave, e que também é justo insistir aqui, esta guerra, que feriu o espírito militar da França, enfureceu o espírito democrático. Foi um empreendimento de encantamento. Nessa campanha, o objetivo do soldado francês, filho da democracia, era a conquista de um jugo para os outros. Uma contradição horrível. A França é feita para despertar a alma das nações, não para sufocá-la. Todas as revoluções da Europa desde 1792 são a Revolução Francesa: raios de dardos da liberdade da França. Isso é um fato solar. Cego é aquele que não verá! Foi Bonaparte quem o disse.

A guerra de 1823, um ultraje à generosa nação espanhola, foi então, ao mesmo tempo, um ultraje à Revolução Francesa. Foi a França que cometeu esta violência monstruosa; por meios sujos, pois, com exceção das guerras de libertação, tudo o que os exércitos fazem é por meios ilícitos. As palavras *obediência passiva* indicam isso. Um exército é uma estranha obra-prima de combinação onde a força resulta de uma enorme soma de impotência. Assim se explica a guerra, feita pela humanidade contra a humanidade, apesar da humanidade.

Quanto aos Bourbons, a guerra de 1823 foi fatal para eles. Levaram-na para um sucesso. Eles não perceberam o perigo que reside em ter uma ideia morta por encomenda. Desviaram-se, na sua inocência, a tal ponto que introduziram o imenso enfraquecimento de um crime no seu estabelecimento como elemento de força. O espírito da emboscada entrou na sua política. 1830 teve o seu germe em 1823. A campanha espanhola tornou-se nos seus conselhos um argumento para a força e para as aventuras por direito divino. A França, tendo restabelecido *el rey netto* em Espanha, poderia muito bem ter restabelecido o rei absoluto em casa. Caíram no erro alarmante de tomar a obediência do soldado para o consentimento da nação. Tal confiança é a ruína dos tronos. Não é permitido adormecer, nem à sombra de uma máquina, nem à sombra de um exército.

Voltemos ao navio *Orion.*

Durante as operações do exército comandado pelo príncipe generalíssimo, uma esquadra navegava no Mediterrâneo. Acabámos de afirmar que o *Orion* pertencia a esta frota e que acidentes do mar o tinham levado ao porto de Toulon.

A presença de um navio de guerra num porto tem algo que atrai e envolve uma multidão. É porque é ótimo, e a galera adora o que é ótimo.

Um navio da linha é uma das mais magníficas combinações do génio do homem com os poderes da natureza.

Um navio da linha é composto, ao mesmo tempo, da matéria mais pesada e leve possível, pois lida ao mesmo tempo com três formas de substância" sólida, líquida e fluida" e deve lutar contra as três. Tem onze garras de ferro com as quais agarrar o granito no fundo do mar, e mais asas e mais antennæ do que insetos alados, para apanhar o vento nas nuvens. Sua respiração jorra através de seus cento e vinte canhões como através de enormes trombetas, e responde orgulhosamente ao trovão. O oceano procura desviar-se na mesmice alarmante dos seus billows, mas a embarcação tem a sua alma, a sua bússola, que o aconselha e lhe mostra sempre o norte. Nas noites mais negras, suas lanternas abastecem o lugar das estrelas. Assim, contra o vento, tem a sua corda e a sua lona; contra a água, madeira; contra as rochas, seu ferro, latão e chumbo; contra as sombras, a sua luz; contra a imensidão, uma agulha.

Se quisermos ter uma ideia de todas aquelas proporções gigantescas que, no seu conjunto, constituem o navio da linha, basta entrar num dos stocks de construção cobertos de seis andares, nos portos de Brest ou Toulon. Os vasos em processo de construção estão sob um vidro de sino lá, por assim dizer. Esta viga colossal é um quintal; Essa grande coluna de madeira que se estende sobre a terra até onde a vista alcança é o mastro principal. Levando-o de sua raiz nos estoques até sua ponta nas nuvens, ele tem sessenta braças de comprimento, e seu diâmetro em sua base é de três pés. O mastro principal inglês eleva-se a uma altura de duzentos e dezassete metros acima da linha de água. A marinha dos nossos pais empregava cabos, a nossa empregava correntes. A pilha simples de correntes em um navio de cem canhões tem quatro metros de altura, vinte metros de largura e oito metros de profundidade. E quanta madeira é necessária para fazer este navio? Três mil metros cúbicos. É uma floresta flutuante.

E, além disso, recorde-se, trata-se aqui apenas do navio militar de há quarenta anos, do simples veleiro; O vapor, então em sua infância, desde então acrescentou novos milagres a esse prodígio que é chamado de navio de guerra. Atualmente, por exemplo, a embarcação mista com parafuso é uma máquina surpreendente, impulsionada por três mil metros quadrados de lona e por um motor de dois mil e quinhentos cavalos de potência.

Para não mencionar estas novas maravilhas, a antiga embarcação de Cristóvão Colombo e de De Ruyter é uma das obras-primas do homem. É tão inesgotável em força como o Infinito em vendavais; armazena o vento nas velas, é preciso na imensa imensidão dos billows, flutua e reina.

Chega uma hora, porém, em que o vendaval quebra aquele quintal de sessenta pés como uma palha, quando o vento dobra aquele mastro de quatrocentos metros de altura, quando aquela âncora, que pesa dezenas de milhares, é torcida nas mandíbulas das ondas como um anzol de pescador nas mandíbulas de um lúcio, quando aqueles canhões monstruosos proferem rugidos claros e fúteis, que o furacão leva para o vazio e para a noite, quando todo esse poder e toda essa majestade estão envolvidos num poder e majestade que são superiores.

Toda vez que essa imensa força é exibida para culminar em uma imensa fraqueza, ela dá aos homens alimento para pensar. Por isso, nos portos, abundam pessoas curiosas à volta destas maravilhosas máquinas de guerra e de navegação, sem serem capazes de explicar perfeitamente porquê. Todos os dias, portanto, de manhã até à noite, os cais, as comportas e os molhes do porto de Toulon eram cobertos com uma infinidade de ociosos e espreguiçadeiras, como se diz em Paris, cujo negócio consistia em olhar para o *Orion*.

O *Orion* era um navio que estava doente há muito tempo, no decurso dos seus cruzeiros anteriores espessas camadas de cracas tinham-se acumulado na quilha a tal ponto que o privavam de metade da sua velocidade, tinha ido para a doca seca no ano anterior, para mandar raspar as cracas, depois pôs-se novamente ao mar; mas esta limpeza tinha afetado os parafusos da quilha: na vizinhança das Ilhas Baleares, os lados tinham sido tensos e tinham sido abertos; e, como o revestimento naqueles dias não era de chapa de ferro, a embarcação tinha vazado. Tinha surgido um violento vendaval equinocial, que primeiro se enfiara numa grade e numa vigia do lado do larboard, e danificara as mortalhas dianteiras; em consequência destes ferimentos, o *Orion* tinha corrido de volta para Toulon.

Ancorou perto do Arsenal; estava totalmente equipado, e os reparos foram iniciados. O casco não tinha sofrido danos a estibordo, mas algumas das tábuas tinham sido despregadas aqui e ali, de acordo com o costume, para permitir a entrada de ar no porão.

Certa manhã, a multidão que olhava para ele testemunhou um acidente.

A tripulação estava ocupada dobrando as velas; o topman, que teve de tomar o canto superior da vela principal a estibordo, perdeu o equilíbrio; viu-se vacilar; a multidão que se aglomerava no cais do Arsenal proferiu um grito; a cabeça do homem sobreequilibrava o corpo; o homem caiu ao redor do quintal, com as mãos estendidas em direção ao abismo; no caminho, agarrou a corda, primeiro com uma mão, depois com a outra, e permaneceu pendurado nela: o mar estava abaixo dele, a uma profundidade vertiginosa; o choque da sua queda tinha transmitido à corda um violento movimento de balanço; O homem balançava para frente e para trás no final daquela corda, como uma pedra numa funda.

Corria um risco terrível ir em seu auxílio; Nenhum dos marinheiros, todos pescadores da costa, recentemente cobrados pelo serviço, ousou tentá-lo. Entretanto, o infeliz topman perdia as forças; a sua angústia não podia ser discernida no seu rosto, mas a sua exaustão era visível em todos os membros; seus braços foram contraídos em contrações horríveis; todos os esforços que ele fez para voltar a subir serviram apenas para aumentar as oscilações da corda-pé; não gritou, por medo de esgotar as suas forças. Todos aguardavam o minuto em que ele deveria soltar o controle sobre a corda e, de instante em instante, as cabeças foram viradas de lado para que sua queda não fosse vista. Há momentos em que um pouco de corda, um poste, o galho de uma árvore, é a própria vida, e é terrível ver um ser vivo se desprender dela e cair como um fruto maduro.

De repente, um homem foi visto subindo no aparelhamento com a agilidade de um gato-tigre; este homem estava vestido de vermelho; era um condenado; usava um boné verde; foi condenado à prisão perpétua. Ao chegar em um nível com o topo, uma rajada de vento levou seu boné e permitiu que uma cabeça perfeitamente branca fosse vista: ele não era um jovem.

Um condenado empregado a bordo com um destacamento das galés tinha, de facto, no primeiro instante, apressado a dirigir-se ao oficial da guarda e, no meio da consternação e da hesitação da tripulação, enquanto todos os marinheiros tremiam e recuavam, pedira autorização ao oficial para arriscar a vida para salvar o topman; a um sinal afirmativo do oficial quebrou a corrente rebitada ao tornozelo com um golpe de martelo, depois pegou numa corda e correu para o aparelhamento: ninguém reparou, no instante, com que facilidade aquela corrente se tinha quebrado; Só mais tarde é que o incidente foi recordado.

Num piscar de olhos, ele estava no quintal; Ele parou por alguns segundos e parecia estar medindo com o olho; Estes segundos, durante os quais a brisa balançava o topman na extremidade de um fio, pareciam séculos para quem olhava. Por fim, o condenado ergueu os olhos para o céu e avançou um passo: a multidão respirou fundo. Viu-se a correr pelo quintal: ao chegar ao ponto, prendeu a corda que lhe tinha trazido e deixou pender a outra extremidade, depois começou a descer a corda, a entregar a mão, e então", e a angústia era indescritível" em vez de um homem suspenso sobre o golfo, eram duas.

Alguém teria dito que era uma aranha vindo para agarrar uma mosca, só que aqui a aranha trouxe vida, não morte. Dez mil olhares foram fixados neste grupo; nem um grito, nem uma palavra; o mesmo tremor contraía todas as sobrancelhas; Todas as bocas prenderam a respiração como se temessem dar o menor sopro ao vento que balançava os dois infelizes.

Entretanto, o condenado conseguiu baixar-se a uma posição perto do marinheiro. Já era tempo; Mais um minuto, e o homem exausto e desesperado ter-se-ia deixado cair no abismo. O condenado tinha-o amarrado em segurança com o cordão a que se agarrava com uma mão, enquanto trabalhava com a outra. Por fim, foi visto a subir de volta ao quintal e a arrastar o marinheiro atrás dele; Segurou-o ali um momento para lhe permitir recuperar as forças, depois agarrou-o nos braços e carregou-o, caminhando no próprio quintal até ao boné, e daí até ao topo principal, onde o deixou nas mãos dos seus camaradas.

Nesse momento, a multidão irrompeu em aplausos: velhos sargentos condenados entre eles choraram, e as mulheres se abraçaram no cais, e todas as vozes foram ouvidas para gritar com uma espécie de raiva terna: "Perdão por esse homem"!

Ele, entretanto, tinha começado imediatamente a descer para voltar a juntar-se ao seu destacamento. Para alcançá-los mais rapidamente, ele caiu no aparelhamento e correu por um dos quintais inferiores; todos os olhos o seguiam. A certa altura, o medo assaltou-os; quer fosse por estar cansado, quer por ter virado a cabeça, pensavam vê-lo hesitar e cambalear. De repente, a multidão proferiu um grito alto: o condenado tinha caído no mar.

A queda foi perigosa. A fragata *Algésiras* estava ancorada ao lado do *Órion*, e o pobre condenado tinha caído entre as duas embarcações: era de recear que escorregasse por baixo de uma ou outra delas. Quatro homens atiraram-se apressadamente para dentro de um barco; a multidão aplaudiu-os; a ansiedade tomou novamente posse de todas as almas; o homem não tinha subido à superfície; desaparecera no mar sem deixar ondulação, como se tivesse caído num barril de óleo: soaram, mergulharam. Em vão. As buscas prosseguiram até à noite: nem sequer encontraram o corpo.

No dia seguinte, o jornal Toulon publicou estas linhas:

"17 de novembro de 1823. Ontem, um condenado pertencente ao destacamento a bordo do *Orion*, ao regressar da prestação de assistência a um marinheiro, caiu no mar e morreu afogado. O corpo ainda não foi encontrado; supõe-se que esteja enredado entre as pilhas do ponto do

Arsenal: este homem foi cometido sob o número 9.430, e seu nome era Jean Valjean".

LIVRO TRÊS

CUMPRIMENTO DA PROMESSA FEITA À MULHER MORTA

CAPÍTULO I

A QUESTÃO DA ÁGUA EM MONTFERMEIL

Montfermeil está situado entre Livry e Chelles, na borda sul daquele terreno de mesa elevado que separa o Ourcq do Marne. Hoje em dia é uma cidade toleravelmente grande, ornamentada durante todo o ano com vilas de gesso, e aos domingos com burgueses radiantes. Em 1823 não havia em Montfermeil nem tantas casas brancas nem tantos cidadãos satisfeitos: era apenas uma aldeia na floresta. Encontrar-se-iam ali algumas casas de recreio do século passado, com certeza, que eram reconhecíveis pelo seu ar grandioso, pelas suas varandas em ferro retorcido e pelas suas longas janelas, cujas minúsculas vidraças lançavam todo o tipo de tons variados de verde sobre o branco das persianas fechadas; mas Montfermeil era, no entanto, uma aldeia. Comerciantes de tecidos aposentados e advogados rústicos ainda não tinham descoberto; Era um lugar tranquilo e encantador, que não estava a caminho de lugar nenhum: lá as pessoas viviam, e barato, aquela vida rústica camponesa que é tão abundante e tão fácil; Só que ali era rara a água, por conta da elevação do planalto.

Era necessário buscá-lo a uma distância considerável; o final da aldeia em direção a Gagny tirou sua água das magníficas lagoas que existem na floresta lá. A outra extremidade, que rodeia a igreja e que fica na direção de Chelles, encontrou água potável apenas numa pequena nascente a meio caminho da encosta, perto da estrada para Chelles, a cerca de um quarto de hora de Montfermeil.

Assim, cada família encontrou trabalho árduo para se manter abastecida com água. As grandes casas, a aristocracia, da qual fazia parte a taberna Thénardier, pagavam meio balde a um homem que fazia negócio dela, e que ganhava cerca de oito sous por dia na sua empresa de abastecimento de água a Montfermeil; mas este bom homem só trabalhava até às sete horas da noite no verão e às cinco no inverno; e a noite chegou e as persianas do rés do chão uma vez fechadas, aquele que não tinha água para beber foi buscá-la para si ou ficou sem ela.

Isso constituiu o terror da pobre criatura que o leitor provavelmente não esqueceu: a pequena Cosette. Recorde-se que Cosette foi útil aos Thénardier de duas maneiras: obrigaram a mãe a pagar-lhes e fizeram com que a criança os servisse. Assim, quando a mãe deixou de pagar totalmente, razão pela qual lemos nos capítulos anteriores, os Thénardier mantiveram Cosette. Ela tomou o lugar de uma criada em sua casa. Nessa qualidade, era ela quem corria para buscar água quando era necessário. Assim, a criança, que estava muito apavorada com a ideia de ir à fonte à noite, tomou muito cuidado para que nunca faltasse água em casa.

O Natal do ano de 1823 foi particularmente brilhante em Montfermeil. O início do inverno tinha sido ameno; Não havia neve nem geada até então. Alguns monteiros de Paris haviam obtido permissão do prefeito para erguer suas cabines na rua principal da vila, e um grupo de comerciantes itinerantes, sob a proteção da mesma tolerância, construíram suas barracas na Praça da Igreja, e até as estenderam até o Beco Boulanger, onde, como o leitor talvez se lembre, a pousada dos Thénardiers estava situada. Essas pessoas enchiam as pousadas e lojas de bebidas, e comunicavam àquele pequeno bairro tranquilo uma vida barulhenta e alegre. Para fazer o papel de historiador fiel, devemos mesmo acrescentar que, entre as curiosidades expostas na praça, havia uma menagerie, na qual palhaços assustadores, vestidos de trapos e que ninguém sabia quando, exibiam aos camponeses de Montfermeil, em 1823, um daqueles horríveis abutres brasileiros, como o nosso Museu Real não possuía até 1845, e que têm um cacau tricolor para um olho. Acredito que os naturalistas chamam esta ave de Caracara Polyborus; pertence à ordem dos Apicidas e à família dos abutres. Alguns bons e velhos soldados bonapartistas, que se tinham retirado para a aldeia, foram ver esta criatura com grande devoção. Os monteiros deram a entender que a cacau tricolor era um fenômeno único feito por Deus expressamente para sua menagerie.

Na própria véspera de Natal, vários homens, carroceiros e mascates, estavam sentados à mesa, bebendo e fumando cerca de quatro ou cinco velas na sala pública da pousada de Thénardier. Esta sala assemelhava-se a todas as salas de bebedouros, - mesas, jarros de estanho, garrafas, bebedores, fumantes; mas pouca luz e muito barulho. A data do ano de 1823 era indicada, no entanto, por dois objetos que então estavam na moda na classe burguesa: a saber, um caleidoscópio e uma lâmpada de estanho nervurado. A fêmea Thénardier assistia à ceia, que estava assando em frente a uma fogueira clara; O marido bebia com os clientes e falava de política.

Além de conversas políticas que tiveram como principais temas a guerra espanhola e M. le Duc d'Angoulême, parênteses estritamente locais, como os seguintes, eram audíveis em meio ao alvoroço:

"Em Nanterre e Suresnes as vinhas floresceram muito. Quando foram contabilizadas dez peças, foram doze. Eles renderam muito suco sob a imprensa". "Mas as uvas não podem estar maduras"? "Nessas partes as uvas não devem estar maduras; o vinho torna-se oleoso assim que chega a primavera". "Então é vinho muito fino"? "Há vinhos mais pobres até do que estes. As uvas devem ser colhidas enquanto verdes". Etc.

Ou um moleiro gritaria: —

"Somos responsáveis pelo que está nos sacos? Encontramos neles uma quantidade de pequenas sementes que não podemos peneirar e que somos obrigados a enviar através das mós; há joio, funcho, ervilhaca, cânhamo, rabo de raposa e uma série de outras ervas daninhas, para não mencionar seixos, que abundam em certos trigos, especialmente no trigo bretão. Não gosto de moer trigo bretão, assim como os long-sawyers gostam de ver vigas com pregos. Você pode julgar a poeira ruim que faz na moagem. E depois as pessoas queixam-se da farinha. Estão enganados. A farinha não é culpa nossa".

Num espaço entre duas janelas, um cortador, que estava sentado à mesa com um proprietário de terras que fixava um preço para algum trabalho de prado a ser realizado na primavera, dizia:

"Não faz mal nenhum ter a relva molhada. Corta melhor. Orvalho é uma coisa boa, senhor. Não faz diferença com essa grama. Sua grama é jovem e

muito difícil de cortar ainda. É terrivelmente terno. Cede antes do ferro".
Etc.

Cosette estava no seu lugar habitual, sentada na barra transversal da mesa da cozinha, perto da chaminé. Ela estava em trapos; seus pés descalços foram empurrados em sapatos de madeira, e pela luz de fogo ela estava envolvida em tricotar meias de lã destinadas aos jovens Thénardiers. Um gatinho muito jovem brincava entre as cadeiras. Risos e conversas eram audíveis na sala ao lado, de duas vozes infantis frescas: era Éponine e Azelma.

No canto da chaminé um gato-o'-nove-caudas estava pendurado num prego.

Nos intervalos, o grito de uma criança muito pequena, que estava em algum lugar da casa, soava através do barulho da loja de carrinhos. Era um menino que tinha nascido para os Thénardier durante um dos invernos anteriores – "ela não sabia porquê", disse ela, "o resultado do frio" – e que tinha pouco mais de três anos. A mãe tinha-o amamentado, mas não o amava. Quando o clamor persistente do pirralho se tornava irritante demais: "Seu filho está esquálido", diria Thénardier; "Vá ver o que ele quer". "Bah"!, responderia a mãe, "ele me incomoda". E a criança negligenciada continuava a gritar no escuro.

CAPÍTULO II

DOIS RETRATOS COMPLETOS

Até agora, neste livro, os Thénardiers foram vistos apenas de perfil; Chegou o momento de fazer o circuito deste casal, e considerá-lo sob todos os seus aspetos.

Thénardier tinha acabado de completar cinquentenário; Madame Thénardier aproximava-se dos quarenta anos, o que equivale a cinquenta numa mulher; para que existisse um equilíbrio de idade entre marido e mulher.

Nossos leitores possivelmente preservaram alguma lembrança dessa mulher Thénardier, desde sua primeira aparição: alta, loira, vermelha, gorda, angular, quadrada, enorme e ágil; ela pertencia, como dissemos, à raça daquelas colossais mulheres selvagens, que se contorcem nas feiras com pedras penduradas nos cabelos. Ela fazia tudo sobre a casa, fazia as camas, fazia a lavagem, a cozinha e tudo mais. Cosette era sua única criada; um rato ao serviço de um elefante. Tudo tremia ao som de sua voz: vidraças, móveis e pessoas. Seu rosto grande, pontilhado de manchas vermelhas, apresentava a aparência de uma escumadeira. Ela tinha barba. Ela era uma porteira de mercado ideal vestida com roupas femininas. Ela jurou esplendidamente; ela se gabava de ser capaz de quebrar uma noz com um golpe de punho. Exceto pelos romances que ela tinha lido, e que faziam a senhora afetada espiar através da ogressa às vezes, de uma forma muito queer, a ideia nunca teria ocorrido a ninguém para dizer dela: "Isso é uma mulher". Esta fêmea Thénardier era como o produto de um wench enxertado em uma peixeira. Quando a ouvimos falar, dissemos: "Isto é um gendarme"; quando alguém a viu beber, disse: "Isso é um carter"; quando alguém viu seu cabo Cosette, um disse: "Esse é o carrasco". Um de seus dentes se projetou quando seu rosto estava em repouso.

Thénardier era um homem pequeno, magro, pálido, angular, ósseo, débil, que tinha um ar doentio e que era maravilhosamente saudável. A sua astúcia começou aqui; sorria habitualmente, por precaução, e era quase educado com todos, até com o mendigo a quem recusava meia coisa. Tinha o olhar de um gato de vara e o porte de um homem de letras. Assemelhava-se muito aos retratos do Abbé Delille. Sua coquetria consistia em beber com os carroceiros. Nunca ninguém conseguira deixá-lo bêbado. Ele fumava um cachimbo grande. Usava uma blusa e, por baixo da blusa, um casaco preto velho. Fez pretensões à literatura e ao materialismo. Havia certos nomes que ele muitas vezes pronunciava para apoiar quaisquer coisas que ele pudesse estar dizendo: Voltaire, Raynal, Parny e, singularmente, Santo Agostinho. Declarou que tinha "um sistema". Além disso, ele era um grande vigarista. Um *filousophe* [philosophe], um ladrão científico. A espécie existe. Recorde-se que fingiu ter servido no exército; tinha o hábito de se relacionar com a exuberância, como, sendo sargento na 6ª ou na 9ª luz uma coisa ou outra, em Waterloo, tinha sozinho, e na presença de um esquadrão de hussardos mortíferos, coberto com o corpo e salvo da morte, no meio do tiro de uva, "um general, que tinha sido perigosamente ferido". Daí surgiu para o seu muro o sinal flamejante, e para a sua pousada o nome que levava no bairro, de "o cabaré do Sargento de Waterloo". Era um liberal, um clássico e um bonapartista. Tinha subscrito o Champ d'Asile. Dizia-se na aldeia que ele tinha estudado para o sacerdócio.

Acreditamos que ele tinha simplesmente estudado na Holanda para um estalajadeiro. Este malandro de ordem composta era, muito provavelmente, algum flamengo de Lille, na Flandres, um francês em Paris, um belga em Bruxelas, estando confortavelmente afastado de ambas as fronteiras. Quanto à sua destreza em Waterloo, o leitor já está familiarizado com isso. Perceber-se-á que ele exagerou uma ninharia. Fluxo e refluxo, errância, aventura, foi o leven da sua existência; uma consciência esfarrapada implica uma vida fragmentária e, aparentemente, na época tempestuosa de 18 de junho de 1815, Thénardier pertencia àquela variedade de saqueadores de que falávamos, batendo no país, vendendo a uns, roubando a outros, e viajando como um homem de família, com esposa e filhos, em um carrinho precário, na retaguarda das tropas em marcha, com instinto de estar sempre ligado ao exército vitorioso. Esta campanha terminou, e tendo, como ele disse, "algum quibus", ele veio a Montfermeil e montou uma pousada lá.

Este *quibus*, composto por bolsas e relógios, por anéis de ouro e cruzes de prata, reunidos em tempo de colheita em sulcos semeados com cadáveres, não chegava a um grande total, e não levava muito longe este sutler transformado em caseiro.

Thénardier tinha aquela peculiar retilínea nos seus gestos que, acompanhados de um juramento, recorda o quartel, e por um sinal da cruz, o seminário. Ele era um bom falador. Ele permitiu que se pensasse que ele era um homem educado. No entanto, o mestre tinha notado que ele se pronunciava indevidamente.

Compunha o cartão tarifário de viagem de forma superior, mas os olhos praticados às vezes espiavam erros ortográficos nele. Thénardier era astuto, ganancioso, preguiçoso e inteligente. Ele não desdenhou de seus servos, o que fez com que sua esposa os dispensasse. Esta gigantesca tinha ciúmes. Pareceu-lhe que aquele homenzinho magro e amarelo devia ser um objeto cobiçado por todos.

Thénardier, que era, acima de tudo, um homem astuto e equilibrado, era um tipo temperado. Esta é a pior espécie; a hipocrisia entra nisso.

Não é que Thénardier não fosse, às vezes, capaz de ira na mesma medida que sua esposa; mas isso era muito raro, e em tais momentos, já que ele estava enfurecido com a raça humana em geral, pois trazia dentro de si uma profunda fornalha de ódio. E como Ele foi uma daquelas pessoas que continuamente vingam os seus erros, que acusam tudo o que passa diante deles de tudo o que lhes sucedeu, e que estão sempre prontos a lançar sobre a primeira pessoa que vem à mão, como uma queixa legítima, a soma total dos enganos, das falências e das calamidades das suas vidas",Quando todo esse fermento foi agitado nele e fervido de sua boca e olhos, ele foi terrível. Ai da pessoa que ficou sob a sua ira em tal momento!

Além de suas outras qualidades, Thénardier era atencioso e penetrante, silencioso ou falador, de acordo com as circunstâncias, e sempre altamente inteligente. Ele tinha algo do olhar dos marinheiros, que estão acostumados a ferrar os olhos para olhar através de óculos marinhos. Thénardier era um estadista.

Todos os recém-chegados que entravam na taberna diziam, ao avistar Madame Thénardier: "Há o dono da casa". Um erro. Ela nem era a amante. O marido era ao mesmo tempo mestre e amante. Ela trabalhava; ele criou. Ele dirigia tudo por uma espécie de ação magnética invisível e constante. Uma palavra lhe bastava, às vezes um sinal; O Mastodon obedeceu. Thénardier era uma espécie de ser especial e soberano aos olhos de Madame Thénardier, embora ela não se desse conta disso. Ela era possuída de virtudes segundo a sua própria espécie; se alguma vez tivesse tido um desacordo quanto a qualquer detalhe com "Monsieur Thénardier" – o que era uma hipótese inadmissível, diga-se de passagem – ela não teria culpado o marido em público por qualquer assunto. Ela nunca teria cometido "diante de estranhos" aquele erro tantas vezes cometido por mulheres, e que é chamado na linguagem parlamentar, de "expor a coroa". Embora a sua concórdia tivesse apenas o mal como resultado, havia contemplação na submissão de Madame Thénardier ao marido. Aquela montanha de barulho e de carne movia-se sob o dedo mínimo daquele déspota frágil. Vista pelo seu lado anão e grotesco, esta era aquela coisa grandiosa e universal, a adoração da mente pela matéria; pois certas feições têm uma causa nas profundezas da beleza eterna. Havia uma quantidade desconhecida sobre Thénardier; daí o império absoluto do homem sobre aquela mulher. Em certos momentos, ela o contemplou como uma vela acesa; em outros, sentia-o como uma garra.

Esta mulher era uma criatura formidável que não amava ninguém além de seus filhos, e que não temia ninguém além de seu marido. Era mãe porque era mamífera. Mas a maternidade não parou com as filhas e, como veremos, não se estendeu aos meninos. O homem tinha apenas um pensamento: como enriquecer-se.

Não conseguiu. Faltava um teatro digno desse grande talento. Thénardier estava arruinando-se em Montfermeil, se a ruína é possível a zero; na Suíça ou nos Pirenéus, este acampamento sem dinheiro ter-se-ia tornado milionário; mas um estalajadeiro deve procurar onde o destino o pegou.

Entender-se-á que a palavra *estalajadeiro* é aqui empregada em sentido restrito, e não se estende a uma classe inteira.

Neste mesmo ano, 1823, Thénardier foi sobrecarregado com cerca de mil e quinhentos francos de pequenas dívidas, o que o deixou ansioso.

Qualquer que tenha sido a obstinada injustiça do destino neste caso, Thénardier foi um daqueles homens que melhor compreendem, com a maior profundidade e da forma mais moderna, aquilo que é uma virtude entre os povos bárbaros e um objeto de mercadoria entre os povos civilizados: a hospitalidade. Além disso, ele era um caçador admirável, e citado por sua habilidade em atirar. Ele tinha uma certa risada fria e tranquila, o que era particularmente perigoso.

Suas teorias como proprietário às vezes irrompiam em relâmpagos. Tinha aforismos profissionais, que inseria na mente da esposa. "O dever do estalajadeiro", disse-lhe ele um dia, violentamente e em voz baixa, "é vender ao primeiro a chegar, ensopados, repouso, luz, fogo, lençóis sujos, um criado, piolhos e um sorriso; parar os transeuntes, esvaziar pequenas bolsas e aliviar honestamente as pesadas; abrigar respeitosamente as famílias que viajam: raspar o homem, arrancar a mulher, limpar a criança; citar a janela aberta, a janela fechada, o canto da chaminé, a poltrona, a cadeira, o otomano, o banquinho, a cama de penas, o colchão e a treliça de palha; saber quanto a sombra consome do espelho e colocar um preço nele; e, por quinhentos mil demônios, fazer o viajante pagar por tudo, até pelas moscas que seu cão come"!

Este homem e esta mulher eram ardilosos e furiosos – uma equipa horrível e terrível.

Enquanto o marido ponderava e combinava, Madame Thénardier não pensava em credores ausentes, não prestava atenção ao ontem nem ao amanhã e vivia num acesso de raiva, tudo num minuto.

Tais eram esses dois seres. Cosette estava entre eles, sujeita à sua dupla pressão, como uma criatura que ao mesmo tempo está sendo moída em um moinho e puxada em pedaços com pinças. O homem e a mulher tinham cada um um método diferente: Cosette era dominada por golpes – este era o da mulher; ela andava descalça no inverno – era o que o homem fazia.

Cosette correu para cima e para baixo, lavou, varreu, esfregou, polvilhou, correu, tremulou, ofegou, moveu artigos pesados e, fraco como estava, fez o trabalho grosseiro. Não havia misericórdia para com ela; uma amante feroz e mestre venenoso. A hospedaria Thénardier era como uma teia de aranha, na qual Cosette tinha sido capturada, e onde ela estava tremendo. O ideal de opressão foi realizado por esta família sinistra. Era algo como a mosca servindo as aranhas.

A pobre criança manteve passivamente a sua paz.

O que acontece dentro dessas almas, quando elas acabaram de abandonar Deus, encontram-se assim, no alvorecer da vida, muito pequenas e no meio de homens todos nus!

CAPÍTULO III

OS HOMENS DEVEM TER VINHO E OS CAVALOS DEVEM TER ÁGUA

Quatro novos viajantes tinham chegado.

Cosette estava meditando tristemente; pois, embora tivesse apenas oito anos de idade, já havia sofrido tanto que refletia com o ar lúgubre de uma velha. Seu olho estava preto em consequência de um golpe do punho de Madame Thénardier, o que fez com que esta comentasse de vez em quando: "Como ela é feia com o punho no olho"!

Cosette pensava que estava escuro, muito escuro, que os cântaros e as carafas nas câmaras dos viajantes que tinham chegado deviam estar cheios e que não havia mais água na cisterna.

Ela ficou um pouco tranquilizada porque ninguém no estabelecimento Thénardier bebeu muita água. Nunca faltou gente sedenta; mas a sua sede era do tipo que se aplica ao jarro e não ao cântaro. Qualquer um que tivesse pedido um copo de água entre todos aqueles copos de vinho teria parecido um selvagem para todos esses homens. Mas chegou um momento em que a criança tremeu; Madame Thénardier levantou a tampa de uma panela que estava fervendo no fogão, depois pegou um copo e se aproximou rapidamente da cisterna. Ela virou a torneira; A criança tinha levantado a cabeça e estava acompanhando todos os movimentos da mulher. Um fluxo fino de água escorria da torneira e metade enchia o copo. "Bem", disse ela, "não há mais água"! Seguiu-se um silêncio momentâneo. A criança não respirava.

"Bah"!, retomou Madame Thénardier, examinando o copo meio cheio, "isso será suficiente".

Cosette aplicou-se mais uma vez ao seu trabalho, mas durante um quarto de hora sentiu o seu coração a saltar no seu peito como um grande floco de neve.

Ela contou os minutos que passaram dessa maneira, e desejou que fosse na manhã seguinte.

De vez em quando, um dos bebedores olhava para a rua e exclamava: "É tão preto como um forno"! ou "É preciso ser um gato para andar pelas ruas sem lanterna a esta hora"! E Cosette tremeu.

De repente, um dos mascates que se alojou na hospedaria entrou, e disse com voz áspera:

"O meu cavalo não foi regado".

"Sim, tem", disse Madame Thénardier.

"Eu te digo que não", retrucou o pedetista.

Cosette emergira debaixo da mesa.

"Oh, sim, senhor"!, disse ela, "o cavalo bebeu; bebeu de um balde, um balde inteiro, e fui eu que levei a água até ele, e falei com ele".

Não era verdade; Cosette mentiu.

"Tem um pirralho do tamanho do meu punho que conta mentiras tão grandes quanto a casa", exclamou o pedetista. "Eu te digo que ele não foi regado, seu jadezinho! Ele tem uma maneira de soprar quando não tem água, o que eu conheço bem".

Cosette persistiu, e acrescentou com uma voz rouca de angústia, e que era quase inaudível:

"E bebeu de coração".

"Venha", disse o mascate, furioso, "isso não vai adiantar nada, que meu cavalo seja regado, e que isso seja o fim"!

Cosette rastejou sob a mesa novamente.

"Na verdade, isso é justo"!, disse Madame Thénardier, "se a besta não foi regada, deve ser".

Então olhando para ela:—

"Bem, agora! Cadê essa outra besta"?

Ela se abaixou e descobriu Cosette encolhida na outra ponta da mesa, quase sob os pés dos bebedores.

"Você está chegando"?, gritou Madame Thénardier.

Cosette rastejou para fora do tipo de buraco em que se escondera. O Thénardier retomou:

"Mademoiselle Dog-lack-name, vá regar esse cavalo".

"Mas, Madame" disse Cosette, fracamente" não há água.

O Thénardier abriu a porta da rua:

"Bem, vá buscar alguns, então"!

Cosette baixou a cabeça e foi buscar um balde vazio que ficava perto do canto da chaminé.

Esse balde era maior do que ela, e a criança poderia ter se colocado nele à vontade.

A Thénardier voltou ao fogão e provou o que havia na panela, com uma colher de pau, resmungando o tempo:

"Há muito na primavera. Nunca houve uma criatura tão maliciosa como aquela. Acho que deveria ter feito melhor para coar minhas cebolas".

Então ela revirou em uma gaveta que continha sous, pimenta e chalotas.

"Veja aqui, Mam'selle Toad", ela acrescentou, "no seu caminho de volta, você receberá um grande pão do padeiro. Aqui está uma peça de quinze sou".

Cosette tinha um pequeno bolso de um lado do avental; Ela pegou a moeda sem dizer uma palavra e a colocou no bolso.

Então ela ficou imóvel, de balde na mão, a porta aberta diante dela. Ela parecia estar esperando que alguém viesse em seu socorro.

"Dá-te bem"!, gritou o Thénardier.

Cosette saiu. A porta fechou-se atrás dela.

CAPÍTULO IV

ENTRADA NA CENA DE UM BONECO

A fila de cabines ao ar livre que começava na igreja, estendia-se, como o leitor se lembrará, até a hospedaria dos Thénardiers. Estas cabines estavam todas iluminadas, porque os cidadãos logo passavam a caminho da missa da meia-noite, com velas acesas em funis de papel, o que, como observou o mestre, então sentado à mesa na casa dos Thénardiers, produzia "um efeito mágico". Em compensação, nem uma estrela era visível no céu.

A última dessas barracas, estabelecida precisamente em frente à porta dos Thénardiers, era uma loja de brinquedos toda reluzente com selinho, vidro e magníficos objetos de estanho. Na primeira fila, e bem à frente, a comerciante tinha colocado sobre um fundo de guardanapos brancos, uma imensa boneca, com quase dois metros de altura, que estava vestida com um manto de crepe rosa, com orelhas de trigo douradas na cabeça, que tinha cabelos reais e olhos de esmalte. Durante todo aquele dia, esta maravilha tinha sido exibida para espanto de todos os transeuntes com menos de dez anos de idade, sem que uma mãe fosse encontrada em Montfermeil suficientemente rica ou extravagante para a dar ao seu filho. Éponine e Azelma tinham passado horas a contemplá-lo, e a própria Cosette tinha-se aventurado a lançar-lhe um olhar, às escondidas, é verdade.

No momento em que Cosette surgiu, de balde na mão, melancólica e superada como estava, não podia deixar de erguer os olhos para aquela boneca maravilhosa, para *a senhora*, como ela a chamava. A pobre criança parou de espanto. Ela ainda não tinha visto aquela boneca perto. Toda a loja lhe parecia um palácio: a boneca não era uma boneca; era uma visão. Era a alegria, o esplendor, as riquezas, a felicidade, que apareciam numa espécie de halo quimérico àquele pequeno ser infeliz tão profundamente mergulhado numa miséria sombria e fria. Com a triste e inocente sagacidade da infância, Cosette mediu o abismo que a separava daquela boneca. Ela disse a si mesma que é preciso ser uma rainha, ou pelo menos uma princesa, para ter uma "coisa" assim. Ela olhou para aquele lindo vestido rosa, aquele lindo cabelo liso, e pensou: "Como essa boneca deve ser feliz"! Ela não conseguia tirar os olhos daquela barraca fantástica. Quanto mais olhava, mais deslumbrada crescia. Ela pensou que estava olhando para o paraíso. Havia outras bonecas atrás da grande, que lhe pareciam fadas e gênios. O comerciante, que andava de um lado para o outro em frente à sua loja, produziu nela um pouco o efeito de ser o Pai Eterno.

Nesta adoração, esqueceu-se de tudo, até da missão de que era acusada.

De repente, a voz grosseira de Thénardier a lembrou para a realidade: "E aí, seu jade bobo! você não foi? Aguarde! Eu vou dar para você! Eu quero saber o que você está fazendo lá! Dá-te bem, seu monstrinho"!

O Thénardier lançara um olhar para a rua e avistara Cosette em êxtase.

Cosette fugiu, arrastando-lhe o pail e dando os passos mais longos de que era capaz.

CAPÍTULO V

O PEQUENO SOZINHO

Como a hospedaria Thénardier ficava naquela parte da aldeia que fica perto da igreja, foi para a nascente na floresta em direção a Chelles que Cosette foi obrigada a ir buscar sua água.

Ela não olhou para a exibição de um único outro comerciante. Enquanto ela estava em Boulanger Lane e no bairro da igreja, as barracas iluminadas iluminavam a estrada; mas logo a última luz da última tenda desapareceu. A pobre criança viu-se no escuro. Ela mergulhou nele. Só que, quando uma certa emoção a venceu, ela fez o máximo de movimento possível com a alça do balde enquanto caminhava. Isso fez um barulho que lhe proporcionou companhia.

Quanto mais ela ia, mais densa se tornava a escuridão. Não havia ninguém nas ruas. No entanto, ela encontrou uma mulher, que se virou ao vê-la, e ficou parada, murmurando entre os dentes: "Para onde essa criança pode ir? É uma criança lobisomem"? Em seguida, a mulher reconheceu Cosette. "Bem", disse ela, "é a Cotovia"!

Desta forma, Cosette atravessou o labirinto de ruas tortuosas e desertas que terminam na aldeia de Montfermeil, ao lado de Chelles. Enquanto ela tinha as casas ou mesmo as paredes apenas em ambos os lados de seu caminho, ela prosseguia com uma ousadia tolerável. De vez em quando, ela captava o cintilar de uma vela através da fenda de um obturador – isso era luz e vida; Havia pessoas lá, e isso a tranquilizou. Mas, na proporção em que ela avançava, seu ritmo diminuía mecanicamente, por assim dizer. Quando passou pela esquina da última casa, Cosette fez uma pausa. Tinha sido difícil avançar mais do que a última estagnação; tornou-se impossível ir mais longe do que a última casa. Ela colocou o balde no chão, enfiou a mão no cabelo e começou lentamente a coçar a cabeça, um gesto peculiar às crianças quando aterrorizadas e indecisas sobre o que fazer. Já não era Montfermeil; eram os campos abertos. O espaço negro e desértico estava diante dela. Ela olhou desesperada para aquela escuridão, onde já não havia ninguém, onde havia bestas, onde havia espectros, possivelmente. Ela olhou bem, e ouviu os animais andando na grama, e ela distintamente viu espectros se movendo nas árvores. Depois, pegou novamente o balde; o medo emprestara-lhe audácia. "Bah"!, disse ela; "Vou dizer-lhe que não havia mais água"! E ela resolutamente reentrou em Montfermeil.

Mal tinha ido cem passos quando fez uma pausa e começou a coçar a cabeça novamente. Agora foi o Thénardier que lhe apareceu, com sua boca horrível de hiena e a ira brilhando em seus olhos. A criança lançou um olhar melancólico diante dela e atrás dela. O que ela deveria fazer? O que seria dela? Para onde ela iria? À sua frente estava o espectro do Thénardier; atrás dela todos os fantasmas da noite e da floresta. Foi diante do Thénardier que ela recuou. Retomou o caminho até à nascente e começou a correr. Saiu da aldeia, entrou na floresta a correr, já sem olhar nem ouvir nada. Ela só parou em seu curso quando sua respiração lhe falhou; mas ela não parou em seu avanço. Ela foi direto à sua frente, em desespero.

Enquanto corria, sentia vontade de chorar.

O tremor noturno da floresta a cercava completamente.

Já não pensava, já não via. A imensidão da noite estava diante desta minúscula criatura. Por um lado, todas as sombras; por outro, um átomo.

Foi apenas sete ou oito minutos a pé da borda da floresta até a primavera. Cosette sabia o caminho, por ter passado por ele muitas vezes à luz do dia. Estranho dizer, ela não se perdeu. Um resquício de instinto guiou-a vagamente. Mas ela não virou os olhos nem para a direita nem para a esquerda, por medo de ver as coisas nos galhos e no mato. Desta forma, ela chegou à primavera.

Era uma bacia estreita e natural, escavada pela água num solo argiloso, com cerca de dois metros de profundidade, rodeada de musgo e daquelas gramíneas altas e frisadas que são chamadas de frescuras de Henrique IV., e pavimentada com várias pedras grandes. Um riacho ficou sem ele, com um pequeno barulho tranquilo.

Cosette não teve tempo para respirar. Estava muito escuro, mas ela tinha o hábito de vir a esta primavera. Sentiu com a mão esquerda no escuro um jovem carvalho que se debruçava sobre a nascente, e que normalmente servia para a apoiar, encontrou um dos seus ramos, agarrou-se a ele, inclinou-se e mergulhou o balde na água. Ela estava em um estado de excitação tão violenta que sua força triplicou. Enquanto assim se curvava, ela não notou que o bolso de seu avental havia se esvaziado na mola. A peça de quinze sou caiu na água. Cosette não viu nem ouviu cair. Ela tirou o balde quase cheio e colocou-o na grama.

Feito isso, ela percebeu que estava desgastada com o cansaço. Teria gostado de partir de novo, mas o esforço necessário para encher o balde tinha sido tal que achou impossível dar um passo. Foi obrigada a sentar-se. Ela caiu na grama e permaneceu agachada lá.

Fechou os olhos; Depois voltou a abri-los, sem saber porquê, mas porque não podia fazer de outra forma. A água agitada no balde ao seu lado descrevia círculos que se assemelhavam a serpentes de estanho.

Por cima, o céu estava coberto de vastas nuvens negras, que eram como massas de fumaça. A trágica máscara de sombra parecia curvar-se vagamente sobre a criança.

Júpiter estava se pondo nas profundezas.

A criança olhou com olhos desnorteados para esta grande estrela, com a qual ela não estava familiarizada, e que a aterrorizava. O planeta estava, de facto, muito perto do horizonte e atravessava uma densa camada de névoa que lhe transmitia uma horrível tonalidade rude. A névoa, melancolicamente roxa, engrandecia a estrela. Alguém lhe teria chamado uma ferida luminosa.

Um vento frio soprava da planície. A floresta estava escura, nem uma folha se movia; não havia nenhum dos vagos e frescos lampejos da maré de verão. Grandes ramos ergueram-se em sábia assustadora. Arbustos esguios e disformes assobiavam nas clareiras. As gramíneas altas ondulavam como enguias sob o vento norte. As urtigas pareciam torcer longos braços providos de garras em busca de presas. Alguns pedaços de urze seca, atirados pela brisa, voaram rapidamente e tinham o ar de fugir aterrorizados diante de algo que viria depois. Por todos os lados havia trechos lúgubres.

A escuridão era desconcertante. O homem precisa de luz. Quem se enterra no oposto do dia sente o seu coração contrair-se. Quando o olho vê preto, o coração vê problemas. Num eclipse à noite, na opacidade suave, há ansiedade até para os corações mais agitados. Ninguém anda sozinho na floresta à noite sem tremer. Sombras e árvores" duas densidades formidáveis. Uma realidade quimérica aparece nas profundezas indistintas. O inconcebível é delineado a poucos passos de distância de você com uma clareza espectral. Contempla-se flutuando, seja no espaço ou no próprio cérebro, não se sabe que coisa vaga e intangível, como os sonhos de flores adormecidas. Há atitudes ferozes no horizonte. Inala-se o eflúvio do grande vazio negro. Teme-se olhar para trás, mas deseja-se fazê-lo. As cavidades da noite, as coisas enrugadas, os perfis taciturnos que desaparecem quando se avança, os desgrenhados obscuros, os tufos irritados, as piscinas lívidas, o lúgubre refletido no fúnebre, a imensidão sepulcral do silêncio, os seres desconhecidos mas possíveis, as curvas de ramos misteriosos, os torsos alarmantes das árvores, os longos punhados de plantas trêmulas, contra tudo isto não há proteção. Não há dureza que não estremeça e que não sinta a proximidade da angústia. A pessoa tem consciência de algo horrível, como se sua alma estivesse se amalgamando com a escuridão. Esta penetração das sombras é indescritivelmente sinistra no caso de uma criança.

As florestas são apocalipses, e o bater das asas de uma alma minúscula produz um som de agonia sob sua abóbada monstruosa.

Sem entender suas sensações, Cosette estava consciente de que estava tomada por aquela enormidade negra da natureza; já não era só o terror que se apoderava dela; era algo mais terrível até do que o terror; ela tremeu. Não há palavras para expressar a estranheza daquele arrepio que a arrepiou até ao fundo do coração; seu olho ficou selvagem; ela pensou que não deveria ser capaz de se abster de voltar lá na mesma hora do dia seguinte.

Então, por uma espécie de instinto, ela começou a contar em voz alta, um, dois, três, quatro e assim por diante até dez, a fim de escapar daquele estado singular que ela não entendia, mas que a aterrorizava, e, quando ela terminou, ela começou de novo; Isso a restaurou a uma verdadeira perceção das coisas sobre ela. Suas mãos, que ela havia molhado ao puxar a água, sentiam frio; levantou-se; O seu terror, um terror natural e invencível, tinha voltado: ela tinha apenas um pensamento agora: fugir a toda velocidade pela floresta, pelos campos para as casas, para as janelas, para as velas acesas. O seu olhar caiu sobre a água que estava diante dela; tal foi o susto que o Thénardier inspirou nela, que ela não ousou fugir sem aquele balde de água: agarrou o cabo com as duas mãos; ela mal conseguia levantar o pail.

Desta forma, avançou uma dúzia de passos, mas o balde estava cheio; era pesado; Ela foi forçada a colocá-lo no chão mais uma vez. Ela respirou por um instante, depois levantou a alça do balde novamente e retomou sua marcha, prosseguindo um pouco mais desta vez, mas novamente foi obrigada a parar. Depois de alguns segundos de repouso, ela partiu novamente. Caminhava curvada para a frente, com a cabeça caída, como uma velha; O peso do balde coou e enrijeceu seus braços finos. O cabo de ferro completava o benumbing e o congelamento de suas mãos molhadas e minúsculas; Ela era forçada a parar de vez em quando, e cada vez que o fazia, a água fria que jorrava do balde caía sobre suas pernas nuas. Isto acontecia nas profundezas de uma floresta, à noite, no inverno, longe de toda a visão humana; ela era uma criança de oito anos: ninguém além de Deus viu aquela coisa triste naquele momento.

E a mãe dela, sem dúvida, infelizmente!

Pois há coisas que fazem os mortos abrirem os olhos em suas sepulturas.

Ela ofegou com uma espécie de chocalho doloroso; soluços contraíram-lhe a garganta, mas ela não ousou chorar, tão receosa era a do Thénardier, mesmo à distância: era seu costume imaginar o Thénardier sempre presente.

No entanto, ela não conseguiu avançar muito dessa maneira, e ela continuou muito lentamente. Apesar de diminuir a duração de suas paradas, e de andar o maior tempo possível entre elas, ela refletiu com angústia que levaria mais de uma hora para voltar a Montfermeil dessa maneira, e que o Thénardier a venceria. Esta angústia misturava-se com o seu terror por estar sozinha na floresta à noite; ela estava desgastada com o cansaço e ainda não tinha saído da floresta. Ao chegar perto de um velho castanheiro que conhecia, fez uma última paragem, mais longa do que as restantes, para que pudesse ficar bem descansada; então ela reuniu todas as suas forças, pegou seu balde novamente e corajosamente retomou sua marcha, mas a pobre criatura, desesperada, não pôde deixar de gritar: "Ó meu Deus! meu Deus"!

Naquele momento, de repente, ela se conscientizou de que seu balde não pesava mais nada: uma mão, que lhe parecia enorme, tinha acabado de agarrar a alça e a levantou vigorosamente. Ela levantou a cabeça. Uma grande forma negra, reta e ereta caminhava ao seu lado através da escuridão; era um homem que tinha vindo atrás dela, e cuja abordagem ela não ouvira. Este homem, sem proferir uma palavra, agarrara o cabo do balde que ela carregava.

Há instintos para todos os encontros da vida.

A criança não tinha medo.

CAPÍTULO VI

O QUE POSSIVELMENTE PROVA A INTELIGÊNCIA DE BOULATRUELLE

Na tarde desse mesmo dia de Natal de 1823, um homem caminhara há bastante tempo na parte mais deserta do Boulevard de l'Hôpital, em Paris. Este homem tinha o ar de uma pessoa que procura alojamento, e parecia parar, por preferência, nas casas mais modestas naquela fronteira dilapidada do faubourg Saint-Marceau.

Veremos mais adiante que este homem tinha, de facto, contratado uma câmara naquele bairro isolado.

Este homem, em seu traje, como em toda a sua pessoa, percebeu o tipo do que pode ser chamado de mendicante bem-criado, - miséria extrema combinada com limpeza extrema. Esta é uma mistura muito rara que inspira corações inteligentes com aquele duplo respeito que se sente pelo homem que é muito pobre e pelo homem que é muito digno. Usava um chapéu redondo muito velho e muito bem escovado; um casaco grosseiro, perfeitamente desgastado, de um amarelo ocre, cor que não era minimamente excêntrica naquela época; um grande colete com bolsos de um corte venerável; bermudas pretas, cinza usado no joelho, meias de preto worsted; e sapatos grossos com fivelas de cobre. Teria sido declarado preceptor em alguma boa família, retornado da emigração. Ele teria sido tirado por mais de sessenta anos de idade, de seus cabelos perfeitamente brancos, sua testa enrugada, seus lábios lívidos e seu semblante, onde tudo respirava depressão e cansaço da vida. A julgar pelo seu passo firme, pelo vigor singular que carimbava todos os seus movimentos, dificilmente se pensaria cinquenta. As rugas em sua testa estavam bem colocadas, e teria disposto a seu favor qualquer um que o observasse atentamente. Seu lábio contraiu-se com uma estranha prega que parecia severa e que era humilde.

Havia no fundo do seu olhar uma indescritível serenidade melancólica. Na mão esquerda carregava um pequeno embrulho amarrado num lenço; à sua direita, apoiava-se numa espécie de cutelo, cortado de alguma sebe. Este bastão tinha sido cuidadosamente aparado e tinha um ar que não era muito ameaçador; o máximo tinha sido feito de seus nós, e recebera uma cabeça semelhante a um coral, feita de cera vermelha: era um cutelo e parecia ser uma bengala.

Há poucos transeuntes naquela avenida, especialmente no inverno. O homem parecia evitá-los em vez de procurá-los, mas isso sem qualquer afetação.

Nessa época, o rei Luís XVIII. ia quase todos os dias a Choisy-le-Roi: era uma das suas excursões favoritas. Por volta das duas horas, quase invariavelmente, a carruagem real e a cavalgada passavam a toda velocidade pelo Boulevard de l'Hôpital.

Isto serviu em vez de um relógio ou relógio para as mulheres pobres do bairro que disseram: "São duas horas; lá está ele de regresso às Tulherias".

E uns apressaram-se a avançar, outros a enfileirar-se, pois um rei que passava cria sempre um tumulto, além disso, o aparecimento e desaparecimento de Luís XVIII produziu um certo efeito nas ruas de Paris. Foi rápido, mas majestoso. Este rei impotente tinha gosto por um galope rápido; Como não conseguia andar, quis correr: aquele aleijado ter-se-ia atraído de bom grado pelo relâmpago. Passou, pacífico e severo, no meio de espadas nuas. O seu enorme sofá, todo coberto de talha dourada, com grandes ramos de lírios pintados nos painéis, trovejava ruidosamente. Quase não houve tempo para lançar um olhar sobre ela. No ângulo traseiro à direita era visível em almofadas tufadas de cetim branco um rosto grande, firme e rude, uma sobrancelha recém-pulverizada à *l'oiseau royal*, um olho orgulhoso, duro e astuto, o sorriso de um homem educado, dois grandes epaulets com franja de barras flutuando sobre um casaco burguês, o Tosão de Ouro, a cruz de São Luís, a cruz da Legião de Honra, a placa de prata do Saint-Esprit, uma barriga enorme e uma larga fita azul: era o rei. Fora de Paris, ele segurava seu chapéu enfeitado com plumas brancas de avestruz sobre os joelhos, envolto em polainas inglesas altas; quando voltou a entrar na cidade, vestiu o chapéu e saudou raramente; Ele olhou friamente para as pessoas, e elas devolveram em espécie. Quando apareceu pela primeira vez no bairro de Saint-Marceau, todo o sucesso que produziu está contido nesta observação de um habitante do faubourg ao seu camarada: "Esse grande companheiro é o governo".

Esta passagem infalível do rei à mesma hora era, portanto, o acontecimento diário do Boulevard de l'Hôpital.

O promenader de casaco amarelo evidentemente não pertencia ao bairro, e provavelmente não pertencia a Paris, pois ignorava esse detalhe. Quando, às duas horas, a carruagem real, rodeada por uma esquadra da guarda-costas toda coberta de rendas prateadas, debochava na avenida, depois de ter feito a curva da Salpêtrière, apareceu surpreendido e quase alarmado. Não havia ninguém além de si mesmo nesta faixa transversal. Ele se apressou atrás do canto da parede de um recinto, embora isso não tenha impedido M. le Duc de Havré de espioná-lo.

M. le Duc de Havré, como capitão da guarda de serviço naquele dia, estava sentado na carruagem, em frente ao rei. Ele disse a Sua Majestade: "Yonder é um homem de aparência maligna". Membros da polícia, que estavam limpando a rota do rei, tomaram igual nota dele: um deles recebeu uma ordem para segui-lo. Mas o homem mergulhou nas ruelas desertas do faubourg e, quando o crepúsculo começava a cair, o agente perdeu o rasto dele, como se afirma num relatório dirigido nessa mesma noite a M. le Comte d'Anglès, Ministro de Estado, Prefeito da Polícia.

Quando o homem de casaco amarelo atirou o agente para fora da pista, redobrou o ritmo, não sem se virar muitas vezes para se assegurar de que não estava a ser seguido. Às quatro e meias, ou seja, quando a noite estava cheia, ele passou em frente ao teatro da Porte Saint-Martin, onde *Os Dois Condenados* estava sendo tocado naquele dia. Este cartaz, iluminado pelas lanternas do teatro, impressionou-o; pois, embora andasse depressa, parou para lê-lo. Um instante depois, ele estava no beco sem saída de La Planchette, e entrou no *Plat d'Etain*, onde se situava o escritório do treinador de Lagny. Este treinador partiu às quatro e meia. Os cavalos foram aproveitados e os viajantes, convocados pelo cocheiro, subiram apressadamente a escada de ferro do veículo.

O homem perguntou: —

"Você tem um lugar"?

"Só um, ao meu lado na caixa", disse o cocheiro.

"Eu vou tomar".

"Suba".

No entanto, antes de partir, o cocheiro lançou um olhar para o vestido surrado do viajante, para o tamanho diminuto de seu pacote, e o fez pagar sua passagem.

"Você vai tão longe quanto Lagny"?, perguntou o cocheiro.

"Sim", disse o homem.

O viajante pagou a Lagny.

Começaram. Quando passaram a barreira, o cocheiro tentou entrar em conversa, mas o viajante só respondeu em monossílabos. O cocheiro começou a assobiar e xingar seus cavalos.

O cocheiro embrulhou-se no seu manto. Estava frio. O homem não parecia estar pensando nisso. Assim, passaram Gournay e Neuilly-sur-Marne.

Por volta das seis horas da noite, chegaram a Chelles. O cocheiro desenhou em frente à pousada dos carroceiros instalada nos antigos edifícios da Abadia Real, para dar aos seus cavalos um feitiço de respiração.

"Eu chego aqui", disse o homem.

Ele pegou a trouxa e o cuzinho e pulou do veículo.

Um instante depois, ele havia desaparecido.

Ele não entrou na pousada.

Quando o treinador partiu para Lagny, poucos minutos depois, não o encontrou na rua principal de Chelles.

O cocheiro virou-se para os viajantes do interior.

"Lá", disse ele, "está um homem que não pertence aqui, pois eu não o conheço. Ele não tinha o ar de possuir um sou, mas ele não considera dinheiro; ele paga a Lagny, e ele vai apenas até Chelles. É noite; todas as casas estão fechadas; Ele não entra na pousada e não é encontrado. Então ele mergulhou através da terra".

O homem não tinha mergulhado na terra, mas tinha ido a passos largos através do escuro, pela rua principal de Chelles, depois virou-se à direita antes de chegar à igreja, na encruzilhada que levava a Montfermeil, como uma pessoa que conhecia o país e tinha estado lá antes.

Ele seguiu esse caminho rapidamente. No local onde é cortada pela antiga estrada arborizada que vai de Gagny a Lagny, ele ouviu pessoas chegando. Escondeu-se precipitadamente numa vala, e lá esperou até que os transeuntes estivessem à distância. No entanto, a precaução era quase supérflua; pois, como já dissemos, foi uma noite de dezembro muito escura. Não mais do que duas ou três estrelas eram visíveis no céu.

É neste ponto que começa a subida da colina. O homem não voltou para a estrada para Montfermeil; Ele atravessou os campos à direita e entrou na floresta a passos largos.

Uma vez na floresta, ele afrouxou o ritmo e começou um exame cuidadoso de todas as árvores, avançando, passo a passo, como se procurasse e seguisse uma estrada misteriosa conhecida apenas por si mesmo. Chegou um momento em que pareceu perder-se e fez uma pausa na indecisão. Por fim, chegou, sentindo o seu caminho centímetro a centímetro, a uma clareira onde havia um grande amontoado de pedras esbranquiçadas. Ele subiu rapidamente para essas pedras, e examinou-as atentamente através das brumas da noite, como se as estivesse passando em revista. Uma grande árvore, coberta daquelas excrescências que são as verrugas da vegetação, ficava a poucos passos de distância da pilha de pedras. Subiu a esta árvore e passou a mão sobre a casca do tronco, como se procurasse reconhecer e contar todas as verrugas.

Em frente a esta árvore, que era uma cinza, havia um castanheiro, sofrendo de uma descasca da casca, à qual tinha sido pregada uma faixa de zinco a título de curativo. Levantou-se na ponta dos pés e tocou nesta faixa de zinco.

Depois pisou durante algum tempo no chão compreendido no espaço entre a árvore e o monte de pedras, como uma pessoa que tenta assegurar-se de que o solo não foi perturbado recentemente.

Feito isso, ele se orientou e retomou sua marcha pela floresta.

Era o homem que acabara de conhecer Cosette.

Enquanto caminhava pelo matagal na direção de Montfermeil, ele espiou aquela pequena sombra movendo-se com um gemido, depositando um fardo no chão, depois pegando-o e partindo novamente. Aproximou-se e percebeu que se tratava de uma criança muito nova, carregada com um enorme balde de água. Em seguida, aproximou-se da criança e, silenciosamente, agarrou o cabo do balde.

CAPÍTULO VII

COSETTE LADO A LADO COM O ESTRANHO NO ESCURO

Cosette, como dissemos, não se assustou.

O homem a abordou. Falava com uma voz grave e quase grave.

"Meu filho, o que você está carregando é muito pesado para você".

Cosette levantou a cabeça e respondeu: —

"Sim, senhor".

"Dá-me" disse o homem; "Vou levá-lo para você".

Cosette soltou o cabo do balde. O homem caminhou ao lado dela.

"É realmente muito pesado", murmurou entre os dentes. Em seguida, acrescentou:

"Quantos anos você tem, pequenina"?

"Oito, senhor".

"E você veio de longe assim"?

"Da nascente na floresta".

"Você vai longe"?

"Um bom quarto de hora a pé daqui".

O homem não disse nada por um momento; Então ele comentou abruptamente: —

"Então você não tem mãe".

"Não sei", respondeu a criança.

Antes que o homem tivesse tempo de falar novamente, ela acrescentou:

"Acho que não. Outras pessoas têm mães. Não tenho nenhuma".

E depois de um silêncio ela continuou:

"Acho que nunca tive nenhuma".

O homem parou; Ele colocou o balde no chão, inclinou-se e colocou as duas mãos nos ombros da criança, fazendo um esforço para olhá-la e ver seu rosto no escuro.

O rosto fino e doentio de Cosette era vagamente delineado pela luz lívida no céu.

"Qual é o seu nome"?, disse o homem.

"Cosette".

O homem parecia ter recebido um choque elétrico. Ele olhou para ela mais uma vez; em seguida, tirou as mãos dos ombros de Cosette, pegou o balde e partiu novamente.

Depois de um momento, ele perguntou: —

"Onde você mora, pequenina"?

"Em Montfermeil, se você souber onde isso está".

"É para lá que vamos"?

"Sim, senhor".

Ele fez uma pausa; depois começou de novo:—

"Quem te mandou numa hora dessas para pegar água na floresta"?

"Era Madame Thénardier".

O homem retomou, com uma voz que se esforçou por tornar indiferente, mas na qual houve, no entanto, um tremor singular:

"O que faz a sua Madame Thénardier"?

"Ela é minha amante", disse a criança. "Ela fica com a pousada".

"A pousada"?, disse o homem, "Bem, vou me hospedar lá hoje à noite. Mostre-me o caminho".

"Estamos a caminho de lá", disse a criança.

O homem andava toleravelmente rápido. Cosette seguiu-o sem dificuldade. Já não sentia cansaço. De vez em quando levantava os olhos para o homem, com uma espécie de tranquilidade e uma confiança indescritível. Nunca tinha sido ensinada a voltar-se para a Providência e a rezar; no entanto, ela sentia dentro de si algo que se assemelhava à esperança e à alegria, e que se elevava para o céu.

Passaram-se vários minutos. O homem retomou: —

"Não há servo na casa de Madame Thénardier"?

"Não, senhor".

"Você está sozinho lá"?

"Sim, senhor".

Seguiu-se outra pausa. Cosette levantou a voz: —

"Ou seja, há duas raparigas".

"Que meninas"?

"Ponine e Zelma".

Foi assim que a criança simplificou os nomes românticos tão caros à mulher Thénardier.

"Quem são Ponine e Zelma"?

"São as jovens damas de Madame Thénardier; suas filhas, como você diria".

"E o que fazem essas raparigas"?

"Oh"!, disse a criança, "eles têm lindas bonecas; coisas com ouro neles, tudo cheio de assuntos. Eles brincam; divertem-se".

"Todo o dia"?

"Sim, senhor".

"E você"?

"Eu? Eu trabalho".

"Todo o dia"?

A criança levantou os grandes olhos, nos quais pendia uma lágrima, que não era visível por causa da escuridão, e respondeu suavemente:

"Sim, senhor".

Depois de um intervalo de silêncio, ela continuou:

"Às vezes, quando termino o meu trabalho e eles me deixam, eu também me divirto".

"Como você se diverte"?

"Da melhor maneira que posso. Deixaram-me em paz; mas não tenho muitos brinquedos. Ponine e Zelma não me deixam brincar com suas bonecas. Só tenho uma pequena espada de chumbo, não mais do que isso".

A criança ergueu o dedo minúsculo.

"E não vai cortar"?

"Sim, senhor" disse a criança; "Corta salada e as cabeças de moscas".

Chegaram à aldeia. Cosette guiou o estranho pelas ruas. Passaram pela padaria, mas Cosette não pensou no pão que lhe mandaram buscar. O homem deixara de lhe fazer perguntas, e agora preservava um silêncio sombrio.

Quando deixaram a igreja para trás, o homem, ao perceber todas as cabines ao ar livre, perguntou a Cosette:

"Então há uma feira acontecendo aqui"?

"Não, senhor; é Natal".

Quando se aproximaram da taberna, Cosette timidamente tocou seu braço:

"Senhor"?

"O quê, meu filho"?

"Estamos bem perto da casa".

"Bem"?

"Você vai me deixar pegar meu balde agora"?

"Porquê"?

"Se Madame vir que alguém carregou isso para mim, ela vai me bater".

O homem entregou-lhe o balde. Um instante depois estavam à porta da taberna.

CAPÍTULO VIII

O DESAGRADO DE RECEBER EM CASA UM POBRE QUE PODE SER UM HOMEM RICO

Cosette não podia deixar de lançar um olhar lateral para a grande boneca, que ainda estava exposta no mercado de brinquedos; Em seguida, ela bateu. A porta abriu-se. A Thénardier apareceu com uma vela na mão.

"Ah! Então é você, seu pequeno desgraçado! Boa misericórdia, mas você tomou o seu tempo! A hussy tem se divertido"!

"Madame" disse Cosette, tremendo todo" aqui está um senhor que quer um alojamento.

O Thénardier rapidamente substituiu seu ar rude por sua careta amável, uma mudança de aspeto comum aos donos de tabernas, e ansiosamente procurou o recém-chegado com seus olhos.

"Este é o cavalheiro"?, disse ela.

"Sim, Madame" respondeu o homem, levantando a mão para o chapéu.

Os viajantes ricos não são tão educados. Este gesto, e uma inspeção do traje e da bagagem do estranho, que o Thénardier passou em revista com um olhar, fez com que a careta amável desaparecesse e o gruff mien reaparecesse. Ela retomou secamente: —

"Entra, meu bom homem".

O "homem bom" entrou. A Thénardier lançou-lhe um segundo olhar, prestou especial atenção ao seu casaco de pedra, que estava absolutamente despojado, e ao seu chapéu, que estava um pouco surrado, e, atirando a cabeça, enrugando o nariz e ferrando os olhos, consultou o marido, que ainda bebia com os carroceiros. O marido respondeu com aquele movimento impercetível do indicador, que, apoiado por uma inflação dos lábios, significa, nesses casos: um mendigo regular. Em seguida, o Thénardier exclamou:

"Ah! veja aqui, meu bom homem; Lamento muito, mas não tenho mais espaço".

"Põe-me onde quiseres", disse o homem; "No sótão, no estábulo. Vou pagar como se ocupasse um quarto".

"Quarenta sous".

"Quarenta sous; concordou".

"Muito bem, então"!

"Quarenta sous"!, disse um carter, em tom baixo, à mulher Thénardier; "Ora, a cobrança é de apenas vinte sous"!

"São quarenta no caso dele", retrucou o Thénardier, no mesmo tom. "Não alojo pobres por menos".

"É verdade" acrescentou o marido, gentilmente; "Estraga uma casa ter essas pessoas nela".

Entretanto, o homem, deitando a trouxa e o cuzinho num banco, sentara-se numa mesa, na qual Cosette se apressou a colocar uma garrafa de vinho e um copo. O comerciante que exigira o balde de água levou-o para o seu cavalo. Cosette retomou seu lugar sob a mesa da cozinha e seu tricô.

O homem, que mal tinha humedecido os lábios no vinho que derramou para si, observou a criança com uma atenção peculiar.

Cosette era feia. Se ela tivesse sido feliz, ela poderia ter sido bonita. Já demos um esboço dessa pequena figura sombria. Cosette era fina e pálida; tinha quase oito anos, mas parecia ter apenas seis. Seus grandes olhos, afundados em uma espécie de sombra, quase foram apagados de choro. Os cantos da boca tinham aquela curva de angústia habitual que se vê em condenados e desesperadamente doentes. Suas mãos estavam, como sua mãe havia adivinhado, "arruinadas com frieiras". O fogo que a iluminou naquele momento trouxe em relevo todos os ângulos de seus ossos, e tornou sua magreza assustadoramente aparente. Como estava sempre a tremer, tinha adquirido o hábito de pressionar os joelhos uns contra os outros. Toda a sua roupa não passava de um pano que teria inspirado pena no verão, e que inspirou horror no inverno. Tudo o que ela tinha era linho furado, não um pedaço de lã. Sua pele era visível aqui e ali e em todos os lugares manchas pretas e azuis podiam ser descidas, o que marcava os lugares onde a mulher Thénardier a havia tocado. Suas pernas nuas eram finas e vermelhas. Os buracos em seu pescoço foram suficientes para fazer chorar. Toda a pessoa desta criança, o seu mien, a sua atitude, o som da sua voz, os intervalos que ela deixava transcorrer entre uma palavra e outra, o seu olhar, o seu silêncio, o seu menor gesto, expressavam e traíam uma única ideia: o medo.

O medo difundiu-se por toda ela; ela estava coberta com ele, por assim dizer; O medo aproximou os cotovelos dos quadris, retirou os calcanhares sob a anágua, fê-la ocupar o menor espaço possível, permitiu-lhe apenas a respiração que era absolutamente necessária e tornou-se o que se poderia chamar o hábito do seu corpo, não admitindo nenhuma variação possível a não ser um aumento. No fundo dos seus olhos havia um recanto espantado onde o terror espreitava.

O seu medo era tal que, à chegada, molhada como estava, Cosette não se atreveu a aproximar-se do fogo e a secar-se, mas sentou-se em silêncio para o seu trabalho novamente.

A expressão no olhar daquela criança de oito anos era habitualmente tão sombria, e por vezes tão trágica, que parecia em certos momentos como se estivesse à beira de se tornar uma ou um demónio.

Como dissemos, ela nunca soube o que é rezar; Nunca tinha posto os pés numa igreja. "Tenho tempo"?, perguntou o Thénardier.

O homem de casaco amarelo nunca tirou os olhos de Cosette.

De uma só vez, o Thénardier exclamou:

"A propósito, onde está esse pão"?

Cosette, de acordo com seu costume sempre que o Thénardier levantava sua voz, emergia com grande pressa de debaixo da mesa.

Ela tinha esquecido completamente o pão. Recorreu ao expediente de crianças que vivem em constante estado de medo. Ela mentiu.

"Madame, a padaria estava fechada".

"Você deveria ter batido".

"Eu bati, Madame".

"Bem"?

"Ele não abriu a porta".

"Vou descobrir até amanhã se isso é verdade", disse o Thénardier; "E se você está me contando uma mentira, eu vou te levar uma dança bonita. Entretanto, devolvam-me o meu pedaço de quinze sou".

Cosette enfiou a mão no bolso do avental e ficou verde. A peça de quinze sou não estava lá.

"Ah, venha agora", disse Madame Thénardier, "você me ouviu"?

Cosette virou o bolso do avesso; não havia nada nele. O que poderia ter sido desse dinheiro? A pequena criatura infeliz não conseguia encontrar uma palavra para dizer. Ela estava petrificada.

"Você perdeu aquele pedaço de quinze sou"?, gritou o Thénardier, rouco, "ou você quer me roubar isso"?

Ao mesmo tempo, estendeu o braço em direção ao gato-o'-nove-caudas que pendia num prego no canto da chaminé.

Este gesto formidável restituiu a Cosette força suficiente para gritar:

"Misericórdia, Madame, Madame! Não o farei mais"!

O Thénardier derrubou o chicote.

Entretanto, o homem de casaco amarelo atrapalhava-se no fob do colete, sem que ninguém se tivesse apercebido dos seus movimentos. Além disso, os outros viajantes estavam bebendo ou jogando cartas, e não estavam prestando atenção em nada.

Cosette contraiu-se numa bola, com angústia, dentro do ângulo da chaminé, esforçando-se por recolher e esconder os seus pobres membros seminus. O Thénardier levantou o braço.

"Perdoe-me, Madame" disse o homem" mas ainda agora avistei algo que havia caído do bolso do avental desse pequeno e rolei para o lado. Talvez seja isso".

Ao mesmo tempo, ele se abaixou e parecia estar procurando no chão por um momento.

"Exatamente; aqui está", prosseguiu, endireitando-se.

E estendeu uma moeda de prata ao Thénardier.

"Sim, é isso", disse ela.

Não era isso, pois era uma peça de vinte e sou; mas o Thénardier achou-o vantajoso. Colocou a moeda no bolso e limitou-se a lançar um olhar feroz para a criança, acompanhado do comentário: "Não deixe que isto volte a acontecer"!

Cosette voltou ao que os Thénardier chamavam de "seu canil", e seus grandes olhos, que estavam rebitados no viajante, começaram a assumir uma expressão como nunca haviam usado antes. Até agora, foi apenas um espanto inocente, mas uma espécie de confiança estupefacta foi misturada com ele.

"A propósito, você gostaria de um jantar"?, perguntou o Thénardier ao viajante.

Não respondeu. Ele parecia estar absorvido pelo pensamento.

"Que tipo de homem é esse"?, ela murmurou entre os dentes. "Ele é um miserável terrivelmente pobre. Ele não tem um sou para pagar por uma ceia. Será que ele vai mesmo pagar-me o seu alojamento? É muita sorte, mesmo assim, que não lhe tenha ocorrido roubar o dinheiro que estava no chão".

Entretanto, uma porta abriu-se e Éponine e Azelma entraram.

Eram duas meninas muito bonitas, mais burguesas do que camponesas na aparência, e muito charmosas; uma com tranças de castanha brilhantes, a outra com longas tranças pretas penduradas nas costas, ambas vivazes, arrumadas, rechonchudas, rosadas e saudáveis, e uma delícia aos olhos. Estavam calorosamente vestidos, mas com tanta arte materna que a espessura dos materiais não prejudicava a coqueteria do arranjo. Havia uma pitada de inverno, embora a primavera não tenha sido totalmente apagada. A luz emanava destes dois pequenos seres. Além disso, estavam no trono. Nas suas toilettes, na sua gayety, no barulho que faziam, havia soberania.

Quando entraram, o Thénardier disse-lhes num tom resmungão cheio de adoração: "Ah! lá estão vocês, seus filhos"!

Em seguida, puxando-os, um após o outro, até os joelhos, alisando os cabelos, amarrando as fitas de novo, e depois soltando-os com aquele jeito suave de sacudir que é peculiar às mães, ela exclamou: "Que sustos eles são"!

Eles foram e sentaram-se no canto da chaminé. Eles tinham uma boneca, que eles viraram de joelhos com todo tipo de conversa alegre. De vez em quando, Cosette levantava os olhos do tricô e assistia ao jogo com um ar melancólico.

Éponine e Azelma não olharam para Cosette. Ela era o mesmo que um cachorro para eles. Estas três raparigas ainda não contavam quatro e vinte anos entre elas, mas já representavam toda a sociedade do homem; inveja de um lado, desdém do outro.

A boneca das irmãs Thénardier estava muito desbotada, muito velha e muito quebrada, mas parecia admirável para Cosette, que nunca tinha tido uma boneca na vida, *uma boneca de verdade*, fazer uso da expressão que todas as crianças entenderão.

De repente, o Thénardier, que andava de um lado para o outro na sala, percebeu que a mente de Cosette estava distraída e que, em vez de trabalhar, ela estava prestando atenção aos pequenos em suas brincadeiras.

"Ah! Eu te peguei"!, gritou ela. "Então é assim que você trabalha! Vou fazê-lo trabalhar ao som do chicote; que eu vou".

O estranho voltou-se para o Thénardier, sem abandonar a cadeira.

"Bah, Madame", disse ele, com um ar quase tímido, "deixe-a brincar"!

Tal desejo expresso por um viajante que tinha comido uma fatia de carneiro e bebido um par de garrafas de vinho com a sua ceia, e que não tinha o ar de ser assustadoramente pobre, teria sido equivalente a uma ordem. Mas que um homem com tal chapéu se permitisse tal desejo, e que um homem com tal casaco se permitisse ter um testamento, era algo que Madame Thénardier não pretendia tolerar. Ela retrucou com acrimônia:—

"Ela tem que trabalhar, já que come. Eu não a alimento para não fazer nada".

"O que ela está fazendo"?, continuou o estranho, com uma voz suave que contrastava estranhamente com suas roupas miseráveis e os ombros de seu porteiro.

O Thénardier dignou-se responder:

"Meias, se quiserem. Meias para as minhas meninas, que não têm nenhuma, por assim dizer, e que estão absolutamente descalças neste momento".

O homem olhou para os pobres pezinhos vermelhos de Cosette e continuou:

"Quando é que ela terá terminado este par de meias"?

"Ela tem pelo menos três ou quatro bons dias de trabalho neles ainda, a criatura preguiçosa"!

"E quanto valerá esse par de meias quando ela as terminar"?

O Thénardier lançou-lhe um olhar de desdém.

"Trinta sous pelo menos".

"Você vai vendê-los por cinco francos"?, continuou o homem.

"Bons céus"!, exclamou um carter que estava ouvindo, com uma gargalhada alta; "Cinco francos! o deuce, eu deveria pensar assim! cinco bolas"!

Thénardier achou que era hora de atacar.

"Sim, senhor; Se tal for a sua fantasia, você poderá ter esse par de meias por cinco francos. Não podemos recusar nada aos viajantes".

"Você deve pagar na hora" disse a Thénardier, com seu jeito ríspido e perentório.

"Vou comprar esse par de meias", respondeu o homem, "e", acrescentou, tirando uma peça de cinco francos do bolso e colocando-a sobre a mesa, "vou pagar por elas".

Depois virou-se para Cosette.

"Agora sou dono do seu trabalho; brincar, meu filho".

O carter ficou tão tocado pela peça de cinco francos, que abandonou o copo e se apressou.

"Mas é verdade"!, exclamou, examinando-a. "Uma verdadeira roda traseira! e não falsificação"!

Thénardier aproximou-se e silenciosamente colocou a moeda no bolso.

O Thénardier não tinha resposta a dar. Mordeu os lábios e o rosto assumiu uma expressão de ódio.

Enquanto isso, Cosette tremia. Aventurou-se a perguntar: —

"É verdade, Madame? Posso jogar"?

"Brinque"!, disse o Thénardier, com uma voz terrível.

"Obrigada, Madame", disse Cosette.

E enquanto sua boca agradecia ao Thénardier, toda a sua pequena alma agradecia ao viajante.

Thénardier tinha retomado a bebida; Sua esposa sussurrou em seu ouvido: —

"Quem pode ser este homem amarelo"?

"Já vi milionários com casacos assim", respondeu Thénardier, de forma soberana.

Cosette tinha largado o tricô, mas não tinha saído do seu lugar. Cosette sempre se moveu o mínimo possível. Ela pegou alguns trapos velhos e sua pequena espada de chumbo de uma caixa atrás dela.

Éponine e Azelma não prestaram atenção ao que estava acontecendo. Tinham acabado de executar uma operação muito importante; eles tinham acabado de pegar o gato. Tinham atirado a boneca ao chão, e Éponine, que era a mais velha, estava a varrer o pequeno gato, apesar do seu miado e das suas contorções, numa quantidade de roupas e retalhos vermelhos e azuis. Enquanto realizava este trabalho sério e difícil, ela dizia à irmã naquela linguagem doce e adorável das crianças, cuja graça, como o esplendor da asa da borboleta, desaparece quando se faz um ensaio para consertá-la rapidamente.

"Veja, irmã, essa boneca é mais divertida que a outra. Ela torce, chora, é calorosa. Veja, irmã, vamos brincar com ela. Ela será minha menina.

Serei uma senhora. Eu virei ver-vos, e vós olhareis para ela. Gradualmente, você perceberá seus bigodes, e isso irá surpreendê-lo. E então você verá seus ouvidos, e então você verá sua cauda e isso irá surpreendê-lo. E você vai me dizer: 'Ah! Mon Dieu"! e eu lhe direi: "Sim, Madame, é minha menina. As raparigas são feitas assim neste momento".

Azelma ouviu com admiração Éponine.

Entretanto, os bebedores começaram a cantar uma canção obscena e a rir dela até o teto tremer. Thénardier acompanhou-os e encorajou-os.

Como os pássaros fazem ninhos de tudo, as crianças fazem uma boneca de qualquer coisa que venha à mão. Enquanto Éponine e Azelma se juntavam ao gato, Cosette, do seu lado, tinha vestido a sua espada. Feito isso, ela o colocou em seus braços, e cantou suavemente, para acalmá-lo para dormir.

A boneca é uma das necessidades mais imperiosas e, ao mesmo tempo, um dos instintos mais encantadores da infância feminina. Cuidar, vestir, vestir, vestir, despir, reparar, ensinar, repreender um pouco, balançar, balançar, acalmar para dormir, imaginar que algo é alguém, aí está o futuro de toda a mulher. Enquanto sonha e tagarela, faz roupas minúsculas e roupas de bebê, enquanto costura vestidos, corsages e corpetes, a criança cresce em uma menina, a jovem em uma menina grande, a menina grande em uma mulher. O primeiro filho é a continuação da última boneca.

Uma menina sem boneca é quase tão infeliz, e tão impossível, como uma mulher sem filhos.

Então Cosette tinha feito de si mesma uma boneca da espada.

Madame Thénardier aproximou-se *do homem amarelo*, "Meu marido tem razão", pensou ela; "talvez seja M. Laffitte; há homens tão ricos queer"!

Ela veio e colocou os cotovelos sobre a mesa.

"Monsieur" disse ela. Com esta palavra, *Monsieur*, o homem virou-se: até então, o Thénardier tinha-se dirigido a ele apenas como *corajoso homme* ou *bonhomme*.

"Veja, senhor" prosseguiu ela, assumindo um ar adocicado que era ainda mais repulsivo de se contemplar do que seu feroz mien" estou disposta a que a criança brinque; Não me oponho, mas é bom por uma vez, porque os senhores são generosos. Veja, ela não tem nada; ela precisa de trabalho".

"Então essa criança não é sua"?, exigiu o homem.

"Ah! mon Dieu! Não, senhor! ela é uma mendiga que acolhemos por caridade; uma espécie de criança. Ela deve ter água no cérebro; ela tem uma cabeça grande, como você vê. Fazemos o que podemos por ela, pois não somos ricos; escrevemos em vão para a sua terra natal, e não recebemos resposta nestes seis meses. Deve ser que a mãe dela esteja morta".

"Ah"!, disse o homem, e caiu em seu devaneio mais uma vez.

"A mãe dela não era muito", acrescentou o Thénardier; "Ela abandonou o filho".

Durante toda esta conversa, Cosette, como que avisada por algum instinto de que estava a ser discutida, não tinha tirado os olhos do rosto do Thénardier; ouviu vagamente; Ela pegou algumas palavras aqui e ali.

Enquanto isso, os bebedores, todos três quartos embriagados, repetiam seu refrão impuro com gayeza redobrada; era um cântico altamente temperado e sem graça, no qual a Virgem e o menino Jesus eram apresentados. O Thénardier saiu para participar dos gritos de riso. Cosette, de seu posto sob a mesa, olhou para o fogo, que se refletia de seus olhos fixos. Ela tinha começado a balançar o tipo de bebê que ela tinha feito, e, enquanto ela balançava, ela cantou em voz baixa: "Minha mãe está morta! Minha mãe morreu! minha mãe morreu"!

Ao ser novamente instado pela anfitriã, o homem amarelo, "o milionário", consentiu finalmente em jantar.

"O que deseja Monsieur"?

"Pão e queijo" disse o homem.

"Decididamente, ele é um mendigo", pensou Madame Thénardier.

Os homens bêbados ainda cantavam a sua música, e a criança debaixo da mesa cantava a dela.

De uma só vez, Cosette fez uma pausa; ela tinha acabado de se virar e avistou a boneca do pequeno Thénardiers, que eles tinham abandonado para o gato e tinham deixado no chão a poucos passos da mesa da cozinha.

Então ela largou a espada enfaixada, que apenas metade atendia às suas necessidades, e lançou os olhos lentamente ao redor da sala. Madame Thénardier sussurrava para o marido e contava com algum dinheiro; Ponine e Zelma estavam brincando com o gato; os viajantes comiam, bebiam ou cantavam; nem um olhar se fixou nela. Ela não tinha um momento a perder; ela saiu de debaixo da mesa com as mãos e os joelhos, certificando-se mais uma vez de que ninguém a observava; Em seguida, ela escorregou rapidamente até a boneca e a agarrou. Um instante depois, ela estava em seu lugar novamente, sentada imóvel, e apenas se virou para lançar uma sombra sobre a boneca que ela segurava em seus braços. A felicidade de brincar com uma boneca era tão rara para ela que continha toda a violência da volúpia.

Ninguém a tinha visto, exceto o viajante, que devorava lentamente a sua parca ceia.

Esta alegria durou cerca de um quarto de hora.

Mas com todas as precauções que Cosette tinha tomado, ela não percebeu que uma das pernas da boneca estava para fora e que o fogo na lareira a iluminava muito vividamente. Aquele pé rosa e brilhante, projetando-se da sombra, de repente atingiu o olho de Azelma, que disse a Éponine: "Olha! irmã".

As duas meninas pararam em estupefação; Cosette tinha ousado levar sua boneca!

Éponine levantou-se e, sem soltar o gato, correu para a mãe e começou a puxar-lhe a saia.

"Deixe-me em paz"!, disse a mãe; "O que você quer"?

"Mãe", disse a criança, "olhe lá"!

E apontou para Cosette.

Cosette, absorvida nos êxtases da possessão, já não via nem ouvia nada.

O semblante de Madame Thénardier assumiu aquela expressão peculiar que se compõe do terrível misturado com as ninharias da vida, e que fez com que este estilo de mulher se chamasse *Megaeras*.

Nesta ocasião, o orgulho ferido exasperou ainda mais a sua ira. Cosette tinha ultrapassado todos os limites; Cosette tinha imposto mãos violentas sobre a boneca pertencente a "essas jovens senhoras". Uma czarina que visse um muzhik experimentando a fita azul de seu filho imperial não usaria outro rosto.

Ela gritou com uma voz rouca de indignação:

"Cosette"!

Cosette começou como se a terra tremesse sob ela; Ela se virou.

"Cosette"!, repetiu o Thénardier.

Cosette pegou na boneca e deitou-a suavemente no chão com uma espécie de veneração, misturada com desespero; depois, sem tirar os olhos, apertou as mãos e, o que é terrível de contar de uma criança daquela idade, torceu-as; então" nem uma das emoções do dia, nem a viagem à floresta, nem o peso do balde de água, nem a perda do dinheiro, nem a visão do chicote, nem mesmo as tristes palavras que ouvira Madame Thénardier proferir tinham sido capazes de arrancar isso dela" ela chorou; Ela explodiu soluçando.

Entretanto, o viajante erguia-se de pé.

"Qual é o problema"?, disse ele ao Thénardier.

"Você não vê"?, disse o Thénardier, apontando para o *corpus delicti* que estava aos pés de Cosette.

"E daí"?, retomou o homem.

"Aquele mendigo", respondeu o Thénardier, "permitiu-se tocar na boneca das crianças"!

"Todo esse barulho para isso"!, disse o homem; "Bem, e se ela brincasse com aquela boneca"?

"Ela tocou-a com as mãos sujas"!, prosseguiu o Thénardier, "com as suas mãos assustadoras"!

Aqui Cosette redobrou os soluços.

"Você vai parar o barulho"?, gritou o Thénardier.

O homem foi direto para a porta da rua, abriu-a e saiu.

Assim que ele se foi, o Thénardier aproveitou sua ausência para dar um chute forte em Cosette debaixo da mesa, o que fez a criança gritar alto.

A porta abriu-se novamente, o homem reapareceu; ele carregava em ambas as mãos a boneca fabulosa que mencionamos, e que todos os brats da aldeia olhavam desde a manhã, e colocou-a de pé na frente de Cosette, dizendo:

"Aqui; isso é para você".

Deve supor-se que, ao longo da hora e mais que ali passara, tinha tomado conhecimento confuso através do seu devaneio daquela loja de brinquedos, iluminada por panelas de fogo e velas de forma tão esplêndida que era visível como uma iluminação através da janela da loja de bebidas.

Cosette levantou os olhos; Ela olhou para o homem que se aproximava dela com aquela boneca como ela poderia ter olhado para o sol; ouviu as palavras inéditas: "É para ti"; Ela olhou para ele; Ela olhou para a boneca; depois recuou lentamente e escondeu-se no extremo, debaixo da mesa num canto da parede.

Ela já não chorava; já não chorava; ela tinha a aparência de não ousar mais respirar.

O Thénardier, Éponine e Azelma também eram como estátuas; os próprios bebedores tinham parado; Um silêncio solene reinou por toda a sala.

Madame Thénardier, petrificada e muda, recomeçou suas conjeturas: "Quem é esse velho sujeito? Ele é um pobre homem? Ele é milionário? Talvez ele seja os dois; ou seja, um ladrão".

O rosto do macho Thénardier apresentava aquela prega expressiva que acentua o semblante humano sempre que o instinto dominante aparece ali em toda a sua força bestial. O taberno olhava alternadamente para o boneco e para o viajante; Ele parecia estar perfumando o homem, pois ele teria perfumado um saco de dinheiro. Isso não durou mais do que o espaço de um relâmpago. Aproximou-se da esposa e disse-lhe em voz baixa:

"Essa máquina custa pelo menos trinta francos. Sem disparates. De barriga para baixo diante daquele homem"!

As naturezas brutas têm isso em comum com as naturezas *ingênuas,* que não possuem estado de transição.

"Bem, Cosette" disse o Thénardier, com uma voz que se esforçava para ser doce, e que era composta pelo mel amargo de mulheres mal-intencionadas", você não vai levar sua boneca?

Cosette aventurou-se a sair do buraco.

"O cavalheiro lhe deu uma boneca, minha pequena Cosette" disse Thénardier, com um ar acariciante. "Tomem; é seu".

Cosette olhou para a maravilhosa boneca numa espécie de terror. Seu rosto ainda estava inundado de lágrimas, mas seus olhos começaram a se encher, como o céu ao amanhecer, com estranhos raios de alegria. O que ela sentiu naquele momento foi um pouco como o que ela teria sentido se lhe tivessem dito abruptamente: "Pequena, você é a rainha da França".

Parecia-lhe que, se tocasse naquela boneca, um raio daria dela.

Isso era verdade, até certo ponto, pois ela disse a si mesma que o Thénardier iria repreendê-la e espancá-la.

No entanto, a atração carregou o dia. Ela terminou aproximando-se e murmurando timidamente quando se virou para Madame Thénardier:

"Pode, Madame"?

Nenhuma palavra pode tornar esse ar, ao mesmo tempo desesperador, aterrorizado e extático.

"Pardi"!, gritou o Thénardier, "é seu. O cavalheiro deu-lhe".

"Verdadeiramente, senhor"?, disse Cosette. "É verdade? A 'senhora' é minha"?

Os olhos do estranho pareciam estar cheios de lágrimas. Ele parecia ter chegado àquele ponto de emoção em que um homem não fala por medo para não chorar. Ele acenou com a cabeça para Cosette, e colocou a mão da "senhora" em sua mão minúscula.

Cosette apressadamente retirou a mão, como se a da "senhora" a queimasse, e começou a olhar para o chão. Somos forçados a acrescentar que, naquele momento, ela esticou a língua imoderadamente. De repente, ela rodou e pegou a boneca em um transporte.

"Vou chamá-la de Catarina" disse ela.

Foi um momento estranho quando os trapos de Cosette se encontraram e apertaram as fitas e musselins rosa frescos da boneca.

"Madame", ela retomou, "posso colocá-la em uma cadeira"?

"Sim, meu filho", respondeu o Thénardier.

Agora foi a vez de Éponine e Azelma olharem para Cosette com inveja.

Cosette colocou Catarina numa cadeira, depois sentou-se no chão à sua frente e permaneceu imóvel, sem pronunciar uma palavra, numa atitude de contemplação.

"Brinca, Cosette", disse o estranho.

"Ah! Estou brincando", devolveu a criança.

Este estranho, este indivíduo desconhecido, que tinha o ar de uma visita que a Providência fazia a Cosette, era a pessoa que os Thénardier odiavam pior do que qualquer outro no mundo naquele momento. No entanto, foi necessário controlar-se. Habituada como estava à dissimulação através do esforço para copiar o marido em todas as suas ações, essas emoções eram mais do que ela poderia suportar. Ela apressou-se a mandar as filhas para a cama, depois pediu permissão ao homem para mandar Cosette embora também; "Porque ela trabalhou duro o dia todo", acrescentou com um ar materno. Cosette foi para a cama, carregando Catarina nos braços.

De vez em quando, a Thénardier ia para o outro lado da sala onde o marido estava, para *aliviar sua alma*, como ela disse. Trocou com o marido palavras que ficaram ainda mais furiosas porque não ousou proferi-las em voz alta.

"Velha besta! O que ele tem na barriga, para vir e nos chatear dessa maneira! Querer aquele monstrinho para jogar! para dar bonecos de quarenta francos para um jade que eu venderia por quarenta sous, então eu iria! Um pouco mais e ele estará dizendo *Vossa Majestade* a ela, como se fosse à Duquesa de Berry! Há algum sentido nisso? Será que ele está louco, então, aquele velho sujeito misterioso"?

"Porquê! é perfeitamente simples", respondeu Thénardier, "se isso o diverte! Diverte-se ter o pequeno a trabalhar; Diverte-o tê-la a jogar. Ele está bem. Um viajante pode fazer o que quiser quando paga por isso. Se o velho sujeito é filantropo, o que é isso para você? Se ele é um, isso não lhe diz respeito. O que você está se preocupando, desde que ele tenha dinheiro"?

A linguagem de um mestre, e o raciocínio de um estalajadeiro, nenhum dos quais admitiu qualquer resposta.

O homem colocou os cotovelos sobre a mesa e retomou sua atitude pensativa. Todos os outros viajantes, vendedores ambulantes e carroceiros, haviam se retirado um pouco, e parado de cantar. Olhavam-no à distância, com uma espécie de admiração respeitosa. Este homem mal vestido, que tirava "rodas traseiras" do bolso com tanta facilidade, e que esbanjava bonecos gigantescos em pequenos brats sujos em sapatos de madeira, era certamente um sujeito magnífico e a ser temido.

Muitas horas se passaram. A missa da meia-noite tinha terminado, os carrilhões tinham cessado, os bebedores tinham saído, a bebedouro estava fechada, a sala pública estava deserta, o fogo extinto, o estranho continuava no mesmo lugar e na mesma atitude. De vez em quando mudava o cotovelo em que se apoiava. Só isso; mas ele não disse uma palavra desde que Cosette deixou a sala.

Só os Thénardier, por cortesia e curiosidade, tinham permanecido na sala.

"Será que ele vai passar a noite dessa maneira"?, resmungou o Thénardier. Quando duas horas da manhã chegaram, ela se declarou vencida e disse ao marido: "Vou para a cama. Faça o que quiser". O marido sentou-se numa mesa no canto, acendeu uma vela e começou a ler o *Courrier Français*.

Uma boa hora passou assim. O digno estalajadeiro havia examinado o *Courrier Français* pelo menos três vezes, desde a data do número até o nome do tipógrafo. O estranho não se mexeu.

Thénardier agitou-se, tossiu, cuspiu, assoou o nariz e rangeu a cadeira. Não é um movimento da parte do homem: "Ele está dormindo"?, pensou

Thénardier. O homem não estava dormindo, mas nada poderia despertá-lo.

Por fim, Thénardier tirou o boné, aproximou-se gentilmente dele e aventurou-se a dizer:

"O Monsieur não vai para o seu repouso"?

Não ir para a cama ter-lhe-ia parecido excessivo e familiar. *Descansar cheirava a* luxo e respeito. Estas palavras possuem a misteriosa e admirável propriedade de inchar a conta no dia seguinte. Uma câmara onde se *dorme* custa vinte sous, uma câmara em que *se descansa* custa vinte francos.

"Bem"!, disse o estranho, "você tem razão. Onde está o seu estábulo"?

"Senhor"!, exclamou Thénardier, com um sorriso, "Eu o conduzirei, senhor".

Pegou na vela; o homem pegou seu pacote e cudgel, e Thénardier o conduziu a uma câmara no primeiro andar, que era de raro esplendor, toda mobiliada em mogno, com uma cama baixa, cortinada com calico vermelho.

"O que é isso"?, disse o viajante.

"É realmente a nossa câmara nupcial", disse o dono da taberna. "Eu e minha esposa ocupamos outra. Isso só é inserido três ou quatro vezes por ano".

"Eu deveria ter gostado muito do estábulo" disse o homem, abruptamente.

Thénardier fingiu não ouvir este comentário pouco amável.

Ele acendeu duas velas de cera perfeitamente frescas que figuravam na peça da chaminé. Um fogo muito bom estava piscando na lareira.

Na chaminé, sob um globo de vidro, estava o vestido de cabeça de uma mulher com arame prateado e flores alaranjadas.

"E o que é isso"?, retomou o desconhecido.

"Isso, senhor", disse Thénardier, "é o boné de casamento da minha esposa".

O viajante examinou o objeto com um olhar que parecia dizer: "Houve realmente um tempo, então, em que aquele monstro era uma donzela"?

Thénardier mentiu, no entanto. Quando arrendara este parco edifício com o propósito de o converter numa taberna, encontrara esta câmara decorada precisamente desta maneira, e comprara os móveis e obtivera as flores laranjas em segunda mão, com a ideia de que isso lançaria uma sombra graciosa sobre "a sua esposa", e resultaria naquilo a que os ingleses chamam respeitabilidade para a sua casa.

Quando o viajante se virou, o anfitrião tinha desaparecido. Thénardier retirou-se discretamente, sem se aventurar a desejar-lhe uma boa noite, pois não queria tratar com desrespeitosa cordialidade um homem a quem se propunha fleecer realmente na manhã seguinte.

O estalajadeiro retirou-se para o seu quarto. Sua esposa estava na cama, mas ela não estava dormindo. Quando ouviu o passo do marido, virou-se e disse-lhe:

"Você sabe, eu vou transformar Cosette fora de portas para morrer".

Thénardier respondeu friamente: —

"Como você continua"!

Não trocaram mais palavras e, instantes depois, a vela apagou-se.

Quanto ao viajante, tinha depositado o seu cudgel e o seu embrulho num canto. O senhorio uma vez foi-se, atirou-se para uma poltrona e permaneceu durante algum tempo enterrado em pensamento. Então tirou os sapatos, pegou uma das duas velas, apagou a outra, abriu a porta e saiu da sala, olhando para ele como uma pessoa que está em busca de algo. Atravessou um corredor e deparou-se com uma escadaria. Lá, ouviu um som muito fraco e suave como a respiração de uma criança. Ele seguiu esse som, e chegou a uma espécie de recesso triangular construído sob a escadaria, ou melhor, formado pela própria escadaria. Este recesso nada mais era do que o espaço sob os degraus. Ali, no meio de toda a espécie de velhos papéis e panelas, entre pó e teias de aranha, havia uma cama – se é que se pode chamar pelo nome de cama uma palete de palha tão cheia de buracos que expõe a palha, e uma capa tão esfarrapada que mostra a palete. Sem folhas. Este foi colocado no chão.

Nesta cama Cosette estava dormindo.

O homem aproximou-se e olhou para ela.

Cosette estava em um sono profundo; ela estava totalmente vestida. No inverno, ela não se despia, para não estar tão fria.

Contra o peito foi pressionada a boneca, cujos olhos grandes, bem abertos, brilhavam no escuro. De vez em quando dava vazão a um suspiro profundo como se estivesse a ponto de acordar, e coava a boneca quase convulsivamente em seus braços. Ao lado de sua cama havia apenas um de seus sapatos de madeira.

Uma porta que estava aberta perto do palete de Cosette permitia uma visão de um quarto bastante grande e escuro. O estranho entrou nele. Na extremidade posterior, através de uma porta de vidro, viu duas camas pequenas e muito brancas. Pertenciam a Éponine e Azelma. Atrás dessas camas, e meio escondido, estava um berço de vime sem cortinas, no qual o menino que chorara a noite toda dormia.

O estranho conjeturou que esta câmara se conectava com a do par Thénardier. Estava a ponto de recuar quando o olho caiu sobre a lareira – uma daquelas vastas chaminés de taberna onde há sempre tão pouco fogo quando há fogo, e que são tão frias de se olhar. Não havia fogo neste, nem sequer cinzas; mas havia algo que atraía o olhar do estranho, no entanto. Eram dois sapatos infantis minúsculos, de forma coquettish e desiguais em tamanho. O viajante recordou o gracioso e imemorial costume segundo o qual as crianças colocam os sapatos na chaminé na véspera de Natal, ali para esperar na escuridão algum presente cintilante da sua boa fada. Éponine e Azelma tiveram o cuidado de não omitir isso, e cada uma delas colocou um de seus sapatos na lareira.

O viajante inclinou-se sobre eles.

A fada, ou seja, a mãe, já tinha feito a sua visita, e em cada uma via uma novíssima e brilhante peça de dez sou.

O homem endireitou-se e estava a ponto de se retirar, quando lá longe, no canto mais escuro da lareira, avistou outro objeto. Olhou para ele e reconheceu um sapato de madeira, um sapato assustador da descrição mais grosseira, meio dilapidado e todo coberto de cinzas e lama seca. Foi o sabot de Cosette. Cosette, com aquela tocante confiança da infância, que sempre pode ser enganada, mas nunca desanimada, também tinha colocado o sapato na pedra da lareira.

A esperança numa criança que nunca conheceu nada além do desespero é uma coisa doce e comovente.

Não havia nada neste sapato de madeira.

O estranho se atrapalhou em seu colete, se inclinou e colocou um louis d'or no sapato de Cosette.

Depois recuperou a sua própria câmara com o passo furtivo de um lobo.

CAPÍTULO IX

THÉNARDIER E AS SUAS MANOBRAS

Na manhã seguinte, pelo menos duas horas antes do amanhecer, Thénardier, sentado ao lado de uma vela na sala pública da taberna, de caneta na mão, fazia a conta para o viajante com o casaco amarelo.

Sua esposa, de pé ao seu lado, e meio curvada sobre ele, seguia-o com os olhos. Não trocaram uma palavra. Por um lado, havia uma profunda meditação, por outro, a admiração religiosa com que se assiste ao nascimento e desenvolvimento de uma maravilha da mente humana. Um barulho era audível na casa; era a cotovia varrendo as escadas.

Após o lapso de um bom quarto de hora, e algumas rasuras, Thénardier produziu a seguinte obra-prima:

PROJETO DE LEI DO CAVALHEIRO NO Nº 1.

Ceia   3 francos.

Câmara 10

Vela   5

Fogo   4

Serviço 1

————

Total   23 francos.

Serviço foi escrito *servisse*.

"Vinte e três francos"!, exclamou a mulher, com um entusiasmo que se misturava com alguma hesitação.

Como todos os grandes artistas, Thénardier estava insatisfeito.

"Peuh"!, exclamou.

Foi o sotaque de Castlereagh auditando o projeto de lei da França no Congresso de Viena.

"Monsieur Thénardier, tem razão; ele certamente deve isso", murmurou a esposa, que estava pensando na boneca dada a Cosette na presença de suas filhas. "É justo, mas é demais. Ele não vai pagar".

Thénardier riu friamente, como de costume, e disse: —

"Ele vai pagar".

Esta gargalhada era a afirmação suprema da certeza e da autoridade. Aquilo que foi afirmado desta forma tem de o ser. Sua esposa não insistiu.

Ela começou a organizar a mesa; O marido andava pelo quarto. Um momento depois, acrescentou:

"Devo mil e quinhentos francos"!

Foi e sentou-se no canto da chaminé, meditando, com os pés entre as cinzas quentes.

"Ah! a propósito", retomou a esposa, "você não esquece que eu vou tirar Cosette de portas hoje? O monstro! Ela parte meu coração com aquela boneca dela! Prefiro casar-me com Luís XVIII. do que mantê-la mais um dia em casa"!

Thénardier acendeu seu cachimbo e respondeu entre dois sopros: —

"Você vai entregar essa conta para o homem".

Depois saiu.

Mal tinha saído do quarto quando o viajante entrou.

Thénardier reapareceu instantaneamente atrás dele e permaneceu imóvel na porta entreaberta, visível apenas para sua esposa.

O homem amarelo carregava a trouxa e o na mão.

"Até tão cedo"?, disse Madame Thénardier; "Monsieur já está nos deixando"?

Enquanto falava assim, ela estava torcendo a conta em suas mãos com um ar envergonhado, e fazendo vincos nela com as unhas. Seu rosto duro apresentava uma sombra que não era habitual com ela: timidez e escrúpulos.

Apresentar tal projeto de lei a um homem que tinha tão completamente o ar "de um pobre desgraçado" parecia-lhe difícil.

O viajante parecia estar preocupado e distraído. Ele respondeu: —

"Sim, Madame, eu vou".

"Então Monsieur não tem negócios em Montfermeil"?

"Não, eu estava de passagem. Só isso. O que lhe devo, Madame", acrescentou.

O Thénardier entregou-lhe silenciosamente a conta dobrada.

O homem desdobrou o papel e olhou para ele; mas seus pensamentos estavam evidentemente em outro lugar.

"Madame", ele retomou, "os negócios são bons aqui em Montfermeil"?

"Então, Monsieur" respondeu o Thénardier, estupefato por não ter testemunhado outro tipo de explosão.

Ela continuou, em tom sombrio e lamentável:

"Ah! Monsieur, os tempos são tão difíceis! e então, temos tão poucos burgueses no bairro! Todas as pessoas são pobres, vejam. Se não tivéssemos, de vez em quando, alguns viajantes ricos e generosos como Monsieur, não nos daríamos bem. Temos tantas despesas. Basta ver, essa criança está nos custando os olhos".

"Que criança"?

"Ora, o pequeno, sabe! Cosette" a Cotovia, como é chamada aqui"!

"Ah"!, disse o homem.

Ela continuou: —

"Como esses camponeses são estúpidos com seus apelidos! Ela tem mais o ar de morcego do que de cotovia. Veja, senhor, não pedimos caridade e não podemos dá-la. Não ganhamos nada e temos de pagar muito. A licença, os impostos, o imposto de porta e janela, os centésimos! Monsieur está ciente de que o governo exige uma quantidade terrível de dinheiro. E depois, tenho as minhas filhas. Não tenho necessidade de criar os filhos dos outros".

O homem retomou, com aquela voz que se esforçou por tornar indiferente, e na qual se prolongou um tremor:

"E se alguém te livrasse dela"?

"Quem? Cosette"?

"Sim".

O rosto vermelho e violento da senhoria iluminava-se horrorosamente.

"Ah! Senhor, meu caro senhor, toma-a, guarda-a, leva-a, leva-a embora, adoça-a, enche-a de trufas, bebe-a, come-a, e as bênçãos da boa Virgem Santa e de todos os santos do paraíso estejam sobre ti"!

"Concordou".

"Sério! Você vai levá-la embora"?

"Vou levá-la embora".

"Imediatamente"?

"Imediatamente. Ligue para a criança".

"Cosette"!, gritou o Thénardier.

"Entretanto", prosseguiu o homem, "pagar-te-ei o que te devo. Quanto custa"?

Ele lançou um olhar sobre a conta, e não conseguiu conter um início de surpresa: —

"Vinte e três francos"!

Olhou para a senhoria e repetiu: —

"Vinte e três francos"?

Havia na enunciação destas palavras, assim repetidas, um acento entre uma exclamação e um ponto de interrogação.

A Thénardier teve tempo para se preparar para o choque. Ela respondeu, com segurança: —

"Bom gracioso, sim, senhor, são vinte e três francos".

O estranho colocou cinco peças de cinco francos sobre a mesa.

"Vá buscar a criança", disse ele.

Nesse momento, Thénardier avançou para o meio da sala e disse:

"O Sr. deve vinte e seis sous".

"Vinte e seis sous"!, exclamou sua esposa.

"Vinte sous para a câmara" retomou Thénardier, friamente" e seis sous para a sua ceia. Quanto à criança, devo discutir um pouco esse assunto com o cavalheiro. Deixa-nos, esposa".

Madame Thénardier ficou deslumbrada como com o choque causado por relâmpagos inesperados de talento. Ela estava consciente de que um grande ator estava fazendo sua entrada no palco, não proferiu uma palavra em resposta e saiu da sala.

Assim que ficaram sozinhos, Thénardier ofereceu uma cadeira ao viajante. O viajante sentou-se; Thénardier permaneceu de pé, e seu rosto assumiu uma expressão singular de bom companheirismo e simplicidade.

"Senhor", disse ele, "o que tenho a dizer-lhe é isto, que adoro aquela criança".

O estranho olhou atentamente para ele.

"Que criança"?

Thénardier continuou:—

"Como é estranho, a gente se apega. Que dinheiro é esse? Recupere a sua peça de cem segundos. Eu adoro a criança".

"A quem você se refere"?, perguntou o estranho.

"Eh! nossa pequena Cosette! Não tencionas tirá-la de nós? Bem, falo francamente; tão verdadeiro quanto você é um homem honesto, eu não vou consentir com isso. Sentirei falta dessa criança. Eu a vi pela primeira vez quando ela era uma coisa pequena. É verdade que ela nos custa dinheiro; É verdade que ela tem os seus defeitos; É verdade que não somos ricos; é verdade que paguei mais de quatrocentos francos por medicamentos para apenas uma das suas doenças! Mas é preciso fazer algo pelo bem de Deus. Não tem pai nem mãe. Eu a criei. Tenho pão suficiente para ela e para mim. Na verdade, penso muito nessa criança. Compreende-se, concebe-se um afeto por uma pessoa; Eu sou um bom tipo de besta, eu sou; Não raciocino; Eu amo essa menina; Minha esposa é de temperamento rápido, mas ela a ama também. Veja, ela é exatamente igual à nossa própria filha. Quero mantê-la a balbuciar sobre a casa".

O estranho manteve o olho fixo em Thénardier. Este último continuou: —

"Com licença, senhor, mas não se entrega o filho a um transeunte, assim. Tenho razão, não estou? Ainda assim, eu não digo – você é rico; você tem o ar de um homem muito bom, se fosse para a felicidade dela. Mas é preciso descobrir isso. Compreendeis: suponhamos que eu a deixasse ir e me sacrificasse, gostaria de saber o que acontece com ela; Não a quero perder de vista; Gostaria de saber com quem ela vive, para poder ir vê-la de vez em quando; para que ela saiba que seu bom pai adotivo está vivo, que ele está cuidando dela. Em suma, há coisas que não são possíveis. Nem sei o seu nome. Se você a levasse embora, eu diria: 'Bem, e a Cotovia, o que aconteceu com ela?' É preciso, pelo menos, ver algum pedaço de papel, alguma ninharia no caminho de um passaporte, sabe"!

O estrangeiro, ainda o perscrutando com aquele olhar que penetra, como diz o ditado, até às profundezas da consciência, respondeu com voz grave e firme:

"Monsieur Thénardier, não é necessário passaporte para viajar cinco léguas de Paris. Se eu tirar Cosette, vou levá-la embora, e isso é o fim da questão. Não saberás o meu nome, não saberás a minha residência, não saberás onde ela está; e a minha intenção é que ela nunca mais vos volte a pôr os olhos enquanto viver. Eu quebro o fio que prende o pé dela, e ela parte. Isso combina com você? Sim ou não"?

Como os gênios, como os demônios, reconhecem a presença de um Deus superior por certos sinais, Thénardier compreendeu que tinha que lidar com uma pessoa muito forte. Era como uma intuição; compreendeu-o com a sua clara e sagaz prontidão. Enquanto bebia com os carroceiros, fumava e cantava canções grosseiras na noite anterior, dedicara todo o tempo a observar o estranho, a observá-lo como um gato e a estudá-lo como um matemático. Ele o observara, tanto por conta própria, pelo prazer da coisa, quanto por instinto, e o espiara como se tivesse sido pago por isso. Nem um movimento, nem um gesto, por parte do homem de casaco amarelo lhe escapou. Mesmo antes de o estranho ter manifestado tão claramente seu interesse em Cosette, Thénardier havia adivinhado seu propósito. Ele havia captado os olhares profundos do velho retornando constantemente para a criança. Quem era esse homem? Porquê este interesse? Por que esse traje horrível, quando ele tinha tanto dinheiro na bolsa? Perguntas que ele colocou a si mesmo sem ser capaz de resolvê-las, e que o irritaram. Ele tinha ponderado a noite toda. Ele não poderia ser o pai de Cosette. Ele era o avô dela? Então, porque não dar-se a conhecer de imediato? Quando se tem um direito, afirma-se. Este homem evidentemente não tinha direito sobre Cosette. O que era, então? Thénardier perdeu-se em conjeturas. Vislumbrou tudo, mas não viu nada. Seja como for, ao entrar em conversa com o homem, certo de que havia algum segredo no caso, de que este tinha algum interesse em permanecer na sombra, sentiu-se forte; Quando ele percebeu, pela resposta clara e firme do estranho, que esse personagem misterioso era misterioso de uma maneira tão simples, ele tomou consciência de que era fraco. Ele não esperava nada disso. Suas conjeturas foram postas à prova. Reuniu as suas ideias. Ele pesou tudo no espaço de um segundo. Thénardier foi um daqueles homens que encaram uma situação num ápice. Decidiu que tinha chegado o momento de proceder de forma simples e rápida. Fez como os grandes líderes fazem no momento decisivo, que sabem que só eles reconhecem; desmascarou abruptamente as baterias.

"Senhor", disse ele, "estou precisando de mil e quinhentos francos".

O estranho tirou do bolso lateral um velho livro de couro preto, abriu-o, sacou três notas bancárias, que deitou sobre a mesa. Em seguida, colocou o polegar grande sobre as notas e disse ao estalajadeiro:

"Vá buscar a Cosette".

Enquanto isso acontecia, o que Cosette vinha fazendo?

Ao acordar, Cosette tinha corrido para pegar seu sapato. Nela ela havia encontrado a peça de ouro. Não era um Napoleão; era uma daquelas peças perfeitamente novas de vinte francos da Restauração, em cuja efígie a pequena fila prussiana substituíra a coroa de louros. Cosette ficou

153

deslumbrada. O seu destino começou a inebriá-la. Ela não sabia o que era uma peça de ouro; ela nunca tinha visto um; escondeu-o rapidamente no bolso, como se o tivesse roubado. Ainda assim, ela sentiu que realmente era dela; adivinhou de onde vinha o seu dom, mas a alegria que experimentou estava cheia de medo. Ela estava feliz; Acima de tudo, ficou estupefacta. Coisas tão magníficas e bonitas não pareciam reais. A boneca assustou-a, a peça de ouro assustou-a. Ela tremia vagamente diante dessa magnificência. Só o estranho não a assustava. Pelo contrário, tranquilizou-a. Desde a noite anterior, no meio de todo o seu espanto, mesmo durante o sono, ela pensava na sua pequena mente infantil naquele homem que parecia ser tão pobre e tão triste, e que era tão rico e tão bondoso. Tudo tinha mudado para ela desde que conheceu aquele homem bom na floresta. Cosette, menos feliz do que a andorinha mais insignificante do céu, nunca soubera o que era refugiar-se sob a sombra de uma mãe e sob uma asa. Nos últimos cinco anos, ou seja, até onde a sua memória corria, a pobre criança tremia e tremia. Ela sempre fora exposta completamente nua ao vento agudo da adversidade; agora parecia-lhe que estava vestida. Antigamente sua alma parecia fria, agora estava quente. Cosette já não tinha medo do Thénardier. Ela não estava mais sozinha; havia alguém lá.

Apressou-se a cumprir os seus deveres matinais regulares. Aquele louis, que ela tinha sobre ela, no próprio bolso do avental de onde a peça de quinze sou tinha caído na noite anterior, distraiu-lhe os pensamentos. Ela não ousou tocá-lo, mas passou cinco minutos olhando para ele, com a língua para fora, se a verdade deve ser dita. Ao varrer a escada, fez uma pausa, permaneceu ali imóvel, esquecida da vassoura e de todo o universo, ocupada em contemplar aquela estrela que ardia no fundo do bolso.

Foi durante um desses períodos de contemplação que o Thénardier se juntou a ela. Ela tinha ido em busca de Cosette a mando do marido. O que era inédito, ela não a atingiu nem lhe disse uma palavra insultuosa.

"Cosette" disse ela, quase gentilmente" venha imediatamente.

Um instante depois, Cosette entrou na sala pública.

O estranho pegou no embrulho que tinha trazido e desamarrou-o. Este pacote continha um pequeno vestido de lã, um avental, um corpete fustiano, um lenço, uma anágua, meias de lã, sapatos - uma roupa completa para uma menina de sete anos. Tudo era preto.

"Meu filho", disse o homem, "pegue esses e vá se vestir rapidamente".

A luz do dia aparecia quando os habitantes de Montfermeil, que tinham começado a abrir as suas portas, contemplaram um velho mal vestido a conduzir uma menina vestida de luto e carregando uma boneca cor-de-rosa nos braços, a passar ao longo da estrada para Paris. Eles estavam indo na direção de Livry.

Era o nosso homem e a Cosette.

Ninguém conhecia o homem; como Cosette já não estava em trapos, muitos não a reconheceram. Cosette estava indo embora. Com quem? Ela não sabia. Whither? Ela não sabia. Tudo o que ela entendia era que estava deixando a taberna Thénardier para trás. Ninguém tinha pensado em despedir-se, nem em despedir-se de ninguém. Ela estava saindo daquela casa odiada e odiada.

Pobre e gentil criatura, cujo coração tinha sido reprimido até aquela hora!

Cosette caminhou gravemente, com os grandes olhos bem abertos e olhando para o céu. Ela tinha colocado seu louis no bolso de seu novo avental. De vez em quando, ela se inclinava e olhava para ele; Então ela olhou para o homem bom. Sentia algo como se estivesse ao lado do bom Deus.

CAPÍTULO X

AQUELE QUE PROCURA MELHORAR A SI MESMO PODE PIORAR A SUA SITUAÇÃO

Madame Thénardier tinha permitido que o marido tivesse o seu próprio caminho, como era seu hábito. Ela esperava grandes resultados. Quando o homem e Cosette partiram, Thénardier deixou passar um quarto de hora completo; depois afastou-a e mostrou-lhe os mil e quinhentos francos.

"Isso é tudo"?, disse ela.

Foi a primeira vez, desde que montaram a arrumação, que ela ousou criticar um dos atos do mestre.

O golpe contado.

"Você tem razão, em calma", disse ele; "Eu sou um tolo. Dá-me o chapéu".

Dobrou as três notas bancárias, enfiou-as no bolso e saiu correndo à pressa; Mas ele cometeu um erro e virou para a direita primeiro. Alguns vizinhos, dos quais ele fez perguntas, o colocaram na pista novamente; a Cotovia e o homem tinham sido vistos indo na direção de Livry. Ele seguiu estas dicas, caminhando a passos largos e falando consigo mesmo o tempo:

"Esse homem é evidentemente um milhão vestido de amarelo, e eu sou um animal. Primeiro deu vinte sous, depois cinco francos, depois cinquenta francos, depois mil e quinhentos francos, todos com igual prontidão. Teria dado quinze mil francos. Mas vou ultrapassá-lo".

E depois, aquele feixe de roupa preparado de antemão para a criança; tudo isso era singular; muitos mistérios estavam escondidos sob ela. Não se deixam escapar mistérios da mão quando já os compreendemos. Os segredos dos ricos são esponjas de ouro; é preciso saber sujeitá-los à pressão. Todos esses pensamentos rodopiavam através de seu cérebro. "Eu sou um animal", disse ele.

Quando se sai de Montfermeil e se chega à curva que a estrada faz para Livry, vê-se estendendo-se antes de se chegar a uma grande distância através do planalto. Ao chegar lá, calculou que deveria poder ver o velho e a criança. Olhou até onde a sua visão chegou e não viu nada. Fez novas indagações, mas perdeu tempo. Alguns transeuntes informaram-no de que o homem e a criança de quem estava à procura tinham ido em direção à floresta na direção de Gagny. Apressou-se nessa direção.

Estavam muito adiantados em relação a ele; mas uma criança anda devagar, e anda depressa; E então, ele conhecia bem o país.

De repente, fez uma pausa e desferiu um golpe na testa como um homem que se esqueceu de algum ponto essencial e que está pronto para refazer os seus passos.

"Eu deveria ter pegado minha arma", disse ele para si mesmo.

Thénardier foi uma daquelas naturezas duplas que às vezes passam pelo nosso meio sem que tenhamos consciência do fato, e que desaparecem sem que as encontremos porque o destino só exibiu um lado delas. É o destino de muitos homens viverem assim meio submersos. Em uma situação calma e equilibrada, Thénardier possuía tudo o que é necessário para fazer – não diremos ser – o que as pessoas concordaram em chamar de um comerciante honesto, um bom burguês. Ao mesmo tempo em que certas circunstâncias eram dadas, certos choques chegavam para trazer sua subnatureza à superfície, ele tinha todos os requisitos para um guarda negro. Ele era um comerciante em quem havia alguma mancha do monstro. Satanás deve ter ocasionalmente agachado em algum canto do casebre em que Thénardier habitava, e ter caído sonhando na presença desta obra-prima horrível.

Depois de uma hesitação momentânea:—

"Bah"!, pensou; "Eles terão tempo para fugir".

E seguiu o seu caminho, caminhando rapidamente em frente, e com quase um ar de certeza, com a sagacidade de uma raposa a perfumar um punhado de perdizes.

Na verdade, quando ele passou pelas lagoas e percorreu em uma direção oblíqua a grande clareira que fica à direita da Avenue de Bellevue, e chegou àquele beco de grama que quase faz o circuito da colina, e cobre o arco do antigo aqueduto da Abadia de Chelles, ele avistou, por cima do mato, do chapéu sobre o qual já erguera tantas conjeturas; era o chapéu daquele homem. O mato não era alto. Thénardier reconheceu o fato de que o homem e Cosette estavam sentados lá. A criança não podia ser vista por causa de seu pequeno tamanho, mas a cabeça de sua boneca era visível.

Thénardier não se enganou. O homem estava sentado lá, e deixando Cosette ficar um pouco descansada. O estalajadeiro andou ao redor do mato e apresentou-se abruptamente aos olhos daqueles que procurava.

"Perdão, desculpe-me, senhor", disse ele, sem fôlego, "mas aqui estão seus mil e quinhentos francos".

Assim dizendo, entregou ao estranho as três notas bancárias.

O homem levantou os olhos.

"Qual é o significado disso"?

Thénardier respondeu respeitosamente: —

"Significa, senhor, que vou retomar Cosette".

Cosette estremeceu e apertou perto do velho.

Ele respondeu, olhando para o fundo dos olhos de Thénardier e enunciando cada sílaba distintamente:

"Você está indo para retomar Co-sette"?

"Sim, senhor, estou. Dir-vos-ei; Debrucei-me sobre o assunto. Na verdade, eu não tenho o direito de dá-la a você. Eu sou um homem honesto, você vê; esta criança não me pertence; ela pertence à sua mãe. Foi a mãe que me confidenciou; Só posso demiti-la à mãe. Você vai me dizer: 'Mas a mãe dela está morta'. Bom; nesse caso, só posso entregar a criança à pessoa que me trouxer um escrito, assinado pela mãe, no sentido de que devo entregar a criança à pessoa mencionada; isso é claro".

O homem, sem dar qualquer resposta, atrapalhou-se no bolso e Thénardier viu o livro de bolso das notas bancárias aparecer mais uma vez.

O dono da taberna tremia de alegria.

"Bom"!, pensou ele; "Mantenhamo-nos firmes; ele vai me subornar"!

Antes de abrir o livro de bolso, o viajante lançou um olhar sobre ele: o local estava absolutamente deserto; não havia alma nem no bosque nem no vale. O homem abriu mais uma vez o livro de bolso e tirou dele, não o punhado de notas que Thénardier esperava, mas um simples papelzinho, que ele desdobrou e apresentou totalmente aberto ao estalajadeiro, dizendo:

"Tem razão; leia"!

Thénardier pegou no papel e leu: —

"M. SUR M., 25 de março de 1823.

"MONSIEUR   THÉNARDIER:—

Você entregará Cosette a esta pessoa. Você será pago por todas as pequenas coisas. Tenho a honra de saudá-lo com respeito,

FANTINE".

"Sabe aquela assinatura"?, retomou o homem.

Certamente foi a assinatura de Fantine; Thénardier reconheceu-o.

Não houve resposta a dar; experimentou dois vexames violentos, o vexame de renunciar ao suborno que esperava e o vexame de ser espancado; O homem acrescentou: —

"Pode guardar este papel como recibo".

Thénardier recuou em boa ordem.

"Esta assinatura é bastante bem imitada", rosnou entre os dentes; "No entanto, deixe-o ir"!

Em seguida, ele ensaiou um esforço desesperado.

"Está bem, senhor", disse ele, "já que você é a pessoa, mas eu devo ser pago por todas essas pequenas coisas. Muito me deve".

O homem ergueu-se de pé, enchendo o pó da manga de rosca:

"Monsieur Thénardier, em janeiro passado, a mãe calculou que lhe devia cento e vinte francos. Em fevereiro, enviou-lhe uma fatura de quinhentos francos; recebeu trezentos francos no final de fevereiro e trezentos francos no início de março. Desde então, decorreram nove meses, a quinze francos por mês, o preço acordado, que ascende a cento e trinta e cinco francos. Recebera cem francos a mais; Isso faz com que trinta e cinco ainda lhe devam. Acabo de vos dar mil e quinhentos francos".

As sensações de Thénardier eram as do lobo no momento em que ele se sente picado e agarrado pela mandíbula de aço da armadilha.

"Quem é esse diabo de homem"?, pensou.

Fez o que o lobo faz: sacudiu-se. Audácia tinha conseguido com ele uma vez.

"Monsieur-I-don't-know-your-name", disse ele resolutamente, e desta vez deixando de lado toda cerimônia respeitosa, "tomarei de volta Cosette se você não me der mil coroas".

O estranho disse tranqüilamente: —

"O quê, Cosette".

Ele pegou Cosette pela mão esquerda e, com a direita, pegou seu, que estava caído no chão.

Thénardier notou o enorme tamanho do cudgel e a solidão do local.

O homem mergulhou na floresta com a criança, deixando o estalajadeiro imóvel e sem palavras.

Enquanto eles se afastavam, Thénardier examinou seus enormes ombros, que eram um pouco arredondados, e seus grandes punhos.

Então, trazendo seus olhos de volta para sua própria pessoa, eles caíram sobre seus braços fracos e suas mãos finas. "Eu realmente devo ter sido extremamente estúpido por não ter pensado em trazer minha arma", disse ele para si mesmo, "já que eu estava indo caçar"!

No entanto, o estalajadeiro não desistiu.

"Quero saber para onde ele vai", disse ele, e partiu para segui-los à distância. Duas coisas ficaram em suas mãos, uma ironia em forma de papel assinado *por Fantine*, e um consolo, os mil e quinhentos francos.

O homem levou Cosette na direção de Livry e Bondy. Caminhava devagar, de cabeça caída, numa atitude de reflexão e tristeza. O inverno tinha desbastado a floresta, para que Thénardier não os perdesse de vista, embora se mantivesse a uma boa distância. O homem virava-se de vez em quando e olhava para ver se estava a ser seguido. De repente, avistou Thénardier. Ele mergulhou de repente no mato com Cosette, onde ambos podiam se esconder. "O deuce"!, disse Thénardier, e ele redobrou o ritmo.

A espessura da vegetação rasteira obrigou-o a aproximar-se deles. Quando o homem chegou à parte mais densa do matagal, rodou. Foi em vão que Thénardier procurou esconder-se nos ramos; não conseguiu impedir que o homem o visse. O homem lançou-lhe um olhar inquieto, depois levantou a cabeça e continuou o seu curso. O estalajadeiro partiu novamente em perseguição. Assim, continuaram por duzentos ou trezentos passos. De repente, o homem virou-se mais uma vez; Ele viu o estalajadeiro. Desta vez, olhou para ele com um ar tão sombrio que Thénardier decidiu que era "inútil" prosseguir. Thénardier refez seus passos.

CAPÍTULO XI

O NÚMERO 9.430 REAPARECE E COSETTE GANHA NA LOTERIA

Jean Valjean não estava morto.

Quando caiu no mar, ou melhor, quando se jogou nele, não foi passado, como vimos. Nadou debaixo de água até chegar a uma embarcação ancorada, à qual estava atracado um barco. Encontrou meios de se esconder neste barco até à noite. À noite, ele nadou novamente, e chegou à costa um pouco longe de Cape Brun. Lá, como não lhe faltava dinheiro, ele adquiria roupas. Uma pequena casa de campo no bairro de Balaguier era, na época, o camarim dos condenados fugidos, uma especialidade lucrativa. Em seguida, Jean Valjean, como todos os tristes fugitivos que procuram escapar à vigilância da lei e da fatalidade social, seguiu um itinerário obscuro e ondulado. Encontrou o seu primeiro refúgio em Pradeaux, perto de Beausset. Em seguida, dirigiu seu curso para Grand-Villard, perto de Briançon, nos Altos Alpes. Foi um voo atrapalhado e inquieto, uma trilha de toupeira, cujos ramos não são rastreáveis. Mais tarde, alguns vestígios de sua passagem para Ain, no território de Civrieux, foram descobertos; nos Pirenéus, em Accons; no local chamado Grange-de-Doumec, perto do mercado de Chavailles, e nos arredores de Perigueux em Brunies, cantão de La Chapelle-Gonaguet. Chegou a Paris. Acabámos de o ver em Montfermeil.

Seu primeiro cuidado ao chegar a Paris tinha sido comprar roupas de luto para uma menina de sete a oito anos de idade; em seguida, para obter um alojamento. Feito isso, ele se entregou a Montfermeil. Recordar-se-á que já durante a sua fuga anterior, fizera uma viagem misteriosa a algum lugar daquele bairro, da qual a lei tinha recolhido uma ideia.

No entanto, pensava-se que ele estava morto, e isso aumentou ainda mais a obscuridade que se acumulava em torno dele. Em Paris, um dos jornais que narravam o fato caiu em suas mãos. Sentia-se tranquilizado e quase em paz, como se estivesse realmente morto.

Na noite do dia em que Jean Valjean resgatou Cosette das garras dos Thénardiers, ele voltou a Paris. Voltou a entrar ao cair da noite, com a criança, através da Barreira Monceaux. Aí entrou num cabriolet, que o levou até à esplanada do Observatório. Lá saiu, pagou ao cocheiro, pegou Cosette pela mão e, juntos, dirigiram os seus passos através da escuridão, pelas ruas desertas que contíguas ao Ourcine e ao Glacière, em direção ao Boulevard de l'Hôpital.

O dia tinha sido estranho e cheio de emoções para Cosette. Tinham comido pão e queijo comprados em tabernas isoladas, atrás de sebes; tinham mudado de carruagem com frequência; tinham percorrido curtas distâncias a pé. Ela não se queixou, mas estava cansada, e Jean Valjean percebeu isso pela maneira como ela arrastava cada vez mais em sua mão enquanto caminhava. Ele a pegou nas costas. Cosette, sem largar Catarina, deitou a cabeça no ombro de Jean Valjean e lá adormeceu.

LIVRO QUATRO

O CASEBRE DE GORBEAU

CAPÍTULO I

MESTRE GORBEAU

Há quarenta anos, um que se tinha aventurado naquele país desconhecido da Salpêtrière, e que tinha subido ao Barrière d'Italie através da avenida, chegou a um ponto em que se pode dizer que Paris desapareceu. Já não era solidão, pois havia transeuntes; não era o país, pois havia casas e ruas; não era a cidade, pois as ruas tinham ruelas como estradas, e nelas crescia a relva; não era uma aldeia, as casas eram demasiado altas. O que era, então? Era um local habitado onde não havia ninguém; era um lugar deserto onde havia alguém; era uma avenida da grande cidade, uma rua de Paris; mais selvagem à noite do que a floresta, mais sombrio de dia do que um cemitério.

Era o bairro antigo do Marché-aux-Chevaux.

O, se arriscasse fora das quatro paredes decrépitas deste Marché-aux-Chevaux; se consentiu mesmo em passar para além da Rue du Petit-Banquier, depois de deixar à sua direita um jardim protegido por muros altos; depois um campo em que moinhos de casca castanha se erguiam como gigantescas cabanas de castores; depois um recinto cheio de madeira, com um monte de cepos, serragem e aparas, sobre o qual estava um grande cão, latindo; depois um muro comprido, baixo, totalmente dilapidado, com uma pequena porta negra em luto, carregada de musgos, que estavam cobertos de flores na primavera; depois, no local mais deserto, um edifício assustador e decrépito, sobre o qual corria a inscrição em letras grandes: POST NO BILLS", este atrevido rambler teria atingido latitudes pouco conhecidas na esquina da Rue des Vignes-Saint-Marcel. Ali, perto de uma fábrica, e entre dois muros de jardim, via-se, naquela época, um edifício mesquinho, que, à primeira vista, parecia tão pequeno como um casebre de colmo, e que era, na realidade, tão grande como uma catedral.

Apresentava o seu lado e empena à via pública; daí a sua aparente diminuição. Quase toda a casa estava escondida. Apenas a porta e uma janela podiam ser vistas.

Este casebre tinha apenas um andar de altura.

O primeiro detalhe que impressionou o observador foi que a porta nunca poderia ter sido outra coisa senão a porta de um casebre, enquanto a janela, se tivesse sido esculpida em pedra vestida em vez de ser em alvenaria áspera, poderia ter sido a estrutura de uma mansão senhorial.

A porta não passava de uma coleção de tábuas comidas por minhocas ligadas grosseiramente por vigas cruzadas que se assemelhavam a troncos grosseiramente lavrados. Abria-se diretamente sobre uma escadaria íngreme de degraus altos, lamacentos, calcários, manchados de gesso, degraus empoeirados, da mesma largura que ele, que podia ser visto da rua, subindo em linha reta como uma escada e desaparecendo na escuridão entre duas paredes. O topo da baía disforme em que esta porta se fechava era mascarado por um estreito decantamento no centro do qual tinha sido serrado um buraco triangular, que servia tanto de vime como orifício de ar quando a porta estava fechada. No interior da porta, as figuras 52 tinham sido traçadas com um par de pincéis mergulhados em tinta e, acima do cantling, a mesma mão tinha espreitado o número 50, de modo que se hesitou. Onde estava um? Acima da porta dizia: "Número 50"; o interior respondeu: "não, número 52". Ninguém sabe que figuras cor de pó foram suspensas como cortinas da abertura triangular.

A janela era grande, suficientemente elevada, decorada com persianas venezianas, e com uma moldura em grandes painéis quadrados; apenas estes grandes painéis sofriam de várias feridas, que eram ocultadas e traídas por um engenhoso curativo de papel. E as persianas, deslocadas e descoladas, ameaçavam os transeuntes em vez de vigiarem os ocupantes. As ripas horizontais faltavam aqui e ali e tinham sido ingenuamente substituídas por tábuas pregadas perpendicularmente; de modo que o que começou como um cego terminou como um obturador. Esta porta com um ar imundo, e esta janela com um ar honesto, embora dilapidado, assim contemplada na mesma casa, produziu o efeito de dois mendigos incompletos caminhando lado a lado, com miens diferentes sob os mesmos trapos, um tendo sido sempre um mendicante, e o outro tendo sido um cavalheiro.

A escadaria levava a um edifício muito vasto que se assemelhava a um galpão que havia sido convertido em uma casa. Este edifício tinha, para o seu tubo intestinal, um longo corredor, no qual se abriam à direita e à esquerda tipos de compartimentos de dimensões variadas que eram habitáveis sob o stress das circunstâncias, e mais parecidos com baias do que células. Estas câmaras receberam a sua luz dos vagos terrenos baldios do bairro.

Tudo isso era sombrio, desagradável, wan, melancólico, sepulcral; atravessadas de acordo com as fendas que jaziam no telhado ou na porta, por raios frios ou por ventos gelados. Uma peculiaridade interessante e pitoresca deste tipo de habitação é o enorme tamanho das aranhas.

À esquerda da porta de entrada, do lado da avenida, a cerca da altura de um homem do chão, uma pequena janela que tinha sido murada formava um nicho quadrado cheio de pedras que as crianças tinham atirado ali quando passavam.

Uma parte deste edifício foi recentemente demolida. A partir do que ainda resta dele, pode-se formar um juízo sobre o que era antigamente. No seu conjunto, não tinha mais de cem anos. Cem anos é juventude numa igreja e idade numa casa. Parece que o alojamento do homem participava de seu caráter efêmero, e a casa de Deus de sua eternidade.

Os carteiros chamaram a casa de número 50-52; mas era conhecida no bairro como a casa Gorbeau.

Expliquemos de onde derivou esta denominação.

Colecionadores de pequenos detalhes, que se tornam herbalistas de anedotas, e picam datas escorregadias em suas memórias com um alfinete, sabem que havia em Paris, durante o século passado, por volta de 1770, dois advogados no Châtelet nomeados, um Corbeau (Corvo), o outro Renard (Fox). Os dois nomes tinham sido defendidos por La Fontaine. A oportunidade era boa demais para os advogados; eles aproveitaram ao máximo. Uma paródia foi imediatamente colocada em circulação nas galerias do tribunal, em versos que mancaram um pouco:

Mestre Corvo, de costas empoleiradas, Segurava no bico
uma apreensão executória; Mestre Fox, pelo cheiro
sedutor,
disse-lhe algo assim: "Ei! Bom dia". Etc.

Os dois praticantes honestos, embaraçados pelas brincadeiras, e
achando o porte da cabeça interferido pelos gritos de riso que se lhes
seguiram, resolveram livrar-se dos seus nomes, e acertaram no expediente
de se candidatarem ao rei.

A petição foi apresentada a Luís XV. no mesmo dia em que o Núncio
Papal, por um lado, e o Cardeal de la Roche-Aymon, por outro, ambos
devotamente ajoelhados, estavam empenhados em vestir, na presença de
Sua Majestade, um chinelo nos pés descalços de Madame du Barry, que
acabara de sair da cama. O rei, que estava rindo, continuou a rir, passou
gaymente dos dois bispos para os dois advogados, e deu a esses membros
da lei seus nomes anteriores, ou quase. Por ordem dos reis, Maître
Corbeau foi autorizado a adicionar uma cauda à sua carta inicial e a chamar-
se Gorbeau. Maître Renard teve menos sorte; tudo o que obteve foi deixar
para colocar um P na frente do seu R, e chamar-se Prenard; de modo que
o segundo nome tinha quase tanta semelhança quanto o primeiro.

Agora, de acordo com a tradição local, este Maître Gorbeau tinha sido
o proprietário do edifício numerado 50-52 no Boulevard de l'Hôpital. Foi
mesmo o autor da janela monumental.

Daí o edifício ter o nome da casa Gorbeau.

Em frente a esta casa, entre as árvores da avenida, ergueu-se um grande
ulmeiro que estava três quartos morto; quase de frente para ela abre a Rue
de la Barrière des Gobelins, uma rua então sem casas, não pavimentada,
plantada com árvores insalubres, que era verde ou lamacenta de acordo
com a estação, e que terminava diretamente na parede exterior de Paris.
Um odor de cobre emitido em sopros dos telhados da fábrica vizinha.

A barreira estava próxima. Em 1823 ainda existia a muralha da cidade.

Essa própria barreira evocava fantasias sombrias na mente. Era o
caminho para Bicêtre. Foi através dela que, sob o Império e a Restauração,

os prisioneiros condenados à morte reentraram em Paris no dia da sua execução. Foi lá, que, por volta de 1829, foi cometido aquele misterioso assassinato, chamado "O assassinato da barreira de Fontainebleau", cujos autores a justiça nunca foi capaz de descobrir; um problema melancólico que nunca foi elucidado, um enigma assustador que nunca foi desvendado. Dê alguns passos, e você se depara com aquela fatal Rue Croulebarbe, onde Ulbach esfaqueou a cabra-menina de Ivry ao som de trovão, como nos melodramas. Mais alguns passos, e chega-se aos abomináveis ulmeiros polidos do Barrière Saint-Jacques, aquele expediente do filantropo para esconder o andaime, aquele miserável e vergonhoso Place de Grève de uma sociedade burguesa e mercantil, que recuou perante a pena de morte, não ousando aboli-la com grandeza, nem defendê-la com autoridade.

Deixando de lado esta Place Saint-Jacques, que era, por assim dizer, predestinada, e que sempre foi horrível, provavelmente o local mais triste daquela avenida triste, sete e trinta anos atrás, era o local que até hoje é tão pouco atraente, onde ficava o edifício número 50-52.

As casas burguesas só começaram a surgir lá vinte e cinco anos depois. O lugar era desagradável. Além dos pensamentos sombrios que ali se assaltavam, tinha-se consciência de estar entre a Salpêtrière, cujo vislumbre se podia ver, e Bicêtre, cujos arredores se tocava bastante; ou seja, entre a loucura das mulheres e a loucura dos homens. Até onde a vista alcançava, não se percebia senão os matadouros, a muralha da cidade e as frentes de algumas fábricas, assemelhando-se a quartéis ou mosteiros; por toda a parte havia casebres, lixo, paredes antigas enegrecidas como cerecloths, novas paredes brancas como lençóis sinuosos; por toda parte fileiras paralelas de árvores, edifícios erguidos sobre uma linha, construções planas, longas fileiras frias e a tristeza melancólica dos ângulos retos. Nem um desnível do terreno, nem um capricho na arquitetura, nem uma dobra. O *conjunto* era glacial, regular, hediondo. Nada oprime o coração como a simetria. É porque a simetria é ennui, e ennui está na própria base do luto. O desespero boceja. Algo mais terrível do que um inferno onde se sofre pode ser imaginado, e isso é um inferno onde se está entediado. Se tal inferno existisse, aquele pedaço do Boulevard de l'Hôpital poderia ter formado a entrada para ele.

No entanto, ao cair da noite, no momento em que a luz do dia está desaparecendo, especialmente no inverno, na hora em que a brisa crepuscular rasga dos ulmeiros suas últimas folhas vermelhas, quando a escuridão é profunda e sem estrelas, ou quando a lua e o vento estão se abrindo nas nuvens e se perdendo nas sombras, esta avenida de repente se torna assustadora. As linhas negras afundam-se para dentro e perdem-se nas sombras, como pedaços do infinito. O transeunte não pode deixar de recordar as inúmeras tradições do lugar que estão ligadas ao gibbet. A solidão deste local, onde tantos crimes foram cometidos, tinha algo de terrível. Quase se tinha um pressentimento de se encontrar com armadilhas naquela escuridão; todas as formas confusas da escuridão pareciam suspeitas, e o longo e oco quadrado, do qual se vislumbrava entre cada árvore, parecia sepultura: de dia era feio; na melancolia noturna; à noite era sinistro.

No verão, ao crepúsculo, via-se, aqui e ali, umas velhinhas sentadas ao pé do ulmeiro, em bancos mofados. Estas boas velhinhas gostavam de mendigar.

No entanto, este trimestre, que tinha um ar mais superanulado do que antigo, tendia mesmo nessa altura para a transformação. Mesmo naquela época, qualquer um que desejasse vê-lo tinha que se apressar. A cada dia algum detalhe de todo o efeito estava desaparecendo. Nos últimos vinte anos, a estação da ferrovia de Orleans ficou ao lado do antigo faubourg e o distraiu, como acontece hoje. Onde quer que seja colocada nas fronteiras de uma capital, uma estação ferroviária é a morte de um subúrbio e o nascimento de uma cidade. Parece que, em torno destes grandes centros de movimentos de um povo, a terra, cheia de germes, tremia e bocejava, para engolir as antigas moradas dos homens e permitir que novas brotassem, ao chocalho destas poderosas máquinas, ao sopro destes monstruosos cavalos de civilização que devoram carvão e vomitam fogo. As casas antigas desmoronam-se e as novas sobem.

Desde que a estrada de ferro de Orleans invadiu a região da Salpêtrière, tremem as antigas e estreitas ruas adjacentes aos fossos Saint-Victor e Jardin des Plantes, que são violentamente atravessadas três ou quatro vezes por dia por aquelas correntes de ônibus fiacres e onibus que, em um determinado tempo, aglomeram as casas à direita e à esquerda; porque há coisas estranhas quando ditas que são rigorosamente exatas; E assim como é verdade dizer que nas grandes cidades o sol faz com que as frentes sul das casas vegetem e cresçam, é certo que a passagem frequente de veículos amplia as ruas. Os sintomas de uma nova vida são evidentes. Neste antigo bairro provinciano, nos recantos mais selvagens, o pavimento mostra-se, os passeios começam a rastejar e a crescer mais, mesmo onde ainda não há peões. Uma manhã, uma manhã memorável em julho de 1845, potes pretos de betume foram vistos fumando lá; nesse dia, poder-se-ia dizer que a civilização tinha chegado à Rue de l'Ourcine, e que Paris tinha entrado no subúrbio de Saint-Marceau.

CAPÍTULO II

UM NINHO PARA CORUJA E UMA TOUTINEGRA

Foi em frente a esta casa de Gorbeau que Jean Valjean parou. Como pássaros selvagens, ele tinha escolhido este lugar deserto para construir seu ninho.

Ele se atrapalhou no bolso do colete, sacou uma espécie de chave de acesso, abriu a porta, entrou, fechou novamente com cuidado e subiu a escada, ainda carregando Cosette.

No topo da escada tirou do bolso outra chave, com a qual abriu outra porta. A câmara em que entrou, e que fechou de novo instantaneamente, era uma espécie de sótão moderadamente espaçoso, mobilado com um colchão colocado no chão, uma mesa e várias cadeiras; um fogão em que um fogo estava queimando, e cujas brasas eram visíveis, estava em um canto. Uma lanterna na avenida lançou uma luz vaga nesta pobre sala. No extremo havia um vestiário com uma cama dobrável; Jean Valjean carregou a criança para esta cama e deitou-a ali sem a acordar.

Ele acertou um fósforo e acendeu uma vela. Tudo isto foi preparado de antemão sobre a mesa e, como fizera na noite anterior, começou a perscrutar o rosto de Cosette com um olhar cheio de êxtase, em que a expressão de bondade e ternura quase equivalia a aberração. A menina, com aquela confiança tranquila que só pertence à força extrema e à fraqueza extrema, adormecera sem saber com quem estava, e continuava a dormir sem saber onde estava.

Jean Valjean inclinou-se e beijou a mão daquela criança.

Nove meses antes tinha beijado a mão da mãe, que também acabara de adormecer.

O mesmo sentimento triste, penetrante e religioso encheu-lhe o coração.

Ajoelhou-se ao lado da cama de Cosette.

Estava em plena luz do dia e a criança ainda dormia. Um raio do sol de dezembro penetrou na janela do sótão e deitou-se sobre o teto em longos fios de luz e sombra. De repente, um carrinho de transporte carregado, que passava ao longo da avenida, sacudiu o leito frágil, como um trovão, e o fez tremer de cima para baixo.

"Sim, madame"!, gritou Cosette, acordando com um começo, "aqui estou! aqui estou"!

E ela saiu da cama, com os olhos ainda meio fechados com o peso do sono, estendendo os braços em direção ao canto da parede.

"Ah! mon Dieu, minha vassoura"!, disse ela.

Ela abriu bem os olhos e contemplou o semblante sorridente de Jean Valjean.

"Ah! então é verdade"!, disse a criança. "Bom dia, Monsieur".

As crianças aceitam a alegria e a felicidade instantaneamente e familiarmente, sendo elas mesmas por natureza alegria e felicidade.

Cosette avistou Catarina ao pé da cama, apoderou-se dela e, enquanto brincava, fez uma centena de perguntas a Jean Valjean. Onde ela estava? Paris era muito grande? Madame Thénardier estava muito longe? Ela era para voltar? etc., etc. De repente, ela exclamou: "Como é bonito aqui"!

Era um buraco assustador, mas ela se sentia livre.

"Devo varrer"?, retomou por fim.

"Joga"!, disse Jean Valjean.

O dia passou assim. Cosette, sem se preocupar em entender nada, estava inexpressivamente feliz com aquela boneca e aquele homem gentil.

CAPÍTULO III

DOIS INFORTÚNIOS FAZEM UM PEDAÇO DE BOA SORTE

Na manhã seguinte, ao amanhecer, Jean Valjean ainda estava ao lado da cama de Cosette; Ele assistiu ali imóvel, esperando que ela acordasse.

Alguma coisa nova tinha entrado em sua alma.

Jean Valjean nunca tinha amado nada; Durante vinte e cinco anos esteve sozinho no mundo. Nunca tinha sido pai, amante, marido, amigo. Na prisão, ele tinha sido cruel, sombrio, casto, ignorante e tímido. O coração daquele ex-presidiário estava cheio de virgindade. A sua irmã e os filhos da sua irmã tinham-lhe deixado apenas uma memória vaga e longínqua que tinha finalmente desaparecido quase completamente; fizera todos os esforços para encontrá-los e, não tendo conseguido encontrá-los, esquecera-se-a. A natureza humana é feita assim; as outras ternas emoções da sua juventude, se é que alguma vez tivera alguma, tinham caído num abismo.

Quando viu Cosette, quando se apoderou dela, a carregou e a libertou, sentiu seu coração se mover dentro dele.

Toda a paixão e carinho dentro dele acordou e correu em direção àquela criança. Aproximou-se da cama, onde ela dormia, e tremeu de alegria. Sofreu todas as dores de uma mãe, e não sabia o que significava; pois esse grande e singular movimento de um coração que começa a amar é uma coisa muito obscura e muito doce.

Pobre velho, com um coração perfeitamente novo!

Só que, como ele tinha cinco e cinquenta anos, e Cosette oito anos de idade, tudo o que poderia ter sido amor em todo o curso de sua vida fluiu junto em uma espécie de luz inefável.

Foi a segunda aparição branca que encontrou. O Bispo fizera-se erguer no seu horizonte a aurora da virtude; Cosette fez nascer a aurora do amor.

Os primeiros dias passaram neste estado deslumbrado.

Cosette, por seu lado, tornara-se também, desconhecida de si mesma, outro ser, coitadinha! Era tão pequena quando a mãe a deixou, que já não se lembrava dela. Como todas as crianças, que se assemelham a rebentos da videira, que se agarram a tudo, ela tentara amar; ela não tinha conseguido. Todos a tinham repelido: os Thénardiers, seus filhos, outras crianças. Ela tinha amado o cachorro, e ele tinha morrido, após o que nada e ninguém teria nada a ver com ela. É triste dizer, e já o insinuámos, que, aos oito anos de idade, o seu coração estava frio. A culpa não foi dela; não era a faculdade de amar que lhe faltava; infelizmente! era a possibilidade. Assim, desde o primeiro dia, todos os seus poderes sencientes e pensantes amaram este homem bondoso. Ela sentiu aquilo que nunca tinha sentido antes: uma sensação de expansão.

O homem já não produzia nela o efeito de ser velho ou pobre; ela achava Jean Valjean bonito, assim como achava o casebre bonito.

Estes são os efeitos da aurora, da infância, da alegria. A novidade da terra e da vida conta para alguma coisa aqui. Nada é tão encantador quanto o reflexo colorido da felicidade em uma guarnição. Todos nós temos no nosso passado uma deliciosa guarnição.

A natureza, uma diferença de cinquenta anos, estabelecera um abismo profundo entre Jean Valjean e Cosette; o destino preencheu este abismo. O destino de repente uniu e uniu com o seu poder irresistível estas duas existências desenraizadas, diferentes em idade, igualmente em tristeza. Um, de fato, completou o outro. O instinto de Cosette procurava um pai, como o instinto de Jean Valjean procurava um filho. Encontrar-se era encontrar-se. No misterioso momento em que suas mãos tocaram, eles foram soldados juntos. Quando essas duas almas se perceberam, reconheceram-se como necessárias uma à outra, e abraçaram-se de perto.

Tomando as palavras no seu sentido mais abrangente e absoluto, podemos dizer que, separado de todos pelas paredes do túmulo, Jean

Valjean era o viúvo, e Cosette era o órfão: esta situação fez com que Jean Valjean se tornasse o pai de Cosette depois de uma forma celestial.

E, na verdade, a impressão misteriosa produzida em Cosette nas profundezas da floresta de Chelles pela mão de Jean Valjean agarrando-a no escuro não era uma ilusão, mas uma realidade. A entrada daquele homem no destino daquela criança tinha sido o advento de Deus.

Além disso, Jean Valjean tinha escolhido bem o seu refúgio. Lá, ele parecia perfeitamente seguro.

A câmara com um camarim, que ocupava com Cosette, era aquela cuja janela se abria na avenida. Sendo esta a única janela da casa, nenhum olhar dos vizinhos era de temer do outro lado do caminho ou ao lado.

O piso térreo do número 50-52, uma espécie de cobertura em ruínas, servia de carroça para os jardineiros, e não existia comunicação entre ele e o primeiro andar. Estava separado pelo piso, que não tinha armadilhas nem escadas, e que formava o diafragma do edifício, por assim dizer. A primeira história continha, como dissemos, numerosas câmaras e vários sótãos, dos quais apenas um era ocupado pela velha que se encarregava da arrumação de Jean Valjean; todo o resto estava desabitado.

Foi esta velha, ornamentada com o nome do *inquilino principal*, e na realidade confiada às funções de porteira, que lhe deixara o alojamento na véspera de Natal. Tinha-se apresentado a ela como um cavalheiro de meios que tinha sido arruinado pelos laços espanhóis, que vinha para lá viver com a sua filhinha. Pagara-lhe seis meses de antecedência e encomendou à velha a mobília da câmara e do camarim, como vimos. Foi esta boa mulher que acendeu o fogo no fogão e preparou tudo na noite da sua chegada.

Semana seguinte; Estes dois seres levavam uma vida feliz naquele casebre.

Cosette riu, tagarelicou e cantou ao amanhecer. As crianças têm o seu canto matinal, bem como os pássaros.

Às vezes acontecia que Jean Valjean apertava sua pequena mão vermelha, toda rachada com frieiras, e a beijava. A pobre criança, acostumada a apanhar, não sabia o significado disso e fugiu confusa.

Às vezes, ela ficava séria e olhava para seu vestidinho preto. Cosette já não estava em trapos; ela estava de luto. Ela tinha saído da miséria e estava entrando na vida.

Jean Valjean tinha-se comprometido a ensiná-la a ler. Às vezes, enquanto fazia a criança enfeitiçar, lembrava-se que era com a ideia de fazer o mal que aprendera a ler na prisão. Esta ideia tinha acabado por ensinar uma criança a ler. Em seguida, o ex-presidiário sorriu com o sorriso pensativo dos anjos.

Sentiu nela uma premeditação vinda do alto, a vontade de alguém que não era homem, e ficou absorvido pelo devaneio. Os bons pensamentos têm os seus abismos, assim como os maus.

Ensinar Cosette a ler, e deixá-la brincar, isso constituiu quase toda a existência de Jean Valjean. E então ele falou de sua mãe, e a fez orar.

Ela o chamava *de pai*, e não sabia outro nome para ele.

Passou horas a vê-la a vestir-se e a despir-se a sua boneca, e a ouvi-la a gozar. A vida, doravante, pareceu-lhe cheia de interesse; os homens lhe pareciam bons e justos; já não censurava ninguém em pensamento; não via razão para não viver para ser um homem muito velho, agora que esta criança o amava. Ele viu todo um futuro se estendendo diante dele, iluminado por Cosette como por uma luz encantadora. Os melhores de nós não estão isentos de pensamentos egoístas. Às vezes, ele refletia com uma espécie de alegria que ela seria feia.

Trata-se apenas de uma opinião pessoal; mas, para exprimir todo o nosso pensamento, no ponto em que Jean Valjean tinha chegado quando começou a amar Cosette, não é de modo algum claro para nós que ele não precisava desse encorajamento para poder perseverar no bem-fazer. Ele acabara de ver a malícia dos homens e a miséria da sociedade sob um novo aspeto – aspetos incompletos, que infelizmente só exibiam um lado da verdade, o destino da mulher como resumido em Fantine, e a autoridade pública como personificada em Javert. Tinha regressado à prisão, desta vez por ter feito bem; tinha uma amargura fresca; o nojo e a lassidão dominavam-no; até mesmo a memória do Bispo provavelmente sofreu um eclipse temporário, embora certamente reaparecerá mais tarde luminoso e triunfante; mas, afinal, essa memória sagrada estava a esbater-se. Quem sabe se Jean Valjean não estava às vésperas de desanimar e de cair mais uma vez? Amou e voltou a ficar forte. Infelizmente! andava com não menos indecisão do que Cosette. Ele a protegeu e ela o fortaleceu. Graças a ele, ela pôde caminhar pela vida; graças a ela, pôde continuar em virtude. Ele era a estadia daquela criança, e ela era o seu adereço. Oh, mistério insondável e divino dos equilíbrios do destino!

CAPÍTULO IV

OBSERVAÇÕES DO INQUILINO PRINCIPAL

Jean Valjean foi prudente o suficiente para nunca sair de dia. Todas as noites, ao crepúsculo, ele caminhava por uma ou duas horas, às vezes sozinho, muitas vezes com Cosette, procurando as vielas laterais mais desertas da avenida e entrando em igrejas ao cair da noite. Gostava de ir a Saint-Médard, que é a igreja mais próxima. Quando ele não levou Cosette consigo, ela permaneceu com a velha; mas o prazer da criança era sair com o homem bom. Preferiu uma hora com ele a todos os seus arrebatadores *tête-à-têtes* com Catarina. Ele segurou a mão dela enquanto eles caminhavam e disse coisas doces para ela.

Descobriu-se que Cosette era uma pequena pessoa muito gay.

A idosa cuidava da arrumação e da cozinha e ia ao mercado.

Viviam sóbrios, sempre com um pouco de fogo, mas como pessoas em circunstâncias muito moderadas. Jean Valjean não fez alterações no mobiliário, pois era o primeiro dia; ele apenas teve a porta de vidro que dava para o camarim de Cosette substituída por uma porta sólida.

Ele ainda usava seu casaco amarelo, suas calças pretas e seu velho chapéu. Na rua, foi levado por um pobre. Às vezes, acontecia que mulheres de bom coração voltavam para dar um sou a ele. Jean Valjean aceitou o sou com uma profunda vénia. Também aconteceu ocasionalmente que ele encontrou algum pobre desgraçado pedindo esmola; Então ele olhou para trás para se certificar de que ninguém o estava observando, furtivamente se aproximou do infeliz, colocou um pedaço de dinheiro em sua mão, muitas vezes uma moeda de prata, e se afastou rapidamente. Isto tinha as suas desvantagens. Começou a ser conhecido no bairro com o nome do *mendigo que dá esmola.*

A velha *hospedeira principal,* uma criatura de aparência cruzada, que estava completamente permeada, no que diz respeito aos seus vizinhos, com a curiosidade peculiar às pessoas invejosas, examinou muito Jean Valjean, sem que ele suspeitasse do fato. Ela era um pouco surda, o que a tornava falante. Restaram-lhe, do seu passado, dois dentes, um acima, outro abaixo, que ela batia continuamente uns contra os outros. Ela tinha questionado Cosette, que não tinha sido capaz de lhe dizer nada, uma vez que ela não sabia nada sozinha, exceto que ela tinha vindo de Montfermeil. Certa manhã, este espião viu Jean Valjean, com um ar que parecia peculiar à velha fofoca, entrando em um dos compartimentos desabitados do casebre. Ela seguiu-o com o passo de um gato velho, e pôde observá-lo sem ser vista, através de uma fenda na porta, que ficava em frente a ele. Jean Valjean estava de costas voltadas para esta porta, por uma questão de maior segurança, sem dúvida. A velha viu-o atrapalhar-se no bolso e desenhar daí um estojo, tesoura e linha; depois começou a rasgar o forro de uma das saias do casaco e, da abertura, tirou um pouco de papel amarelado, que desdobrou. A velha reconheceu, com terror, que se tratava de uma conta bancária de mil francos. Era a segunda ou terceira que ela tinha visto ao longo de sua existência. Ela fugiu alarmada.

Um momento depois, Jean Valjean abordou-a e pediu-lhe para ir buscar esta nota de mil francos para ele, acrescentando que era o seu rendimento trimestral, que tinha recebido no dia anterior. "Onde"?, pensou a idosa. "Ele só saiu às seis da noite, e o banco do governo certamente não está aberto a essa hora". A idosa foi buscar a mudança na conta e mencionou suas suposições. Essa nota de mil francos, comentada e multiplicada, produziu uma vasta discussão aterrorizada entre os fofoqueiros da Rue des Vignes Saint-Marcel.

Alguns dias depois, por acaso, Jean Valjean estava serrando um pouco de madeira, nas mangas da camisa, no corredor. A velha estava na sala, colocando as coisas em ordem. Ela estava sozinha. Cosette estava ocupada em admirar a madeira enquanto era serrada. A velha avistou o casaco pendurado numa unha e examinou-o. O forro tinha sido costurado novamente. A boa mulher sentiu-o cuidadosamente, e pensou que observava nas saias e inverte as espessuras do papel. Mais contas bancárias de mil francos, sem dúvida!

Ela também notou que havia todos os tipos de coisas nos bolsos. Não só as agulhas, linha e tesoura que ela tinha visto, mas um grande livro de bolso, uma faca muito grande e, uma circunstância suspeita, várias perucas de várias cores. Cada bolso deste casaco tinha o ar de estar de uma forma proporcionada contra acidentes inesperados.

Assim, os habitantes da casa chegaram aos últimos dias de inverno.

CAPÍTULO V

UMA PEÇA DE CINCO FRANCOS CAI NO CHÃO E PRODUZ UM TUMULTO

Perto da igreja de Saint-Médard havia um pobre homem que tinha o hábito de agachar-se à beira de um poço público que tinha sido condenado, e a quem Jean Valjean gostava de conceder caridade. Ele nunca passou por este homem sem lhe dar alguns sous. Às vezes falava com ele. Aqueles que invejavam este mendicante diziam que ele pertencia à polícia. Era um ex-beadle de setenta e cinco anos, que murmurava constantemente as suas orações.

Certa noite, quando Jean Valjean estava passando, quando não tinha Cosette com ele, viu o mendigo em seu lugar habitual, sob a lanterna que acabara de ser acesa. O homem parecia empenhado em oração, de acordo com seu costume, e estava muito curvado. Jean Valjean aproximou-se dele e colocou-lhe a habitual esmola na mão. O mendicante levantou os olhos de repente, olhou atentamente para Jean Valjean e, em seguida, baixou a cabeça rapidamente. Este movimento foi como um relâmpago. Jean Valjean foi apanhado com um susto. Pareceu-lhe que acabara de avistar, pela luz da lanterna da rua, não a visão plácida e radiante do velho talão, mas de um rosto bem conhecido e surpreendente. Ele experimentou a mesma impressão que alguém teria ao se encontrar, de repente, cara a cara, no escuro, com um tigre. Recuou, apavorado, petrificado, não ousando nem respirar, falar, nem permanecer, nem fugir, olhando para o mendigo que deixara cair a cabeça, envolta num trapo, e já não parecia saber que estava ali. Neste estranho momento, um instinto – possivelmente o misterioso instinto de autopreservação – impediu Jean Valjean de proferir uma palavra. O mendigo tinha a mesma figura, os mesmos trapos, a mesma aparência que tinha todos os dias. "Bah"!, disse Jean Valjean, "Estou louco! Estou sonhando! Impossível"! E voltou profundamente perturbado.

Mal ousou confessar, mesmo a si próprio, que o rosto que pensava ter visto era o rosto de Javert.

Naquela noite, ao refletir sobre o assunto, lamentou não ter questionado o homem, a fim de obrigá-lo a levantar a cabeça uma segunda vez.

No dia seguinte, ao cair da noite, voltou. O mendigo estava em seu posto: "Bom dia, meu bom homem", disse Jean Valjean, resolutamente, entregando-lhe um sou. O mendigo levantou a cabeça e respondeu com voz choramingada: "Obrigado, meu bom senhor". Era inequivocamente o ex-beadle.

Jean Valjean sentiu-se completamente tranquilo. Começou a rir. "Como é que eu poderia ter pensado que vi Javert lá"?, pensou. "Vou perder a visão agora"? E não pensou mais nisso.

Alguns dias depois", podia ter sido às oito horas da noite" ele estava em seu quarto, e empenhado em fazer Cosette encantar em voz alta, quando ouviu a porta da casa abrir e depois fechar novamente. Isso pareceu-lhe singular. A velha, que era a única habitante da casa, exceto ele próprio, ia sempre para a cama ao cair da noite, para não queimar as velas. Jean Valjean fez um sinal para Cosette ficar quieta. Ouviu alguém subir as escadas. Pode ser a velha, que pode ter adoecido e saído para o boticário. Jean Valjean ouviu.

O passo era pesado e soava como o de um homem; mas a velha usava sapatos robustos, e não há nada que se assemelhe tanto ao passo de um homem como o de uma velha. No entanto, Jean Valjean apagou a vela.

Ele mandou Cosette para a cama, dizendo-lhe em voz baixa: "Entra na cama muito suavemente"; e enquanto ele beijava sua testa, os passos pararam.

Jean Valjean permaneceu em silêncio, imóvel, de costas para a porta, sentado na cadeira da qual não se mexera, e prendendo a respiração no escuro.

Findo um intervalo bastante longo, virou-se, não ouvindo mais nada, e, ao erguer os olhos em direção à porta de sua câmara, viu uma luz através do buraco da fechadura. Esta luz formava uma espécie de estrela sinistra na escuridão da porta e da parede. Evidentemente, havia alguém lá, que estava segurando uma vela na mão e ouvindo.

Passaram-se vários minutos e a luz recuou. Mas não ouviu nenhum som de passos, o que parecia indicar que a pessoa que estava ouvindo na porta havia tirado seus sapatos.

Jean Valjean atirou-se, todo vestido como estava, na sua cama, e não conseguiu fechar os olhos a noite toda.

Ao amanhecer, no momento em que caía num dedo por cansaço, foi acordado pelo ranger de uma porta que se abria num sótão no final do corredor, depois ouviu o mesmo passo masculino que tinha subido as escadas na noite anterior. O passo aproximava-se. Levantou-se da cama e aplicou o olho no buraco da fechadura, que era toleravelmente grande, na esperança de ver a pessoa que entrara de noite na casa e ouvira à sua porta, enquanto passava. Foi um homem, de facto, que passou, desta vez sem parar, em frente à câmara de Jean Valjean. O corredor era demasiado escuro para permitir distinguir o rosto da pessoa; mas quando o homem chegou à escada, um raio de luz de fora fez com que ela se destacasse como uma silhueta, e Jean Valjean teve uma visão completa de suas costas. O homem era de estatura elevada, vestido com um longo casaco de pedra, com um debaixo do braço. O formidável pescoço e ombros pertenciam a Javert.

Jean Valjean poderia ter tentado vislumbrá-lo através de sua janela que se abria na avenida, mas ele teria sido obrigado a abrir a janela: ele não ousou.

Era evidente que este homem tinha entrado com uma chave, e como ele. Quem lhe dera essa chave? Qual era o significado disso?

Quando a velha veio fazer o trabalho, às sete horas da manhã, Jean Valjean lançou-lhe um olhar penetrante, mas não a questionou. A boa mulher apareceu como de costume.

Quando ela se levantou, ela comentou com ele:

"Possivelmente Monsieur pode ter ouvido alguém entrar ontem à noite"?

Naquela idade, e naquela avenida, oito horas da noite era a calada da noite.

"É verdade, diga-se de passagem", respondeu, no tom mais natural possível. "Quem era"?

"Foi um novo inquilino que entrou na casa", disse a idosa.

"E qual é o seu nome"?

"Não sei exatamente; Dumont, ou Daumont, ou algum nome desse tipo".

"E quem é este Monsieur Dumont"?

A velha olhou para ele com seus olhinhos de polega, e respondeu: —

"Um cavalheiro de propriedade, como você".

Talvez ela não tivesse nenhum significado secundário. Jean Valjean pensou ter percebido um.

Quando a velha partiu, ele subiu cem francos que tinha num armário, num rolo, e colocou-o no bolso. Apesar de todas as precauções que tomou nesta operação para não ser ouvido a chocalhar prata, uma peça de cem sou escapou das suas mãos e rolou ruidosamente no chão.

Quando a escuridão chegou, ele desceu e examinou cuidadosamente os dois lados da avenida. Não viu ninguém. A avenida parecia estar absolutamente deserta. É verdade que uma pessoa pode esconder-se atrás de árvores.

Ele subiu as escadas novamente.

"Venha", disse ele a Cosette.

Ele a pegou pela mão e ambos saíram.

LIVRO CINCO

PARA UMA CAÇA NEGRA, UM PACOTE MUDO

CAPÍTULO I

OS ZIGUEZAGUES DA ESTRATÉGIA

Impõe-se aqui uma observação, tendo em vista as páginas que o leitor está prestes a folhear, e outras que serão encontradas mais adiante.

O autor deste livro, que lamenta a necessidade de se mencionar, está ausente de Paris há muitos anos. Paris transformou-se desde que ele a abandonou. Surgiu uma nova cidade, que é, depois de uma moda, desconhecida para ele. Não há necessidade de ele dizer que ama Paris: Paris é a cidade natal de sua mente. Em consequência de demolições e reconstruções, a Paris da sua juventude, aquela Paris que ele carregou religiosamente na sua memória, é agora uma Paris de outros tempos. Deve permitir-lhe falar dessa Paris como se ela ainda existisse. É possível que, quando o autor conduz seus leitores a um local e diz: "Em tal rua há tal e tal casa", nem rua nem casa existirão mais naquela localidade. Os leitores podem verificar os fatos se quiserem resolver o problema. Por seu lado, desconhece a nova Paris e escreve com a velha Paris diante dos seus olhos, numa ilusão que lhe é preciosa. É para ele uma delícia sonhar que ainda resta atrás de si algo daquilo que viu quando estava no seu próprio país, e que nem tudo desapareceu. Contanto que você vá e venha em sua terra natal, você imagina que essas ruas são uma questão de indiferença para você; que aquelas janelas, aqueles telhados e aquelas portas não são nada para você; que essas paredes são estranhas para você; que essas árvores são apenas as primeiras encontradas ao acaso; que aquelas casas, nas quais não entrais, vos são inúteis; que os pavimentos que pisa são meras pedras. Mais tarde, quando já não estás lá, percebes que as ruas te são queridas; que você sente falta daqueles telhados, daquelas portas; e que esses muros são necessários para ti, essas árvores são bem amadas por ti; que entraste naquelas casas em que nunca entraste, todos os dias, e que deixaste uma parte do teu coração, do teu sangue, da tua alma, naquelas calçadas. Todos aqueles lugares que já não contemplais, que talvez nunca mais vejais, por acaso, e cuja memória guardastes, assumem um encanto melancólico, repetem-se à vossa mente com a melancolia de uma aparição, tornam visível a terra santa para vós, e são, por assim dizer, a própria forma da França, e vós os amais; e tu os chamaste como são, como eram, e persistes nisto, e não te submeterás a nenhuma mudança: porque estás apegado à figura da tua pátria como ao rosto da tua mãe.

Podemos, então, ser autorizados a falar do passado no presente? Dito isto, imploramos ao leitor que tome nota e continuamos.

Jean Valjean abandonou instantaneamente a avenida e mergulhou nas ruas, tomando as linhas mais intrincadas que podia traçar, retornando à sua pista às vezes, para se certificar de que não estava sendo seguido.

Esta manobra é peculiar ao veado caçado. Em solos onde uma marca da pista pode ser deixada, esta manobra possui, entre outras vantagens, a de enganar os caçadores e os cães, jogando-os no cheiro errado. Em vingança, isso é chamado de *falsa re-embuste*.

A lua estava cheia naquela noite. Jean Valjean não se arrependeu. A lua, ainda muito próxima do horizonte, lançou grandes massas de luz e sombra nas ruas. Jean Valjean podia deslizar perto das casas no lado escuro, e ainda vigiar o lado claro. Talvez não tenha levado suficientemente em consideração o fato de que o lado negro lhe escapou. Ainda assim, nas ruas desertas que ficam perto da Rue Poliveau, ele pensou que se sentia seguro de que ninguém o estava seguindo.

Cosette seguiu em frente sem fazer perguntas. Os sofrimentos dos primeiros seis anos de sua vida haviam incutido algo passivo em sua natureza. Além disso", e esta é uma observação a que frequentemente teremos ocasião de nos repetir", ela habituara-se, sem ela própria se aperceber disso, às peculiaridades deste homem de bem e às aberrações do destino. E então ela estava com ele, e ela se sentiu segura.

Jean Valjean não sabia mais para onde ia do que Cosette. Ele confiou em Deus, como ela confiou nele. Parecia que ele também estava agarrado à mão de alguém maior do que ele; pensava que sentia um ser a guiá-lo, embora invisível. No entanto, ele não tinha uma ideia definida, nenhum plano, nenhum projeto. Ele nem tinha certeza absoluta de que era Javert, e então poderia ter sido Javert, sem Javert saber que ele era Jean Valjean. Não estava disfarçado? Não se acreditava que ele estava morto? Ainda assim, as coisas queer estavam acontecendo há vários dias. Ele não queria mais deles. Ele estava determinado a não voltar para a casa Gorbeau. Como o animal selvagem perseguido de seu covil, ele estava procurando um buraco no qual pudesse se esconder até encontrar um onde pudesse habitar.

Jean Valjean descreveu muitos e variados labirintos no bairro de Mouffetard, que já estava adormecido, como se a disciplina da Idade Média e o jugo do toque de recolher ainda existissem; combinou de várias maneiras, com estratégia ardilosa, a Rue Censier e a Rue Copeau, a Rue du Battoir-Saint-Victor e a Rue du Puits l'Ermite. Existem casas de alojamento nesta localidade, mas nem sequer entrou numa delas, não encontrando nada que lhe convinha. Ele não tinha dúvidas de que, se alguém tivesse a chance de estar em seu caminho, eles a teriam perdido.

Quando as onze horas chegavam de Saint-Étienne-du-Mont, atravessava a Rue de Pontoise, em frente ao gabinete do comissário de polícia, situado no n.º 14. Alguns instantes depois, o instinto de que falámos acima fê-lo dar a volta. Nesse momento viu distintamente, graças à lanterna do comissário, que os traiu, três homens que o seguiam de perto, passarem, um após o outro, sob aquela lanterna, no lado escuro da rua. Um dos três entrou no beco que leva à casa do comissário. Aquele que marchou à sua cabeça pareceu-lhe decididamente suspeito.

"Vem, criança", disse ele a Cosette; e apressou-se a abandonar a Rue Pontoise.

Pegou num circuito, transformou-se na Passage des Patriarches, que estava fechada por causa da hora, percorreu a Rue de l'Épée-de-Bois e a Rue de l'Arbalète, e mergulhou na Rue des Postes.

Naquela época, havia uma praça formada pelo cruzamento de ruas, onde fica hoje o Colégio Rollin, e onde a Rue Neuve-Sainte-Geneviève se desliga.

Entende-se, é claro, que a Rue Neuve-Sainte-Geneviève é uma rua antiga, e que uma chaise de postagem não passa pela Rue des Postes uma vez em dez anos. No século XIII esta Rue des Postes era habitada por oleiros, e o seu verdadeiro nome é Rue des Pots.

A lua lançou uma luz lívida neste espaço aberto. Jean Valjean entrou em emboscada numa porta, calculando que, se os homens ainda o seguiam, não poderia deixar de olhar bem para eles, enquanto atravessavam este espaço iluminado.

De facto, não tinham decorrido três minutos quando os homens apareceram. Eram quatro agora. Todos eram altos, vestidos com casacos longos e castanhos, com chapéus redondos e enormes cutelos nas mãos. A sua grande estatura e os seus vastos punhos não os tornavam menos alarmantes do que o seu sinistro passo através da escuridão. Alguém os teria pronunciado quatro espectros disfarçados de burgueses.

Eles pararam no meio do espaço e formaram um grupo, como homens em consulta. Tinham um ar de indecisão. Aquele que parecia ser o seu líder virou-se e apontou apressadamente com a mão direita na direção que Jean Valjean tomara; outro parecia indicar a direção contrária com considerável obstinação. No momento em que o primeiro homem rodou, a lua caiu cheia em seu rosto. Jean Valjean reconheceu Javert perfeitamente.

CAPÍTULO II

É UMA SORTE QUE A PONT D'AUSTERLITZ TENHA CARRUAGENS

A incerteza estava no fim para Jean Valjean: felizmente ainda durou para os homens. Aproveitou a hesitação deles. Foi tempo perdido para eles, mas ganho para ele. Escorregou de debaixo do portão onde se escondera e desceu a Rue des Postes, em direção à região do Jardin des Plantes. Cosette estava começando a ficar cansada. Pegou-a nos braços e carregou-a. Não havia transeuntes e as lanternas da rua não tinham sido acesas por causa da lua.

Redobrou o ritmo.

Em poucos passos chegara às olarias do cálice, em cuja frente o luar tornava nitidamente legível a antiga inscrição:

De Goblet fils é a fábrica aqui; Venha escolher jarros e cântaros, vasos de flores, cachimbos, tijolos.
Para todos os que chegam, o Coração vende telhas.

Deixou para trás a Rue de la Clef, depois a Fonte Saint-Victor, contornou o Jardin des Plantes pelas ruas mais baixas e chegou ao cais. Lá, ele se virou. O cais estava deserto. As ruas estavam desertas. Não havia ninguém atrás dele. Respirou fundo.

Ganhou a Pont d'Austerlitz.

Naquela época, ainda ali se cobravam portagens.

Apresentou-se na portagem e entregou um sou.

"São dois sous", disse o velho soldado encarregado da ponte. "Você está carregando uma criança que pode andar. Pague por dois".

Ele pagou, irritado por sua passagem ter despertado comentários. Cada voo deve ser um deslize impercetível.

Uma carroça pesada atravessava o Sena ao mesmo tempo que ele próprio e a caminho, como ele, para a margem direita. Isso foi útil para ele. Ele podia atravessar a ponte à sombra do carrinho.

Em direção ao meio da ponte, Cosette, cujos pés estavam entorpecidos, queria caminhar. Ele a colocou no chão e pegou sua mão novamente.

Uma vez atravessada a ponte, ele percebeu alguns pátios de madeira à sua direita. Dirigiu o seu curso a três. Para alcançá-los, era necessário arriscar-se num espaço toleravelmente grande, desprotegido e iluminado. Não hesitou. Aqueles que estavam em sua pista evidentemente perderam o cheiro, e Jean Valjean acreditava estar fora de perigo. Caçado, sim; seguiu, não.

Uma pequena rua, a Rue du Chemin-Vert-Saint-Antoine, abria-se entre dois pátios de madeira fechados em muros. Esta rua era escura e estreita e parecia feita expressamente para ele. Antes de entrar, lançou um olhar atrás de si.

Do ponto em que estava, podia ver toda a extensão da Pont d'Austerlitz.

Quatro sombras estavam apenas entrando na ponte.

Estas sombras tinham as costas viradas para o Jardin des Plantes e estavam a caminho da margem direita.

Estas quatro sombras eram os quatro homens.

Jean Valjean estremeceu como a fera que é recapturada.

Uma esperança lhe restou; era que os homens não tinham, talvez, pisado na ponte, e não o tinham avistado enquanto atravessava o grande espaço iluminado, segurando Cosette pela mão.

Nesse caso, mergulhando na pequena rua à sua frente, ele poderia escapar, se pudesse alcançar os pátios de madeira, os pântanos, os mercados-jardins, o terreno desabitado que não foi construído.

Pareceu-lhe que poderia comprometer-se com aquela ruazinha silenciosa. Ele entrou.

CAPÍTULO III

A SABER, O PLANO DE PARIS EM 1727

Trezentos passos mais à frente, chegou a um ponto onde a rua se bifurcava. Separou-se em duas ruas, que corriam em linha inclinada, uma para a direita e outra para a esquerda.

Jean Valjean tinha diante de si o que se assemelhava aos dois ramos de um Y. Qual ele deve escolher? Não hesitou, mas pegou o da direita.

Porquê?

Porque a esquerda corria para um subúrbio, isto é, para as regiões habitadas, e a direita para o campo aberto, isto é, para as regiões desertas.

No entanto, já não andavam muito depressa. O ritmo de Cosette retardou o de Jean Valjean.

Ele a pegou e a carregou novamente. Cosette deitou a cabeça no ombro do homem bom e não disse uma palavra.

Virou-se de vez em quando e olhou para trás. Teve o cuidado de se manter sempre do lado escuro da rua. A rua era reta em sua retaguarda. Nas primeiras duas ou três vezes em que se virou, não viu nada; O silêncio era profundo, e ele continuou sua marcha um tanto tranquilizado. De repente, ao virar-se, pensou ter percebido na parte da rua por onde acabara de passar, longe na obscuridade, algo que se movia.

Ele correu para a frente precipitadamente em vez de caminhar, na esperança de encontrar alguma rua lateral, para fazer sua fuga através dela e, assim, quebrar seu cheiro mais uma vez.

Chegou a um muro.

Este muro, no entanto, não impediu absolutamente novos progressos; era um muro que margeava uma rua transversal, na qual terminava a que ele tomara.

Também aqui foi obrigado a tomar uma decisão; deve ir para a direita ou para a esquerda.

Ele olhou para a direita. A pista fragmentada foi prolongada entre edifícios que eram galpões ou celeiros, depois terminou em um beco sem saída. A extremidade do beco sem saída era distintamente visível, uma parede branca elevada.

Ele olhou para a esquerda. Desse lado a pista estava aberta e, cerca de duzentos passos mais adiante, esbarrou em uma rua da qual era o afluente. Desse lado estava a segurança.

No momento em que Jean Valjean meditava uma curva à esquerda, num esforço para chegar à rua que via no final da pista, percebeu uma espécie de estátua negra e imóvel na esquina da pista com a rua para a qual estava a ponto de dirigir os seus passos.

Era alguém, um homem, que evidentemente tinha acabado de ser colocado lá, e que estava barrando a passagem e esperando.

Jean Valjean recuou.

O ponto de Paris onde Jean Valjean se encontrou, situado entre o Faubourg Saint-Antoine e la Râpée, é um dos que as melhorias recentes transformaram de cima para baixo, resultando em desfiguração, segundo uns, e numa transfiguração, segundo outros. Os jardins do mercado, os pátios de madeira e os edifícios antigos foram apagados. Hoje em dia, há ruas novas e largas, arenas, circos, hipódromos, estações ferroviárias e uma prisão, Mazas, lá; progresso, como vê o leitor, com o seu antídoto.

Há meio século, naquela língua comum e popular, toda composta de tradições, que persiste em chamar o Institut *les Quatre-Nations*, e a Opera-Comique *Feydeau*, o local preciso onde Jean Valjean tinha chegado chamava-se *le Petit-Picpus*. A Porte Saint-Jacques, a Porte Paris, o Barrière des Sergents, os Porcherons, la Galiote, les Célestins, les Capucins, le Mail, la Bourbe, l'Arbre de Cracovie, la Petite-Pologne, estes são os nomes da velha Paris que sobrevivem no meio do novo. A memória da população paira sobre essas relíquias do passado.

Le Petit-Picpus, que, além disso, quase nunca teve existência, e nunca foi mais do que o contorno de um quarto, tinha quase o aspeto monge de uma cidade espanhola. As estradas não eram muito pavimentadas; as ruas não estavam muito construídas. Com exceção das duas ou três ruas, das quais falaremos agora, tudo ali era muro e solidão. Nem uma loja, nem um veículo, dificilmente uma vela acesa aqui e ali nas janelas; todas as luzes se apagam depois das dez horas. Jardins, conventos, quintais de madeira, sapais; habitações humildes ocasionais e grandes muros tão altos quanto as casas.

Assim foi este quarteirão no século passado. A Revolução esnobou-o profundamente. O governo republicano demoliu-a e cortou-a. Rebentos de lixo foram estabelecidos lá. Há trinta anos, este bairro estava a desaparecer sob o processo de apagamento de novos edifícios. Hoje, foi totalmente apagado. O Petit-Picpus, do qual nenhum plano existente preservou um traço, é indicado com suficiente clareza no plano de 1727, publicado em Paris por Denis Thierry, Rue Saint-Jacques, em frente à Rue du Plâtre; e em Lyon, por Jean Girin, Rue Mercière, ao sinal da Prudência. Petit-Picpus tinha, como acabamos de mencionar, um Y de ruas, formado pela Rue du Chemin-Vert-Saint-Antoine, que se estendia em dois ramos, tomando à esquerda o nome de Little Picpus Street, e à direita o nome da Rue Polonceau. Os dois membros do Y estavam ligados no vértice como por uma barra; este bar chamava-se Rue Droit-Mur. A Rue Polonceau terminava aí; Rue Petit-Picpus passou, e subiu em direção ao mercado Lenoir. Uma pessoa vinda do Sena chegou à extremidade da Rue Polonceau, e tinha à sua direita a Rue Droit-Mur, virando abruptamente em ângulo reto, à sua frente o muro daquela rua, e à sua direita um prolongamento truncado da Rue Droit-Mur, que não tinha problema e era chamada de Cul-de-Sac Genrot.

Era aqui que Jean Valjean estava.

Como acabamos de dizer, ao avistar aquela silhueta negra de guarda no ângulo da Rue Droit-Mur e da Rue Petit-Picpus, ele recuou. Não poderia haver dúvida disso. Aquele fantasma estava à sua espera.

O que ele deveria fazer?

O tempo para recuar já passou. O que ele havia percebido em movimento um instante antes, na escuridão distante, era Javert e seu esquadrão, sem dúvida. Javert provavelmente já estava no início da rua em cujo final Jean Valjean estava. Javert, ao que tudo indica, conhecia este pequeno labirinto e tomara as suas precauções enviando um dos seus homens para vigiar a saída. Essas suposições, que tanto se assemelhavam a provas, rodopiaram repentinamente, como um punhado de poeira apanhada por uma inesperada rajada de vento, através do cérebro triste de Jean Valjean. Ele examinou o Cul-de-Sac Genrot; Lá, ele foi cortado. Examinou a Rue Petit-Picpus; ali estava uma sentinela. Viu aquela forma negra destacando-se em relevo contra o pavimento branco, iluminado pela lua; avançar era cair nas mãos deste homem; recuar era atirar-se para os braços de Javert. Jean Valjean sentiu-se apanhado, como numa rede, que se contraía lentamente; Ele olhou para o céu em desespero.

CAPÍTULO IV

AS TATEADAS DO VOO

Para compreender o que se segue, é necessário formar uma ideia exata da pista Droit-Mur e, em particular, do ângulo que se deixa à esquerda quando se sai da Rue Polonceau para esta faixa. A pista Droit-Mur era quase inteiramente limitada à direita, até a Rue Petit-Picpus, por casas de aspeto médio; à esquerda, por um edifício solitário de contornos severos, composto por numerosas partes que foram aumentando gradualmente por um ou dois andares à medida que se aproximavam do lado da Rue Petit-Picpus; de modo que este edifício, que era muito elevado no lado da Rue Petit-Picpus, era toleravelmente baixo no lado adjacente à Rue Polonceau. Ali, no ângulo de que falámos, desceu a tal ponto que consistia apenas numa parede. Este muro não ficava diretamente na rua; formava um nicho profundamente recuado, escondido pelos seus dois cantos de dois observadores que poderiam ter sido, um na Rue Polonceau, o outro na Rue Droit-Mur.

Começando por estes ângulos do nicho, o muro estendia-se ao longo da Rue Polonceau até uma casa que ostentava o número 49, e ao longo da Rue Droit-Mur, onde o fragmento era muito mais curto, até ao edifício sombrio que mencionámos e cuja empena se cruzava, formando assim outro ângulo de recuo na rua. Esta empena era sombria de aspeto; apenas uma janela era visível, ou, para falar mais corretamente, duas persianas cobertas com uma folha de zinco e mantidas constantemente fechadas.

O estado dos lugares de que estamos aqui a descrever é rigorosamente exato, e certamente despertará uma memória muito precisa na mente dos antigos habitantes do bairro.

O nicho era inteiramente preenchido por uma coisa que se assemelhava a uma porta colossal e miserável; Era um vasto conjunto sem forma de tábuas perpendiculares, sendo as superiores mais largas que as inferiores, unidas por longas tiras transversais de ferro. De um lado havia um portão de carruagem das dimensões comuns, e que evidentemente não tinha sido cortado mais de cinquenta anos antes.

Uma tília mostrava sua crista acima do nicho, e a parede estava coberta de hera ao lado da Rue Polonceau.

No perigo iminente em que Jean Valjean se encontrava, este edifício sombrio tinha sobre si um olhar solitário e desabitado que o tentava. Passou rapidamente os olhos por cima dela; disse a si mesmo que, se conseguisse entrar nela, poderia salvar-se a si mesmo. Primeiro concebeu uma ideia, depois uma esperança.

Na parte central da frente deste edifício, no lado da Rue Droit-Mur, havia em todas as janelas dos diferentes andares antigos tubos de cisterna de chumbo. Os vários ramos dos tubos que levavam de um tubo central a todas essas pequenas bacias esboçavam uma espécie de árvore na frente. Estas ramificações de cachimbos com os seus cem cotovelos imitavam aqueles velhos vinhas sem folhas que se contorcem sobre as frentes de velhas casas de fazenda.

Este estranho espalier, com seus ramos de chumbo e ferro, foi a primeira coisa que atingiu Jean Valjean. Sentou Cosette de costas contra um poste de pedra, com uma ordem para ficar em silêncio, e correu para o local onde a conduta tocou a calçada. Talvez houvesse alguma maneira de subir por ele e entrar na casa. Mas o tubo estava degradado e passado serviço, e mal pendurado em suas fixações. Além disso, todas as janelas desta habitação silenciosa estavam raladas com pesadas barras de ferro, até mesmo as janelas do sótão no telhado. E então, a lua caiu cheia sobre aquela fachada, e o homem que estava observando na esquina da rua teria visto Jean Valjean no ato de escalar. E, finalmente, o que fazer com Cosette? Como ela foi desenhada até o topo de uma casa de três andares?

Ele desistiu de qualquer ideia de escalar por meio do cano de drenagem, e rastejou ao longo do muro para voltar para a Rue Polonceau.

Quando chegou à inclinação do muro onde deixara Cosette, reparou que ninguém o podia ver ali. Como acabamos de explicar, ele estava escondido de todos os olhos, não importando de que direção eles estavam se aproximando; além disso, ele estava na sombra. Finalmente, havia duas portas; talvez possam ser forçados. O muro acima do qual ele via a tília e a hera evidentemente ficava em um jardim onde ele podia, pelo menos, esconder-se, embora ainda não houvesse folhas nas árvores, e passar o resto da noite.

O tempo foi passando; tem de agir rapidamente.

Sentiu-se por cima da porta da carruagem, e imediatamente reconheceu o fato de que era impraticável fora e dentro.

Aproximou-se da outra porta com mais esperança; foi assustadoramente decrépito; a sua própria imensidão tornava-a menos sólida; as tábuas estavam podres; as bandas de ferro – eram apenas três – estavam enferrujadas. Parecia que poderia ser possível furar essa barreira devorada por vermes.

Ao examiná-la, constatou que a porta não era uma porta; não tinha dobradiças, barras transversais, fechadura, nem fissura no meio; as bandas de ferro atravessavam-na de um lado para o outro sem qualquer rutura. Através das fendas nas tábuas, ele avistou lajes não talhadas e blocos de pedra grosseiramente cimentados, que os transeuntes ainda poderiam ter visto lá dez anos atrás. Ele foi forçado a reconhecer com consternação que esta porta aparente era simplesmente a decoração de madeira de um edifício contra o qual foi colocada. Era fácil arrancar uma tábua; Mas então, a pessoa se viu cara a cara com uma parede.

CAPÍTULO V

O QUE SERIA IMPOSSÍVEL COM LANTERNAS A GÁS

Nesse momento um som pesado e medido começou a ser audível a alguma distância. Jean Valjean arriscou um olhar na esquina da rua. Sete ou oito soldados, formados num pelotão, tinham acabado de entrar na Rue Polonceau. Ele viu o brilho de suas baionetas. Avançavam em sua direção; estes soldados, em cuja cabeça distinguia a figura alta de Javert, avançavam lenta e cautelosamente. Eles paravam com frequência; era evidente que vasculhavam todos os recantos das paredes e todos os abraços das portas e becos.

Esta era uma patrulha que Javert tinha encontrado - não podia haver erro quanto a esta suposição - e cuja ajuda ele tinha exigido.

Os dois acólitos de Javert marchavam em suas fileiras.

Ao ritmo a que marchavam, e tendo em conta as paragens que estavam a fazer, demoravam cerca de um quarto de hora a chegar ao local onde Jean Valjean estava. Foi um momento assustador. Alguns minutos apenas separaram Jean Valjean daquele terrível precipício que bocejou diante dele pela terceira vez. E as galés agora significavam não apenas as galés, mas Cosette perdeu para ele para sempre; ou seja, uma vida que se assemelha ao interior de um túmulo.

Havia apenas uma coisa que era possível.

Jean Valjean tinha essa peculiaridade, que carregava, como se poderia dizer, duas bolsas de mendigo: em uma guardava seus santos pensamentos; no outro, os talentos duvidosos de um condenado. Ele revirava um ou outro, de acordo com as circunstâncias.

Entre os seus outros recursos, graças às suas numerosas fugas da prisão de Toulon, foi, como se recordará, um mestre do passado na incrível arte de rastejar sem escadas nem ferros de escalada, por pura força muscular, apoiando-se na nuca, nos ombros, nas ancas e nos joelhos, ajudando-se nas raras projeções da pedra, no ângulo reto de uma parede, tão alto quanto o sexto andar, se necessário; uma arte que tornou tão célebre e tão alarmante aquele canto do muro da Conciergerie de Paris pelo qual Battemolle, condenado à morte, fugiu há vinte anos.

Jean Valjean mediu com os olhos o muro acima do qual espiava a tília; tinha cerca de dezoito metros de altura. O ângulo que se formou com a empena do grande edifício foi preenchido, na sua extremidade inferior, por uma massa de alvenaria de forma triangular, provavelmente destinada a preservar aquele canto demasiado conveniente do lixo daquelas criaturas sujas chamadas transeuntes. Esta prática de encher cantos do muro é muito usada em Paris.

Esta massa tinha cerca de cinco metros de altura; O espaço acima do cume desta massa que era necessário subir não era superior a catorze pés.

O muro foi encimado por uma pedra plana sem enfrentamento.

Cosette era a dificuldade, pois não sabia escalar uma parede. Deveria abandoná-la? Jean Valjean não pensou nisso uma única vez. Era impossível carregá-la. Toda a força de um homem é necessária para realizar com sucesso essas subidas singulares. O menor fardo perturbaria seu centro de gravidade e o puxaria para baixo.

Teria sido necessária uma corda; Jean Valjean não tinha nenhuma. Onde foi buscar uma corda à meia-noite, na Rue Polonceau? Certamente, se Jean Valjean tivesse tido um reino, ele o teria dado por uma corda naquele momento.

Todas as situações extremas têm os seus relâmpagos que ora deslumbram, ora nos iluminam.

O olhar desesperado de Jean Valjean caiu no poste da rua do beco cego Genrot.

Naquela época, não havia jatos de gás nas ruas de Paris. Ao cair da noite, lanternas colocadas a distâncias regulares eram acesas; subiam e desciam por meio de uma corda, que atravessava a rua de um lado para o outro, e era ajustada numa ranhura do poste. A polia sobre a qual esta corda corria estava presa sob a lanterna em uma pequena caixa de ferro, cuja chave era mantida pelo isqueiro, e a própria corda era protegida por uma caixa de metal.

Jean Valjean, com a energia de uma luta suprema, atravessou a rua de uma só vez, entrou no beco sem saída, quebrou o trinco da caixinha com a ponta da faca e, um instante depois, estava ao lado de Cosette mais uma vez. Ele tinha uma corda. Estes sombrios inventores de expedientes trabalham rapidamente quando lutam contra a fatalidade.

Já explicamos que as lanternas não tinham sido acesas naquela noite. A lanterna no Cul-de-Sac Genrot foi, portanto, naturalmente extinta, como as outras; e podia-se passar diretamente por baixo dela sem sequer perceber que ela não estava mais em seu lugar.

No entanto, a hora, o lugar, a escuridão, a absorção de Jean Valjean, seus gestos singulares, suas idas e vindas, tudo começou a deixar Cosette inquieta. Qualquer outra criança que não ela teria dado vazão a gritos altos muito antes. Contentou-se em arrancar Jean Valjean pela saia do casaco. Eles podiam ouvir o som da aproximação da patrulha cada vez mais distintamente.

"Pai", disse ela, em voz muito baixa, "tenho medo. Quem está chegando"?

"Hush"!, respondeu o homem infeliz; "é Madame Thénardier".

Cosette estremeceu. E acrescentou:

"Não diga nada. Não interfira comigo. Se você gritar, se você chorar, o Thénardier está deitado esperando por você. Ela está vindo para te levar de volta".

Então, sem pressa, mas sem fazer um movimento inútil, com precisão firme e curtíssima, o mais notável num momento em que a patrulha e Javert poderiam vir sobre ele a qualquer momento, ele desfez seu cravat, passou-o ao redor do corpo de Cosette sob as axilas, tomando cuidado para que não machucasse a criança, prendeu esse cravat a uma extremidade da corda, Por meio daquele nó que os marinheiros chamam de "nó de andorinha", tomou a outra ponta da corda nos dentes, tirou os sapatos e as meias, que jogou sobre o muro, pisou sobre a massa de alvenaria e começou a erguer-se no ângulo da parede e da empena com tanta solidez e certeza como se tivesse as voltas de uma escada sob os pés e cotovelos. Meio minuto não tinha decorrido quando ele estava descansando de joelhos na parede.

Cosette olhou para ele com espanto estúpido, sem proferir uma palavra. A injunção de Jean Valjean, e o nome de Madame Thénardier, tinham-lhe arrefecido o sangue.

De repente, ouviu a voz de Jean Valjean a chorar-lhe, embora num tom muito baixo:

"Coloque as costas contra a parede".

Ela obedeceu.

"Não diga uma palavra e não se assuste", continuou Jean Valjean.

E sentiu-se levantada do chão.

Antes de ter tempo para se recuperar, ela estava em cima do muro.

Jean Valjean agarrou-a, colocou-a de costas, pegou-lhe duas mãos minúsculas na sua grande mão esquerda, deitou-se de bruços e rastejou por cima da parede até ao canto. Como ele tinha adivinhado, havia um edifício cujo telhado começava do topo da barricada de madeira e descia a uma distância muito curta do solo, com um declive suave que pastava a tília. Uma circunstância de sorte, pois o muro era muito mais alto deste lado do que do lado da rua. Jean Valjean só conseguia ver o chão a uma grande profundidade abaixo dele.

Tinha acabado de chegar à encosta do telhado, e ainda não tinha saído da crista do muro, quando um violento tumulto anunciou a chegada da patrulha. A voz estrondosa de Javert era audível:—

"Procure o beco sem saída! A Rue Droit-Mur é vigiada! assim é a Rue Petit-Picpus. Vou responder por isso que ele está no beco sem saída".

Os soldados correram para o beco Genrot.

Jean Valjean deixou-se deslizar pelo telhado, ainda agarrado a Cosette, alcançou a tília e saltou para o chão. Seja por terror ou coragem, Cosette não tinha respirado um som, embora suas mãos estivessem um pouco abrasadas.

CAPÍTULO VI

O INÍCIO DE UM ENIGMA

Jean Valjean encontrava-se numa espécie de jardim muito vasto e de aspeto singular; um daqueles jardins melancólicos que parecem feitos para serem olhados no inverno e à noite. Este jardim tinha uma forma oblonga, com um beco de grandes choupos na extremidade posterior, árvores florestais toleravelmente altas nos cantos, e um espaço sem sombra no centro, onde se podia ver uma árvore muito grande e solitária, depois várias árvores de fruto, retorcidas e eriçadas como arbustos, canteiros de legumes, uma mancha de melão, cujas molduras de vidro brilhavam ao luar, e um poço velho. Aqui e ali havia bancos de pedra que pareciam pretos com musgo. As vielas eram cercadas por pequenos arbustos sombrios e muito eretos. A grama tinha metade tomado posse deles, e um molde verde cobria o resto.

Jean Valjean tinha ao seu lado o edifício cujo telhado lhe servira como meio de descida, uma pilha de bichas e, atrás das bichas, diretamente contra a parede, uma estátua de pedra, cujo rosto mutilado já não era mais do que uma máscara disforme que pairava vagamente através da escuridão.

O edifício era uma espécie de ruína, onde se distinguiam câmaras desmontadas, uma das quais, muito onerada, parecia servir de galpão.

O grande edifício da Rue Droit-Mur, que tinha uma ala na Rue Petit-Picpus, virou duas fachadas, em ângulos retos, para este jardim. Estas fachadas interiores eram ainda mais trágicas do que as exteriores. Todas as janelas foram raladas. Nenhum brilho de luz era visível em nenhum deles. O andar superior tinha escudos como prisões. Uma dessas fachadas projetava a sua sombra sobre a outra, que caía sobre o jardim como uma imensa vala negra.

Nenhuma outra casa era visível. O fundo do jardim estava perdido na névoa e na escuridão. No entanto, as paredes podiam ser confusamente feitas, que se cruzavam como se houvesse mais terras cultivadas além, e os telhados baixos da Rue Polonceau.

Nada mais selvagem e solitário do que este jardim poderia ser imaginado. Não havia ninguém nele, o que era bastante natural tendo em vista a hora; mas não parecia que este local fosse feito para qualquer um entrar, mesmo em plena luz do dia.

O primeiro cuidado de Jean Valjean tinha sido pegar seus sapatos e colocá-los novamente, em seguida, pisar sob o galpão com Cosette. Um homem que está fugindo nunca se acha suficientemente escondido. A criança, cujos pensamentos ainda estavam sobre o Thénardier, compartilhava seu instinto de se retirar da vista tanto quanto possível.

Cosette tremeu e pressionou perto dele. Ouviram o barulho tumultuado da patrulha vasculhando o beco sem saída e as ruas; os golpes de suas armas contra as pedras; Os apelos de Javert aos espiões da polícia que ele havia postado, e suas imprecações se misturavam com palavras que não podiam ser distinguidas.

Ao fim de um quarto de hora, parecia que aquela espécie de rugido tempestuoso estava a tornar-se mais distante. Jean Valjean prendeu a respiração.

Ele havia colocado a mão levemente na boca de Cosette.

No entanto, a solidão em que se encontrava era tão estranhamente calma, que esse alvoroço assustador, por mais próximo e furioso que fosse, não o perturbava tanto quanto a sombra de uma apreensão. Parecia que aqueles muros tinham sido construídos com as pedras surdas de que falam as Escrituras.

De repente, no meio desta profunda calma, surgiu um novo som; um som tão celestial, divino, inefável, arrebatador, como o outro tinha sido horrível. Era um hino que emanava da melancolia, uma explosão deslumbrante de oração e harmonia no silêncio obscuro e alarmante da noite; vozes femininas, mas vozes compostas ao mesmo tempo pelos sotaques puros das virgens e pelos sotaques inocentes das crianças, vozes que não são da terra, e que se assemelham àquelas que o recém-nascido ainda ouve, e que o moribundo já ouve. Esta canção procedia do edifício sombrio que se elevava acima do jardim. No momento em que o burburinho dos demônios recuou, alguém teria dito que um coro de anjos estava se aproximando através da escuridão.

Cosette e Jean Valjean caíram de joelhos.

Não sabiam o que era, não sabiam onde estavam; mas ambos, o homem e a criança, o penitente e o inocente, sentiram que deviam ajoelhar-se.

Estas vozes tinham esta estranha característica, que não impediam que o edifício parecesse deserto. Era um canto sobrenatural numa casa desabitada.

Enquanto essas vozes cantavam, Jean Valjean não pensava em nada. Já não contemplava a noite; contemplou um céu azul. Pareceu-lhe que sentia as asas que todos temos dentro de nós, a desdobrar-se.

A canção morreu. Pode ter durado muito tempo. Jean Valjean não poderia ter contado. Horas de êxtase nunca são mais do que um momento.

Todos voltaram a calar-se. Já não havia nada na rua; não havia nada no jardim. O que o ameaçara, o que o tranquilizara, tudo desaparecera. A brisa balançava algumas ervas daninhas secas na crista da parede, e elas emitiam um som fraco, doce e melancólico.

CAPÍTULO VII

CONTINUAÇÃO DO ENIGMA

O vento noturno tinha subido, o que indicava que devia ser entre uma e duas horas da manhã. A pobre Cosette não disse nada. Como ela se sentou ao lado dele e encostou a cabeça nele, Jean Valjean imaginou que ela estava dormindo. Ele se abaixou e olhou para ela. Os olhos de Cosette estavam bem abertos e seu ar pensativo doía Jean Valjean.

Ela ainda tremia.

"Você está com sono"?, disse Jean Valjean.

"Estou muito fria", respondeu.

Um momento depois, ela retomou:

"Ela ainda está lá"?

"Quem"?, perguntou Jean Valjean.

"Madame Thenardier".

Jean Valjean já se tinha esquecido dos meios que tinha utilizado para fazer Cosette calar-se.

"Ah"!, disse ele, "ela se foi. Você não precisa temer mais nada".

A criança suspirou como se uma carga tivesse sido levantada de seu seio.

O chão estava úmido, o galpão aberto por todos os lados, a brisa ficava mais aguda a cada instante. O mocinho tirou o casaco e enrolou-o em volta de Cosette.

"Você está menos frio agora"?, disse ele.

"Ah, sim, pai".

"Bem, espere por mim um momento. Em breve voltarei".

Abandonou a ruína e rastejou ao longo do grande edifício, procurando um abrigo melhor. Deparou-se com portas, mas estavam fechadas. Havia bares em todas as janelas do piso térreo.

Logo depois de ter virado o ângulo interno do edifício, observou que estava chegando a algumas janelas arqueadas, onde percebeu uma luz. Ele ficou na ponta dos pés e espiou por uma dessas janelas. Todos eles se abriram num salão toleravelmente vasto, pavimentado com grandes lajes, cortadas por arcadas e pilares, onde apenas uma pequena luz e grandes sombras eram visíveis. A luz vinha de um cone que ardia num canto. O apartamento estava deserto, e nada estava mexendo nele. No entanto, ao olhar atentamente, pensou ter percebido no chão algo que parecia estar coberto por um lençol enrolado e que se assemelhava a uma forma humana. Esta forma estava deitada de bruços para baixo, plana na calçada, com os braços estendidos em forma de cruz, na imobilidade da morte. Alguém teria dito, a julgar por uma espécie de serpente que ondulava sobre o chão, que essa forma sinistra tinha uma corda ao redor do pescoço.

Toda a câmara foi banhada por aquela névoa de lugares que são espaçadamente iluminados, o que aumenta o horror.

Jean Valjean disse muitas vezes depois que, embora muitos espectros fúnebres tivessem cruzado seu caminho na vida, ele nunca tinha visto nada mais sangrento e terrível do que aquela forma enigmática realizando algum mistério inexplicável naquele lugar sombrio, e contemplado assim à noite. Era alarmante supor que aquela coisa talvez estivesse morta; e ainda mais alarmante pensar que talvez estivesse vivo.

Teve a coragem de rebocar o rosto no vidro e de ver se a coisa se movia. Apesar de ter permanecido assim o que lhe parecia muito tempo, a forma estendida não fazia movimento. De repente, sentiu-se dominado por um terror inexprimível e fugiu. Começou a correr em direção ao galpão, sem ousar olhar para trás. Pareceu-lhe que, se virasse a cabeça, veria aquela forma seguindo-o a passos largos e agitando os braços.

Chegou à ruína todo sem fôlego. Seus joelhos estavam cedendo abaixo dele; a transpiração jorrava dele.

Onde ele estava? Quem poderia imaginar algo como esse tipo de sepulcro no meio de Paris! Que casa estranha era essa? Um edifício cheio de mistério noturno, chamando as almas através das trevas com a voz dos anjos, e quando elas vieram, oferecendo-lhes abruptamente aquela visão terrível; prometendo abrir os portais radiantes do céu e, em seguida, abrindo os horríveis portões do túmulo! E na verdade era um edifício, uma casa, que tinha um número na rua! Não era um sonho! Ele teve que tocar as pedras para se convencer de que tal era o fato.

O frio, a ansiedade, o mal-estar, as emoções da noite, tinham-lhe dado uma febre genuína, e todas estas ideias se chocavam no seu cérebro.

Ele se aproximou de Cosette. Ela estava dormindo.

CAPÍTULO VIII

O ENIGMA TORNA-SE DUPLAMENTE MISTERIOSO

A criança tinha deitado a cabeça sobre uma pedra e adormecido.

Sentou-se ao lado dela e começou a pensar. Pouco a pouco, enquanto olhava para ela, ele se acalmou e recuperou a posse de sua liberdade de espírito.

Ele percebeu claramente esta verdade, o fundamento de sua vida doravante, que enquanto ela estivesse lá, enquanto ele a tivesse perto dele, ele não deveria precisar de nada além dela, ele não deveria temer nada além dela, exceto por ela. Nem sequer tinha consciência de que estava muito frio, já que tinha tirado o casaco para a cobrir.

No entanto, contrariando este devaneio em que tinha caído, ouvira durante algum tempo um barulho peculiar. Era como o tilintar de um sino. Este som procedia do jardim. Podia ser ouvido distintamente, embora de forma ténue. Assemelhava-se à música ténue e vaga produzida pelos sinos do gado à noite nos pastos.

Esse barulho fez Valjean girar.

Ele olhou e viu que havia alguém no jardim.

Um ser parecido com um homem caminhava entre os copos de sino dos canteiros de melão, levantando-se, inclinando-se, parando, com movimentos regulares, como se estivesse arrastando ou espalhando algo no chão. Esta pessoa parecia mancar.

Jean Valjean estremeceu com o tremor contínuo dos infelizes. Para eles, tudo é hostil e suspeito. Desconfiam do dia porque permite que as pessoas os vejam, e da noite porque ajuda a surpreendê-los. Um pouco antes ele tinha tremido porque o jardim estava deserto, e agora ele tremia porque havia alguém lá.

Caiu de terrores quiméricos para verdadeiros terrores. Ele disse a si mesmo que Javert e os espiões talvez não tivessem partido de lá; que tinham, sem dúvida, deixado as pessoas de vigia na rua; que se este homem o descobrisse no jardim, clamaria por socorro contra os ladrões e o libertaria. Ele pegou a Cosette adormecida suavemente em seus braços e a carregou atrás de um monte de móveis velhos, que estavam fora de uso, no canto mais remoto do galpão. Cosette não mexeu.

A partir daí, ele examinou a aparência do ser na mancha de melão. O estranho era que o som do sino seguia cada um dos movimentos desse homem. Quando o homem se aproximou, o som se aproximou; quando o homem recuou, o som recuou; se ele fez algum gesto apressado, um tremolo acompanhou o gesto; Quando parou, o som cessou. Parecia evidente que o sino estava ligado àquele homem; Mas o que isso poderia significar? Quem era esse homem que tinha um sino suspenso ao seu redor como um carneiro ou um boi?

Ao fazer essas perguntas a si mesmo, ele tocou as mãos de Cosette. Estavam gelados.

"Ah! bom Deus"!, exclamou.

Falou-lhe em voz baixa:

"Cosette"!

Ela não abriu os olhos.

Ele a sacudiu vigorosamente.

Ela não acordou.

"Ela está morta"?, ele disse a si mesmo, e levantou-se, tremendo da cabeça aos pés.

Os pensamentos mais assustadores correram pell-mell através de sua mente. Há momentos em que suposições hediondas nos assaltam como uma coorte de fúrias e forçam violentamente as partições de nossos cérebros. Quando aqueles que amamos estão em causa, a nossa prudência inventa todo o tipo de loucura. Ele lembrou que dormir ao ar livre em uma noite fria pode ser fatal.

Cosette estava pálido e tinha caído a todo o comprimento no chão a seus pés, sem movimento.

Ouviu-a respirar: ela ainda respirava, mas com uma respiração que lhe parecia fraca e à beira da extinção.

Como ele foi aquecê-la de volta à vida? Como ele a despertou? Tudo o que não estava relacionado com isso desapareceu de seus pensamentos. Ele correu descontroladamente da ruína.

Era absolutamente necessário que Cosette estivesse na cama e ao lado de um incêndio em menos de um quarto de hora.

CAPÍTULO IX

O HOMEM DO SINO

Ele caminhou direto até o homem que viu no jardim. Tinha levado na mão o rolo de prata que estava no bolso do colete.

A cabeça do homem estava inclinada e ele não o viu se aproximar. Em poucos passos, Jean Valjean ficou ao seu lado.

Jean Valjean abordou-o com o grito: —

"Cem francos"!

O homem deu um pontapé inicial e levantou os olhos.

"Você pode ganhar cem francos", continuou Jean Valjean, "se me conceder abrigo para esta noite".

A lua brilhou cheia no semblante aterrorizado de Jean Valjean.

"O quê! então é você, padre Madeleine"!, disse o homem.

Esse nome, assim pronunciado, naquela hora obscura, naquele lugar desconhecido, por aquele homem estranho, fez Jean Valjean recomeçar.

Ele esperava tudo menos isso. A pessoa que assim se dirigia a ele era um velho curvado e coxo, vestido quase como um camponês, que usava no joelho esquerdo uma rótula de couro, de onde pendia um sino moderadamente grande. Seu rosto, que estava na sombra, não era distinguível.

No entanto, o mocinho tinha tirado o boné e exclamou, tremendo todo:

"Ah, bom Deus! Como é que você está aqui, Padre Madeleine? Onde entrou? Dieu-Jésus! Você caiu do céu? Não há problema nisso: se alguma vez cair, será a partir daí. E que estado você está! Você não tem cravat; você não tem chapéu; você não tem casaco! Você sabe, você teria assustado qualquer um que não o conhecesse? Sem casaco! Senhor Deus! Os santos estão enlouquecendo hoje em dia? Mas como você entrou aqui"?

Suas palavras caíram umas sobre as outras. O mocinho falava com uma volubilidade rústica, em que não havia nada de alarmante. Tudo isso foi proferido com um misto de estupefação e *bondade* ingênua.

"Quem é você? e que casa é essa"?, exigiu Jean Valjean.

"Ah! pardieu, isso é demais"!, exclamou o velho, "Eu sou a pessoa para quem você conseguiu o lugar aqui, e esta casa é aquela onde você me colocou. O quê! Você não me reconhece"?

"Não", disse Jean Valjean; "E como é que você me conhece"?

"Você salvou minha vida", disse o homem.

Ele se virou. Um raio de luar delineou seu perfil, e Jean Valjean reconheceu o velho Fauchelevent.

"Ah"!, disse Jean Valjean, "então é você? Sim, lembro-me de ti".

"Isso é muita sorte" disse o velho, em tom de reprovação.

"E o que você está fazendo aqui"?, retomou Jean Valjean.

"Ora, estou cobrindo meus melões, claro"!

De fato, no momento em que Jean Valjean o abordou, o velho Fauchelevent segurava em sua mão a ponta de um tapete de palha que ele estava ocupado em espalhar sobre a cama de melão. Durante a hora em que esteve no jardim, já tinha espalhado vários deles. Foi esta operação que o levou a executar os movimentos peculiares observados a partir do barracão por Jean Valjean.

Ele continuou: —

"Eu disse a mim mesmo: 'A lua está brilhante: vai congelar. E se eu pusesse meus melões em seus casacos"? E", acrescentou, olhando para Jean Valjean com um largo sorriso, "pardieu! Você deveria ter feito o mesmo! Mas como é que se chega aqui"?

Jean Valjean, achando-se conhecido deste homem, pelo menos apenas sob o nome de Madeleine, avançou a partir daí apenas com cautela. Multiplicou as perguntas. Estranho dizer, seus papéis pareciam estar invertidos. Foi ele, o intruso, que interrogou.

215

"E que sino é esse que você usa no joelho"?

"Isto", respondeu Fauchel, "é para que eu possa ser evitado".

"O quê! para que sejas evitado"?

O velho Fauchelevent piscou com um ar indescritível.

"Ah, meu Deus! só há mulheres nesta casa, muitas raparigas. Parece que eu deveria ser uma pessoa perigosa de conhecer. O sino alerta-os. Quando eu venho, eles vão".

"Que casa é essa"?

"Venha, você sabe bem o suficiente".

"Mas eu não".

"Não quando você me conseguiu o lugar aqui como jardineiro"?

"Responda-me como se eu não soubesse nada".

"Bem, então, este é o convento de Petit-Picpus".

As memórias repercutem-se em Jean Valjean. O acaso, isto é, a Providência, lançou-o precisamente naquele convento do Quartier Saint-Antoine onde o velho Fauchelevent, aleijado pela queda do seu carrinho, fora admitido por sua recomendação dois anos antes. Ele repetiu, como se estivesse falando consigo mesmo:

"O convento de Petit-Picpus".

"Exatamente", devolveu o velho Fauchel. "Mas para chegar ao ponto, como o deuce você conseguiu entrar aqui, você, padre Madeleine? Não importa se você é um santo; você também é um homem, e nenhum homem entra aqui".

"Você certamente está aqui".

"Não há ninguém além de mim".

"Ainda assim", disse Jean Valjean, "devo ficar aqui".

"Ah, bom Deus"!, gritou Fauchel.

Jean Valjean aproximou-se do velho e disse-lhe com voz grave:

"Padre Fauchel, salvei a sua vida".

"Fui o primeiro a recordá-lo", devolveu Fauchel.

"Bem, você pode fazer hoje por mim o que eu fiz por você antigamente".

Fauchelevent tomou em suas mãos envelhecidas, trêmulas e enrugadas as duas mãos robustas de Jean Valjean, e ficou por vários minutos como se fosse incapaz de falar. Por fim, exclamou:

"Ah! isso seria uma bênção do bom Deus, se eu pudesse lhe fazer algum pequeno retorno por isso! Salve a sua vida! Monsieur le Maire, descartem o velho"!

Uma alegria maravilhosa transfigurara este velho. Seu semblante parecia emitir um raio de luz.

"O que você deseja que eu faça"?, retomou.

"Isso eu vou te explicar. Você tem uma câmara"?

"Tenho um casebre isolado, atrás das ruínas do antigo convento, num canto que ninguém nunca olha. Há três quartos".

A cabana estava, de facto, tão bem escondida atrás das ruínas, e tão habilmente arranjada para evitar que fosse vista, que Jean Valjean não a tinha percebido.

"Bom", disse Jean Valjean. "Agora vou pedir-vos duas coisas".

"O que são, senhor prefeito"?

"Em primeiro lugar, você não deve contar a ninguém o que sabe sobre mim. No segundo, você não deve tentar descobrir mais nada".

"Como quiserem. Eu sei que você não pode fazer nada que não seja honesto, que você sempre foi um homem segundo o bom coração de Deus. E depois, aliás, foi você quem me colocou aqui. Isso preocupa-o. Estou ao vosso serviço".

"Isso está resolvido então. Agora, vem comigo. Vamos buscar a criança".

"Ah"!, disse Fauchel, "então há uma criança"?

Ele não acrescentou mais uma palavra, e seguiu Jean Valjean como um cão segue seu mestre.

Menos de meia hora depois, Cosette, que tinha voltado a ficar rosada antes da chama de um bom fogo, estava dormindo na cama do velho jardineiro. Jean Valjean tinha vestido o seu cravat e casaco mais uma vez; O chapéu, que tinha atirado por cima do muro, tinha sido encontrado e apanhado. Enquanto Jean Valjean vestia o casaco, Fauchelevent tinha retirado o sino e a rótula, que agora estavam pendurados num prego ao lado de um cesto vintage que adornava a parede. Os dois homens estavam a aquecer-se com os cotovelos apoiados numa mesa sobre a qual Fauchelevent tinha colocado um pouco de queijo, pão preto, uma garrafa de vinho e dois copos, e o velho dizia a Jean Valjean, enquanto punha a mão no joelho deste último: "Ah! Padre Madeleine! Você não me reconheceu imediatamente; Você salva a vida das pessoas e depois as esquece! Isso é mau! Mas eles se lembram de você! Você é um ingrata"!

CAPÍTULO X

O QUE EXPLICA COMO JAVERT ENTROU NO CHEIRO

Os acontecimentos de que acabámos de ver o reverso, por assim dizer, realizaram-se da forma mais simples possível.

Quando Jean Valjean, na noite do mesmo dia em que Javert o prendera ao lado do leito de morte de Fantine, escapou da prisão da cidade de M. sur M., a polícia supôs que ele se tinha levado para Paris. Paris é um turbilhão onde tudo se perde, e tudo desaparece nesta barriga do mundo, como na barriga do mar. Nenhuma floresta esconde um homem como aquela multidão. Fugitivos de todos os tipos sabem disso. Vão para Paris como um abismo; há golfos que salvam. A polícia também sabe disso, e é em Paris que procura o que perdeu noutros lugares. Eles procuraram o ex-prefeito de M. sur M. Javert foi convocado a Paris para lançar luz sobre suas pesquisas. Javert tinha, de facto, prestado uma ajuda poderosa na recaptura de Jean Valjean. O zelo e a inteligência de Javert naquela ocasião haviam sido comentados por M. Chabouillet, secretário da Prefeitura sob Comte Anglès. M. Chabouillet, que, além disso, já tinha sido patrono de Javert, mandou anexar o inspetor de M. sur M. à força policial de Paris. Lá, Javert se prestou útil em mergulhadores e, embora a palavra possa parecer estranha para tais serviços, maneiras honrosas.

Já não pensava em Jean Valjean" o lobo de hoje faz esquecer o lobo de ontem" quando, em dezembro de 1823, leu um jornal, ele que nunca leu jornais; mas Javert, um homem monárquico, tinha o desejo de conhecer os detalhes da entrada triunfal do "Príncipe Generalíssimo" em Bayonne. No momento em que terminava o artigo, o que lhe interessava; um nome, o nome de Jean Valjean, atraiu sua atenção no final de uma página. O jornal anunciou que o condenado Jean Valjean estava morto e publicou o fato em termos tão formais que Javert não duvidou. Limitou-se à observação: "É uma boa entrada". Então ele jogou fora o papel, e não pensou mais sobre isso.

Algum tempo depois, foi transmitido um relatório policial da prefeitura do Sena e Oise para a prefeitura da polícia de Paris, relativo ao rapto de uma criança, que tinha ocorrido, em circunstâncias peculiares, como se dizia, na comuna de Montfermeil. Uma menina de sete ou oito anos de idade, segundo o relatório, que tinha sido confiada pela mãe a um estalajadeiro daquele bairro, tinha sido roubada por um desconhecido; esta criança respondeu ao nome de Cosette, e era filha de uma menina chamada Fantine, que tinha morrido no hospital, não se sabia onde ou quando.

Este relatório ficou sob o olhar de Javert e levou-o a pensar.

O nome de Fantine era bem conhecido por ele. Lembrou-se que Jean Valjean o fizera, Javert, cair na gargalhada, pedindo-lhe uma pausa de três dias, com o propósito de ir buscar o filho daquela criatura. Recordou o facto de Jean Valjean ter sido detido em Paris no preciso momento em que entrava no autocarro de Montfermeil. Alguns sinais tinham-no feito suspeitar, na altura, que aquela era a segunda ocasião em que entrava naquele autocarro, e que já no dia anterior tinha feito uma excursão ao bairro daquela aldeia, pois não tinha sido visto na própria aldeia. O que pretendia ele fazer naquela região de Montfermeil? Nem sequer se podia supor. Javert entendeu agora. A filha de Fantine estava lá. Jean Valjean estava indo lá em busca dela. E agora esta criança tinha sido roubada por um estranho! Quem poderia ser esse estranho? Poderia ser Jean Valjean? Mas Jean Valjean estava morto. Javert, sem dizer nada a ninguém, pegou o ônibus do *Pewter Platter*, Cul-de-Sac de la Planchette, e fez uma viagem a Montfermeil.

Ele esperava encontrar uma grande luz sobre o assunto lá; Encontrou muita obscuridade.

Nos primeiros dias, os Thénardiers tinham falado em sua raiva. O desaparecimento da Cotovia tinha criado uma sensação na aldeia. Ele imediatamente obteve inúmeras versões da história, que terminou no sequestro de uma criança. Daí o boletim de ocorrência. Mas passado o seu primeiro vexame, Thénardier, com o seu maravilhoso instinto, compreendeu muito rapidamente que nunca é aconselhável agitar o procurador da Coroa, e que as suas queixas a respeito do *rapto* de Cosette teriam como primeiro resultado fixar-se em si mesmo, e em muitos assuntos obscuros que tinha à mão, o olho cintilante da justiça. A última coisa que as corujas desejam é ter uma vela trazida para elas. E, em primeiro lugar, como explicar os mil e quinhentos francos que recebera? Ele se virou bruscamente, colocou uma mordaça na boca de sua esposa e fingiu espanto quando a *criança roubada* foi mencionada a ele. Ele não entendia nada sobre isso; sem dúvida, ele resmungou por algum tempo por ter aquela pequena criatura querida "tirada dele" tão apressadamente; ele deveria ter gostado de mantê-la mais dois ou três dias, por ternura; mas o seu "avô" tinha vindo atrás dela da forma mais natural do mundo. Acrescentou o "avô", que produziu um bom efeito. Esta foi a história que Javert encontrou quando chegou a Montfermeil. O avô fez com que Jean Valjean desaparecesse.

No entanto, Javert deixou algumas perguntas, como despencas, na história de Thénardier. "Quem era esse avô? e qual era o seu nome"? Thénardier respondeu com simplicidade: "Ele é um fazendeiro rico. Vi o passaporte dele. Acho que o nome dele era M. Guillaume Lambert".

Lambert é um nome respeitável e extremamente tranquilizador. Em seguida, Javert retornou a Paris.

"Jean Valjean certamente está morto", disse ele, "e eu sou um nono".

Começara de novo a esquecer esta história, quando, no decurso de março de 1824, ouviu falar de uma personagem singular que residia na freguesia de Saint-Médard e que tinha sido apelidada de "o mendicante que dá esmolas". Essa pessoa, segundo a história, era um homem de meios, cujo nome ninguém sabia exatamente, e que vivia sozinho com uma menina de oito anos, que nada sabia sobre si mesma, exceto que ela tinha vindo de Montfermeil. Montfermeil! esse nome estava sempre surgindo, e isso fez Javert furar suas orelhas. Um velho espião da polícia mendigo, um ex-beadle, a quem esta pessoa tinha dado esmola, acrescentou mais alguns detalhes. Este senhor de propriedade era muito tímido, nunca saindo a não ser à noite, não falando com ninguém, exceto, ocasionalmente, com os pobres, e nunca permitindo que ninguém se aproximasse dele. Ele usava um casaco amarelo horrível, que valia muitos milhões, sendo todo coberto com contas bancárias. Isso despertou a curiosidade de Javert de uma maneira decidida. A fim de ver de perto este fantástico cavalheiro sem alarmá-lo, ele emprestou a roupa do beadle por um dia, e o lugar onde o velho espião tinha o hábito de agachar-se todas as noites, choramingar orixás pelo nariz e jogar o espião sob a capa da oração.

"O indivíduo suspeito" de fato se aproximou de Javert disfarçado e lhe deu esmola. Nesse momento, Javert levantou a cabeça, e o choque que Jean Valjean recebeu ao reconhecer Javert foi igual ao recebido por Javert quando ele pensou que ele reconhecia Jean Valjean.

No entanto, a escuridão pode tê-lo enganado; A morte de Jean Valjean foi oficial; Javert nutria sérias dúvidas; e na dúvida, Javert, o homem dos escrúpulos, nunca pôs o dedo no colarinho de ninguém.

Seguiu o seu homem até à casa de Gorbeau e pôs "a velha" a falar, o que não foi difícil. A idosa confirmou o fato em relação ao casaco forrado com milhões, e narrou-lhe o episódio da nota de mil francos. Ela tinha visto! Ela tinha lidado com isso! Javert contratou um quarto; naquela noite, instalou-se nela. Ele veio e ouviu na porta do misterioso inquilino, na esperança de captar o som de sua voz, mas Jean Valjean viu sua vela através do buraco da fechadura, e frustrou o espião mantendo-se em silêncio.

No dia seguinte, Jean Valjean descampou; mas o barulho causado pela queda da peça de cinco francos foi notado pela velha, que, ouvindo o barulho da moeda, suspeitou que ele poderia estar pretendendo ir embora, e se apressou em avisar Javert. À noite, quando Jean Valjean saiu, Javert o esperava atrás das árvores da avenida com dois homens.

Javert pedira ajuda na Prefeitura, mas não mencionara o nome do indivíduo que esperava apreender, esse era o seu segredo, e ele o tinha guardado por três razões: em primeiro lugar, porque a menor indiscrição poderia colocar Jean Valjean em alerta, em seguida, porque, para impor as mãos a um ex-presidiário que havia fugido e era dado como morto, sobre um criminoso que a justiça havia classificado para sempre como *um dos malfeitores do tipo mais perigoso*, foi um sucesso magnífico que os antigos membros da polícia parisiense certamente não deixariam a um recém-chegado como Javert, e ele tinha medo de ser privado de seu condenado; e, por último, porque Javert, sendo artista, tinha gosto pelo imprevisto. Ele odiava aqueles sucessos bem anunciados de que se fala com muita antecedência e que tiveram a flor da pele. Preferiu elaborar as suas obras-primas no escuro e desvendá-las subitamente no final.

Javert seguira Jean Valjean de árvore em árvore, depois de esquina em esquina da rua, e não o perdera de vista por um único instante; mesmo nos momentos em que Jean Valjean acreditava ser o olho mais seguro de Javert estava nele. Por que Javert não prendeu Jean Valjean? Porque ele ainda estava em dúvida.

Recorde-se que, naquela época, a polícia não estava precisamente à vontade; a imprensa livre envergonhou-a; várias prisões arbitrárias denunciadas pelos jornais, ecoaram até as Câmaras e tornaram a Prefeitura tímida. A interferência na liberdade individual era uma questão grave. Os agentes da polícia tinham medo de errar; o prefeito colocou-lhes a culpa; Um erro significou demissão. O leitor pode imaginar o efeito que este breve parágrafo, reproduzido por vinte jornais, teria causado em Paris: "Ontem, um avô idoso, de cabelos brancos, um senhor respeitável e abastado, que caminhava com o neto, de oito anos, foi preso e conduzido à agência da Prefeitura como um condenado foragido"!

Repita-se, além disso, que Javert tinha escrúpulos próprios; injunções de sua consciência foram acrescentadas às injunções do prefeito. Ele estava realmente em dúvida.

Jean Valjean virou-lhe as costas e andou no escuro.

A tristeza, o mal-estar, a ansiedade, a depressão, esta nova desgraça de ser forçado a fugir à noite, a procurar um refúgio casual em Paris para Cosette e para si próprio, a necessidade de regular o seu ritmo ao ritmo da criança – tudo isto, sem que ele se apercebesse, alterara o andar de Jean Valjean e imprimiu-lhe tamanha senilidade, que a própria polícia, encarnada na pessoa de Javert, poderia, e de fato cometeu, um erro. A impossibilidade de se aproximar demais, seu traje de preceptor *emigrado*, a declaração de Thénardier que fez dele um avô e, finalmente, a crença em sua morte na prisão, aumentaram ainda mais a incerteza que se acumulava na mente de Javert.

Por um instante ocorreu-lhe fazer uma exigência abrupta de seus papéis; mas se o homem não era Jean Valjean, e se este homem não era um bom e honesto velho sujeito que vivia de sua renda, ele provavelmente era alguma lâmina alegre profunda e ardilosamente implicada na obscura teia de malfeitos parisienses, algum chefe de um bando perigoso, que dava esmolas para esconder seus outros talentos, o que era uma velha esquiva. Tinha companheiros de confiança, retiros cúmplices em caso de emergência, nos quais se refugiava, sem dúvida. Todas essas voltas que ele estava fazendo pelas ruas pareciam indicar que ele não era um homem simples e honesto. Prendê-lo demasiado apressadamente seria "matar a galinha que pôs os ovos de ouro". Onde estava o inconveniente em esperar? Javert tinha certeza de que não escaparia.

Assim, procedeu num estado de espírito toleravelmente perplexo, colocando-se uma centena de perguntas sobre esta enigmática personagem.

Foi só muito tarde, na Rue de Pontoise, que, graças à luz brilhante lançada de uma loja de carrinhos, ele reconheceu decididamente Jean Valjean.

Há neste mundo dois seres que dão um começo profundo: a mãe que recupera seu filho e o tigre que recupera sua presa. Javert deu esse início profundo.

Assim que reconheceu positivamente Jean Valjean, o formidável condenado, percebeu que havia apenas três e pediu reforços na delegacia da Rue de Pontoise. Colocam-se luvas antes de agarrar um cutelo de espinho.

Essa demora e a parada no Carrefour Rollin para consultar seus agentes chegaram perto fazendo com que ele perdesse o rastro. Ele rapidamente adivinhou, no entanto, que Jean Valjean gostaria de colocar o rio entre seus perseguidores e ele mesmo. Ele dobrou a cabeça e refletiu como um cão de sangue que coloca o nariz no chão para se certificar de que ele está no cheiro certo. Javert, com sua poderosa retidão de instinto, foi direto para a ponte de Austerlitz. Uma palavra com o porteiro forneceu-lhe a informação que ele exigia: "Já viste um homem com uma menina"? "Eu o fiz pagar dois sous", respondeu o pedágio. Javert chegou à ponte na estação para ver Jean Valjean atravessar o pequeno ponto iluminado do outro lado da água, conduzindo Cosette pela mão. Viu-o entrar na Rue du Chemin-Vert-Saint-Antoine; lembrou-se do Cul-de-Sac Genrot ali organizado como uma armadilha, e da única saída da Rue Droit-Mur para a Rue Petit-Picpus. *Certificou-se das tocas traseiras*, como dizem os caçadores, despachou apressadamente um dos seus agentes, por via rotunda, para guardar aquela questão. Uma patrulha que regressava ao posto do Arsenal depois de o ter passado, fez uma requisição e fez com que o acompanhasse. Em tais jogos, os soldados são ases. Além disso, o princípio é que, para obter o melhor de um javali, deve-se empregar a ciência da vingança e muitos cães. Feitas essas combinações, sentindo que Jean Valjean estava preso entre o beco cego Genrot à direita, seu agente à esquerda e ele mesmo, Javert, na retaguarda, ele deu uma pitada de rapé.

Depois começou o jogo. Viveu um momento de êxtase e infernal; permitiu que o seu homem prosseguisse, sabendo que o tinha a salvo, mas desejoso de adiar o momento da prisão o máximo de tempo possível, feliz por pensar que tinha sido levado e, no entanto, por o ver livre, regozijando-se com o seu olhar, com aquela volúpia da aranha que permite que a mosca tremule, e do gato que deixa o rato correr. Garras e garras possuem uma sensualidade monstruosa: os movimentos obscuros da criatura aprisionada em suas pinças. Que delícia é esse estrangulamento!

Javert estava se divertindo. As malhas de sua rede estavam firmemente entrelaçadas. Tinha a certeza do sucesso; tudo o que tinha de fazer agora era fechar a mão.

Acompanhado como estava, a própria ideia de resistência era impossível, por mais vigoroso, enérgico e desesperado que Jean Valjean fosse.

Javert avançou lentamente, soando, procurando em seu caminho todos os cantos da rua como tantos bolsões de ladrões.

Quando chegou ao centro da rede, encontrou a mosca que já não estava lá.

Sua exasperação pode ser imaginada.

Interrogou a sua sentinela das Rues Droit-Mur e Petit-Picpus; Esse agente, que permanecera imperturbavelmente no seu posto, não tinha visto o homem passar.

Às vezes acontece que um veado é perdido cabeça e chifres; ou seja, ele escapa embora tenha a matilha em seus calcanhares, e então os caçadores mais antigos não sabem o que dizer. Duvivier, Ligniville e Desprez param. Num descontentamento deste tipo, Artonge exclama: "Não era um veado, mas um feiticeiro". Javert teria gostado de proferir o mesmo grito.

Sua deceção beirava por um momento o desespero e a raiva.

É certo que Napoleão cometeu erros durante a guerra com a Rússia, que Alexandre cometeu erros na guerra da Índia, que César cometeu erros na guerra em África, que Ciro teve culpa na guerra da Cítia e que Javert errou nesta campanha contra Jean Valjean. Enganou-se, talvez, ao hesitar em reconhecer o ex-presidiário. O primeiro olhar deveria ter-lhe bastado. Enganou-se ao não prendê-lo pura e simplesmente no antigo edifício; errou ao não prendê-lo quando o reconheceu positivamente na Rue de Pontoise. Ele estava errado ao se aconselhar com seus auxiliares à luz plena da lua no Carrefour Rollin. Os conselhos são certamente úteis; é bom conhecer e interrogar os cães que merecem confiança; mas o caçador não pode ser muito cauteloso quando está perseguindo animais inquietos como o lobo e o condenado. Javert, ao pensar demais em como ele deveria colocar os cães de sangue da matilha na trilha, alarmou a besta dando-lhe vento do dardo, e assim o fez correr. Acima de tudo, enganou-se porque, depois de ter apanhado novamente o cheiro na ponte de Austerlitz, jogou aquele jogo formidável e pueril de manter tal homem no fim de um fio. Julgava-se mais forte do que era e acreditava que podia jogar no jogo do rato e do leão. Ao mesmo tempo, considerou-se demasiado fraco, quando julgou necessário obter reforços. Precaução fatal, perda de tempo precioso! Javert cometeu todos esses erros e, no entanto, foi um dos espiões mais inteligentes e corretos que já existiram. Ele era, com toda a força do termo, o que se chama por vingança de cão *conhecedor*. Mas o que há de perfeito?

Grandes estrategistas têm seus eclipses.

As maiores loucuras são muitas vezes compostas, como as maiores cordas, por uma infinidade de fios. Pegue o cabo fio a fio, pegue todos os pequenos motivos determinantes separadamente, e você pode quebrá-los um após o outro, e você diz, "Isso é tudo o que há dele"! Trança-os, torça-os juntos; o resultado é enorme: é Átila hesitando entre Marciano, a leste, e Valentiniano, a oeste; é Aníbal a tardar em Cápua; é Danton adormecendo em Arcis-sur-Aube.

Seja como for, mesmo no momento em que viu que Jean Valjean lhe tinha escapado, Javert não perdeu a cabeça. Certo de que o condenado que havia quebrado sua proibição não poderia estar longe, ele estabeleceu sentinelas, organizou armadilhas e ambuscadas, e bateu no quarteirão toda aquela noite. A primeira coisa que viu foi a desordem na lanterna da rua cuja corda tinha sido cortada. Um sinal precioso que, no entanto, o levou ao erro, pois o levou a voltar todas as suas pesquisas na direção do Genrot Cul-de-Sac. Neste beco sem saída havia muros toleravelmente baixos que se debruçavam sobre jardins cujos limites contíguos aos imensos trechos de terrenos baldios. Jean Valjean evidentemente deve ter fugido nessa direção. O fato é que, se ele tivesse penetrado um pouco mais no Cul-de-Sac Genrot, ele provavelmente teria feito isso e se perdido. Javert explorou esses jardins e esses trechos de lixo como se estivesse caçando uma agulha.

Ao amanhecer, deixou dois homens inteligentes à vista e regressou à Prefeitura da Polícia, tão envergonhado como um espião da polícia que tinha sido capturado por um assaltante poderia ter sido.

LIVRO SEIS

O PETIT-PICPUS

CAPÍTULO I

NÚMERO 62 RUE PETIT-PICPUS

Nada, há meio século, se assemelhava mais a qualquer outro portão de carruagem do que o portão de carruagem do número 62 da Rue Petit-Picpus. Esta entrada, que geralmente ficava entreaberta da forma mais convidativa, permitia uma visão de duas coisas, nenhuma das quais tem nada de muito fúnebre: um pátio cercado por paredes penduradas com videiras e o rosto de um porteiro descontraído. Acima do muro, na parte inferior da quadra, árvores altas eram visíveis. Quando um raio de sol animou o pátio, quando um copo de vinho animou o porteiro, foi difícil passar pelo número 62 da Little Picpus Street sem levar uma impressão sorridente dele. No entanto, era um lugar sombrio do qual se tinha tido um vislumbre.

O umbral sorriu; A casa rezou e chorou.

Se alguém conseguisse passar o carregador, o que não era fácil, o que era quase impossível para todos, pois havia um *gergelim aberto!* o que era necessário saber", se, uma vez passado o porteiro, entrava-se num pequeno vestíbulo à direita, no qual se abria uma escada fechada entre duas paredes e tão estreita que só uma pessoa podia subi-la de cada vez, se não se deixasse alarmar por uma dobradinha de amarelo canário, Com um dado de chocolate que revestia esta escadaria, se alguém se aventurasse a subi-la, atravessava-se um primeiro pouso, depois um segundo, e chegava-se no primeiro andar a um corredor onde a lavagem amarela e o plinto em tons de chocolate o perseguiam com uma persistência pacífica. Escadaria e corredor foram iluminados por duas belas janelas. O corredor deu uma volta e ficou escuro. Se alguém dobrasse essa capa, chegava alguns passos mais adiante, em frente a uma porta que era ainda mais misteriosa porque não estava presa. Se alguém a abrisse, encontrava-se numa pequena câmara com cerca de seis metros quadrados, de azulejos, bem esfregada, limpa, fria e pendurada com papel nankin com flores verdes, às quinze sous o rolo. Uma luz branca e sem brilho caiu de uma grande janela, com pequenas vidraças, à esquerda, que usurpou toda a largura da sala. Olhava-se em volta, mas não se via ninguém; ouvia-se, não se ouvia nem um passo nem um murmúrio humano. As paredes estavam nuas, a câmara não estava mobilada; não havia sequer uma cadeira.

Olhou-se de novo, e contemplou-se na parede voltada para a porta um buraco quadrangular, com cerca de um metro quadrado, com uma grade de barras de ferro entrelaçadas, pretas, nodosas, sólidas, que formavam quadrados – eu quase tinha dito malhas – de menos de uma polegada e meia de comprimento diagonal. As pequenas flores verdes do papel nankin corriam de forma calma e ordenada para aquelas barras de ferro, sem serem assustadas ou lançadas em confusão pelo seu contacto fúnebre. Supondo que um ser vivo tivesse sido tão maravilhosamente magro a ponto de ensaiar uma entrada ou uma saída pelo buraco quadrado, essa grade teria impedido isso. Não permitia a passagem do corpo, mas permitia a passagem dos olhos; ou seja, da mente. Isto parece ter-lhes ocorrido, pois tinha sido reforçado por uma folha de estanho inserida na parede um pouco na traseira, e perfurada com mil orifícios mais microscópicos do que os orifícios de um coador. Na parte inferior desta placa, uma abertura tinha sido perfurada exatamente semelhante ao orifício de uma caixa de correio. Um pouco de fita presa a um fio de sino pendurado à direita da abertura ralada.

Se a fita foi puxada, uma campainha tocou, e ouviu-se uma voz muito próxima, o que fez com que se começasse.

"Quem está lá"?, perguntou a voz.

Era uma voz de mulher, uma voz suave, tão suave que era triste.

Aqui, novamente, havia uma palavra mágica que era necessário conhecer. Se não se sabia, a voz cessava, o muro voltava a calar-se, como se a obscuridade aterrorizada do sepulcro estivesse do outro lado dele.

Se alguém soubesse a senha, a voz retomava: "Entre à direita".

Percebeu-se então à direita, virada para a janela, uma porta de vidro encimada por uma moldura envidraçada e pintada de cinzento. Ao levantar o trinco e cruzar o umbral, experimentou-se precisamente a mesma impressão de quando se entra no teatro em um *baignoire ralado*, antes que a grade seja abaixada e o lustre seja iluminado. Uma estava, de facto, numa espécie de caixa-teatro, estreita, mobilada com duas cadeiras velhas, e um tapete de palha muito desgastado, iluminado pela luz vaga da porta de vidro; uma caixa normal, com a frente apenas de uma altura para se apoiar, com uma tabuleta de madeira preta. Esta caixa foi ralada, só que o ralo dela não era de madeira dourada, como na ópera; Era uma rede monstruosa de barras de ferro, terrivelmente entrelaçadas e rebitadas à parede por enormes fixações que se assemelhavam a punhos cerrados.

Os primeiros minutos passaram; Quando os olhos começaram a habituar-se a este meio crepúsculo semelhante a uma adega, tentou-se passar a grade, mas não conseguiu mais do que seis centímetros além dela. Lá encontrou uma barreira de persianas pretas, reforçadas e fortificadas com vigas transversais de madeira pintadas de amarelo pão de gengibre. Essas persianas eram divididas em ripas longas e estreitas, e mascaravam todo o comprimento da grade. Estavam sempre fechados. Ao fim de alguns instantes, ouviu-se uma voz que vinha de trás destas persianas e dizia:

"Estou aqui. O que você deseja comigo"?

Era uma voz amada, às vezes adorada. Ninguém era visível. Dificilmente o som de uma respiração era audível. Parecia que se tratava de um espírito evocado, que vos falava através das paredes do sepulcro.

Se alguém por acaso estivesse dentro de certas condições prescritas e muito raras, a fenda de uma das persianas abria-se em frente a você; o espírito evocado tornou-se uma aparição. Atrás da grade, atrás do obturador, percebia-se até onde a grade permitia a visão, uma cabeça, da qual apenas a boca e o queixo eram visíveis; o resto estava coberto com um véu negro. Vislumbrou-se um guimpe negro, e uma forma mal definida, coberta por uma mortalha preta. Essa cabeça falou contigo, mas não olhou para ti e nunca sorriu para ti.

A luz que vinha de trás de você foi ajustada de tal maneira que você a viu no branco, e ela viu você no preto. Esta luz era simbólica.

No entanto, seus olhos mergulharam ansiosamente através daquela abertura que foi feita naquele lugar desligado de todos os olhares. Uma profunda imprecisão envolvia aquela forma revestida de luto. Seus olhos procuraram essa imprecisão e procuraram perceber o entorno da aparição. Ao fim de muito pouco tempo, descobriu que não conseguia ver nada. O que se via era a noite, o vazio, as sombras, uma névoa invernal misturada com um vapor do túmulo, uma espécie de paz terrível, um silêncio do qual não se podia recolher nada, nem mesmo suspiros, uma escuridão em que nada se podia distinguir, nem mesmo fantasmas.

O que se viu foi o interior de um claustro.

Era o interior daquele edifício severo e sombrio que se chamava Convento dos Bernardinos da Adoração Perpétua. A caixa em que você estava era o salão. A primeira voz que vos dirigira era a da porteira que se sentava sempre imóvel e silenciosa, do outro lado da parede, perto da abertura quadrada, blindada pela grade de ferro e pela placa com os seus mil buracos, como por uma viseira dupla. A obscuridade que banhava a caixa ralada surgiu do facto de o salão, que tinha uma janela do lado do mundo, não ter nenhuma do lado do convento. Os olhos profanos não devem ver nada daquele lugar sagrado.

No entanto, havia algo além dessa sombra; havia uma luz; Havia vida no meio daquela morte. Embora este tenha sido o mais rigorosamente murado de todos os conventos, esforçar-nos-emos por penetrar nele, e por levar o leitor para dentro, e dizer, sem transgredir os limites adequados, coisas que os contadores de histórias nunca viram e, portanto, nunca descreveram.

CAPÍTULO II

A OBEDIÊNCIA DE MARTIN VERGA

Este convento, que em 1824 já existia há muitos anos na Rue Petit-Picpus, era uma comunidade de Bernardinos da obediência de Martinho Verga.

Estes bernardinos estavam ligados, em consequência, não a Claraval, como os monges bernardinos, mas a Cîteaux, como os monges beneditinos. Por outras palavras, eram os súbditos, não de São Bernardo, mas de São Benoît.

Qualquer pessoa que tenha entregado fólios antigos, em alguma medida, sabe que Martin Verga fundou em 1425 uma congregação de bernardinos-beneditinos, com Salamanca como chefe da ordem, e Alcala como o estabelecimento do ramo.

Esta congregação tinha enviado ramificações por todos os países católicos da Europa.

Não há nada de anormal na Igreja latina nestes enxertos de uma ordem sobre outra. Para mencionar apenas uma única ordem de Saint-Benoît, que está aqui em questão: há anexados a esta ordem, sem contar a obediência de Martinho Verga, quatro congregações", duas na Itália, Mont-Cassin e Sainte-Justine de Pádua; dois em França, Cluny e Saint-Maur; e nove ordens: Vallombrosa, Granmont, os Célestins, os Camaldules, os Cartuxos, os Humiliés, os Olivateurs, os Silvestrins e, por último, Cîteaux; para o próprio Cîteaux, um baú para outras ordens, é apenas um desdobramento de Saint-Benoît. Cîteaux data de São Roberto, Abbé de Molesme, na diocese de Langres, em 1098. Ora, foi em 529 que o diabo, tendo-se retirado para o deserto de Subiaco" era velho" tornara-se eremita" foi expulso do antigo templo de Apolo, onde habitava, por Saint-Benoît, então com dezassete anos.

Depois do governo dos carmelitas, que andam descalços, usam um pouco de salgueiro na garganta e nunca se sentam, a regra mais dura é a dos bernardinos-beneditinos de Martinho Verga. Eles estão vestidos de preto, com um guimpe, que, de acordo com a ordem expressa de Saint-Benoît, monta no queixo. Um manto de serge com mangas grandes, um grande véu de lã, o guimpe que se eleva ao queixo cortado quadrado no peito, a faixa que desce sobre a testa até aos olhos, este é o seu vestido. Tudo é preto, exceto a banda, que é branca. Os noviços usam o mesmo hábito, mas todos de branco. As freiras professas também usam um terço ao seu lado.

Os bernardinos-beneditinos de Martinho Verga praticam a Adoração Perpétua, como os beneditinos chamados Damas do Santíssimo Sacramento, que, no início deste século, tinham duas casas em Paris, uma no Templo, outra na Rue Neuve-Sainte-Geneviève. No entanto, as Bernardinas-Beneditinas do Petit-Picpus, de que estamos a falar, eram uma ordem totalmente diferente das Senhoras do Santíssimo Sacramento, enclausuradas na Rue Neuve-Sainte-Geneviève e no Templo. Havia inúmeras diferenças em seu governo; havia alguns em seu traje. Os bernardinos-beneditinos do Petit-Picpus usavam o guime preto, e os beneditinos do Santíssimo Sacramento e da Rue Neuve-Sainte-Geneviève usavam um branco, e tinham, além disso, em seus seios, um Santíssimo Sacramento com cerca de três centímetros de comprimento, em prata dourada ou cobre dourado. As freiras do Petit-Picpus não usavam este Santíssimo Sacramento. A Adoração Perpétua, que era comum à casa do Petit-Picpus e à casa do Templo, deixa essas duas ordens perfeitamente distintas. A sua única semelhança reside nesta prática das Senhoras do Santíssimo Sacramento e das Bernardinas de Martinho Verga, assim como existia uma semelhança no estudo e na glorificação de todos os mistérios relativos à infância, à vida e à morte de Jesus Cristo e da Virgem, entre as duas ordens, que eram: no entanto, amplamente separado e, por vezes, até hostil. O Oratório da Itália, estabelecido em Florença por Philip de Neri, e o Oratório da França, estabelecido por Pierre de Bérulle. O Oratório da França reivindicou a precedência, uma vez que Filipe de Neri era apenas um santo, enquanto Bérulle era um cardeal.

Voltemos ao duro domínio espanhol de Martin Verga.

Os bernardinos-beneditinos desta obediência jejuam durante todo o ano, abstêm-se de carne, jejuam na Quaresma e em muitos outros dias que lhes são peculiares, levantam-se do seu primeiro sono, de uma a três horas da manhã, para ler o seu breviário e cantar matinas, dormem em todas as estações entre lençóis de serge e em palha, não façam uso do banho, nunca acendam uma fogueira, açoitem-se todas as sextas-feiras, observem a regra do silêncio, falem uns com os outros apenas durante as horas de recreação, que são muito breves, e usem chemises durante seis meses no ano, desde 14 de setembro, que é a Exaltação da Santa Cruz, até à Páscoa. Estes seis meses são uma modificação: a regra diz todo o ano, mas esta droga, intolerável no calor do verão, produziu febres e espasmos nervosos. O seu uso teve de ser restringido. Mesmo com esta paliação, quando as freiras colocam esta quimia no dia 14 de setembro, sofrem de febre durante três ou quatro dias. Obediência, pobreza, castidade, perseverança na reclusão, são estes os seus votos, que a regra agrava muito.

A prioresa é eleita por três anos pelas mães, que são chamadas de *mères vocales* porque têm voz no capítulo. Uma prioresa só pode ser reeleita duas vezes, o que fixa o reinado mais longo possível de uma prioresa em nove anos.

Nunca vêem o sacerdote oficiante, que está sempre escondido deles por uma cortina de serge de nove metros de altura. Durante o sermão, quando o pregador está na capela, eles deixam cair o véu sobre o rosto. Devem sempre falar baixo, andar com os olhos no chão e a cabeça baixa. Só é permitida a entrada de um homem no convento: o arcebispo da diocese.

Há realmente um outro, o jardineiro. Mas ele é sempre um homem velho e, para que ele possa estar sempre sozinho no jardim, e para que as freiras possam ser avisadas para evitá-lo, um sino é preso ao seu joelho.

A sua submissão à prioresa é absoluta e passiva. É a sujeição canônica em plena força de sua abnegação. Como à voz de Cristo, *ut voci Christi*, a um gesto, ao primeiro sinal, *ad nutum, ad primum signum*, imediatamente, com alegria, com perseverança, com uma certa obediência cega, *pronta, hilariter, perseveranter et cæca quadam obedientia*, como o arquivo na mão do operário, *quase limam in manibus fabri*, sem poder ler ou escrever sem permissão expressa, *legere vel scribere non addiscerit sine expressa superioris licentia.*

Cada um deles, por sua vez, faz o que chama de *reparação.* A reparação é a oração por todos os pecados, por todas as faltas, por todas as dissensões, por todas as violações, por todas as iniquidades, por todos os crimes cometidos na terra. No espaço de doze horas consecutivas, das quatro da tarde às quatro da manhã, ou das quatro da manhã às quatro da tarde, a irmã que está a reparar permanece de joelhos sobre a pedra diante do Santíssimo Sacramento, com as mãos apertadas, uma corda ao pescoço. Quando o cansaço se torna insuportável, prostra-se de face contra a terra, com os braços estendidos em forma de cruz; este é o seu único alívio. Nesta atitude, ela reza por todos os culpados do universo. Isso é ótimo para a sublimidade.

Como este ato é realizado em frente a um poste no qual queima uma vela, é chamado, sem distinção, *para fazer reparação* ou *para estar no posto.* As freiras até preferem, por humildade, esta última expressão, que contém uma ideia de tortura e humilhação.

Reparar é uma função na qual toda a alma é absorvida. A irmã no posto não se viraria se um raio caísse diretamente atrás dela.

Além disso, há sempre uma irmã ajoelhada diante do Santíssimo Sacramento. Esta estação dura uma hora. Eles aliviam-se uns aos outros como soldados em guarda. Esta é a Adoração Perpétua.

As prioressas e as mães quase sempre ostentam nomes estampados com solenidade peculiar, recordando, não os santos e mártires, mas momentos da vida de Jesus Cristo: como Mãe Natividade, Mãe Conceição, Mãe Apresentação, Mãe Paixão. Mas os nomes dos santos não são interditados.

Quando os vemos, nunca vemos nada além de suas bocas.

Todos os seus dentes são amarelos. Nunca entrou naquela escova de dentes aquele convento. Escovar os dentes está no topo de uma escada em cujo fundo está a perda da alma.

Nunca dizem o *meu.* Não possuem nada de próprio e não devem apegar-se a nada. Chamam tudo de *nosso*, assim: nosso véu, nosso terço, se estivessem falando de sua chemise, diriam *nossa chemise*. Às vezes, eles se apegam a algum objeto mesquinho, a um livro de horas, a uma relíquia, a uma medalha que foi abençoada. Assim que se aperceberem de que estão a ficar cada vez mais apegados a este objeto, devem abandoná-lo. Recordam as palavras de Santa Teresa, a quem uma grande senhora disse, quando estava prestes a entrar na sua ordem: "Permita-me, mãe, enviar uma Bíblia à qual estou muito ligado". "Ah, você está apegado a alguma coisa! Nesse caso, não insira a nossa encomenda"!

Cada pessoa é proibida de se fechar, de ter *um lugar próprio, uma câmara*. Vivem com as células abertas. Quando se encontram, diz-se: "Bendito e adorado seja o Santíssimo Sacramento do altar"! O outro responde: "Para sempre". A mesma cerimónia quando um bate à porta do outro. Mal tocou na porta quando se ouve uma voz suave do outro lado a dizer apressadamente: "Para sempre"! Como todas as práticas, esta torna-se mecânica por força do hábito; e um às vezes diz *para sempre* antes que o outro tenha tido tempo de dizer a frase bastante longa: "Louvado e adorado seja o Santíssimo Sacramento do altar".

Entre os visitandinos, aquele que entra diz: "Ave Maria", e aquele cuja cela está inserida diz: "Gratia plena". É a sua maneira de dizer o bom dia, que é de facto cheio de graça.

A cada hora do dia, três toques suplementares soam do sino da igreja do convento. Neste sinal, prioresas, mães vocais, freiras professas, irmãs leigas, noviças, postulantes, interrompem o que dizem, o que fazem ou o que pensam, e todos dizem em uníssono se forem cinco horas, por exemplo: "Às cinco horas e a todas as horas louvado e adorado seja o Santíssimo Sacramento do altar"! Se são oito horas, "Às oito horas e a todas as horas"! e assim por diante, de acordo com a hora.

Este costume, cujo objetivo é quebrar o fio do pensamento e conduzi-lo constantemente de volta a Deus, existe em muitas comunidades; a fórmula por si só varia. Assim, no Menino Jesus, eles dizem: "A esta hora e a cada hora, o amor de Jesus acenda o meu coração"! Os bernardinos-beneditinos de Martinho Verga, enclausurados, há cinquenta anos em Petit-Picpus, entoam os ofícios com uma salmodia solene, um canto gregoriano puro, e sempre com voz plena durante todo o curso do ofício. Em todos os lugares do missal onde ocorre um asterisco, eles fazem uma pausa e dizem em voz baixa: "Jesus-Marie-Joseph". Para o ofício dos mortos, adotam um tom tão baixo que as vozes das mulheres dificilmente conseguem descer a tal profundidade. O efeito produzido é marcante e trágico.

As freiras do Petit-Picpus tinham feito uma abóbada sob o seu grande altar para o enterro da sua comunidade. *O Governo*, como se costuma dizer, não permite que este cofre receba caixões para que saiam do convento quando morrem. Isso é uma aflição para eles, e causa-lhes consternação como uma violação das regras.

Eles tinham obtido um consolo medíocre, na melhor das hipóteses: permissão para serem enterrados em uma hora especial e em um canto especial no antigo cemitério de Vaugirard, que era feito de terras que anteriormente pertenciam à sua comunidade.

Às sextas-feiras as freiras ouvem missa, vésperas e todos os ofícios, como no domingo. Além disso, observam escrupulosamente todas as pequenas festas desconhecidas dos povos do mundo, das quais a Igreja da França era tão pródiga nos velhos tempos, e das quais ainda é pródiga na Espanha e na Itália. Suas estações na capela são intermináveis. Quanto ao número e à duração de suas orações, não podemos transmitir melhor ideia delas do que citando a ingênua observação de uma delas: "As orações dos postulantes são assustadoras, as orações das noviças ainda são piores e as orações das freiras professas são ainda piores".

Uma vez por semana o capítulo reúne-se: preside a prioresa; as mães vocais assistem. Cada irmã ajoelha-se por sua vez sobre as pedras, e confessa em voz alta, na presença de todos, as faltas e os pecados que cometeu durante a semana. As mães vocais consultam-se após cada confissão e infligem a penitência em voz alta.

Além desta confissão em tom alto, para a qual todas as faltas menos graves são reservadas, eles têm por suas ofensas veniais o que chamam de *coulpe. Fazer o coulpe* significa prostrar-se no rosto durante o escritório em frente à prioresa até que esta, que nunca é chamada de nada além de *nossa mãe*, notifique o culpado com um leve toque do pé contra a madeira de sua barraca que ela pode se levantar. O *coulpe* ou *peccavi*, é feito para uma questão muito pequena – um vidro quebrado, um véu rasgado, um atraso involuntário de alguns segundos em um escritório, uma nota falsa na igreja, etc., isso basta, e o *coulpe* é feito. O *coulpe* é inteiramente espontâneo, é a própria pessoa culpada (a palavra está etimologicamente em seu lugar aqui) que se julga e a inflige a si mesma. Nos dias de festa e aos domingos, quatro mães precentores entoam os escritórios diante de uma grande mesa de leitura com quatro lugares. Um dia, uma das mães precentores entoou um salmo que começava com *Ecce*, e em vez de *Ecce* pronunciou em voz alta as três notas *do si sol*, por este pedaço de distração ela sofreu um *coulpe* que durou durante todo o culto: o que tornou a culpa enorme foi o fato de o capítulo ter rido.

Quando uma freira é convocada para o salão, mesmo que fosse a própria prioresa, ela deixa cair o véu, como será lembrado, para que apenas sua boca seja visível.

Só a prioresa pode manter a comunicação com estranhos. Os outros podem ver apenas a sua família imediata, e isso muito raramente. Se, por acaso, uma forasteira se apresentar para ver uma freira, ou alguém que ela conheceu e amou no mundo exterior, é necessária uma série regular de negociações. Se for uma mulher, a autorização pode, por vezes, ser concedida; A freira vem, e eles falam com ela através das persianas, que são abertas apenas para uma mãe ou irmã. É desnecessário dizer que a permissão é sempre recusada aos homens.

Tal é a regra de Saint-Benoît, agravada por Martin Verga.

Essas freiras não são gays, rosadas e frescas, como as filhas de outras ordens muitas vezes são. São pálidos e graves. Entre 1825 e 1830, três deles enlouqueceram.

CAPÍTULO III

AUSTERIDADES

Um é postulante por dois anos pelo menos, muitas vezes por quatro; um novato para quatro. É raro que os votos definitivos possam ser pronunciados antes dos vinte e três ou vinte e quatro anos de idade. Os bernardinos-beneditinos de Martinho Verga não admitem viúvas à sua ordem.

Nas suas celas, entregam-se a muitas macerações desconhecidas, das quais nunca devem falar.

No dia em que uma noviça faz sua profissão, ela está vestida com seu traje mais bonito, ela é coroada com rosas brancas, seu cabelo é escovado até brilhar, e enrolado. Então ela se prostra; um grande véu negro é jogado sobre ela, e o ofício para os mortos é cantado. Em seguida, as freiras se separam em dois arquivos; um arquivo passa perto dela, dizendo com sotaques: "Nossa irmã está morta"; e o outro arquivo responde em voz de êxtase: "Nossa irmã está viva em Jesus Cristo"!

Na época em que esta história se passa, um internato foi anexado ao convento - um internato para jovens meninas de famílias nobres e principalmente ricas, entre as quais poderiam ser notadas Mademoiselle de Saint-Aulaire e de Bélissen, e uma menina inglesa com o ilustre nome católico de Talbot. Estas jovens, criadas por estas freiras entre quatro paredes, cresceram com horror ao mundo e à época. Um deles disse-nos um dia: "A visão da calçada da rua fez-me estremecer da cabeça aos pés". Vestiam-se de azul, com um boné branco e um Espírito Santo de prata dourada ou de cobre no peito. Em certos dias grandiosos de festa, particularmente no dia de Santa Marta, foi-lhes permitido, como um grande favor e uma felicidade suprema, vestirem-se de freiras e exercerem os ofícios e a prática de Saint-Benoît durante um dia inteiro. Nos primeiros dias, as freiras tinham o hábito de lhes emprestar as suas vestes pretas. Isso parecia profano, e a prioresa proibiu. Apenas os noviços tinham permissão para emprestar. É notável que estas performances, toleradas e incentivadas, sem dúvida, no convento por um espírito secreto de proselitismo e para dar a estas crianças uma prévia do santo hábito, foram uma felicidade genuína e uma verdadeira recreação para os estudiosos. Eles simplesmente se divertiram com isso. *Era novo, deu-lhes uma mudança.* Razões sinceras da infância, que não conseguem, no entanto, fazer com que nós, mundanos, compreendamos a felicidade de segurar um aspersor de água benta na mão e ficar horas juntos cantando duro o suficiente para quatro em frente a uma mesa de leitura.

Os alunos conformavam-se, com exceção das austeridades, a todas as práticas do convento. Houve uma certa jovem que entrou no mundo, e que depois de muitos anos de vida conjugal não conseguiu quebrar-se do hábito de dizer apressadamente sempre que alguém lhe batia à porta: "para sempre"! Tal como as freiras, as alunas só viam os seus familiares no salão. Suas próprias mães não obtiveram permissão para abraçá-los. O que se segue ilustra até que ponto a severidade nesse ponto foi carregada. Um dia, uma jovem recebeu a visita da mãe, que estava acompanhada de uma irmãzinha de três anos de idade. A jovem chorou, pois desejava muito abraçar a irmã. Impossível. Ela implorou que, pelo menos, a criança pudesse passar sua mãozinha pelas grades para que ela pudesse beijá-la. Isso foi quase indignadamente recusado.

CAPÍTULO IV

GAYETIES

No entanto, estas jovens encheram esta casa de sepultura com lembranças encantadoras.

Em certas horas, a infância brilhava naquele claustro. Chegou a hora do recreio. Uma porta balançava em suas dobradiças. Os pássaros disseram: "Bom; aqui vêm as crianças"! Uma irrupção da juventude inundou aquele jardim cruzado com uma cruz como uma mortalha. Rostos radiantes, testas brancas, olhos inocentes, cheios de luz alegre, todos os tipos de auroras, estavam espalhados por entre essas sombras. Depois das salmosdias, dos sinos, das ervilhas, dos anéis e dos escritórios, o som dessas meninas irrompeu de repente mais docemente do que o barulho das abelhas. Abriu-se a colmeia da alegria e cada um trouxe o seu mel. Brincavam, chamavam-se uns aos outros, formavam-se em grupos, corriam; pequenos dentes brancos tagarelando nos cantos; os véus sobrepunham-se às gargalhadas à distância, as sombras vigiavam os raios de sol, mas o que importava? Ainda assim, eles sorriram e riram. Aquelas quatro paredes lúgubres tiveram o seu momento de brilho deslumbrante. Eles olhavam, vagamente branqueados com o reflexo de tanta alegria com aquele doce enxame de colmeias. Foi como uma chuva de rosas caindo sobre esta casa de luto. As jovens brincavam sob os olhos das freiras; O olhar da impecabilidade não envergonha a inocência. Graças a estas crianças, houve, entre tantas horas austeras, uma hora de ingenuidade. Os mais pequenos saltavam; os mais velhos dançavam. Neste claustro o jogo misturava-se com o céu. Nada é tão delicioso e tão augusto quanto todas essas almas jovens frescas e em expansão. Homero teria vindo rir com Perrault; e havia naquele jardim negro, a juventude, a saúde, o ruído, os gritos, a vertigem, o prazer, a felicidade suficiente para suavizar as rugas de todos os seus antepassados, os da epopeia e os do conto de fadas, os do trono, bem como os da cabana de palha de Hécuba a la Mère-Grand.

Naquela casa, mais do que em qualquer outro lugar, talvez surjam aqueles ditos infantis tão graciosos e que evocam um sorriso cheio de reflexão. Foi entre aquelas quatro paredes sombrias que uma criança de cinco anos exclamou um dia: "Mãe! uma das grandes raparigas acaba de me dizer que tenho apenas mais nove anos e dez meses para ficar aqui. Que felicidade"!

Foi também aqui que teve lugar este memorável diálogo:

Uma mãe vocal. Por que você está chorando, meu filho?

A criança (seis anos). Eu disse a Alix que conhecia minha história francesa. Ela diz que eu não sei, mas eu sei.

Alix, a menina grande (nove anos). Não; ela não sabe.

A Mãe. Como é isso, meu filho?

Alix. Ela disse-me para abrir o livro aleatoriamente e fazer-lhe qualquer pergunta no livro, e ela responderia.

"Bem"?

"Ela não respondeu".

"Vamos ver sobre isso. O que você perguntou a ela"?

"Abri o livro aleatoriamente, como ela propôs, e coloquei a primeira pergunta com que me deparei".

"E qual era a questão"?

"Foi: 'O que aconteceu depois disso?'"

Foi aí que essa profunda observação foi feita num paroquete bastante ganancioso que pertencia a uma senhora pensionista:

"Que bem criado! come o topo da fatia de pão com manteiga como uma pessoa"!

Foi numa das lajes deste claustro que uma vez se apanhou uma confissão que fora escrita antecipadamente, para que ela não a esquecesse, por um pecador de sete anos:

"Pai, acuso-me de ter sido avarento.

"Pai, acuso-me de ter sido adúltera.

"Pai, acuso-me de ter levantado os olhos para os senhores".

Foi num dos bancos de relva deste jardim que uma boca rosada de seis anos de idade improvisou o seguinte conto, que foi ouvido pelos olhos azuis de quatro e cinco anos:

"Havia três galinhos que possuíam um país onde havia muitas flores. Arrancaram as flores e colocaram-nas nos bolsos. Depois disso, arrancaram as folhas e colocaram-nas nos seus brinquedos. Havia um lobo naquele país; havia muita floresta; e o lobo estava na floresta; e comeu os galinhos".

E este outro poema:—

"Veio um golpe com um pau.

"Foi Punchinello quem deu ao gato.

"Não foi bom para ela; magoou-a.

"Então uma senhora colocou Punchinello na prisão".

Foi lá que uma criança abandonada, fundadora que o convento criava por caridade, proferiu este doce e dilacerante ditado. Ela ouviu os outros falando de suas mães, e murmurou em seu canto: —

"Quanto a mim, a minha mãe não estava lá quando eu nasci"!

Havia uma porteira robusta que sempre podia ser vista correndo pelos corredores com seu monte de chaves, e cujo nome era Irmã Agatha. As *grandes garotas* – aquelas com mais de dez anos de idade – chamavam-lhe *Agathocles*.

O refeitório, um grande apartamento de forma quadrada oblonga, que não recebia luz a não ser através de um claustro abobadado ao nível do jardim, era escuro e úmido e, como dizem as crianças, cheio de feras. Todos os lugares ao redor mobiliaram seu contingente de insetos.

Cada um dos seus quatro cantos recebera, na língua dos alunos, um nome especial e expressivo. Havia o canto da aranha, o canto da lagarta, o canto do piolho de madeira e o canto do grilo.

Cricket canto foi perto da cozinha e foi altamente estimado. Não estava tão frio lá como em outros lugares. Do refeitório os nomes tinham passado

244

para o internato-escola, e lá serviu como no antigo Colégio Mazarin para distinguir quatro nações. Cada aluna pertencia a uma dessas quatro nações, segundo o canto do refeitório em que se sentava às refeições. Um dia, Monsenhor Arcebispo, ao fazer sua visita pastoral, viu uma linda menina rosada de lindos cabelos dourados entrar na sala de aula por onde ele estava passando.

Perguntou a outro aluno, uma morena encantadora de bochechas rosadas, que estava perto dele:

"Quem é isso"?

"Ela é uma aranha, Monseigneur".

"Bah! E esse yonder"?

"Ela é um grilo".

"E aquele"?

"Ela é uma lagarta".

"Sério! e você mesmo"?

"Eu sou um piolho de madeira, Monseigneur".

Cada casa deste tipo tem as suas peculiaridades. No início deste século, Écouen era um daqueles lugares rigorosos e graciosos onde as jovens passam a infância numa sombra que é quase augusta. Em Écouen, para tomar posição na procissão do Santíssimo Sacramento, foi feita uma distinção entre virgens e floristas. Havia também os "dais" e os "censores" – os primeiros que seguravam as cordas dos dais, e os outros que carregavam incenso diante do Santíssimo Sacramento. As flores pertenciam por direito às floristas. Quatro "virgens" caminharam com antecedência. Na manhã daquele grande dia, não era raro ouvir a pergunta feita no dormitório: "Quem é virgem"?

Madame Campan costumava citar este ditado de uma "pequena" de sete anos, a uma "menina grande" de dezesseis anos, que tomava a cabeça da procissão, enquanto ela, a pequena, permanecia na retaguarda: "Você é virgem, mas eu não sou".

CAPÍTULO V

DISTRAÇÕES

Acima da porta do refeitório, esta oração, que era chamada de *Paternoster branco*, e que possuía a propriedade de levar as pessoas diretamente ao paraíso, estava inscrita em grandes letras pretas:

"Pequeno Paternoster branco, que Deus fez, que Deus disse, que Deus colocou no paraíso. À noite, quando fui para a cama, encontrei três anjos sentados na minha cama, um ao pé, dois à cabeça, a boa Virgem Maria no meio, que me disse para me deitar sem hesitar. O bom Deus é meu pai, a boa Virgem é minha mãe, os três apóstolos são meus irmãos, as três virgens são minhas irmãs. A camisa em que Deus nasceu envolve meu corpo; A cruz de Santa Margarida está escrita no meu peito. Madame a Virgem caminhava pelos prados, chorando por Deus, quando conheceu M. São João. «Monsieur Saint John, de onde vem?» "Venho da *Ave Salus*". "Não viste o bom Deus; onde ele está?' "Ele está na árvore da cruz, com os pés pendurados, as mãos pregadas, um barrete de espinhos brancos na cabeça". Quem disser isto três vezes na eventide, três vezes pela manhã, ganhará o paraíso na última".

Em 1827, este orixá característico tinha desaparecido da parede sob um revestimento triplo de tinta dupla. Neste momento, está finalmente a desaparecer das memórias de várias que eram raparigas na altura e que agora são mulheres idosas.

Um grande crucifixo preso à parede completou a decoração deste refeitório, cuja única porta, como pensamos ter mencionado, se abriu no jardim. Duas mesas estreitas, cada uma ladeada por dois bancos de madeira, formavam duas longas linhas paralelas de uma extremidade à outra do refeitório. As paredes eram brancas, as mesas eram pretas; Estas duas cores de luto constituem a única variedade nos conventos. As refeições eram simples, e a comida das próprias crianças severa. Um único prato de carne e legumes combinados, ou peixe salgado – tal era o seu luxo. Esta escassa tarifa, reservada apenas aos alunos, era, no entanto, uma exceção. As crianças comiam em silêncio, sob o olhar da mãe de quem era a vez, que, se uma mosca levava uma noção para voar ou para cantarolar contra a regra, abria e fechava um livro de madeira de vez em quando. Este silêncio foi temperado com a vida dos santos, lido em voz alta de um pequeno púlpito com uma mesa, que estava situada ao pé do crucifixo. A leitora era uma das grandes raparigas, por sua vez, semanalmente. A distâncias regulares, sobre as mesas nuas, havia grandes tigelas envernizadas nas quais os alunos lavavam seus próprios copos de prata, facas e garfos, e nas quais às vezes jogavam algum pedaço de carne dura ou peixe estragado; isso foi punido. Estas tigelas eram chamadas *ronds d'eau*. A criança que quebrou o silêncio "fez uma cruz com a língua". Onde? No chão. Ela lambeu a calçada. O pó, esse fim de todas as alegrias, foi encarregado do castigo daquelas pobres folhas de rosa que tinham sido culpadas de chilrear.

Havia no convento um livro que nunca foi impresso a não ser como uma *cópia única*, e que é proibido ler. É a regra de Saint-Benoît. Um arcano que nenhum olho profano deve penetrar. *Nemo regulas, seu constitutiones nostras, externis communicabit.*

Os alunos um dia conseguiram apoderar-se deste livro, e começaram a lê-lo com avidez, uma leitura muitas vezes interrompida pelo medo de serem apanhados, o que os levou a fechar o volume precipitadamente.

Do grande perigo assim incorrido, derivaram apenas uma quantidade muito moderada de prazer. A coisa mais "interessante" que encontraram foram algumas páginas ininteligíveis sobre os pecados dos rapazes.

Brincavam num beco do jardim delimitado por algumas árvores frutíferas gastas. Apesar da extrema vigilância e da severidade dos castigos aplicados, quando o vento sacudia as árvores, por vezes conseguiam apanhar uma maçã verde ou um damasco estragado ou uma pera habitada às escondidas. Vou agora ceder o privilégio da fala a uma carta que está diante de mim, uma carta escrita há cinco e vinte anos por uma antiga aluna, agora Madame la Duchesse de ——, uma das mulheres mais elegantes de Paris. Passo a citar literalmente: "Esconde-se a pera ou a maçã da melhor forma possível. Quando se sobe as escadas para colocar o véu na cama antes do jantar, enfia-se debaixo do travesseiro e à noite come-se na cama e, quando não se pode fazer isso, come-se no armário". Esse era um dos seus maiores luxos.

Certa vez, na época da visita do arcebispo ao convento, uma das jovens, Mademoiselle Bouchard, ligada à família Montmorency, apostou que pediria um dia de licença – uma enormidade em uma comunidade tão austera. A aposta foi aceite, mas nenhum dos que apostou acreditou que o faria. Quando chegou o momento, quando o arcebispo passava na frente dos alunos, Mademoiselle Bouchard, para o terror indescritível de seus companheiros, saiu das fileiras e disse: "Monseigneur, um dia de licença". Mademoiselle Bouchard era alta, florida, com o rostinho mais bonito do mundo. M. de Quélen sorriu e disse: "O que, meu querido filho, um dia de licença! Três dias, se quiser. Concedo-lhe três dias". A prioresa nada podia fazer; O arcebispo falara. Horror do convento, mas alegria do aluno. O efeito pode ser imaginado.

No entanto, este claustro severo não estava tão bem murado, mas a vida das paixões do mundo exterior, o drama e até o romance, não entravam. Para o provar, limitar-nos-emos a registar aqui e a mencionar brevemente um facto real e incontestável, que, no entanto, não tem qualquer referência em si mesmo, e não está ligado por qualquer fio à história que estamos a relatar. Mencionamos o fato para completar a fisionomia do convento na mente do leitor.

Por esta altura havia no convento uma pessoa misteriosa que não era freira, que era tratada com grande respeito, e que era tratada como *Madame Albertine*. Nada se sabia sobre ela, exceto que ela estava louca, e que no mundo ela passou por morta. Por baixo desta história dizia-se que havia os arranjos de fortuna necessários para um grande casamento.

Esta mulher, de quase trinta anos de idade, de tez escura e toleravelmente bonita, tinha um olhar vago em seus grandes olhos negros. Será que ela conseguia ver? Havia alguma dúvida a este respeito. Ela deslizava em vez de andar, nunca falava; não se sabia bem se ela respirava. Suas narinas estavam lívidas e apertadas como depois de ceder seu último suspiro. Tocar a mão dela era como tocar na neve. Ela possuía uma estranha graça espectral. Onde quer que ela entrasse, as pessoas sentiam frio. Um dia, uma irmã, ao vê-la passar, disse a outra irmã: "Ela passa por uma mulher morta". "Talvez ela seja uma", respondeu o outro.

Cem contos foram contados sobre Madame Albertine. Isso surgiu da eterna curiosidade dos alunos. Na capela havia uma galeria chamada *L'Œil de Bœuf.* Era nesta galeria, que tinha apenas uma baía circular, um *œil de bœuf,* que Madame Albertine ouvia os escritórios. Ocupou-a sempre sozinha porque esta galeria, estando ao nível do primeiro conto, podia ver-se o pregador ou o padre oficiante, que era interditado às freiras. Um dia, o púlpito foi ocupado por um jovem sacerdote de alta patente, M. Le Duc de Rohan, par da França, oficial dos Mosqueteiros Vermelhos em 1815, quando era príncipe de Léon, e que morreu depois, em 1830, como cardeal e arcebispo de Besançon. Foi a primeira vez que M. de Rohan pregou no convento de Petit-Picpus. Madame Albertine geralmente preservou perfeita calma e completa imobilidade durante os sermões e cultos. Naquele dia, assim que avistou M. de Rohan, levantou-se e disse, em voz alta, em meio ao silêncio da capela: "Ah! Augusto"! Toda a comunidade virou a cabeça de espanto, o pregador levantou os olhos, mas Madame Albertine tinha recaído na sua imobilidade. Um sopro do mundo exterior, um lampejo de vida, passara por um instante naquele rosto frio e sem vida e depois desaparecera, e a louca tornara-se um cadáver novamente.

Essas duas palavras, no entanto, haviam colocado todos no convento que tinham o privilégio de falar para tagarelar. Quantas coisas estavam contidas naquele "Ah! Auguste"! que revelações! O nome de M. de Rohan era mesmo Auguste. Era evidente que Madame Albertine pertencia à mais alta sociedade, uma vez que conhecia M. de Rohan, e que a sua própria posição ali era da mais alta, uma vez que ela falava assim familiarmente de um grande senhor, e que existia entre eles alguma ligação, de relacionamento, talvez, mas muito próximo em qualquer caso, já que ela sabia seu "nome de estimação".

Duas duquesas muito severas, Mesdames de Choiseul e de Sérent, visitavam frequentemente a comunidade, onde penetravam, sem dúvida, em virtude do privilégio *Magnates mulieres,* e causavam grande consternação no internato. Quando estas duas velhinhas passaram, todas as pobres jovens tremeram e deixaram cair os olhos.

Além disso, M. de Rohan, bastante desconhecido para si mesmo, era um objeto de atenção para as alunas. Nessa época acabara de ser feito, enquanto aguardava o episcopado, vigário-geral do arcebispo de Paris. Era um dos seus hábitos vir com frequência para celebrar os ofícios na capela das freiras do Petit-Picpus. Nenhum dos jovens reclusos podia vê-lo, por causa da cortina de serge, mas ele tinha uma voz doce e bastante estridente, que eles tinham vindo a conhecer e distinguir. Ele tinha sido um mousquetaire, e então, dizia-se que ele era muito coquettish, que seu belo cabelo castanho estava muito bem vestido em um rolo em torno de sua cabeça, e que ele tinha uma cintura larga de moire magnífico, e que sua batina preta era do corte mais elegante do mundo. Ele ocupou um grande lugar em todas essas imaginações de dezesseis anos.

Nem um som de fora entrou no convento. Mas houve um ano em que o som de uma flauta penetrou. Este foi um acontecimento, e as raparigas que lá estavam na escola na altura ainda se lembram dele.

Era uma flauta que se tocava no bairro. Esta flauta tocava sempre o mesmo ar, um ar que hoje está muito longe – "Meu Zétulbé, vem reinar a minha alma" – e ouvia-se duas ou três vezes por dia. As jovens passavam horas a ouvi-lo, as mães vocais ficavam chateadas com isso, os cérebros estavam ocupados, os castigos desciam nos chuveiros. Isso durou vários meses. As meninas estavam todas mais ou menos apaixonadas pelo músico desconhecido. Cada um sonhava que era Zétulbé. O som da flauta procedeu da direção da Rue Droit-Mur; e teriam dado qualquer coisa, comprometido tudo, tentado qualquer coisa para ver, para dar uma olhada, nem que seja por um segundo, ao "jovem" que tocava aquela flauta tão deliciosamente, e que, sem dúvida, tocava em todas essas almas ao mesmo tempo. Houve alguns que conseguiram escapar por uma porta dos fundos, e subiram para o terceiro andar do lado da Rue Droit-Mur, a fim de tentar vislumbrar através das lacunas. Impossível! Uma chegou ao ponto de empurrar o braço através da grade e acenar com o lenço branco. Dois foram ainda mais ousados. Eles encontraram meios de subir em um telhado, e arriscaram suas vidas lá, e conseguiram finalmente ver "o jovem".

Era um velho *senhor emigrado*, cego e sem dinheiro, que tocava flauta no sótão, para passar o tempo.

CAPÍTULO VI

O PEQUENO CONVENTO

Neste recinto do Petit-Picpus existiam três edifícios perfeitamente distintos: o Grande Convento, habitado pelas freiras, o Internato, onde estavam alojados os eruditos; e, por último, o que se chamava Pequeno Convento. Era um edifício com jardim, no qual viviam todo o tipo de freiras envelhecidas de várias ordens, as relíquias de claustros destruídos na Revolução; uma reunião de todos os medleys pretos, cinzentos e brancos de todas as comunidades e todas as variedades possíveis; o que se poderia chamar, se tal acoplamento de palavras é permitido, uma espécie de convento arlequim.

Quando o Império foi estabelecido, todas essas pobres mulheres idosas dispersas e exiladas receberam permissão para vir e se abrigar sob as asas dos bernardinos-beneditinos. O governo pagou-lhes uma pequena pensão, as senhoras do Petit-Picpus receberam-nas cordialmente. Era um pell-mell singular. Cada um seguiu a sua própria regra. Por vezes, os alunos do internato eram autorizados, como grande recreação, a visitar-lhes; o resultado é que todas essas memórias jovens guardaram, entre outras lembranças, as de Madre Sainte-Bazile, Madre Sainte-Scolastique e Madre Jacó.

Uma dessas refugiadas viu-se quase em casa. Ela era uma freira de Sainte-Aure, a única de sua ordem que havia sobrevivido. O antigo convento das senhoras de Sainte-Aure ocupou, no início do século XVIII, esta mesma casa do Petit-Picpus, que pertenceu mais tarde aos beneditinos de Martinho Verga. Esta santa mulher, pobre demais para usar o magnífico hábito de sua ordem, que era um manto branco com uma escápula escarlate, tinha piamente colocado um pequeno manequim, que ela exibiu com complacência e que ela legou à casa quando de sua morte. Em 1824, restava apenas uma freira desta ordem; hoje, resta apenas uma boneca.

Além destas dignas mães, algumas mulheres da velha sociedade tinham obtido permissão da prioresa, como Madame Albertine, para se retirarem para o Pequeno Convento. Entre o número estavam Madame Beaufort d'Hautpoul e Marquise Dufresne. Outra nunca foi conhecida no convento, exceto pelo barulho formidável que ela fazia quando assoava o nariz. Os alunos chamavam-lhe Madame Vacarmini (burburinho).

Por volta de 1820 ou 1821, Madame de Genlis, que na época editava uma pequena publicação periódica chamada *l'Intrépide*, pediu para ser autorizada a entrar no convento do Petit-Picpus como senhora residente. O Duque de Orleães recomendou-a. Alvoroço na colmeia; as mães-vocais estavam todas agitadas; Madame de Genlis tinha feito romances. Mas ela declarou que ela era a primeira a detestá-los, e então, ela tinha chegado ao seu feroz estágio de devoção. Com a ajuda de Deus e do Príncipe, ela entrou. Partiu ao fim de seis ou oito meses, alegando como razão que não havia sombra no jardim. As freiras ficaram encantadas. Apesar de muito velha, ainda tocava harpa, e fazia-o muito bem.

Quando foi embora, deixou a sua marca na cela. Madame de Genlis era supersticiosa e latinista. Estas duas palavras fornecem um perfil toleravelmente bom dela. Há alguns anos, ainda havia para ver, colados no interior de um pequeno armário da sua cela em que trancava os seus talheres e as suas joias, estas cinco linhas em latim, escritas com a sua própria mão em tinta vermelha sobre papel amarelo, e que, na sua opinião, possuíam a propriedade de assustar os ladrões:

> Imparibus meritis pendent tria corpora ramis:Dismas et
> Gesmas, media est divina potestas; Alta petit Dismas,
> infelix, infima, Gesmas; Nos et res nostras conservet
> summa potestas. Hos versus dicas, ne tu furto tua perdas.

Estes versos em latim do século VI levantam a questão se os dois ladrões do Calvário foram nomeados, como é comumente acreditado, Dismas e Gestas, ou Dismas e Gesmas. Esta ortografia pode ter confundido as pretensões apresentadas no século passado pelo Vicomte de Gestas, de uma descendência do ladrão perverso. No entanto, a virtude útil ligada a esses versículos forma uma regra de fé na ordem dos Hospitalários.

A igreja da casa, construída de modo a separar o Grande Convento do Internato como uma verdadeira trincheira, era, naturalmente, comum ao Internato, ao Grande Convento e ao Pequeno Convento. O público chegou a ser admitido por uma espécie de lazaretto de entrada na rua. Mas tudo estava tão organizado, que nenhum dos habitantes do claustro podia ver um rosto do mundo exterior. Suponhamos uma igreja cujo coro é agarrado numa mão gigantesca, e dobrado de modo a formar, não como nas igrejas comuns, um prolongamento atrás do altar, mas uma espécie de salão, ou adega obscura, à direita do sacerdote oficiante; suponhamos que este salão esteja fechado por uma cortina de sete metros de altura, da qual já falámos; à sombra dessa cortina, amontoe-se em barracas de madeira as freiras no coro à esquerda, as alunas à direita, as irmãs leigas e as noviças na parte inferior, e você terá alguma ideia das freiras do Petit-Picpus ajudando no serviço divino. Aquela caverna, que se chamava coro, comunicava com o claustro por um átrio. A igreja foi iluminada do jardim. Quando as freiras estavam presentes nos cultos onde seu governo exigia silêncio, o público era avisado de sua presença apenas pelos assentos dobráveis das barracas subindo e descendo ruidosamente.

CAPÍTULO VII

ALGUMAS SILHUETAS DESTA ESCURIDÃO

Durante os seis anos que separaram 1819 de 1825, a prioresa do Petit-Picpus foi Mademoiselle de Blemeur, cujo nome, na religião, era Madre Inocente. Ela veio da família de Marguerite de Blemeur, autora de *Lives of the Saints of the Order of Saint-Benoît*. Tinha sido reeleita. Era uma mulher com cerca de sessenta anos de idade, baixa, grossa, "cantando como uma panela rachada", diz a carta que já citamos; uma excelente mulher, aliás, e a única alegre em todo o convento, e por isso adorada. Ela era culta, erudita, sábia, competente, curiosamente proficiente em história, abarrotada de latim, recheada de grego, cheia de hebraico, e mais monge beneditino do que freira beneditina.

A subprioresa era uma velha freira espanhola, Madre Cineres, que era quase cega.

As mais estimadas entre as mães vocais foram Madre Sainte-Honorine; a tesoureira, Madre Sainte-Gertrude, a principal amante das noviças; Mãe-Saint-Ange, a amante assistente; Mãe Anonciação, o sacristão; Madre Saint-Augustin, a enfermeira, a única no convento que era maliciosa; depois Madre Sainte-Mechtilde (Mademoiselle Gauvain), muito jovem e com uma bela voz; Madre des Anges (Mademoiselle Drouet), que tinha estado no convento dos Filles-Dieu, e no convento du Trésor, entre Gisors e Magny; Madre São José (Mademoiselle de Cogolludo), Madre Sainte-Adélaide (Mademoiselle d'Auverney), Madre Miséricorde (Mademoiselle de Cifuentes, que não resistiu às austeridades), Madre Compaixão (Mademoiselle de la Miltière, recebida aos sessenta anos desafiando a regra, e muito rica); Madre Providência (Mademoiselle de Laudinière), Madre

Présentation (Mademoiselle de Siguenza), que foi prioresa em 1847; e, finalmente, Madre Sainte-Céligne (irmã do escultor Ceracchi), que enlouqueceu; Madre Sainte-Chantal (Mademoiselle de Suzon), que enlouqueceu.

Havia também, entre os mais bonitos, uma menina encantadora de três e vinte anos, que era da Ilha de Bourbon, descendente do Chevalier Roze, cujo nome tinha sido Mademoiselle Roze, e que se chamava Madre Assunção.

Madre Sainte-Mechtilde, encarregada do canto e do coro, gostava de fazer uso dos alunos deste bairro. Ela geralmente pegava uma escala completa deles, ou seja, sete, dos dez aos dezesseis anos de idade, inclusive, de vozes e tamanhos variados, que ela fazia cantar em pé, desenhados em uma linha, lado a lado, de acordo com a idade, do menor ao maior. Isto apresentava aos olhos, algo na natureza de um caniço de raparigas, uma espécie de Pan-pipe vivo feito de anjos.

As das irmãs leigas que os estudiosos mais amavam eram a Irmã Euphrasie, a Irmã Sainte-Marguérite, a Irmã Sainte-Marthe, que estava em seu pontilhado, e a Irmã Sainte-Michel, cujo nariz comprido as fazia rir.

Todas essas mulheres eram gentis com as crianças. As freiras eram severas apenas consigo mesmas. Nenhum fogo foi aceso, exceto na escola, e a comida foi escolhida em comparação com a do convento. Além disso, esbanjavam mil cuidados com seus estudiosos. Só que, quando uma criança passava perto de uma freira e se dirigia a ela, a freira nunca respondia.

Esta regra do silêncio tinha tido este efeito, que em todo o convento, a fala tinha sido retirada das criaturas humanas, e conferida a objetos inanimados. Agora era o sino da igreja que falava, agora era o sino do jardineiro. Um sino muito sonoro, colocado ao lado da porteira, e que era audível por toda a casa, indicado pelas suas variadas ervilhas, que formavam uma espécie de telégrafo acústico, todas as ações da vida material que deviam ser realizadas, e convocado para o salão, em caso de necessidade, tal ou tal habitante da casa. Cada pessoa e cada coisa tinha a sua própria ervilha. A prioresa tinha uma e uma, a subprioresa uma e duas. Seis-cinco anunciavam aulas, de modo que os alunos nunca diziam "para ir às aulas", mas "para ir às seis-cinco". Quatro e quatro foi o sinal de Madame de Genlis. Ouviu-se com muita frequência. "C'est le diable a quatre"", é o próprio deuce" dizia o caridoso. Tennine strokes anunciou um grande evento. Era a abertura da *porta da reclusão*, uma assustadora folha de ferro eriçada com parafusos que só se ligava nas dobradiças na presença do arcebispo.

Com exceção do arcebispo e do jardineiro, nenhum homem entrou no convento, como já dissemos. As alunas viram outras duas: uma, o capelão, o Abbé Banés, velho e feio, que lhes foi permitido contemplar no coro, através de um gradil; o outro, o mestre de desenho, M. Ansiaux, a quem a carta, da qual folheamos algumas linhas, chama *M. Anciot*, e descreve como *um velho corcunda assustador.*

Veremos que todos estes homens foram cuidadosamente escolhidos.

Tal era esta curiosa casa.

CAPÍTULO VIII

PÓS LAPIDES DE CORDA

Depois de esboçar a sua face moral, não será inútil apontar, em poucas palavras, a sua configuração material. O leitor já tem alguma ideia disso.

O convento do Petit-Picpus-Sainte-Antoine encheu quase todo o vasto trapézio que resultou do cruzamento da Rue Polonceau, da Rue Droit-Mur, da Rue Petit-Picpus e da pista não utilizada, chamada Rue Aumarais em planos antigos. Estas quatro ruas rodeavam este trapézio como um fosso. O convento era composto por vários edifícios e um jardim. O edifício principal, tomado na sua totalidade, era uma justaposição de construções híbridas que, vistas de uma vista panorâmica, delineavam, com considerável exatidão, um gibbet deitado no chão. O braço principal do gibbet ocupava todo o fragmento da Rue Droit-Mur compreendido entre a Rue Petit-Picpus e a Rue Polonceau; o braço menor era uma fachada alta, cinzenta e severa ralada que dava para a Rue Petit-Picpus; a entrada da carruagem n.º 62 marcava a sua extremidade. No centro desta fachada havia uma porta baixa, arqueada, branqueada de pó e cinzas, onde as aranhas teciam as suas teias, e que ficava aberta apenas durante uma ou duas horas aos domingos, e em raras ocasiões, quando o caixão de uma freira saía do convento. Esta era a entrada pública da igreja. O cotovelo da gibbet era um salão quadrado que era usado como salão dos criados, e que as freiras chamavam de *amanteigado*. No braço principal estavam as celas das mães, das irmãs e das noviças. No braço menor estavam as cozinhas, o refeitório, apoiado pelos claustros e pela igreja. Entre a porta nº 62 e a esquina da fechada Aumarais Lane, estava a escola, que não era visível de fora. O restante do trapézio formava o jardim, que era muito mais baixo do que o nível da Rue Polonceau, o que fazia com que as paredes fossem muito mais altas no interior do que no exterior. O jardim, ligeiramente arqueado, tinha no centro, no cume de uma colina, um fino abeto pontiagudo e cónico, de onde corriam, a partir do patrão de um escudo, quatro ruelas grandiosas, e, entre as ramificações destas, oito ruelas pequenas, de modo que, se o recinto fosse circular, a planta geométrica das ruelas assemelhar-se-ia a uma cruz sobreposta numa roda. Como as vielas terminavam todas nas paredes muito irregulares do jardim, tinham um comprimento desigual. Eles eram cercados por arbustos de groselha. No fundo, um beco de altos choupos corria das ruínas do antigo convento, que ficava no ângulo da Rue Droit-Mur até a casa do Pequeno Convento, que ficava no ângulo da Aumarais Lane. Em frente ao Pequeno Convento ficava o que se chamava o pequeno jardim. A este conjunto, acrescente ao leitor um pátio, de todos os tipos de ângulos variados formados pelos edifícios interiores, pelas paredes da prisão, pela longa linha negra de telhados que margeava o outro lado da Rue Polonceau pela sua única perspetiva e bairro, e ele será capaz de formar para si mesmo uma imagem completa do que era a casa dos Bernardinos do Petit-Picpus há quarenta anos. Esta casa santa tinha sido construída no local preciso de um famoso campo de ténis do século XIV ao XVI, que foi chamado de "campo de ténis dos onze mil diabos".

Todas essas ruas, aliás, eram mais antigas do que Paris. Estes nomes, Droit-Mur e Aumarais, são muito antigos; as ruas que os ostentam são muito mais antigas ainda. Aumarais Lane chamava-se Maugout Lane; a Rue Droit-Mur era chamada de Rue des Églantiers, pois Deus abriu flores antes que o homem cortasse pedras.

CAPÍTULO IX

UM SÉCULO SOB UM GUIMPE

Uma vez que estamos empenhados em dar pormenores sobre o que era o convento do Petit-Picpus em tempos passados, e já que nos aventurámos a abrir uma janela sobre esse retiro discreto, o leitor permitir-nos-á mais uma pequena digressão, totalmente estranha a este livro, mas característica e útil, pois mostra que o claustro até tem as suas figuras originais.

No Pequeno Convento havia um centenário que vinha da Abadia de Fontevrault. Ela até já estava na sociedade antes da Revolução. Falava muito de M. de Miromesnil, Guardião dos Selos sob Luís XVI. e de uma Presidentess Duplat, com quem tinha sido muito íntima. Era seu prazer e sua vaidade arrastar esses nomes sob todos os pretextos. Ela contou maravilhas da Abadia de Fontevrault, que era como uma cidade, e que havia ruas no mosteiro.

Ela falava com um sotaque de Picard que divertia os alunos. Todos os anos, ela renovava solenemente os seus votos e, no momento do juramento, dizia ao sacerdote: "Monseigneur Saint-François deu-o a Monseigneur Saint-Julien, Monseigneur Saint-Julien deu-o a Monseigneur Saint-Eusebius, Monseigneur Saint-Eusebius deu-o a Monseigneur Saint-Procopius, etc., etc., e assim o dou, pai". E as alunas começavam a rir, não nas mangas, mas debaixo do véu; pequenas risadas sufocadas encantadoras que fizeram as mães vocais franzirem a testa.

Noutra ocasião, o centenário contava histórias. Ela disse que, *em sua juventude, os monges bernardinos eram tão bons quanto os mousquetários.* Era um século que falava através dela, mas era o século XVIII. Ela contou sobre o costume dos quatro vinhos, que existia antes da Revolução em Champagne e Borgonha. Quando um grande personagem, um marechal da França, um príncipe, um duque e um par, atravessaram uma cidade na

Borgonha ou em Champagne, os pais da cidade saíram para arengá-lo e presentearam-no com quatro gôndolas de prata nas quais haviam derramado quatro tipos diferentes de vinho. No primeiro cálice podia ler-se esta inscrição, *vinho de macaco*, no segundo, *vinho de leão*, no terceiro, *vinho de ovelha*, no quarto, *vinho de porco*. Estas quatro lendas expressam os quatro estágios descendentes pelo bêbado; o primeiro, a intoxicação, que anima; o segundo, o que irrita; a terceira, a que embota; e o quarto, o que brutaliza.

Num armário, a sete chaves, guardava um objeto misterioso do qual pensava muito. O governo de Fontevrault não proibia isso. Ela não mostraria esse objeto a ninguém. Calou-se, o que a sua regra lhe permitia fazer, e escondeu-se, sempre que quisesse contemplá-lo. Se ouvisse um passo no corredor, fechava o armário novamente o mais apressadamente possível com as mãos envelhecidas. Assim que lhe foi mencionado, calou-se, ela que tanto gostava de falar. Os mais curiosos ficaram perplexos com o seu silêncio e os mais tenazes com a sua obstinação. Assim, forneceu um assunto de comentário para todos aqueles que estavam desocupados ou entediados no convento. Que tesouro do centenário poderia ser, tão precioso e tão secreto? Algum livro sagrado, sem dúvida? Algum terço único? Alguma relíquia autêntica? Perdiam-se em conjeturas. Quando a pobre velhinha morreu, correram para o armário dela mais apressadamente do que caberia, talvez, e abriram-no. Eles encontraram o objeto sob um pano de linho triplo, como um pato consagrado. Era um prato de Faenza representando os pequenos Amores fugindo perseguidos por rapazes boticários armados com enormes seringas. A perseguição abunda em caretas e em posturas cómicas. Um dos pequenos amores encantadores já está bastante cuspido. Ele está resistindo, batendo suas asas minúsculas e ainda fazendo um esforço para voar, mas o dançarino está rindo com um ar satânico. Moral: Amor vencido pela cólica. Este prato, que é muito curioso, e que teve, possivelmente, a honra de dotar Molière de uma ideia, ainda existia em setembro de 1845; estava à venda por um comerciante de bric-à-brac no Boulevard Beaumarchais.

Esta boa velhinha não receberia visitas de fora *porque*, disse ela, o *salão é muito sombrio*.

CAPÍTULO X

ORIGEM DA ADORAÇÃO PERPÉTUA

No entanto, este salão quase sepulcral, do qual procurámos transmitir uma ideia, é um traço puramente local que não é reproduzido com a mesma severidade noutros conventos. No convento da Rue du Temple, em particular, que pertencia, na verdade, a outra ordem, as persianas pretas foram substituídas por cortinas castanhas, e o salão em si era um salão com um piso de madeira polida, cujas janelas estavam cobertas por cortinas de musselina branca e cujas paredes admitiam todo o tipo de molduras, um retrato de uma freira beneditina com rosto desvendado, buquês pintados, e até mesmo a cabeça de um turco.

É naquele jardim do convento do Templo, que se erguia aquele famoso castanheiro que era reconhecido como o melhor e o maior de França, e que ostentava a reputação entre as pessoas de bem do século XVIII de ser *o pai de todos os castanheiros do reino.*

Como dissemos, este convento do Templo foi ocupado por beneditinos da Adoração Perpétua, beneditinos bem diferentes daqueles que dependiam de Cîteaux. Esta ordem da Adoração Perpétua não é muito antiga e não remonta a mais de duzentos anos. Em 1649, o santo sacramento foi profanado em duas ocasiões, com poucos dias de intervalo, em duas igrejas em Paris, em Saint-Sulpice e em Saint-Jean en Grève, um raro e assustador sacrilégio que deixou toda a cidade em alvoroço. M. o Prior e Vigário-Geral de Saint-Germain des Prés ordenou uma procissão solene de todo o seu clero, na qual o Núncio do Papa oficiou. Mas esta expiação não satisfez duas santas, Madame Courtin, Marquesa de Boucs e a Condessa de Châteauvieux. Este ultraje cometido sobre "o santíssimo sacramento do altar", embora temporário, não se afastaria dessas santas almas, e pareceu-lhes que só poderia ser atenuado por uma "Adoração

Perpétua" em algum mosteiro feminino. Ambos, um em 1652, outro em 1653, fizeram doações de notáveis quantias a Madre Catarina de Bar, chamada do Santíssimo Sacramento, freira beneditina, com o propósito de fundar, para este piedoso fim, um mosteiro da ordem de Saint-Benoît; a primeira permissão para esta fundação foi dada a Madre Catarina de Bar por M. de Metz, Abbé de Saint-Germain, "com a condição de que nenhuma mulher pudesse ser recebida sem contribuir com trezentos livres, o que equivale a seis mil livres, para o principal". Depois do Abbé de Saint-Germain, o rei concedeu cartas-patente; e todo o resto, carta abbatial e cartas reais, foi confirmado em 1654 pela Câmara de Contas e pelo Parlamento.

Tal é a origem da consagração legal do estabelecimento dos beneditinos da Adoração Perpétua do Santíssimo Sacramento em Paris. O seu primeiro convento foi "um novo edifício" na Rue Cassette, a partir das contribuições de Mesdames de Boucs e de Châteauvieux.

Esta ordem, como se verá, não devia ser confundida com as freiras beneditinas de Cîteaux. Remonta ao Abade de Saint-Germain des Prés, da mesma forma que as damas do Sagrado Coração voltam ao general dos jesuítas, e as irmãs de caridade ao general dos lazaristas.

Também era totalmente diferente dos Bernardinos do Petit-Picpus, cujo interior acabamos de mostrar. Em 1657, o Papa Alexandre VII. tinha autorizado, por um briefing especial, os Bernardinos da Rue Petit-Picpus, a praticar a Adoração Perpétua como as freiras beneditinas do Santíssimo Sacramento. Mas as duas ordens permaneceram distintas.

CAPÍTULO XI

FIM DO PETIT-PICPUS

No início da Restauração, o convento do Petit-Picpus estava em decadência; Isto faz parte da morte geral da Ordem, que, após o século XVIII, foi desaparecendo como todas as ordens religiosas. A contemplação é, como a oração, uma das necessidades da humanidade; mas, como tudo o que a Revolução tocou, transformar-se-á e, de hostil ao progresso social, tornar-se-á favorável a ela.

A casa do Petit-Picpus estava a ficar rapidamente despovoada. Em 1840, o Pequeno Convento tinha desaparecido, a escola tinha desaparecido. Já não havia mulheres idosas, nem raparigas; os primeiros estavam mortos, os segundos tinham partido deles. *Volaverunt.*

A regra da Adoração Perpétua é tão rígida em sua natureza que alarma, as vocações recuam diante dela, a ordem não recebe recrutas. Em 1845, ainda obteve irmãs leigas aqui e ali. Mas das freiras professas, nenhuma. Há quarenta anos, as freiras eram quase uma centena; Há quinze anos, não eram mais de vinte e oito. Quantos existem hoje? Em 1847, a prioresa era jovem, sinal de que o círculo de escolha estava restrito. Ela não tinha quarenta anos. À medida que o número diminui, o cansaço aumenta, o serviço de cada um torna-se mais doloroso; aproximava-se então o momento em que haveria apenas uma dúzia de ombros dobrados e doloridos para suportar o pesado domínio de Saint-Benoît. O fardo é implacável e continua a ser o mesmo para poucos e para muitos. Pesa, esmaga. Assim morrem. No período em que o autor deste livro ainda vivia em Paris, dois morreram. Um tinha vinte e cinco anos, o outro vinte e três. Esta última pode dizer, como Julia Alpinula: *"Hic jaceo. Vixi annos viginti et tres"*. É em consequência desta decadência que o convento desistiu da educação das raparigas.

Não nos sentimos capazes de passar diante desta casa extraordinária sem entrar nela, e sem introduzir as mentes que nos acompanham, e que estão ouvindo nossa história, para o benefício de alguns, por acaso, da história melancólica de Jean Valjean. Penetrámos nesta comunidade, cheia daquelas velhas práticas que hoje parecem tão novas. É o jardim fechado, *hortus conclusus*. Falámos deste lugar singular em pormenor, mas com respeito, pelo menos até agora, pois detalhe e respeito são compatíveis. Não compreendemos tudo, mas não insultamos nada. Estamos igualmente distantes da hosana de José de Maistre, que acabou ungindo o carrasco, e do escárnio de Voltaire, que chega ao ponto de ridicularizar a cruz.

Um ato ilógico da parte de Voltaire, diga-se de passagem; pois Voltaire teria defendido Jesus como defendeu Calas; E mesmo para aqueles que negam encarnações sobre-humanas, o que representa o crucifixo? O sábio assassinado.

Neste século XIX, a ideia religiosa atravessa uma crise. As pessoas estão desaprendendo certas coisas, e fazem bem, desde que, ao desaprendê-las, aprendam o seguinte: não há vácuo no coração humano. Certas demolições acontecem, e é bom que o façam, mas com a condição de serem seguidas de reconstruções.

Entretanto, estudemos as coisas que já não existem. É necessário conhecê-los, nem que seja apenas com o propósito de evitá-los. As falsificações do passado assumem nomes falsos e, de bom grado, chamam-se de futuro. Este espectro, este passado, é dado à falsificação do seu próprio passaporte. Informemo-nos da armadilha. Estejamos atentos. O passado tem uma visão, uma superstição, uma máscara, uma hipocrisia. Denunciemos a visagem e rasguemos a máscara.

Quanto aos conventos, apresentam um problema complexo: uma questão de civilização, que os condena; uma questão de liberdade, que os protege.

LIVRO SETE

PARÊNTESE

CAPÍTULO I

O CONVENTO COMO IDEIA ABSTRATA

Este livro é um drama, cujo personagem principal é o Infinito.

O homem é o segundo.

Assim sendo, e tendo acontecido um convento estar na nossa estrada, tem sido nosso dever entrar nele. Porquê? Porque o convento, comum tanto ao Oriente como ao Ocidente, à antiguidade e aos tempos modernos, ao paganismo, ao budismo, ao mahometanismo, bem como ao cristianismo, é um dos aparelhos óticos aplicados pelo homem ao Infinito.

Este não é o lugar para ampliar desproporcionalmente certas ideias; no entanto, mantendo absolutamente nossas reservas, nossas restrições e até mesmo nossas indignações, devemos dizer que toda vez que encontramos o homem no Infinito, bem ou mal compreendido, nos sentimos dominados pelo respeito. Há, na sinagoga, na mesquita, no pagode, na peruca, um lado hediondo que execramos, e um lado sublime, que adoramos. Que contemplação para a mente, e que alimento infinito para o pensamento, é a reverberação de Deus sobre o muro humano!

CAPÍTULO II

O CONVENTO COMO FACTO HISTÓRICO

Do ponto de vista da história, da razão e da verdade, condena-se o monaquismo. Os mosteiros, quando abundam numa nação, são entupimentos na sua circulação, estabelecimentos pesados, centros de ociosidade onde deveriam existir centros de trabalho. As comunidades monásticas são para a grande comunidade social o que o visco é para o carvalho, o que a verruga é para o corpo humano. A sua prosperidade e a sua gordura significam o empobrecimento do país. O regime monástico, bom no início da civilização, útil na redução do brutal pelo espiritual, é mau quando os povos atingem a sua masculinidade. Além disso, quando se relaxa, e quando entra no seu período de desordem, torna-se mau pelas mesmas razões que o tornaram salutar no seu período de pureza, porque ainda continua a dar o exemplo.

A claustração teve o seu dia. Os claustros, úteis na educação inicial da civilização moderna, têm embaraçado o seu crescimento, e são prejudiciais ao seu desenvolvimento. No que diz respeito à instituição e formação em relação ao homem, os mosteiros, que eram bons no século X, questionáveis no XV, são detestáveis no XIX. A lepra do monaquismo roeu quase até um esqueleto duas nações maravilhosas, a Itália e a Espanha; um a luz, o outro o esplendor da Europa durante séculos; e, nos dias de hoje, estes dois povos ilustres estão apenas começando a convalescer, graças à saudável e vigorosa higiene de 1789.

O convento – o antigo convento feminino em particular, tal como ainda se apresenta no limiar deste século, em Itália, na Áustria, em Espanha – é uma das concreções mais sombrias da Idade Média. O claustro, esse claustro, é o ponto de intersecção dos horrores. O claustro católico, propriamente dito, está inteiramente cheio do esplendor negro da morte.

O convento espanhol é o mais fúnebre de todos. Erguem-se, na obscuridade, sob abóbadas cheias de melancolia, sob cúpulas vagas de sombra, altares maciços de Babel, tão altos como catedrais; ali imensos crucifixos brancos pendem de correntes no escuro; há estendidos, todos nus sobre o ébano, grandes Cristos de marfim; mais do que sangrar,— sangrento; hediondos e magníficos, com os cotovelos exibindo os ossos, as joelheiras mostrando seus tegumentos, suas feridas mostrando sua carne, coroadas de espinhos de prata, pregadas com pregos de ouro, com gotas de sangue de rubis nas sobrancelhas e lágrimas de diamante nos olhos. Os diamantes e rubis parecem molhados, e fazem chorar os seres velados na sombra abaixo, seus lados machucados com a camisa de cabelo e seus flagelos de ponta de ferro, seus seios esmagados com obstáculos de vime, seus joelhos execrados com oração; mulheres que se julgam esposas, espectros que se julgam serafins. Será que essas mulheres pensam? Não. Têm alguma vontade? Não. Eles amam? Não. Eles vivem? Não. Os seus nervos viraram-se para os ossos; os seus ossos transformaram-se em pedra. O seu véu é de noite tecida. A sua respiração sob o véu assemelha-se à respiração indescritivelmente trágica da morte. A abadessa, um espectro, santifica-os e aterroriza-os. O imaculado está lá, e muito feroz. Tais são os antigos mosteiros da Espanha. Mentirosos de terrível devoção, cavernas de virgens, lugares ferozes.

A Espanha católica é mais romana do que a própria Roma. O convento espanhol era, acima de todos os outros, o convento católico. Havia um sabor do Oriente sobre isso. O arcebispo, o kislar-aga do céu, trancou e vigiava este seraglio de almas reservado a Deus. A freira era a odalisca e o sacerdote era o eunuco. Os fervorosos foram escolhidos em sonhos e possuíam Cristo. À noite, o belo jovem nu desceu da cruz e tornou-se o êxtase do claustro. Altas muralhas protegiam a mística sultana, que tinha o crucificado por seu sultão, de toda distração viva. Um olhar sobre o mundo exterior era a infidelidade. O *in pace* substituiu o saco de couro. O que foi lançado ao mar no Oriente foi jogado no chão no Ocidente. Em ambos os quadrantes, as mulheres torciam as mãos; as ondas para a primeira, a sepultura para a última; aqui o afogado, lá o enterrado. Paralelo monstruoso.

Hoje em dia, os defensores do passado, incapazes de negar estas coisas, adotaram o expediente de lhes sorrir. Entrou na moda uma maneira estranha e fácil de suprimir as revelações da história, de invalidar os comentários da filosofia, de elidir todos os fatos embaraçosos e todas as perguntas sombrias. *Uma questão para declamações*, dizem os espertos. Declamações, repita o tolo. Jean-Jacques um declamador; Diderot um declamador; Voltaire em Calas, Labarre e Sirven, declamadores. Não sei quem descobriu recentemente que Tácito era um declamador, que Nero era uma vítima, e que a pena se deve decididamente a "aquele pobre Holofernes".

Os factos, no entanto, são coisas estranhas para desconcertar, e são obstinados. O autor deste livro viu, com os seus próprios olhos, a oito léguas de distância de Bruxelas", há relíquias da Idade Média que são alcançáveis para todos" na Abadia de Villers, o buraco das oubliettes, no meio do campo que antigamente era o pátio do claustro, e nas margens do Thil, quatro masmorras de pedra, metade debaixo de terra, metade debaixo de água. Eles estavam *no ritmo*. Cada uma dessas masmorras tem os restos de uma porta de ferro, uma abóbada e uma abertura ranada que, por fora, está dois metros acima do nível do rio e, por dentro, seis metros acima do nível do solo. Quatro metros de rio passam ao longo da parede externa. O chão está sempre encharcado. O ocupante do *em ritmo* tinha este solo molhado para a sua cama. Em uma dessas masmorras, há um fragmento de um colar de ferro rebitado à parede; noutro, vê-se uma caixa quadrada feita de quatro lajes de granito, demasiado curta para uma pessoa se deitar, demasiado baixa para se manter de pé. Um ser humano foi colocado dentro, com uma tampa de pedra em cima. Isso existe. Vê-se. Pode ser tocado. Estas masmorras, estas dobradiças de ferro, estes decotes, aquele buraco elevado ao nível da corrente do rio, aquela caixa de pedra fechada com uma tampa de granito como um túmulo, com esta diferença, que o morto aqui era um ser vivo, aquele solo que não é senão lama, aquele buraco de abóbada, aquelas paredes escorrendo",que declamadores!

CAPÍTULO III

EM QUE CONDIÇÕES SE PODE RESPEITAR O PASSADO

O monaquismo, tal como existia em Espanha, e tal como ainda existe em Thibet, é uma espécie de phthisis para a civilização. Interrompe a vida curta. Simplesmente despovoa. Claustração, castração. Foi o flagelo da Europa. Acrescente-se a isto a violência tantas vezes feita à consciência, as vocações forçadas, o feudalismo reforçado pelo claustro, o direito do primogênito despejando o excesso da família no monaquismo, as ferocidades de que acabamos de falar, o *ritmo*, as bocas fechadas, os cérebros murados, tantas mentes infelizes colocadas no calabouço dos votos eternos, a tomada do hábito, o enterro de almas vivas. Acrescente torturas individuais às degradações nacionais e, seja quem for, estremecerá diante da pedra e do véu, aquelas duas folhas sinuosas de desígnio humano. No entanto, em certos pontos e em certos lugares, apesar da filosofia, apesar do progresso, o espírito do claustro persiste em meados do século XIX, e um singular recrudescimento ascético é, neste momento, surpreendente o mundo civilizado. A obstinação das instituições antiquadas em perpetuar-se assemelha-se à teimosia do perfume rançoso que deve reclamar os nossos cabelos, às pretensões dos peixes mimados que devem persistir em ser comidos, à perseguição da roupa da criança que deve insistir em vestir o homem, à ternura dos cadáveres que devem voltar a abraçar os vivos.

"Ingrates"!, diz a roupa, "Eu te protegi nas intempéries. Por que você não terá nada a ver comigo"? "Acabei de vir do mar profundo", diz o peixe. "Eu fui uma rosa", diz o perfume. "Eu te amei", diz o cadáver. "Eu te civilizei", diz o convento.

A isto só há uma resposta: "Antigamente".

Sonhar com o prolongamento indefinido das coisas extintas, e com o governo dos homens embalsamando, restaurar dogmas em mau estado, remendar santuários, remendar claustros, renegar relicários, reabastecer superstições, reabastecer fanatismos, pôr novas alças nos pincéis de água benta e no militarismo, reconstituir o monaquismo e o militarismo, acreditar na salvação da sociedade pela multiplicação de parasitas, forçar o passado sobre o presente, isso parece estranho. Ainda assim, há teóricos que sustentam tais teorias. Estes teóricos, que são, sob outros aspetos, pessoas de inteligência, têm um processo muito simples; aplicam ao passado uma vidraça a que chamam ordem social, direito divino, moralidade, família, respeito pelos anciãos, autoridade antiga, tradição sagrada, legitimidade, religião; e eles vão gritando: "Olha! tomem isso, pessoas honestas". Esta lógica era conhecida pelos antigos. Os adivinhos praticam-no. Eles esfregaram uma novilha preta com giz e disseram: "Ela é branca, *Bos cretatus*".

Quanto a nós, respeitamos o passado aqui e ali, e poupamo-lo, acima de tudo, desde que consinta em estar morto. Se ele insiste em estar vivo, nós o atacamos e tentamos matá-lo.

Superstições, intolerâncias, devoção afetada, preconceitos, essas formas, todas as formas como são, são tenazes da vida; têm dentes e unhas na fumaça, e devem ser apertados de corpo a corpo, e a guerra deve ser feita sobre eles, e isso sem trégua; pois é uma das fatalidades da humanidade ser condenada ao eterno combate com fantasmas. É difícil agarrar a escuridão pela garganta e lançá-la à terra.

Um convento na França, em plena luz do dia do século XIX, é um colégio de corujas de frente para a luz. Um claustro, apanhado no próprio ato de ascetismo, no coração da cidade de 89 e de 1830 e de 1848, Roma a florescer em Paris, é um anacronismo. Em tempos normais, para dissolver um anacronismo e fazê-lo desaparecer, basta fazê-lo soletrar a data. Mas não estamos em tempos normais.

Vamos lutar.

Lutemos, mas façamos uma distinção. A propriedade peculiar da verdade é nunca cometer excessos. Que necessidade tem de exagero? Há aquilo que é necessário destruir, e há aquilo que é simplesmente necessário elucidar e examinar. Que força é um exame gentil e sério! Não apliquemos uma chama onde apenas é necessária uma luz.

Assim, dado o século XIX, opomo-nos, como proposição geral, e entre todos os povos, tanto na Ásia como na Europa, na Índia e na Turquia, à claustração ascética. Quem diz claustro, diz pântano. A sua putrescência é evidente, a sua estagnação não é saudável, a sua fermentação infeta as pessoas com febre e etioliza-as; sua multiplicação torna-se uma praga do Egito. Não podemos pensar sem aflição naquelas terras onde faquires, bonzes, santons, monges gregos, marabouts, talapoínos e dervixes se multiplicam como enxames de vermes.

Dito isto, a questão religiosa permanece. Esta questão tem certos lados misteriosos, quase formidáveis; que nos seja permitido analisá-la fixamente.

CAPÍTULO IV

O CONVENTO DO PONTO DE VISTA DOS PRINCÍPIOS

Os homens unem-se e habitam em comunidades. Em virtude de que direito? Por força do direito de associação.

Fecham-se em casa. Em virtude de que direito? Em virtude do direito que cada homem tem de abrir ou fechar a sua porta.

Eles não saem. Em virtude de que direito? Em virtude do direito de ir e vir, o que implica o direito de permanecer em casa.

Lá, em casa, o que fazem?

Falam em tons baixos; deixam cair os olhos; eles labutam. Renunciam ao mundo, às cidades, às sensualidades, aos prazeres, às vaidades, ao orgulho, aos interesses. Estão vestidos com lã grossa ou linho grosso. Nenhum deles possui por direito próprio nada. Ao entrar lá, cada um que era rico faz-se pobre. O que tem, dá a todos. Aquele que era o que se chama nobre, cavalheiro e senhor, é igual àquele que era camponês. A célula é idêntica para todos. Todos passam pela mesma tonsura, vestem o mesmo frock, comem o mesmo pão preto, dormem na mesma palha, morrem nas mesmas cinzas. O mesmo saco nas costas, a mesma corda em torno dos lombos. Se a decisão foi andar descalço, todos vão descalços. Pode haver um príncipe entre eles; Esse príncipe é a mesma sombra que os outros. Até os nomes de família desapareceram. Têm apenas nomes próprios. Todos estão curvados sob a igualdade dos nomes de batismo. Dissolveram a família carnal e constituíram na sua comunidade uma família espiritual. Eles não têm outros parentes além de todos os homens. Socorrem os pobres, cuidam dos doentes. Elegem aqueles a quem obedecem. Eles se chamam de "meu irmão".

Você me para e exclama: "Mas esse é o convento ideal"!

Basta que seja o possível convento, que eu tome conhecimento dele.

Daí resulta que, no livro anterior, falei de um convento com respeitosos sotaques. A Idade Média posta de lado, a Ásia posta de lado, a questão histórica e política mantida em reserva, do ponto de vista puramente filosófico, fora das exigências da política militante, com a condição de que o mosteiro seja absolutamente voluntário e contenha apenas partes consentidas, considerarei sempre uma comunidade de clausura com um certo atenta, e, em alguns aspectos, uma gravidade deferente.

Onde quer que haja uma comunidade, há uma comuna; onde há uma comuna, há direito. O mosteiro é o produto da fórmula: Igualdade, Fraternidade. Ah! quão grandiosa é a liberdade! E que esplêndida transfiguração! A liberdade é suficiente para transformar o mosteiro numa república.

Continuemos.

Mas estes homens, ou estas mulheres que estão atrás destas quatro paredes. Veste-se de lã grossa, são iguais, chamam-se uns aos outros irmãos, isso é bom; mas eles fazem outra coisa?

Sim.

O quê?

Olham para a escuridão, ajoelham-se e apertam as mãos.

O que isso significa?

CAPÍTULO V

ORAÇÃO

Eles rezam.

A quem?

A Deus.

Orar a Deus, qual é o significado dessas palavras?

Existe um infinito além de nós? É esse infinito ali, inerente, permanente; necessariamente substancial, pois é infinito; e porque, se lhe faltasse matéria, estaria limitada; necessariamente inteligente, já que é infinito, e porque, se lhe faltasse inteligência, terminaria aí? Será que este infinito desperta em nós a ideia de essência, enquanto podemos atribuir a nós mesmos apenas a ideia de existência? Em outros termos, não é o absoluto, do qual somos apenas o relativo?

Ao mesmo tempo que há um infinito sem nós, não há um infinito dentro de nós? Não se sobrepõem estes dois infinitos (que plural alarmante!), um sobre o outro? Não é este segundo infinito, por assim dizer, subjacente ao primeiro? Não é o espelho, o reflexo, o eco deste último, um abismo concêntrico com outro abismo? Este segundo infinito também é inteligente? Será que acha? Será que ama? Será que vai? Se essas duas infinidades são inteligentes, cada uma delas tem um princípio de vontade, e há um *eu* no infinito superior como há um *eu* no infinito inferior. O *Eu* abaixo é a alma, o *Eu* no alto é Deus.

Colocar o infinito aqui embaixo em contato, por meio do pensamento, com o infinito no alto, chama-se orar.

Não retiremos nada da mente humana; suprimir é ruim. Temos de reformar e transformar. Certas faculdades no homem dirigem-se ao Desconhecido; pensamento, devaneio, oração. O Desconhecido é um oceano. O que é a consciência? É a bússola do Desconhecido. Pensamento, devaneio, oração, são radiações grandes e misteriosas. Respeitemo-los. Vão essas irradiações majestosas da alma? Na sombra; ou seja, à luz.

A grandeza da democracia é não renegar nada e nada negar à humanidade. Perto da direita do homem, ao lado dela, pelo menos, existe o direito da alma.

Esmagar o fanatismo e venerar o infinito, tal é a lei. Não nos limitemos a prostrar-nos diante da árvore da criação e à contemplação dos seus ramos cheios de estrelas. Temos o dever de trabalhar sobre a alma humana, de defender o mistério contra o milagre, de adorar o incompreensível e rejeitar o absurdo, de admitir, como fato inexplicável, apenas o necessário, purificar a crença, remover superstições do alto da religião; para limpar Deus das lagartas.

CAPÍTULO VI

A BONDADE ABSOLUTA DA ORAÇÃO

Quanto aos modos de oração, todos são bons, desde que sejam sinceros. Vire seu livro de cabeça para baixo e esteja no infinito.

Existe, como sabemos, uma filosofia que nega o infinito. Há também uma filosofia, patologicamente classificada, que nega o sol; Esta filosofia chama-se cegueira.

Erigir um sentido que nos falta numa fonte de verdade é a autossuficiência de um belo cego.

O curioso são os ares altivos, superiores e compassivos que esta filosofia tateante assume em relação à filosofia que contempla Deus. Imagina-se que ouve uma toupeira a gritar: "Tenho pena deles com o seu sol"!

Há, como sabemos, ateus poderosos e ilustres. No fundo, levados de volta à verdade pela sua própria força, não têm a certeza absoluta de que são ateus; é com eles apenas uma questão de definição, e em qualquer caso, se eles não acreditam em Deus, sendo grandes mentes, eles provam Deus.

Saudamo-los como filósofos, ao mesmo tempo que denunciamos inexoravelmente a sua filosofia.

Continuemos.

O que é notável é também a sua facilidade em se pagarem com palavras. Uma escola metafísica do Norte, impregnada até certo ponto de nevoeiro, imaginou ter operado uma revolução na compreensão humana ao substituir a palavra Força pela palavra Vontade.

Dizer: "a planta quer", em vez de: "a planta cresce": isso seria fecundo em resultados, na verdade, se acrescentasse: "o universo quer". Porquê? Porque chegaria a isto: a planta quer, portanto tem um *Eu*, o universo quer, portanto tem um Deus.

Quanto a nós, que, no entanto, contrariamente a esta escola, não rejeitamos nada *a priori*, uma vontade na planta, aceite por esta escola, parece-nos mais difícil de admitir do que uma vontade no universo negada por ela.

Negar a vontade do infinito, isto é, Deus, é impossível em qualquer outra condição que não seja a negação do infinito. Demonstrámo-lo.

A negação do infinito leva diretamente ao niilismo. Tudo se torna "uma conceção mental".

Com o niilismo, nenhuma discussão é possível; pois a lógica niilista duvida da existência de seu interlocutor, e não tem certeza de que ele mesmo exista.

Do seu ponto de vista, é possível que seja para si mesmo, apenas "uma conceção mental".

Só que não percebe que tudo o que negou admite no caroço, simplesmente pela pronúncia da palavra, mente.

Em suma, de modo algum está aberto ao pensamento por uma filosofia que faz com que tudo termine na monossílaba, Não.

Para Não, há apenas uma resposta, Sim.

O niilismo não faz sentido.

Não existe nada. Zero não existe. Tudo é alguma coisa. Nada é nada.

O homem vive mais da afirmação do que do pão.

Nem mesmo ver e mostrar basta. A filosofia deve ser uma energia; deve ter por esforço e efeito melhorar a condição do homem. Sócrates deveria entrar em Adão e produzir Marco Aurélio; Em outras palavras, o homem de sabedoria deve ser feito emergir do homem de felicidade. O Éden deve ser transformado num Liceu. A ciência deve ser cordial. Desfrutar, que triste objetivo e que ambição irrisória! O bruto gosta. Pensar na sede dos homens, dar-lhes a todos como elixir a noção de Deus, fazer confraternizar neles a consciência e a ciência, torná-los justos por este misterioso confronto; Tal é a função da filosofia real. A moral é um florescimento de verdades. A contemplação leva à ação. O absoluto deve ser praticável. É necessário que o ideal seja respirável, bebível e comestível para a mente humana. É o ideal que tem o direito de dizer: *Toma, este é o meu corpo, este é o meu sangue.* A sabedoria é a santa comunhão. É nesta condição que deixa de ser um amor estéril pela ciência e se torna o modo único e soberano de mobilização humana, e que a própria filosofia é promovida à religião.

A filosofia não deve ser uma corbel erguida sobre o mistério para contemplá-lo à sua vontade, sem outro resultado que não seja o de ser conveniente à curiosidade.

Pela nossa parte, adiando o desenvolvimento do nosso pensamento para outra ocasião, limitar-nos-emos a dizer que não entendemos o homem como ponto de partida nem progresso como fim, sem aquelas duas forças que são os seus dois motores: a fé e o amor.

O progresso é o objetivo, o ideal é o tipo.

Qual é esse ideal? É Deus.

Ideal, absoluto, perfeição, infinito: palavras idênticas.

CAPÍTULO VII

PRECAUÇÕES A OBSERVAR NA CULPA

A história e a filosofia têm deveres eternos, que são, ao mesmo tempo, deveres simples; para combater Caiphas o Sumo Sacerdote, Draco o Legislador, Trimalcion o Legislador, Tibério o Imperador; isso é claro, direto e límpido, e não oferece obscuridade.

Mas o direito a viver separado, mesmo com os seus inconvenientes e abusos, insiste em ser afirmado e tido em conta. O cenobitismo é um problema humano.

Quando se fala de conventos, aquelas moradas do erro, mas da inocência, da aberração mas da boa vontade, da ignorância mas da devoção, da tortura mas do martírio, torna-se sempre necessário dizer sim ou não.

Um convento é uma contradição. Seu objeto, a salvação; os seus meios, o sacrifício. O convento é egoísmo supremo tendo como resultado suprema abnegação.

Abdicar com o objetivo de reinar parece ser o artifício do monaquismo.

No claustro, sofre-se para desfrutar. Desenha-se uma letra de câmbio sobre a morte. Desconta-se na luz celeste terrestre sombria. No claustro, o inferno é aceito antecipadamente como um post obit sobre o paraíso.

Tirar o véu ou a pedra é um suicídio pago com a eternidade.

Não nos parece que, sobre tal assunto, seja admissível o escárnio. Tudo é sério, tanto o bom como o mau.

O homem justo franze a testa, mas nunca sorri com um deboche malicioso. Compreendemos a ira, mas não a malícia.

CAPÍTULO VIII

FÉ, LEI

Mais algumas palavras.

Culpamos a igreja quando ela está saturada de intrigas, desprezamos o espiritual que é duro para com o temporal; mas nós em toda parte honramos o homem pensativo.

Saudamos o homem que se ajoelha.

Uma fé; Esta é uma necessidade para o homem. Ai daquele que nada crê.

Não se está desocupado porque se é absorvido. Há trabalho visível e trabalho invisível.

Contemplar é trabalhar, pensar é agir.

Braços cruzados labutam, mãos apertadas trabalham. Um olhar fixo no céu é uma obra.

Thales permaneceu imóvel por quatro anos. Fundou a filosofia.

Em nossa opinião, os cenobitas não são homens preguiçosos e os reclusos não são ociosos.

Meditar sobre a Sombra é uma coisa séria.

Sem invalidar nada do que acabamos de dizer, acreditamos que uma memória perpétua do túmulo é própria dos vivos. Neste ponto, o padre e o filósofo concordam. *Temos de morrer.* O Abade de la Trappe responde a Horácio.

Misturar com a vida uma certa presença do sepulcro, esta é a lei do sábio; e é a lei do asceta. A este respeito, o asceta e o sábio convergem. Há um crescimento material; nós admitimos. Há uma grandeza moral; mantemo-nos fiéis a isso. Espíritos impensados e vivazes dizem: —

"De que servem aquelas figuras imóveis do lado do mistério? Para que servem? O que eles fazem"?

Infelizmente! Na presença das trevas que nos rodeiam, e que nos esperam, na nossa ignorância do que a imensa dispersão fará de nós, respondemos: "Não há provavelmente obra mais divina do que a realizada por estas almas". E acrescentamos: "Provavelmente não há trabalho que seja mais útil".

Certamente deve haver alguns que oram constantemente por aqueles que nunca rezam de todo.

Em nossa opinião, toda a questão reside na quantidade de pensamento que se mistura com a oração.

Leibnitz rezando é grandioso, Voltaire adorando é bom. *Deo erexit Voltaire.*

Somos a favor da religião contra as religiões.

Somos do número dos que acreditam na miséria dos orixás e na sublimidade da oração.

Além disso, neste minuto que agora atravessamos", um minuto que, felizmente, não deixará a sua marca no século XIX —, nesta hora, em que tantos homens têm sobrancelhas e almas baixas, mas pouco elevadas, entre tantos mortais cuja moralidade consiste no gozo, e que estão ocupados com as coisas breves e disformes da matéria, quem se exila parece-nos digno de veneração.

O mosteiro é uma renúncia. Sacrifício mal dirigido ainda é sacrifício. Confundir um erro grave com um dever tem uma grandeza própria.

Tomado por si mesmo, e idealmente, e a fim de examinar a verdade por todos os lados até que todos os aspetos tenham sido imparcialmente esgotados, o mosteiro, o convento feminino em particular, - pois no nosso século é a mulher que mais sofre, e neste exílio do claustro há algo de protesto, - o convento feminino tem incontestavelmente uma certa majestade.

Esta existência de clausura, tão austera, tão deprimente, cujas características acabamos de traçar, não é vida, porque não é liberdade; não é o sepulcro, porque não é plenitude; é o estranho lugar onde se vê, como da crista de uma montanha alta, de um lado o abismo onde estamos, do outro, o abismo para onde iremos; é a fronteira estreita e enevoada que separa dois mundos, iluminados e obscurecidos por ambos ao mesmo tempo, onde o raio da vida que se enfraqueceu se mistura com o vago raio da morte; é a meia obscuridade do túmulo.

Nós, que não acreditamos no que estas mulheres acreditam, mas que, como elas, vivemos pela fé, nunca fomos capazes de pensar sem uma espécie de terror terno e religioso, sem uma espécie de piedade, cheia de inveja, daquelas criaturas dedicadas, trêmulas e confiantes, destas almas humildes e augustas, que ousam habitar à beira do mistério, esperando entre o mundo que está fechado e o céu que ainda não está aberto, voltados para a luz que não se pode ver, possuindo a única felicidade de pensar que sabem onde ela está, aspirando para o golfo, e o desconhecido, seus olhos fixos imóveis na escuridão, ajoelhados, desnorteados, estupefatos, estremecidos, meio erguidos, às vezes, pelas respirações profundas da eternidade.

LIVRO OITO

OS CEMITÉRIOS TOMAM O QUE LHES É COMPROMETIDO

CAPÍTULO I

QUE TRATA DA MANEIRA DE ENTRAR EM UM CONVENTO

Foi nesta casa que Jean Valjean tinha, como disse Fauchelevent, "caído do céu".

Ele tinha escalado a parede do jardim que formava o ângulo da Rue Polonceau. Aquele hino dos anjos que ouvira a meio da noite, eram as freiras a cantar matinas; aquele salão, do qual ele tinha vislumbrado na escuridão, era a capela. Aquele fantasma que ele tinha visto esticado no chão era a irmã que estava fazendo a reparação; aquele sino, cujo som tão estranhamente o surpreendera, era o sino do jardineiro preso ao joelho do Padre Fauchelevent.

Cosette uma vez deitada, Jean Valjean e Fauchelevent tinham, como já vimos, bebido um copo de vinho e um pouco de queijo antes de um bom fogo crepitante; depois, a única cama da cabana ocupada por Cosette, cada um atirou-se sobre uma treliça de palha.

Antes de fechar os olhos, Jean Valjean disse: "Devo permanecer aqui daqui em diante". Este comentário passou pela cabeça de Fauchelevent durante toda a noite.

Para dizer a verdade, nenhum dos dois dormiu.

Jean Valjean, sentindo que estava descoberto e que Javert estava em seu cheiro, entendeu que ele e Cosette estavam perdidos se voltassem para Paris. Então a nova tempestade que acabara de irromper sobre ele o deixara preso naquele claustro. Jean Valjean tinha, doravante, apenas um pensamento: permanecer lá. Ora, para um infeliz na sua posição, este convento era ao mesmo tempo o mais seguro e o mais perigoso dos lugares; o mais perigoso, porque, como nenhum homem poderia entrar lá, se fosse descoberto, era uma ofensa flagrante, e Jean Valjean encontraria apenas um passo intervindo entre o convento e a prisão; o mais seguro, porque, se ele conseguisse ser aceito lá e permanecer lá, quem o procuraria em tal lugar? Morar em um lugar impossível era segurança.

Do seu lado, Fauchelevent estava a acariciar os seus cérebros. Começou por declarar a si próprio que não entendia nada do assunto. Como é que M. Madeleine tinha chegado lá, quando as paredes eram o que eram? As paredes do claustro não devem ser pisadas. Como ele chegou lá com uma criança? Não se pode escalar uma parede perpendicular com uma criança nos braços. Quem era essa criança? De onde vieram os dois? Uma vez que Fauchelevent tinha vivido no convento, ele não tinha ouvido nada de M. sur M., e ele não sabia nada do que tinha acontecido lá. Padre Madeleine tinha um ar que desencorajava perguntas; e, além disso, Fauchelevent disse a si mesmo: "Não se questiona um santo". M. Madeleine tinha preservado todo o seu prestígio aos olhos de Fauchelevent. Só que, a partir de algumas palavras que Jean Valjean deixara cair, o jardineiro pensou que poderia tirar a conclusão de que M. Madeleine provavelmente havia falido durante os tempos difíceis, e que ele era perseguido por seus credores; ou que se comprometera em algum assunto político e estava escondido; o que não desagradou a Fauchelevent, que, como muitos dos nossos camponeses do Norte, tinha um velho fundo de bonapartismo sobre ele. Enquanto estava escondido, M. Madeleine tinha escolhido o convento como refúgio, e era muito simples que ele desejasse permanecer lá. Mas o ponto inexplicável, ao qual Fauchelevent voltava constantemente e sobre o qual ele cansava o cérebro, era que M. Madeleine deveria estar lá, e que ele deveria ter aquela garotinha com ele. Fauchelevent viu-os, tocou-os, falou com eles e ainda não acreditou que fosse possível. O incompreensível acabara de entrar na cabana de Fauchelevent. Fauchelevent tateou em meio a conjeturas, e não conseguia ver nada claramente além disso: "M. Madeleine salvou minha vida". Só esta certeza era suficiente e decidiu o seu rumo. Ele disse a si mesmo: "Agora é a minha vez". E acrescentou, em consciência: "M. Madeleine não parou para deliberar quando se tratava de se atirar para debaixo do carrinho com o propósito de me arrastar para fora". Ele decidiu salvar M. Madeleine.

No entanto, ele fez muitas perguntas a si mesmo e fez com que ele respondesse: "Depois do que ele fez por mim, eu o salvaria se ele fosse um ladrão? Exatamente o mesmo. Se ele fosse um assassino, eu o salvaria? Exatamente o mesmo. Já que ele é um santo, devo salvá-lo? Exatamente o mesmo".

Mas que problema foi conseguir que ele permanecesse no convento! Fauchelevent não recuou perante esta empreitada quase quimérica; este pobre camponês da Picardia sem outra escada que não fosse a sua auto-devoção, a sua boa vontade e um pouco daquela velha astúcia rústica, nesta ocasião alistado ao serviço de um empreendimento generoso, comprometeu-se a escalar as dificuldades do claustro e as escarpas íngremes do governo de Saint-Benoît. O Padre Fauchelevent era um velho egoísta durante toda a sua vida, e que, no fim dos seus dias, parava, enfermo, sem lhe interessar pelo mundo, achava doce agradecer, e percebendo uma ação generosa a ser realizada, lançou-se sobre ela como um homem, que no momento em que está morrendo, deve encontrar perto de sua mão um copo de bom vinho que ele nunca provou, e deve engoli-lo com avidez. Podemos acrescentar, que o ar que ele respirara durante muitos anos neste convento tinha destruído toda a personalidade que nele havia, e acabara por lhe tornar absolutamente necessária uma boa ação de algum tipo.

Por isso, tomou a sua decisão: dedicar-se a M. Madeleine.

Acabamos de chamá-lo de *pobre camponês da Picardia*. Essa descrição é justa, mas incompleta. No ponto desta história a que agora chegámos, torna-se útil um pouco da fisiologia do Padre Fauchelevent. Era camponês, mas tinha sido notário, o que acrescentava malandragem à sua astúcia e penetração à sua ingenuidade. Tendo, por várias causas, fracassado em seus negócios, ele desceu ao chamado de um carter e um trabalhador. Mas, apesar dos juramentos e chicotadas, que os cavalos parecem exigir, algo do notário tinha permanecido nele. Ele tinha alguma inteligência natural; falava boa gramática; conversou, o que é uma coisa rara numa aldeia; e os outros camponeses disseram dele: "Ele fala quase como um cavalheiro com chapéu". Fauchelevent pertencia, de facto, àquela espécie, que o vocabulário impertinente e irreverente do século passado qualificava como *demi-burguês, demi-lout*, e que as metáforas derramadas pelo castelo sobre a cabana de colmo se enfiavam no pombo-buraco do plebeu: *bastante rústico, antes citado; pimenta e sal.* Fauchelevent, embora duramente tentado e duramente usado pelo destino, desgastado, uma espécie de alma velha pobre e sem fios, era, no entanto, um homem impulsivo e extremamente espontâneo em suas ações; uma qualidade preciosa que impede que alguém seja perverso. Seus defeitos e seus vícios, pois ele tinha alguns, eram todos superficiais; Em suma, a sua fisionomia era do tipo que sucede com um observador. Seu rosto envelhecido não tinha nenhuma daquelas rugas desagradáveis no topo da testa, que significam malícia ou estupidez.

Ao amanhecer, o Padre Fauchel abriu os olhos, depois de ter pensado muito, e viu M. Madeleine sentada na sua treliça de palha e observando o sono de Cosette. Fauchelevent sentou-se e disse: —

"Agora que você está aqui, como você vai inventar para entrar"?

Esta observação resumiu a situação e despertou Jean Valjean do seu devaneio.

Os dois homens se aconselharam juntos.

"Em primeiro lugar", disse Fauchelevent, "você começará por não colocar os pés fora desta câmara, nem você nem a criança. Um passo no jardim e estamos prontos".

"É verdade".

"Monsieur Madeleine", retomou Fauchelevent, "você chegou em um momento muito auspicioso, quero dizer um momento muito inauspicioso; Uma das senhoras está muito doente. Isso impedirá que olhem muito na nossa direção. Parece que ela está morrendo. As orações das quarenta horas estão sendo feitas. Toda a comunidade está confusa. Isso ocupa-os. Quem está no ponto de partida é um santo. Na verdade, somos todos santos aqui; toda a diferença entre eles e eu é que eles dizem 'nossa célula', e que eu digo 'minha cabine'. As orações pelos moribundos devem ser feitas, e depois as orações pelos mortos. Estaremos aqui em paz até hoje; mas eu não vou responder por to-morrow".

"Ainda assim", observou Jean Valjean, "esta casa está no nicho da parede, está escondida por uma espécie de ruína, há árvores, não é visível do convento".

"E acrescento que as freiras nunca chegam perto disso".

"Bem"?, disse Jean Valjean.

O ponto de interrogação que acentuava este "bem" significava: "parece-me que se pode ficar escondido aqui"? Foi a este ponto de interrogatório que Fauchelevent respondeu:

"Há as raparigas".

"Que meninas"?, perguntou Jean Valjean.

Assim que Fauchelevent abriu a boca para explicar as palavras que proferira, um sino emitiu um golpe.

"A freira está morta", disse ele. "Há o nó".

E fez um sinal a Jean Valjean para ouvir.

O sino tocou uma segunda vez.

"É o knell, Monsieur Madeleine. O sino continuará a tocar uma vez por minuto durante vinte e quatro horas, até que o corpo seja retirado da igreja.—Veja, eles tocam. Nas horas de recreação, basta ter uma bola rolando de lado, para mandar todos eles até aqui, apesar das proibições, caçar e vasculhar tudo por aqui. Esses querubins são demônios".

"Quem"?, perguntou Jean Valjean.

"As meninas. Você seria descoberto muito rapidamente. Eles gritavam: 'Oh! um homem"! Hoje em dia não há perigo. Não haverá hora de recreação. O dia será inteiramente dedicado às orações. Ouve-se a campainha. Como lhe disse, um golpe a cada minuto. É a sentença de morte".

"Eu entendo, padre Fauchel. Há alunos".

E Jean Valjean pensou consigo mesmo:

"Aqui está a educação de Cosette já fornecida".

Fauchelevent exclamou:—

"Pardine! Há raparigas de facto! E eles batiam em torno de você! E eles saíam correndo! Ser homem aqui é ter a peste. Você vê como eles prendem um sino na minha pata como se eu fosse uma fera".

Jean Valjean caiu em pensamentos cada vez mais profundos.—"Este convento seria a nossa salvação", murmurou.

Então ele levantou a voz: —

"Sim, a dificuldade é permanecer aqui".

"Não", disse Fauchel, "a dificuldade é sair".

Jean Valjean sentiu o sangue correr de volta ao seu coração.

"Para sair"!

"Sim, Monsieur Madeleine. Para voltar aqui é preciso primeiro sair".

E depois de esperar até que outro golpe do knell tivesse soado, Fauchelevent continuou:

"Você não deve ser encontrado aqui desta maneira. De onde vem? Por mim, cais do céu, porque eu vos conheço; mas as freiras exigem que se entre pela porta".

De repente, ouviram um toque bastante complicado de outro sino.

"Ah"!, disse Fauchel, "eles estão tocando as mães vocais. Eles estão indo para o capítulo. Eles sempre têm um capítulo quando alguém morre. Ela morreu ao amanhecer. As pessoas geralmente morrem ao amanhecer. Mas não consegue sair pela forma como entrou? Venha, eu não peço para te questionar, mas como você entrou"?

Jean Valjean ficou pálido; O simples pensamento de descer novamente àquela rua terrível o fez estremecer. Você sai de uma floresta cheia de tigres e, uma vez fora dela, imagine um conselho amigável que o aconselhará a voltar mais tarde! Jean Valjean retratou para si toda a força policial ainda envolvida em enxames naquele bairro, agentes em vigilância, sentinelas por toda parte, punhos assustadores estendidos em direção ao seu colarinho, Javert na esquina do cruzamento das ruas talvez.

"Impossível"!, disse ele. "Padre Fauchel, diga que eu caí do céu".

"Mas eu acredito, eu acredito", retrucou Fauchel. "Você não tem necessidade de me dizer isso. O bom Deus deve ter tomado você em sua mão com o propósito de ter um bom olhar para você perto e, em seguida, deixá-lo cair. Apenas, ele quis colocá-lo no convento de um homem; ele cometeu um erro. Venha, lá vai outra ervilha, que é mandar o porteiro ir e informar o município que o médico-morto é para vir aqui e ver um cadáver. Tudo isso é a cerimônia da morte. Estas boas senhoras não gostam nada dessa visita. Um médico é um homem que não acredita em nada. Ele levanta o véu. Às vezes ele levanta outra coisa também. Quão rápido eles tiveram o médico convocado desta vez! Qual é a questão? O seu bebé ainda está a dormir. Qual é o nome dela"?

"Cosette".

"Ela é sua filha? Você é o avô dela, quer dizer"?

"Sim".

"Vai ser fácil para ela sair daqui. Eu tenho a minha porta de serviço que se abre no pátio. Eu bato. O porteiro abre; Tenho o meu cesto vintage nas costas, a criança está nele, eu saio. O Padre Fauchelevent sai com o seu cesto – isso é perfeitamente natural. Você vai dizer à criança para ficar muito quieto. Ela estará debaixo da coberta. Vou deixá-la para o tempo que for necessário com um bom e velho amigo, um vendedor de frutas que conheço na Rue Chemin-Vert, que é surdo e que tem uma pequena cama. Vou gritar no ouvido da vendedora de frutas, que ela é uma sobrinha minha, e que ela deve guardá-la para mim até amanhã. Então o pequeno voltará a entrar consigo; pois farei com que você volte a entrar. Tem de ser feito. Mas como você vai conseguir sair"?

Jean Valjean balançou a cabeça.

"Ninguém deve me ver, o objetivo está aí, padre Fauchelevent. Encontre algum meio de me colocar em uma cesta, disfarçada, como a Cosette".

Fauchelevent arranhou o lóbulo da orelha com o dedo médio da mão esquerda, um sinal de grave constrangimento.

Uma terceira ervilha criou um desvio.

"Esse é o médico morto que está a partir", disse Fauchelevent. "Ele deu uma olhada e disse: 'Ela está morta, está bem'. Quando o médico assina o passaporte para o paraíso, a empresa do agente funerário envia um caixão. Se for mãe, as mães colocam-na; se ela é uma irmã, as irmãs a colocam.

Depois disso, eu prego ela. Isso faz parte do dever do meu jardineiro. Um jardineiro é um pouco coveiro. Ela é colocada em um salão inferior da igreja que se comunica com a rua, e no qual nenhum homem pode entrar a não ser o médico dos mortos. Eu não conto os homens do agente funerário e eu como homens. É nesse salão que prego o caixão. Os homens do agente funerário vêm buscá-lo, e chicoteiam, cocheiro! É assim que se vai para o céu. Vão buscar uma caixa sem nada, levam-na de novo com alguma coisa dentro. É assim que é um enterro. *De profundis*".

Um raio de sol horizontal tocou levemente o rosto da adormecida Cosette, que estava com a boca vagamente aberta, e tinha o ar de um anjo bebendo na luz. Jean Valjean tinha caído a olhar para ela. Já não ouvia Fauchel.

O facto de não se ser ouvido não é razão para preservar o silêncio. O bom e velho jardineiro prosseguiu tranquilamente com o seu balbucio: —

"A sepultura está cavada no cemitério de Vaugirard. Eles declaram que vão suprimir aquele cemitério de Vaugirard. É um cemitério antigo que está fora dos regulamentos, que não tem uniforme e que vai se aposentar. É uma pena, pois é conveniente. Tenho um amigo lá, o padre Mestienne, o coveiro. As freiras aqui possuem um privilégio, é ser levado para aquele cemitério ao cair da noite. Há uma permissão especial da Prefeitura em seu nome. Mas quantos eventos aconteceram desde ontem! A Mãe Crucificação está morta, e o Padre Madeleine—"

"Está enterrado" disse Jean Valjean, sorrindo tristemente.

Fauchelevent pegou a palavra.

"Nossa! se você estivesse aqui para sempre, seria um verdadeiro enterro".

Uma quarta ervilha irrompeu. Fauchelevent apressou-se a separar a rótula da unha e apertou-a novamente no joelho.

"Desta vez é para mim. A Mãe Prioresa quer-me. Bom, agora estou me picando na língua da minha fivela. Monsieur Madeleine, não mexa daqui, e espere por mim. Algo novo surgiu. Se você está com fome, há vinho, pão e queijo".

E apressou-se a sair da cabana, gritando: "Vem! vindo"!

293

Jean Valjean o observou correndo pelo jardim tão rápido quanto sua perna torta permitiria, lançando um olhar lateral pelo caminho em seu remendo de melão.

Menos de dez minutos depois, o padre Fauchelevent, cujo sino colocou as freiras em seu caminho para fugir, bateu suavemente em uma porta, e uma voz suave respondeu: *"Para sempre! Para sempre"!* ou seja: *"Entrar".*

A porta era a que dava para o salão reservado para ver o jardineiro a negócios. Este salão contíguo à sala do capítulo. A prioresa, sentada na única cadeira do salão, esperava por Fauchelevent.

CAPÍTULO II

FAUCHELEVENT NA PRESENÇA DE UMA DIFICULDADE

É peculiaridade de certas pessoas e de certas profissões, nomeadamente sacerdotes e freiras, vestir um ar grave e agitado em ocasiões críticas. No momento em que Fauchelevent entrou, esta dupla forma de preocupação ficou impressa no semblante da prioresa, que era aquela sábia e encantadora Mademoiselle de Blemeur, Madre Inocente, que era ordinariamente alegre.

O jardineiro fez uma tímida reverência e permaneceu à porta da cela. A prioresa, que lhe contava contas, levantou os olhos e disse:

"Ah! és tu, Pai Fauvent".

Esta abreviatura tinha sido adotada no convento.

Fauchelevent curvou-se novamente.

"Pai Fauvent, eu te enviei".

"Aqui estou, reverenda Mãe".

"Tenho algo a dizer-lhe".

"E eu também" disse Fauchel, com uma ousadia que lhe causou terror interior", tenho algo a dizer à reverenda Mãe.

A prioresa olhou fixamente para ele.

"Ah! você tem uma comunicação a fazer comigo".

"Um pedido".

"Muito bem, fale".

Goodman Fauchelevent, o ex-notário, pertencia à categoria dos camponeses que têm garantia. Uma certa ignorância inteligente constitui uma força; Você não desconfia dele, e você é pego por ele. Fauchelevent tinha sido um sucesso durante os mais de dois anos que passou no convento. Sempre solitário e ocupado com a sua jardinagem, não tinha mais nada a fazer senão satisfazer a sua curiosidade. Como ele estava a uma distância de todas aquelas mulheres veladas que passavam de um lado para o outro, ele viu diante dele apenas uma agitação de sombras. Por força da atenção e da nitidez, ele conseguira vestir todos aqueles fantasmas com carne, e aqueles cadáveres estavam vivos para ele. Ele era como um homem surdo cuja visão se torna mais aguçada, e como um cego cuja audição se torna mais aguda. Tinha-se empenhado em adivinhar o significado das diferentes ervilhas, e conseguira, de modo que este claustro taciturno e enigmático não possuía segredos para ele; A esfinge balbuciou todos os seus segredos em seu ouvido. Fauchelevent sabia tudo e tudo escondia; que constituía a sua arte. Todo o convento o achava estúpido. Um grande mérito na religião. As mães vocais fizeram muito de Fauchelevent. Era um mudo curioso. Inspirou confiança. Além disso, ele era regular, e nunca saiu, exceto por requisitos bem demonstrados do pomar e horta. Esta discricionariedade de conduta tinha-lhe dado crédito. No entanto, ele tinha posto dois homens para tagarelar: o porteiro, no convento, e ele conhecia as singularidades de seu salão, e o coveiro, no cemitério, e ele conhecia as peculiaridades de sua sepultura; Desta forma, ele possuía uma dupla luz sobre o assunto dessas freiras, uma quanto à sua vida, outra quanto à sua morte. Mas não abusou do seu conhecimento. A congregação pensava muito nele. Velho, coxo, cego para tudo, provavelmente um pouco surdo na pechincha", que qualidades! Teriam tido dificuldade em substituí-lo.

O mocinho, com a certeza de uma pessoa que se sente apreciada, entrou numa arenga rústica bastante difusa e muito profunda para a reverenda prioresa. Falava muito da sua idade, das suas enfermidades, da sobretaxa dos anos que lhe contavam o dobro daqui para a frente, das exigências crescentes do seu trabalho, da grande dimensão do jardim, das noites que deviam passar, como a última, por exemplo, em que tinha sido obrigado a colocar esteiras de palha sobre as camas de melão, por causa da lua, e ele terminou da seguinte forma: "Que ele tinha um irmão" - (a prioresa fez um movimento),- "um irmão não mais jovem" - (um segundo movimento por parte da prioresa, mas um expressivo de tranquilização),- "que, se lhe fosse permitido, este irmão viria viver com ele e ajudá-lo, que era um excelente jardineiro, que a comunidade receberia dele um bom serviço, melhor do que o seu; que, caso contrário, se o seu irmão não fosse admitido, pois ele, o mais velho, sentia que a sua saúde estava debilitada e que era insuficiente para o trabalho, deveria ser obrigado, para grande pesar, a ir embora; e que seu irmão tinha uma filhinha que ele traria consigo, que poderia ser criada por Deus na casa, e que poderia, quem sabe, tornar-se freira algum dia".

Quando terminou de falar, a prioresa ficou com o rosário entre os dedos, e disse-lhe:

"Você poderia comprar uma barra de ferro robusta entre hoje e esta noite"?

"Com que propósito"?

"Para servir de alavanca".

"Sim, reverenda mãe", respondeu Fauchel.

A prioresa, sem acrescentar uma palavra, levantou-se e entrou na sala adjacente, que era o salão do capítulo, e onde provavelmente estavam reunidas as mães vocais. Fauchelevent ficou sozinho.

CAPÍTULO III

MÃE INOCENTE

Decorreu cerca de um quarto de hora. A prioresa voltou e sentou-se mais uma vez em sua cadeira.

Os dois interlocutores pareciam preocupados. Apresentaremos, da melhor forma possível, um relatório estenográfico do diálogo que se seguiu.

"Pai Fauvent"!

"Reverenda Mãe"!

"Conhece a capela"?

"Tenho uma pequena gaiola lá, onde ouço a missa e os escritórios".

"E estiveste no coro no cumprimento dos teus deveres"?

"Duas ou três vezes".

"Há uma pedra a ser levantada".

"Pesado"?

"A laje do pavimento que está ao lado do altar".

"A laje que fecha o cofre"?

"Sim".

"Seria bom ter dois homens para isso".

"A Mãe Ascensão, que é tão forte como um homem, ajudar-vos-á".

"Uma mulher nunca é um homem".

"Só temos uma mulher aqui para te ajudar. Cada um faz o que pode. Porque Dom Mabillon dá quatrocentas e dezessete epístolas de São Bernardo, enquanto Merlonus Horstius só dá trezentos e sessenta e sete, eu não desprezo Merlonus Horstius".

"Nem eu".

"O mérito consiste em trabalhar de acordo com as forças de cada um. Um claustro não é um estaleiro".

"E uma mulher não é um homem. Mas o meu irmão é o mais forte"!

"E você consegue uma alavanca"?

"Esse é o único tipo de chave que se encaixa nesse tipo de porta".

"Há um anel na pedra".

"Vou colocar a alavanca através dele".

"E a pedra está tão arranjada que balança num pivô".

"Isso é bom, reverenda mãe. Vou abrir o cofre".

"E as quatro Mães Precentores vos ajudarão".

"E quando o cofre estiver aberto"?

"Deve ser fechado novamente".

"Será que vai ser tudo"?

"Não".

"Dá-me as tuas ordens, muito reverenda Mãe".

"Fauvent, temos confiança em você".

"Estou aqui para fazer o que quiserem".

"E para manter a paz sobre tudo"!

"Sim, reverenda mãe".

"Quando o cofre está aberto—"

"Vou fechá-lo novamente".

"Mas antes disso—"

"O quê, reverenda mãe"?

"Algo deve ser rebaixado nele".

Seguiu-se um silêncio. A prioresa, depois de um bico do lábio inferior que parecia hesitação, quebrou-o.

"Pai Fauvent"!

"Reverenda Mãe"!

"Sabe que uma mãe morreu esta manhã"?

"Não".

"Não ouviste a campainha"?

"Nada se ouve no fundo do jardim".

"Sério"?

"Mal consigo distinguir o meu próprio sinal".

"Ela morreu ao amanhecer".

"E então, o vento não soprava na minha direção esta manhã".

"Foi a Mãe Crucificação. Uma mulher abençoada".

A prioresa fez uma pausa, moveu os lábios, como se estivesse em oração mental, e retomou:

"Há três anos, Madame de Béthune, uma jansenista, tornou-se ortodoxa, simplesmente por ter visto a Mãe Crucificação em oração".

"Ah! Sim, agora ouço o nó, reverenda Mãe".

"As mães levaram-na para o quarto morto, que se abre sobre a igreja".

"Eu sei".

"Nenhum outro homem além de você pode ou deve entrar naquela câmara. Cuidem-se. Uma bela visão seria, ver um homem entrar na sala morta"!

"Mais vezes"!

"Ei"?

"Mais vezes"!

"O que você diz"?

"Digo mais vezes".

"Mais vezes do que o quê"?

"Reverenda mãe, eu não disse mais vezes do que o quê, eu disse mais vezes".

"Eu não entendo você. Por que você diz mais vezes"?

"Para falar como tu, reverenda Mãe".

"Mas eu não disse 'mais vezes'".

Nesse momento, marcaram nove horas.

"Às nove horas da manhã e a todas as horas, louvado e adorado seja o Santíssimo Sacramento do altar", disse a prioresa.

"Amém", disse Fauchelevent.

O relógio bateu oportunamente. Cortou "mais vezes" curto. É provável que, se não fosse por isso, a prioresa e Fauchelevent nunca teriam desvendado essa meada.

Fauchelevent esfregou a testa.

A prioresa entregou-se a outro pequeno murmúrio interior, provavelmente sagrado, e levantou a voz:

"Em vida, a Mãe Crucificação converteu-se; depois de sua morte, ela fará milagres".

"Ela vai"!, respondeu o padre Fauchel, caindo no degrau e esforçando-se para não vacilar novamente.

"Padre Fauvent, a comunidade foi abençoada na Mãe Crucificação. Sem dúvida, não é concedido a cada um morrer, como o Cardeal de Bérulle, enquanto reza a santa missa, e respirar suas almas a Deus, pronunciando estas palavras: *Hanc igitur oblationem*. Mas, sem alcançar tal felicidade, a morte da Mãe Crucificação foi muito preciosa. Ela manteve sua consciência até o último momento. Ela falou connosco, depois falou aos anjos. Ela nos deu seus últimos comandos. Se você tivesse um pouco mais de fé, e se pudesse estar na cela dela, ela teria curado sua perna apenas tocando-a. Ela sorriu. Sentimos que ela estava recuperando sua vida em Deus. Havia algo de paraíso naquela morte".

Fauchelevent pensou que era um orixá que ela estava terminando.

"Amém", disse ele.

"Pai Fauvent, o que os mortos desejam deve ser feito".

A prioresa tirou várias contas de seu terço. Fauchelevent manteve a paz.

Ela continuou: —

"Consultei sobre este ponto muitos eclesiásticos que trabalham em Nosso Senhor, que se ocupam dos exercícios da vida clerical e que dão frutos maravilhosos".

"Reverenda Mãe, você pode ouvir o barulho muito melhor aqui do que no jardim".

"Além disso, ela é mais do que uma mulher morta, é uma santa".

"Como você, reverenda Mãe".

"Ela dormiu em seu caixão por vinte anos, por permissão expressa de nosso Santo Padre, Pio VII".

"Aquele que coroou o Emp—Buonaparte".

Para um homem inteligente como Fauchel, esta alusão era estranha. Felizmente, a prioresa, completamente absorvida em seus próprios pensamentos, não a ouviu. Ela continuou: —

"Pai Fauvent"?

"Reverenda mãe"?

"São Didoro, arcebispo da Capadócia, desejava que esta única palavra fosse inscrita no seu túmulo: *Ácaro*, que significa, um verme da terra; assim foi feito. Isso é verdade"?

"Sim, reverenda mãe".

"O bem-aventurado Mezzocane, abade de Áquila, quis ser enterrado sob a forca; isso foi feito".

"É verdade".

"São Terêncio, bispo do Porto, onde a foz do Tibre deságua no mar, pediu que no seu túmulo fosse gravado o sinal que foi colocado nas sepulturas dos parricidas, na esperança de que os transeuntes cuspissem no seu túmulo. Assim foi feito. Os mortos devem ser obedecidos".

"Assim seja".

"O corpo de Bernard Guidonis, nascido em França, perto de Roche-Abeille, foi, como ele tinha ordenado, e apesar do rei de Castela, transportado para a igreja dos dominicanos em Limoges, embora Bernard Guidonis fosse bispo de Tuy, em Espanha. Pode afirmar-se o contrário"?

"Aliás, não, reverenda mãe".

"O fato é atestado por Plantavit de la Fosse".

Várias contas do terço foram apagadas, ainda em silêncio. A prioresa retomou:

"Pai Fauvent, Mãe Crucificação será enterrada no caixão em que ela dormiu nos últimos vinte anos".

"Isso é justo".

"É uma continuação do sono dela".

"Então vou ter que pregar esse caixão"?

"Sim".

"E devemos rejeitar o caixão do agente funerário"?

"Precisamente".

"Estou sob as ordens da comunidade muito reverenda".

"As quatro Mães Precentores vão ajudá-lo".

"Em pregar o caixão? Não preciso deles".

"Não. Ao baixar o caixão".

"Onde"?

"Dentro do cofre".

"Que cofre"?

"Sob o altar".

Fauchelevent começou.

"A abóbada debaixo do altar"?

"Sob o altar".

"Mas—"

"Você terá uma barra de ferro".

"Sim, mas—"

"Você levantará a pedra com a barra por meio do anel".

"Mas—"

"Os mortos devem ser obedecidos. Ser sepultado na abóbada sob o altar da capela, não ir para a terra profana; permanecer ali na morte, onde rezou enquanto vivia; tal era o último desejo da Mãe Crucificação. Ela pediu-nos isso; ou seja, mandou-nos".

"Mas é proibido".

"Proibido pelos homens, ordenado por Deus".

"E se se tornasse conhecido"?

"Temos confiança em si".

"Ah! Eu sou uma pedra nas vossas paredes".

"O capítulo reunido. As mães vocais, que acabei de consultar novamente, e que agora estão deliberando, decidiram que a Mãe Crucificação será enterrada, de acordo com seu desejo, em seu próprio caixão, sob nosso altar. Pense, Pai Fauvent, se ela fizesse milagres aqui! Que glória de Deus para a comunidade! E milagres saem dos túmulos".

"Mas, reverenda Mãe, se o agente da comissão sanitária—"

"São Benoît II., em matéria de sepultura, resistiu a Constantino Pogonatus".

"Mas o comissário da polícia—"

"Chonodemaire, um dos sete reis alemães que entraram entre os gauleses sob o Império de Constâncio, reconheceu expressamente o direito das freiras a serem enterradas na religião, isto é, sob o altar".

"Mas o inspetor da Prefeitura—"

"O mundo não é nada na presença da cruz. Martinho, o décimo primeiro general dos cartuxos, deu à sua ordem este dispositivo: *Stat crux dum volvitur orbis*".

"Amém" disse Fauchelevent, que imperturbavelmente se desvencilhou assim do dilema, sempre que ouvia latim.

Qualquer audiência é suficiente para uma pessoa que manteve a paz por muito tempo. No dia em que o retórico Gymnastoras deixou sua prisão, carregando em seu corpo muitos dilemas e numerosos silogismos que haviam atingido, ele parou em frente à primeira árvore a que chegou, arengou-a e fez grandes esforços para convencê-la. A prioresa, geralmente submetida à barreira do silêncio, e cujo reservatório estava superlotado, levantou-se e exclamou com a loquacidade de uma barragem que se rompeu:

"Tenho à direita Benoît e à esquerda Bernard. Quem foi Bernardo? O primeiro abade de Claraval. Fontaines, na Borgonha, é um país que é abençoado porque lhe deu à luz. Seu pai se chamava Técelin e sua mãe Alèthe. Começou em Cîteaux, para terminar em Claraval; foi ordenado abade pelo bispo de Châlon-sur-Saône, Guillaume de Champeaux; teve setecentos noviços e fundou cento e sessenta mosteiros; ele derrubou Abeilard no concílio de Sens em 1140, e Pierre de Bruys e Henrique seu discípulo, e outro tipo de espíritos errantes que foram chamados de Apostólicos; confundiu Arnauld de Brescia, lançou relâmpagos no monge Raoul, o assassino dos judeus, dominou o concílio de Reims em 1148, causou a condenação de Gilberto de Poréa, bispo de Poitiers, causou a condenação de Éon de l'Étoile, organizou as disputas dos príncipes, iluminou o rei Luís, o Jovem, aconselhou o Papa Eugênio III., regulamentou o Templo, pregou a cruzada, realizou duzentos e cinquenta milagres durante sua vida, e até trinta e nove em um dia. Quem foi Benoît? Ele era o patriarca de Mont-Cassin; foi o segundo fundador do Sainteté Claustrale, foi o Basílio do Ocidente. Sua ordem produziu quarenta papas, duzentos cardeais, cinquenta patriarcas, dezesseis arcebispos, quatro mil e seiscentos bispos, quatro imperadores, doze imperatrizes, quarenta e seis reis, quarenta e uma rainhas, três mil e seiscentos santos canonizados, e existe há catorze anos. De um lado São Bernardo, do outro o agente do departamento sanitário! De um lado São Benoît, do outro o inspetor das vias públicas! O Estado, os comissários rodoviários, o agente público, os regulamentos, a administração, o que sabemos de tudo isso? Não há uma chance de transeunte que não ficaria indignado ao ver como somos tratados. Não temos sequer o direito de dar o nosso pó a Jesus Cristo! O seu departamento sanitário é uma invenção revolucionária. Deus subordinado ao comissário de polícia; tal é a idade. Silêncio, Fauvent"!

Fauchelevent estava mas mal à vontade sob este banho de chuveiro. A prioresa continuou: —

"Ninguém duvida do direito do mosteiro à sepultura. Só os fanáticos e os que estão em erro o negam. Vivemos tempos de terrível confusão. Não sabemos aquilo que é necessário saber, e sabemos aquilo que devemos ignorar. Somos ignorantes e ímpios. Nesta época existem pessoas que não distinguem entre o grande São Bernardo e o São Bernardo denominado dos católicos pobres, um certo bom eclesiástico que viveu no século XIII. Outros são tão blasfemos que comparam o andaime de Luís XVI à cruz de Jesus Cristo. Luís XVI. era apenas um rei. Tenhamos cuidado com Deus! Não há mais justo nem injusto. O nome de Voltaire é conhecido, mas não o nome de César de Bus. No entanto, César de Bus é um homem de memória abençoada, e Voltaire um de memória inabençoada. O último arcebispo, o Cardeal de Périgord, nem sequer sabia que Carlos de Gondren sucedeu a Berulle, e François Bourgoin a Gondren, e Jean-François Senault a Bourgoin, e o Padre Sainte-Marthe a Jean-François Senault. O nome do Padre Coton é conhecido, não porque tenha sido um dos três que insistiram na fundação do Oratório, mas porque forneceu a Henrique IV., o rei huguenote, o material para um juramento. O que agrada as pessoas do mundo em Saint François de Sales, é que ele trapaceou no jogo. E então, a religião é atacada. Porquê? Porque houve maus sacerdotes, porque Sagittaire, bispo de Gap, era irmão de Salone, bispo de Embrun, e porque ambos seguiam Mommol. O que isso tem a ver com a pergunta? Isso impede Martin de Tours de ser santo e dar metade do seu manto a um mendigo? Perseguem os santos. Fechou os olhos para a verdade. A escuridão é a regra. Os animais mais ferozes são os animais cegos. Ninguém pensa no inferno como uma realidade. Ah! como as pessoas são más! Por ordem do rei significa hoje, por ordem da revolução. Já não se sabe o que é devido aos vivos ou aos mortos. Uma morte santa é proibida. O enterro é uma questão civil. Isso é horrível. São Leão II. escreveu duas cartas especiais, uma a Pierre Notaire, outra ao rei dos visigodos, com o propósito de combater e rejeitar, em questões que tocam os mortos, a autoridade do exarca e a supremacia do imperador. Gauthier, bispo de Châlons, manteve-se nesta questão contra Otão, Duque da Borgonha. A antiga magistratura concordou com ele. Antigamente tínhamos vozes no capítulo, mesmo sobre assuntos do dia. O abade de Cîteaux, o general da ordem, foi conselheiro por direito de nascimento do parlamento da Borgonha. Fazemos o que nos agrada com os nossos mortos. Não é o próprio corpo de São Benoît na França, na abadia de Fleury, chamado São Benoît-sur-Loire, embora ele tenha morrido na Itália, em

Mont-Cassin, no sábado, dia 21 do mês de março, do ano 543? Tudo isto é incontestável. Abomino cantores de salmos, odeio priores, execro hereges, mas devo detestar ainda mais qualquer um que deva sustentar o contrário. Basta ler Arnoul Wion, Gabriel Bucelin, Trithemus, Maurólicos e Dom Luc d'Achery".

A prioresa respirou, depois virou-se para Fauchelevent.

"Está resolvido, padre Fauvent?

"Está resolvido, reverenda mãe".

"Podemos depender de você"?

"Vou obedecer".

"Está tudo bem".

"Sou inteiramente devotado ao convento".

"Compreende-se. Você vai fechar o caixão. As irmãs vão levá-lo para a capela. O ofício para os mortos será então dito. Depois, voltaremos ao claustro. Entre onze horas e meia-noite, você virá com sua barra de ferro. Tudo será feito no mais profundo sigilo. Haverá na capela apenas as quatro Mães Precentores, a Mãe Ascensão e você mesmo".

"E a irmã no posto"?

"Ela não vai se virar".

"Mas ela vai ouvir".

"Ela não vai ouvir. Além disso, o que o claustro conhece o mundo não aprende".

Seguiu-se uma pausa. A prioresa prosseguiu:

"Você vai tirar a campainha. Não é necessário que a irmã no posto perceba a sua presença".

"Reverenda mãe"?

"O quê, Pai Fauvent"?

"O médico dos mortos fez a sua visita"?

"Ele vai pagar às quatro horas do dia de hoje. A ervilha que ordena ao médico que os mortos sejam convocados já foi deflagrada. Mas você não entende nenhuma das ervilhas"?

"Não presto atenção a ninguém além do meu".

"Está bem, padre Fauvent".

"Reverenda mãe, será necessária uma alavanca de pelo menos seis metros de comprimento".

"Onde você vai obtê-lo"?

"Onde não faltam grades, barras de ferro não faltam. Tenho o meu monte de ferro velho no fundo do jardim".

"Cerca de três quartos de hora antes da meia-noite; não se esqueçam".

"Reverenda mãe"?

"O quê"?

"Se alguma vez tiveres outros trabalhos deste tipo, o meu irmão é o homem forte para ti. Um turco perfeito"!

"Fá-lo-ão o mais rapidamente possível".

"Não consigo trabalhar muito rápido. Estou enfermo; é por isso que eu preciso de um assistente. Eu manco".

"Mancar não é pecado, e talvez seja uma bênção. O imperador Henrique II., que combateu o antipapa Gregório e restabeleceu Benoît VIII., tem dois sobrenomes, o Santo e o Lame".

"Dois surtouts são uma coisa boa", murmurou Fauchelevent, que realmente estava um pouco difícil de ouvir.

"Agora que penso nisso, padre Fauvent, vamos dar uma hora inteira para ele. Não é muito. Esteja perto do altar principal, com a sua barra de ferro, às onze horas. O escritório começa à meia-noite. Tudo deve ter sido concluído um bom quarto de hora antes disso".

"Tudo farei para provar o meu zelo para com a comunidade. Estas são as minhas ordens. Estou para pregar o caixão. Às onze horas exatamente, estarei na capela. As Mães Precentoras estarão lá. A Mãe Ascensão estará lá. Dois homens seriam melhores. No entanto, não importa! Vou ter a minha alavanca. Vamos abrir o cofre, vamos baixar o caixão, e vamos fechar o cofre novamente. Depois disso, não haverá vestígios de nada. O governo não terá suspeitas. Assim tudo foi arranjado, reverenda Mãe"?

"Não"!

"O que mais resta"?

"O caixão vazio permanece".

Isso produziu uma pausa. Fauchelevent meditava. A prioresa meditava.

"O que fazer com esse caixão, padre Fauvent"?

"Será dado à terra".

"Vazio"?

Mais um silêncio. Fauchelevent fez, com a mão esquerda, esse tipo de gesto que dispensa um assunto problemático.

"Reverenda Mãe, sou eu que devo pregar o caixão no porão da igreja, e ninguém pode entrar lá além de mim, e cobrirei o caixão com o caixão".

"Sim, mas os portadores, quando o colocarem no carro funerário e o baixarem na sepultura, certamente sentirão que não há nada nele".

"Ah! o de—"!, exclamou Fauchelevent.

A prioresa começou a fazer o sinal da cruz e olhou fixamente para o jardineiro. O *vil* enfiou-se depressa na garganta.

Apressou-se a improvisar um expediente para fazê-la esquecer o juramento.

"Vou colocar terra no caixão, reverenda mãe. Isso produzirá o efeito de um cadáver".

"Tem razão. Terra, isso é a mesma coisa que o homem. Então você vai administrar o caixão vazio"?

"Vou fazer disso o meu negócio especial".

O rosto da prioresa, até aquele momento perturbado e turvo, tornou-se sereno mais uma vez. Ela fez o sinal de um superior dispensando um inferior a ele. Fauchelevent foi em direção à porta. Quando ele estava prestes a desmaiar, a prioresa levantou a voz suavemente:

"Estou contente contigo, Padre Fauvent; traga o seu irmão até mim, depois do enterro, e diga-lhe para ir buscar a sua filha".

CAPÍTULO IV

EM QUE JEAN VALJEAN TEM BASTANTE AR DE TER LIDO AUSTIN CASTILLEJO

Os passos de um coxo são como os olhares de um homem de um olho só; eles não atingem seu objetivo muito rapidamente. Além disso, Fauchelevent estava em um dilema. Demorou quase um quarto de hora a regressar à sua casa no jardim. Cosette tinha acordado. Jean Valjean colocou-a perto do fogo. No momento em que Fauchelevent entrou, Jean Valjean estava apontando para ela a cesta de vintner na parede e dizendo-lhe: "Ouça-me atentamente, minha pequena Cosette. Temos de nos afastar desta casa, mas voltaremos a ela, e aqui ficaremos muito felizes. O homem bom que mora aqui vai te levar nas costas nisso. Você vai me esperar na casa de uma senhora. Eu virei buscá-lo. Obedeça e não diga nada, acima de tudo, a menos que queira que Madame Thénardier o pegue novamente"!

Cosette assentiu gravemente.

Jean Valjean virou-se perante o barulho feito por Fauchel, abrindo a porta.

"Bem"?

"Tudo está arranjado e nada está", disse Fauchelevent. "Eu tenho permissão para trazê-lo; mas antes de trazê-lo você deve ser retirado. É aí que reside a dificuldade. É bastante fácil com a criança".

"Você vai levá-la adiante"?

"E ela vai segurar a língua?

"Eu respondo por isso".

"Mas você, padre Madeleine?

E, depois de um silêncio, carregado de ansiedade, Fauchelevent exclamou:

"Ora, saia como entrou"!

Jean Valjean, como em primeira instância, contentou-se em dizer: "Impossível".

Fauchelevent resmungou, mais para si do que para Jean Valjean:

"Há outra coisa que me incomoda. Eu disse que colocaria terra nele. Quando eu pensar nisso, a terra em vez do cadáver não vai parecer a coisa real, não vai fazer, vai ficar deslocada, vai se mover. Os homens vão suportá-lo. Você entende, padre Madeleine, o governo vai notar isso".

Jean Valjean olhou-o fixamente nos olhos e pensou que ele estava delirando.

Fauchelevent continuou:—

"Como é que você vai sair? Tudo deve ser feito até amanhã de manhã. É para amanhã que vos trago para dentro. A prioresa espera por você".

Em seguida, explicou a Jean Valjean que esta era a sua recompensa por um serviço que ele, Fauchelevent, deveria prestar à comunidade. Que cabia entre as suas funções participar nos enterros, que pregava os caixões e ajudava o coveiro no cemitério. Que a freira que morrera naquela manhã pedira para ser enterrada no caixão que lhe servira de cama, e enterrada na abóbada sob o altar da capela. Que o regulamento policial proibia isso, mas que ela era uma das mortas a quem nada é recusado. Que a prioresa e as mães vocais pretendiam realizar o desejo do falecido. Que foi muito pior para o governo. Que ele, Fauchelevent, deveria pregar o caixão na cela, levantar a pedra na capela e abaixar o cadáver na abóbada. E que, a título de agradecimento, a prioresa devia admitir o irmão na casa como jardineiro e a sobrinha como aluna. Que seu irmão era M. Madeleine, e que sua sobrinha era Cosette. Que a prioresa lhe dissera para trazer o irmão na noite seguinte, após o enterro falsificado no cemitério. Mas que ele não poderia trazer M. Madeleine de fora se M. Madeleine não estivesse do lado de fora. Esse foi o primeiro problema. E depois, que havia outro: o caixão vazio.

"O que é esse caixão vazio"?, perguntou Jean Valjean.

Fauchelevent respondeu:—

"O caixão da administração".

"Que caixão? Que administração"?

"Morre uma freira. O médico municipal chega e diz: 'Morreu uma freira'. O governo envia um caixão. No dia seguinte, envia um carro funerário e agentes funerários para pegar o caixão e levá-lo ao cemitério. Os homens do agente funerário virão e levantarão o caixão; não haverá nada nele".

"Coloque alguma coisa nele".

"Um cadáver? Não tenho nenhuma".

"Não".

"E então"?

"Uma pessoa viva".

"Que pessoa"?

"Eu"!, disse Jean Valjean.

Fauchelevent, que estava sentado, surgiu como se uma bomba tivesse estourado sob sua cadeira.

"Você"!

"Por que não"?

Jean Valjean deu lugar a um daqueles raros sorrisos que lhe iluminavam o rosto como um clarão do céu no inverno.

"Sabes, Fauchel, o que disseste: 'A mãe crucificação está morta', e eu acrescento: 'e o padre Madeleine está enterrado'".

"Ah! bom, você pode rir, você não está falando sério".

"Muito a sério, tenho de sair deste sítio".

"Com certeza".

"Eu disse para você encontrar uma cesta, e uma cobertura para mim também".

"Bem"?

"O cesto será de pinho e a capa um pano preto".

312

"Em primeiro lugar, será um pano branco. As freiras são enterradas de branco".

"Que seja um pano branco, então".

"Você não é como os outros homens, padre Madeleine".

Contemplar tais artifícios, que nada mais são do que as invenções selvagens e ousadas das galés, brotam das coisas pacíficas que o cercavam e se misturam com o que ele chamou de "pequeno curso de vida no convento", causou tanto espanto quanto uma pesca de gaivota na sarjeta da Rue Saint-Denis inspiraria em um transeunte.

Jean Valjean prosseguiu:—

"O problema é sair daqui sem ser visto. Isto oferece os meios. Mas dêem-me algumas informações, em primeiro lugar. Como é gerido? Onde está esse caixão"?

"O vazio"?

"Sim".

"No andar de baixo, no que se chama de sala morta. Ergue-se sobre dois cavaletes, debaixo do palco".

"Quanto tempo dura o caixão"?

"Seis pés".

"O que é este quarto morto"?

"É uma câmara no rés do chão que tem uma janela ralada que se abre no jardim, que é fechada no exterior por uma persiana, e duas portas; um conduz ao convento, o outro à igreja".

"Que igreja"?

"A igreja na rua, a igreja em que qualquer um pode entrar".

"Você tem as chaves dessas duas portas"?

"Não; Tenho a chave da porta que comunica com o convento; o porteiro tem a chave da porta que comunica com a igreja".

"Quando é que o porteiro abre essa porta"?

"Só para permitir que os homens do agente funerário entrem, quando vêm buscar o caixão. Quando o caixão é retirado, a porta é fechada novamente".

"Quem prega o caixão"?

"Eu faço".

"Quem espalha o fel sobre ele"?

"Eu faço".

"Você está sozinho"?

"Nenhum outro homem, exceto o médico da polícia, pode entrar na sala morta. Isso até está escrito na parede".

"Você poderia me esconder naquele quarto esta noite quando todos estão dormindo"?

"Não. Mas eu poderia escondê-lo em um pequeno recanto escuro que se abre na sala morta, onde guardo minhas ferramentas para usar em enterros, e do qual tenho a chave".

"A que horas virá o carro funerário para o caixão"?

"Por volta das três horas da tarde. O enterro ocorrerá no cemitério de Vaugirard um pouco antes do anoitecer. Não está muito perto".

"Ficarei escondido no seu armário de ferramentas a noite toda e toda a manhã. E a comida? Vou ter fome".

"Vou trazer-lhe alguma coisa".

"Você pode vir me pregar no caixão às duas horas".

Fauchelevent recuou e quebrou as articulações dos dedos.

"Mas isso é impossível"!

"Bah! Impossível pegar um martelo e cravar uns pregos numa prancha"?

O que parecia inédito para Fauchelevent era, repetimos, uma questão simples para Jean Valjean. Jean Valjean tinha estado numa situação pior do que esta. Qualquer homem que tenha sido prisioneiro sabe como se contrair para caber no diâmetro da fuga. O prisioneiro está sujeito a fuga, pois o doente está sujeito a uma crise que o salva ou mata. Uma fuga é uma cura. O que é que um homem não se submete por causa da cura? Ter sido pregado num estojo e levado como um fardo de mercadorias, viver muito tempo numa caixa, encontrar ar onde não há, poupar fôlego durante horas, saber sufocar sem morrer – este era um dos talentos sombrios de Jean Valjean.

Além disso, um caixão contendo um ser vivo, expediente desse condenado, é também um expediente imperial. Se quisermos creditar ao monge Austin Castillejo, este foi o meio empregado por Carlos, o Quinto, desejoso de ver os Plombes pela última vez após sua abdicação.

Ele mandou trazê-la e levá-la para fora do mosteiro de Saint-Yuste desta maneira.

Fauchelevent, que se tinha recuperado um pouco, exclamou:

"Mas como você vai conseguir respirar"?

"Vou respirar".

"Nessa caixa! O simples pensamento disso me sufoca".

"Você certamente deve ter uma luva, você vai fazer alguns buracos aqui e ali, ao redor da minha boca, e você vai pregar a prancha superior frouxamente".

"Bom! E se acontecer de tossir ou espirrar"?

"Um homem que está a fugir não tosse nem espirra".

E Jean Valjean acrescentou: –

"Padre Fauchel, temos de chegar a uma decisão: ou sou apanhado aqui, ou aceito esta fuga pelo carro funerário".

Todos já repararam no gosto que os gatos têm por parar e descansar entre as duas folhas de uma porta semi-fechada. Quem está lá que não disse a um gato: "Entre"! Há homens que, quando um incidente está semiaberto diante deles, têm a mesma tendência a parar na indecisão entre duas resoluções, correndo o risco de serem esmagados pelo encerramento abrupto da aventura pelo destino. Os excessivamente prudentes, gatos como são, e porque são gatos, às vezes incorrem em mais perigo do que os audaciosos. Fauchelevent era dessa natureza hesitante. Mas a frieza de Jean Valjean prevaleceu sobre ele, apesar de si mesmo. Ele resmungou: –

"Bem, já que não há outros meios".

Jean Valjean retomou:—

"A única coisa que me incomoda é o que vai acontecer no cemitério".

"Esse é o ponto que não é problemático", exclamou Fauchelevent. "Se você tem certeza de sair bem do caixão, eu tenho certeza de tirá-lo do túmulo. O coveiro é um bêbado e um amigo meu. Ele é o Padre Mestienne. Um velho companheiro da velha escola. O coveiro coloca os cadáveres na sepultura, e eu coloco o coveiro no bolso. Vou dizer-vos o que vai acontecer. Eles chegarão um pouco antes do anoitecer, três quartos de hora antes do fechamento dos portões do cemitério. O carro funerário irá diretamente até a sepultura. Seguirei; esse é o meu negócio. Vou ter um martelo, um cinzel e umas pinças no bolso. O carro funerário para, os homens do agente funerário amarram uma corda em torno do seu caixão e abaixam-no. O sacerdote faz as orações, faz o sinal da cruz, asperge a água benta e parte dele. Fico sozinho com o Padre Mestienne. Ele é meu amigo, digo-lhe. Uma das duas coisas acontecerá, ou ele estará sóbrio, ou não estará sóbrio. Se ele não estiver bêbado, dir-lhe-ei: 'Venha beber enquanto o *Bon Coing* [o Marmelo Bom] estiver aberto'. Eu o carrego, eu o pego bêbado", não demora muito para deixar o padre Mestienne bêbado, ele sempre tem o começo disso sobre ele", eu o deito debaixo da mesa, pego seu cartão, para que eu possa entrar no cemitério novamente, e volto sem ele. Então você não tem mais ninguém além de mim para lidar. Se estiver bêbado, dir-lhe-ei: 'Afasta-te; Eu farei o seu trabalho por você'. Fora ele vai, e eu te arrasto para fora do buraco".

Jean Valjean estendeu a mão e Fauchelevent precipitou-se sobre ela com a comovente efusão de um camponês.

"Isso está resolvido, padre Fauchelevent. Tudo vai correr bem".

"Desde que nada corra mal", pensou Fauchelevent. "Nesse caso, seria terrível".

CAPÍTULO V

NÃO É NECESSÁRIO ESTAR BÊBADO PARA SER IMORTAL

No dia seguinte, quando o sol estava diminuindo, os raros transeuntes no Boulevard du Maine tiraram o chapéu para um carro funerário antiquado, ornamentado com caveiras, ossos cruzados e lágrimas. Este carro funerário continha um caixão coberto com um pano branco sobre o qual se estendia uma grande cruz negra, como um enorme cadáver com os braços caídos. Seguiu-se um treinador de luto, no qual se podia ver um padre na sua súplica, e um menino de coro no seu boné vermelho. Dois agentes funerários com uniformes cinzas guarnecidos de preto caminhavam à direita e à esquerda do carro funerário. Atrás dela vinha um velho vestido de operário, que mancava junto. O cortejo seguia em direção ao cemitério de Vaugirard.

O cabo de um martelo, a lâmina de um cinzel frio e a antennæ de um par de pinças eram visíveis, salientes do bolso do homem.

O cemitério de Vaugirard formou uma exceção entre os cemitérios de Paris. Tinha seus usos peculiares, assim como tinha sua entrada de carruagem e sua porta de casa, que os velhos do bairro, que se agarravam tenazmente a palavras antigas, ainda chamavam de *porte cavalière* e *porte piétonne*.16 Os bernardinos-beneditinos da Rue Petit-Picpus tinham obtido autorização, como já referimos, para aí serem enterrados num canto à parte, e à noite, tendo o terreno pertencido anteriormente à sua comunidade. Sendo os coveiros assim obrigados a prestar serviço à noite no verão e à noite no inverno, neste cemitério, eram submetidos a uma disciplina especial. Os portões dos cemitérios de Paris fecharam-se, naquela época, ao pôr-do-sol, e sendo este um regulamento municipal, o cemitério de Vaugirard estava vinculado a ele como os outros. O portão da carruagem e a porta da casa eram dois portões ralados contíguos, contíguos a um pavilhão construído pelo arquiteto Perronet, e habitados pelo porteiro do cemitério. Esses portões, portanto, balançaram inexoravelmente sobre suas dobradiças no instante em que o sol desapareceu atrás da cúpula dos Inválidos. Se algum coveiro se atrasasse depois daquele momento no cemitério, só havia uma maneira de ele sair: o cartão de coveiro fornecido pelo departamento de funerais públicos. Uma espécie de caixa de correio foi construída na janela do porteiro. O coveiro deixou cair o cartão nesta caixa, o porteiro ouviu-o cair, puxou a corda e a pequena porta abriu-se. Se o homem não tinha o seu cartão, mencionou o seu nome, o porteiro, que às vezes estava na cama e dormindo, levantou-se, saiu e identificou o homem, e abriu o portão com a sua chave; O coveiro saiu, mas teve de pagar uma multa de quinze francos.

Este cemitério, com suas peculiaridades fora dos regulamentos, embaraçava a simetria da administração. Foi suprimido pouco depois de 1830. O cemitério de Mont-Parnasse, chamado de cemitério oriental, sucedeu-lhe, e herdou aquela famosa loja de carrinhos ao lado do cemitério de Vaugirard, que era encimada por um marmelo pintado em uma tábua, e que formava um ângulo, um lado nas mesas dos bebedores, e o outro nos túmulos, com este sinal: *Au Bon Coing*.

O cemitério de Vaugirard era o que pode ser chamado de cemitério desbotado. Estava caindo em desuso. A humidade invadia-a, as flores desertavam-na. Os burgueses não se importavam muito em ser enterrados no Vaugirard; insinuava pobreza. Père-Lachaise, se quiser! ser enterrado em Père-Lachaise equivale a ter móveis de mogno. É reconhecido como elegante. O cemitério de Vaugirard era um recinto venerável, plantado como um jardim francês à moda antiga. Becos retos, caixa, thuya-árvores, azevinho, túmulos antigos sob ciprestes envelhecidos e grama muito alta. À noite foi trágico lá. Havia linhas muito lúgubres sobre isso.

O sol ainda não se tinha posto quando o carro funerário com o fel branco e a cruz negra entrou na avenida do cemitério de Vaugirard. O coxo que o seguiu não foi outro senão Fauchelevent.

O enterro da Mãe Crucificação na abóbada sob o altar, a saída de Cosette, a introdução de Jean Valjean no quarto morto, tudo tinha sido executado sem dificuldade, e não tinha havido problemas.

Observemos, de passagem, que o enterro da Mãe Crucificação sob o altar do convento é uma ofensa perfeitamente venial aos nossos olhos. É uma das falhas que se assemelham a um dever. As freiras tinham-no cometido, não só sem dificuldade, mas até com o aplauso das suas próprias consciências. No claustro, aquilo a que se chama "governo" não passa de uma intromissão na autoridade, uma interferência sempre questionável. Em primeiro lugar, a regra; Quanto ao código, veremos. Fazei quantas leis quiserdes, homens; mas guardai-os para vós. O tributo a César nunca é nada além dos restos do tributo a Deus. Um príncipe não é nada na presença de um princípio.

Fauchelevent mancava atrás do carro funerário num estado de espírito muito contente. As suas tramas gémeas, uma com as freiras, uma para o convento, outra contra, outra com M. Madeleine, tinham conseguido, ao que tudo indica. A compostura de Jean Valjean era uma daquelas tranquilidades poderosas que são contagiosas. Fauchelevent já não duvidava do seu sucesso.

O que faltava fazer era um mero nada. Nos últimos dois anos, ele tinha feito bem Padre Mestienne, uma pessoa gordinha, bêbado pelo menos dez vezes. Tocou com o Padre Mestienne. Fazia o que gostava com ele. Fê-lo dançar de acordo com o seu capricho. A cabeça de Mestienne ajustou-se ao limite da vontade de Fauchelevent. A confiança de Fauchelevent era perfeita.

No momento em que o comboio entrou na avenida que leva ao cemitério, Fauchelevent olhou alegremente para o carro funerário e disse meio em voz alta, enquanto esfregava as grandes mãos:

"Aqui está uma bela farsa"!

De repente, o carro funerário parou; tinha chegado ao portão. A autorização para o enterro deve ser exibida. O agente funerário dirigiu-se ao porteiro do cemitério. Durante este colóquio, que é sempre produtivo de um atraso de um a dois minutos, alguém, um estranho, veio e colocou-se atrás do carro funerário, ao lado de Fauchelevent. Era uma espécie de homem trabalhador, que usava um colete com grandes bolsos e carregava um colchão debaixo do braço.

Fauchelevent inquiriu este estranho.

"Quem é você"?, exigiu.

"O homem respondeu: —

"O coveiro".

Se um homem pudesse sobreviver ao golpe de uma bola de canhão cheia no peito, ele faria a mesma cara que Fauchel fez.

"O coveiro"?

"Sim".

"Você"?

"Eu".

"O padre Mestienne é o coveiro".

"Ele estava".

"O quê! Ele estava"?

"Ele está morto".

Fauchelevent esperava tudo menos isso, que um coveiro pudesse morrer. É verdade, no entanto, que os coveiros morrem eles próprios. Ao escavar sepulturas para outras pessoas, esvazia-se a sua.

Fauchelevent ficou ali de boca aberta. Ele mal tinha forças para gaguejar:—

"Mas não é possível"!

"É assim".

"Mas", insistiu fracamente, "o padre Mestienne é o coveiro".

"Depois de Napoleão, Luís XVIII. Depois de Mestienne, Gribier. Camponesa, meu nome é Gribier".

Fauchel, que estava mortalmente pálido, olhou para este Gribier.

Era um homem alto, magro, lívido e totalmente fúnebre. Tinha o ar de médico malsucedido que se tornara coveiro.

Fauchelevent caiu na gargalhada.

"Ah"!, disse ele, "que coisas queer acontecem! Padre Mestienne está morto, mas viva o pequeno Padre Lenoir! Sabe quem é o pequeno Padre Lenoir? Ele é um jarro de vinho tinto. É um jarro de Surêne, morbigou! de Paris Surêne real? Ah! Tão velha Mestienne está morta! Lamento por isso; Era um sujeito alegre. Mas você também é um sujeito alegre. Não és, camarada? Vamos tomar uma bebida juntos agora".

O homem respondeu: —

"Já fui estudante. Passei no meu quarto exame. Eu nunca bebo".

O carro funerário tinha partido de novo, e estava rolando pelo grande beco do cemitério.

Fauchelevent tinha abrandado o ritmo. Mancava mais por ansiedade do que por enfermidade.

O coveiro caminhou à sua frente.

Fauchelevent passou o inesperado Gribier mais uma vez em revisão.

Ele era um daqueles homens que, embora muito jovens, têm ar de idade e que, embora esguios, são extremamente fortes.

"Camarada"!, gritou Fauchelevent.

O homem virou-se.

"Eu sou o coveiro do convento".

"Meu colega" disse o homem.

Fauchel, que era analfabeto, mas muito perspicaz, entendeu que tinha que lidar com uma espécie formidável de homem, com um bom falador. Ele murmurou:

"Então o padre Mestienne está morto".

O homem respondeu: —

"Completamente. O bom Deus consultou o seu caderno de notas que mostra quando o tempo acabou. Foi a vez do Padre Mestienne. O padre Mestienne morreu".

Fauchelevent repetiu mecanicamente: "O bom Deus—"

"O bom Deus" disse o homem com autoridade. "Segundo os filósofos, o Pai Eterno; segundo os jacobinos, o Ser Supremo".

"Não vamos nos conhecer"?, gaguejou Fauchel.

"Está feito. Você é camponês, eu sou parisiense".

"As pessoas não se conhecem até terem bebido juntas. Quem esvazia o copo esvazia o coração. Você deve vir e tomar uma bebida comigo. Tal coisa não pode ser recusada".

"Negócios em primeiro lugar".

Fauchelevent pensou: "Estou perdido".

Eram apenas algumas voltas da roda distantes do pequeno beco que levava ao canto das freiras.

O coveiro retomou:

"Camponesa, tenho sete filhos pequenos que devem ser alimentados. Como eles têm de comer, eu não posso beber".

E acrescentou, com a satisfação de um homem sério que está a virar bem uma frase:

"A fome deles é inimiga da minha sede".

O carro funerário contornou um amontoado de ciprestes, abandonou o grande beco, transformou-se num estreito, entrou no terreno baldio e mergulhou num matagal. Isso indicava a proximidade imediata do local da sepultura. Fauchelevent afrouxou o ritmo, mas não conseguiu deter o carro funerário. Felizmente, o solo, que estava leve e molhado com as chuvas de inverno, entupiu as rodas e retardou sua velocidade.

Aproximou-se do coveiro.

"Eles têm um pequeno vinho Argenteuil tão bom", murmurou Fauchelevent.

"Villager", retrucou o homem, "eu não deveria ser coveiro. O meu pai era porteiro no Prytaneum [Câmara Municipal]. Ele me destinou para a literatura. Mas teve retrocessos. Ele teve perdas na 'mudança'. Fui obrigado a renunciar à profissão de autor. Mas continuo a ser um escritor público".

"Então você não é coveiro, então"?, devolveu Fauchel, agarrado a este ramo, débil como era.

"Um não atrapalha o outro. Eu acumulo".

Fauchelevent não entendeu esta última palavra.

"Venha tomar uma bebida", disse ele.

Neste caso, torna-se necessária uma observação. Fauchel, qualquer que fosse a sua angústia, ofereceu uma bebida, mas não se explicou em um ponto; Quem devia pagar? Geralmente, Fauchelevent oferecia e o Padre Mestienne pagava. Uma oferta de bebida foi o resultado evidente da nova situação criada pelo novo coveiro, e foi necessário fazer essa oferta, mas o velho jardineiro deixou o proverbial quarto de hora com o nome de Rabelais no escuro, e isso não sem querer. Quanto a si próprio, Fauchel não quis pagar, perturbado como estava.

O coveiro prosseguiu com um sorriso superior:

"É preciso comer. Aceitei a reversão do Padre Mestienne. Chega-se a ser filósofo quando se está quase a concluir as aulas. Ao trabalho da mão junto-me o trabalho do braço. Tenho a minha banca de escrivão no mercado da Rue de Sèvres. Tu sabes? o Mercado dos Guarda-Chuvas. Todos os cozinheiros da Cruz Vermelha se aplicam a mim. Rabisco as suas declarações de amor aos soldados crus. De manhã escrevo cartas de amor; à noite cavo sepulturas. Assim é a vida, rústica".

O carro funerário continuava a avançar. Fauchelevent, inquieto até o último grau, olhava para ele por todos os lados. Grandes gotas de transpiração escorriam de sua testa.

"Mas", continuou o coveiro, "um homem não pode servir duas amantes. Tenho de escolher entre a caneta e o mattock. O mattock está arruinando minha mão".

O carro funerário parou.

O menino do coro desceu do treinador de luto, depois o padre.

Uma das pequenas rodas dianteiras do carro funerário tinha subido um pouco sobre uma pilha de terra, além da qual era visível uma sepultura aberta.

"Que farsa é essa"!, repetiu Fauchel, consternado.

CAPÍTULO VI

ENTRE QUATRO TÁBUAS

Quem estava no caixão? O leitor sabe. Jean Valjean.

Jean Valjean tinha arranjado as coisas para que ele pudesse existir lá, e ele quase pudesse respirar.

É estranho o grau de segurança de consciência que confere segurança ao resto. Todas as combinações pensadas por Jean Valjean vinham progredindo, e progredindo favoravelmente, desde o dia anterior. Ele, como Fauchelevent, contava com o padre Mestienne. Não teve dúvidas quanto ao fim. Nunca houve uma situação tão crítica, nunca uma compostura tão completa.

As quatro tábuas do caixão exalam uma espécie de paz terrível. Parecia que algo do repouso dos mortos entrava na tranquilidade de Jean Valjean.

Das profundezas daquele caixão conseguira acompanhar, e acompanhara, todas as fases do terrível drama que brincava com a morte.

Pouco depois de Fauchelevent ter terminado de pregar na prancha superior, Jean Valjean sentiu-se executado, depois expulso. Sabia, pela diminuição do solavanco, quando saíram das calçadas e chegaram à estrada de terra. Ele adivinhara, de um barulho enfadonho, que eles estavam atravessando a ponte de Austerlitz. Na primeira parada, ele tinha entendido que eles estavam entrando no cemitério; Na segunda paragem, disse a si mesmo:

"Aqui está a sepultura".

De repente, sentiu as mãos agarrarem o caixão, depois uma grade dura contra as tábuas; Ele explicou a si mesmo como a corda que estava sendo presa ao redor do caixão, a fim de baixá-lo na cavidade.

Então ele experimentou uma vertigem.

O agente funerário e o coveiro provavelmente permitiram que o caixão perdesse o equilíbrio e baixaram a cabeça antes do pé. Recuperou-se totalmente quando se sentiu horizontal e imóvel. Ele tinha acabado de tocar o fundo.

Tinha uma certa sensação de frio.

Uma voz ergueu-se sobre ele, glacial e solene. Ouviu palavras latinas, que não compreendia, passarem por cima dele, tão lentamente que conseguiu apanhá-las uma a uma:

"Qui dormiunt in terræ pulvere, evigilabunt; alii in vitam æternam, et alii in approbrium, ut videant semper".

A voz de uma criança disse: —

"De profundis".

A voz grave recomeçou:

"Requiem æternam dona ei, Domine".

A voz da criança respondeu: —

"Et lux perpetua luceat ei".

Ouviu algo como o suave respingo de várias gotas de chuva na prancha que o cobria. Provavelmente era a água benta.

Ele pensou: "Isso vai acabar em breve. Paciência por mais algum tempo. O padre vai partir. Fauchelevent vai levar Mestienne para beber. Ficarei à esquerda. Então Fauchelevent voltará sozinho, e eu sairei. Esse será o trabalho de uma boa hora".

A voz grave retomou

"Requiescat no ritmo".

E a voz da criança disse: —

"Amém".

Jean Valjean coou os ouvidos e ouviu algo como recuar passos.

"Lá, eles estão indo agora", pensou ele. "Estou sozinho".

De repente, ouviu sobre a cabeça um som que lhe pareceu um trovão.

Era uma pá de terra caindo sobre o caixão.

Uma segunda pá caiu.

Um dos orifícios por onde respirava tinha acabado de ser parado.

Uma terceira pá de terra caiu.

Depois, um quarto.

Há coisas que são fortes demais para o homem mais forte.

CAPÍTULO VII

EM QUE SE ENCONTRA A ORIGEM DO DITADO: NÃO PERCA O CARTÃO

Foi o que aconteceu por cima do caixão em que jazia Jean Valjean.

Quando o carro funerário partiu, quando o padre e o menino do coro entraram novamente na carruagem e partiram, Fauchel, que não tinha tirado os olhos do coveiro, viu este curvar-se e agarrar a pá, que se enfiava de pé no monte de terra.

Então Fauchelevent tomou uma decisão suprema.

Colocou-se entre a sepultura e o coveiro, cruzou os braços e disse:

"Quem paga sou eu"!

O coveiro olhou-o espantado e respondeu: —

"O que é isso, camponês"?

Fauchelevent repetiu:—

"Quem paga sou eu"!

"O quê"?

"Para o vinho".

"Que vinho"?

"Aquele vinho Argenteuil".

"Onde está o Argenteuil"?

"No *Bon Coing*".

"Vá para o diabo"!, disse o coveiro.

E jogou uma pá de terra no caixão.

O caixão devolveu um som oco. Fauchelevent sentiu-se cambaleante e a ponto de cair de cabeça na sepultura. Ele gritou com uma voz em que o som estrangulado do chocalho da morte começou a se misturar:

"Camarada! Antes que o *Bon Coing* seja fechado"!

O coveiro levou mais terra na pá. Fauchelevent continuou.

"Vou pagar".

E agarrou o braço do homem.

"Ouça-me, camarada. Eu sou o coveiro do convento, vim para ajudar-vos. É um negócio que pode ser realizado à noite. Comecemos, então, por tomar uma bebida".

E enquanto falava, e se agarrava a essa insistência desesperada, ocorreu-lhe esta reflexão melancólica: "E se ele beber, vai ficar bêbado"?

"Provinciano", disse o homem, "se você insistir positivamente, eu concordo. Nós vamos beber. Depois do trabalho, nunca antes".

E ele floresceu sua pá rapidamente. Fauchelevent o conteve.

"É o vinho Argenteuil, às seis".

"Oh, venha", disse o coveiro, "você é um sineiro. Ding dong, ding dong, isso é tudo o que você sabe dizer. Vá se enforcar".

E jogou uma segunda pá.

Fauchelevent tinha chegado a um ponto em que já não sabia o que estava a dizer.

"Vem beber", gritou, "já que sou eu que pago a conta".

"Quando colocamos a criança na cama", disse o coveiro.

Ele arremessou em uma terceira pá.

Então ele jogou sua pá na terra e acrescentou: —

"Está frio esta noite, você vê, e o cadáver gritaria atrás de nós se fôssemos plantá-la lá sem uma capa".

Nesse momento, enquanto carregava a pá, o coveiro inclinou-se e o bolso do colete abriu-se. O olhar selvagem de Fauchelevent caiu mecanicamente naquele bolso, e lá parou.

O sol ainda não estava escondido atrás do horizonte; ainda havia luz suficiente para lhe permitir distinguir algo branco no fundo daquele bolso bocejando.

A soma total de relâmpagos que o olho de um camponês Picard pode conter, atravessou as pupilas de Fauchelevent. Acabara de lhe ocorrer uma ideia.

Enfiou a mão no bolso por trás, sem que o coveiro, que estava totalmente absorvido em sua pá de terra, observando-a, e puxou o objeto branco que estava no fundo dela.

O homem mandou uma quarta pá cair na sepultura.

Assim que se virou para conseguir o quinto, Fauchel olhou calmamente para ele e disse:

"A propósito, seu novo homem, você tem seu cartão"?

O coveiro fez uma pausa.

"Que cartão"?

"O sol está a ponto de se pôr".

"Isso é bom, vai colocar a sua touca".

"O portão do cemitério fechará imediatamente".

"Bem, e então"?

"Tem o seu cartão"?

"Ah! meu cartão"?, disse o coveiro.

E ele se atrapalhou no bolso.

Tendo revistado um bolso, passou a revistar o outro. Passou para os seus fobs, explorou o primeiro, voltou para o segundo.

"Ora, não", disse ele, "eu não tenho o meu cartão. Devo tê-lo esquecido".

"Quinze francos de multa", disse Fauchelevent.

O coveiro ficou verde. O verde é a palidez das pessoas lívidas.

"Ah! Jesus-meu-Deus-banco-abaixo-da-lua"![17] exclamou. "Quinze francos bem"!

"Três pedaços de cem sous", disse Fauchelevent.

O coveiro largou a pá.

Chegara a vez de Fauchelevent.

"Ah, venha agora, recruta", disse Fauchel, "nada desse desespero. Não se trata de cometer suicídio e beneficiar a sepultura. Quinze francos é quinze francos e, além disso, você pode não ser capaz de pagá-lo. Eu sou uma mão velha, você é uma mão nova. Eu conheço todas as cordas e os dispositivos. Vou dar-lhe alguns conselhos amigáveis. Uma coisa é clara, o sol está a ponto de se pôr, está tocando a cúpula agora, o cemitério será fechado em mais cinco minutos".

"Isso é verdade", respondeu o homem.

"Mais cinco minutos e você não terá tempo de encher a sepultura, ela é tão oca quanto o diabo, esta sepultura, e chegar ao portão na época para passá-la antes que ela seja fechada".

"É verdade".

"Nesse caso, uma multa de quinze francos".

"Quinze francos".

"Mas você tem tempo. Onde você mora"?

"A alguns passos da barreira, a um quarto de hora daqui. Nº 87 Rue de Vaugirard".

"Você tem apenas tempo para sair, levando para seus calcanhares na sua melhor velocidade".

"É exatamente assim".

"Uma vez fora do portão, você galopa para casa, recebe seu cartão, volta, o porteiro do cemitério te admite. Como tem o seu cartão, não haverá nada a pagar. E enterrarás o teu cadáver. Enquanto isso, velarei por você, para que não fuja".

"Estou em dívida contigo pela minha vida, camponês".

"Decamp"!, disse Fauchelevent.

O coveiro, tomado de gratidão, apertou a mão e saiu correndo.

Quando o homem desapareceu no matagal, Fauchelevent ouviu até ouvir seus passos morrerem ao longe, então ele se debruçou sobre a sepultura e disse em tom baixo:

"Padre Madeleine"!

Não houve resposta.

Fauchelevent foi tomado com um susto. Ele tombou em vez de subir na sepultura, atirou-se sobre a cabeça do caixão e gritou:

"Você está lá"?

Silêncio no caixão.

Fauchel, mal conseguindo respirar para tremer, agarrou seu cinzel frio e seu martelo, e levantou a tampa do caixão.

O rosto de Jean Valjean apareceu no crepúsculo; estava pálido e os olhos fechados.

Os cabelos de Fauchelevent ergueram-se na cabeça, ele saltou para os pés, depois caiu de volta contra o lado da sepultura, pronto para desmaiar no caixão. Ele olhou para Jean Valjean.

Jean Valjean jazia ali pálido e imóvel.

Fauchelevent murmurou com uma voz tão ténue como um suspiro: —

"Ele está morto"!

E, levantando-se e cruzando os braços com tanta violência que os punhos cerrados entraram em contato com os ombros, gritou:

"E é assim que eu salvei a vida dele"!

Então o pobre homem caiu a soluçar. Ele soliloquizou o tempo, pois é um erro supor que o solilóquio não é natural. Emoções poderosas muitas vezes falam em voz alta.

"A culpa é do padre Mestienne. Por que esse tolo morreu? Que necessidade havia para ele desistir do fantasma no exato momento em que ninguém estava esperando? Foi ele que matou M. Madeleine. Padre Madeleine! Ele está no caixão. É bastante útil. Tudo acabou. Ora, há algum sentido nestas coisas? Ah! Meu Deus! ele está morto! Pois bem! e sua menina, o que devo fazer com ela? O que dirá o vendedor de frutas? A ideia de ser possível um homem assim morrer assim! Quando penso como ele se colocou debaixo daquele carrinho! Padre Madeleine! Padre Madeleine! Pardine! Ele estava sufocado, eu disse isso. Ele não acreditaria em mim. Pois bem! Aqui está um truque bonito para jogar! Ele está morto, esse homem bom, o melhor homem de todas as pessoas boas de Deus! E sua menina! Ah! Em primeiro lugar, eu não voltarei lá sozinho. Ficarei aqui. Depois de ter feito uma coisa dessas! De que adianta sermos dois velhos, se somos dois velhos tolos! Mas, em primeiro lugar, como conseguiu entrar no convento? Esse foi o início de tudo. Não se deve fazer essas coisas. Padre Madeleine! Padre Madeleine! Padre Madeleine! Madeleine! Monsieur Madeleine! Monsieur le Maire! Ele não me ouve. Agora saia desse arranhão se puder"!

E rasgou o cabelo.

Um som de ralar tornou-se audível através das árvores ao longe. Era o portão do cemitério fechando.

Fauchelevent inclinou-se sobre Jean Valjean, e de repente ele se limitou e recuou até os limites de uma sepultura.

Os olhos de Jean Valjean estavam abertos e olhando para ele.

Ver um cadáver é alarmante, contemplar uma ressurreição é quase tanto. Fauchelevent tornou-se como pedra, pálido, barulhento, esmagado por todos esses excessos de emoção, sem saber se tinha a ver com um homem vivo ou morto, e olhando para Jean Valjean, que estava olhando para ele.

"Adormeci", disse Jean Valjean.

E elevou-se a uma postura sentada.

Fauchelevent caiu de joelhos.

"Apenas, boa Virgem! Como você me assustou"!

Então levantou-se e gritou: —

"Obrigado, padre Madeleine"!

Jean Valjean tinha apenas desmaiado. O ar fresco reanimara-o.

A alegria é o refluxo do terror. Fauchelevent encontrou quase tanta dificuldade em se recuperar quanto Jean Valjean.

"Então você não está morto! Ah! Como você é sábio! Eu te liguei tanto que você voltou. Quando vi os seus olhos fechados, disse: 'Bom! lá está ele, sufocado', eu deveria ter enlouquecido, louco o suficiente para uma camisa de força. Teriam me colocado em Bicêtre. O que você acha que eu deveria ter feito se você estivesse morto? E a sua menina? Tem aquela vendedora de frutas, ela nunca teria entendido! A criança é empurrada para os seus braços, e então – o avô está morto! Que história! Bons santos do paraíso, que conto! Ah! você está vivo, isso é o melhor de tudo"!

"Estou com frio", disse Jean Valjean.

Esta observação recordou completamente Fauchelevent à realidade, e havia uma necessidade premente dela. As almas desses dois homens estavam perturbadas mesmo quando se recuperaram, embora não percebessem, e havia sobre eles algo estranho, que era a perplexidade sinistra inspirada no lugar.

"Vamos sair daqui rapidamente", exclamou Fauchelevent.

Atrapalhou-se no bolso e puxou uma cabaça com a qual se tinha fornecido.

"Mas primeiro, tome uma gota", disse ele.

O frasco terminou o que o ar fresco tinha começado, Jean Valjean engoliu um bocado de aguardente, e recuperou a plena posse de suas faculdades.

Ele saiu do caixão e ajudou Fauchelevent a pregar a tampa novamente.

Três minutos depois, estavam fora da sepultura.

Além disso, Fauchelevent foi perfeitamente composto. Demorou o seu tempo. O cemitério estava fechado. A chegada do coveiro Gribier não foi apreendida. Esse "recruta" estava em casa ocupado em procurar o seu cartão, e com alguma dificuldade em encontrá-lo nos seus alojamentos, uma vez que estava no bolso de Fauchelevent. Sem cartão, não conseguia voltar ao cemitério.

Fauchelevent pegou a pá, e Jean Valjean a picareta, e juntos enterraram o caixão vazio.

Quando a sepultura estava cheia, Fauchelevent disse a Jean Valjean:

"Vamos lá. Vou ficar com a pá; você carrega o colchão".

A noite estava caindo.

Jean Valjean sentiu alguma dificuldade em mover-se e em andar. Tinha-se enrijecido naquele caixão, e tornara-se um pouco como um cadáver. A rigidez da morte tinha-o agarrado entre aquelas quatro tábuas. Teve, de certa forma, de descongelar do túmulo.

"Você está envergonhado", disse Fauchelevent. "É uma pena que eu tenha uma perna de jogo, caso contrário podemos sair rapidamente".

"Bah"!, respondeu Jean Valjean, "quatro passos vão colocar vida nas minhas pernas mais uma vez".

Partiram pelas ruelas por onde o carro funerário tinha passado. Ao chegar antes do portão fechado e do pavilhão do porteiro Fauchelevent, que segurava o cartão do coveiro na mão, largou-o na caixa, o porteiro puxou a corda, o portão abriu-se e eles saíram.

"Como tudo está indo bem"!, disse Fauchelevent; "Que ideia maiúscula foi sua, Padre Madeleine"!

Eles passaram a barreira de Vaugirard da maneira mais simples do mundo. No bairro do cemitério, uma pá e uma picareta equivalem a dois passaportes.

A Rue Vaugirard estava deserta.

"Padre Madeleine" disse Fauchel, erguendo os olhos para as casas" Seus olhos são melhores que os meus. Mostre-me o n.º 87".

"Aqui está", disse Jean Valjean.

"Não há ninguém na rua", disse Fauchelevent. "Dê-me o seu colchão e espere alguns minutos por mim".

Fauchelevent entrou no n.º 87, subiu ao topo, guiado pelo instinto que sempre conduz o pobre homem à guarita, e bateu no escuro, à porta de um sótão.

Uma voz respondeu: "Entre".

Era a voz de Gribier.

Fauchelevent abriu a porta. A habitação do coveiro era, como todas essas habitações miseráveis, uma guarnição sem mobília e sobrecarregada. Um estojo de embalagem – um caixão, talvez – tomou o lugar de uma cômoda, um pote de manteiga servido para um bebedouro, um colchão de palha servido para uma cama, o chão servido em vez de mesas e cadeiras. Num canto, num fragmento esfarrapado que tinha sido um pedaço de um tapete velho, uma mulher magra e várias crianças estavam empilhadas num monte. Todo este interior pobre trazia vestígios de ter sido derrubado. Alguém teria dito que tinha havido um terramoto "por um". As cobertas estavam deslocadas, os trapos espalhados, o jarro quebrado, a mãe chorava, as crianças provavelmente tinham sido espancadas; vestígios de uma busca vigorosa e mal-humorada. Era evidente que o coveiro tinha feito uma busca desesperada pelo seu cartão, e tinha responsabilizado todos os que se encontravam na guarita, desde o jarro à sua mulher, pela sua perda. Usava um ar de desespero.

Mas Fauchelevent estava com muita pressa em terminar esta aventura para tomar conhecimento deste lado triste do seu sucesso.

Ele entrou e disse: —

"Eu te trouxe de volta sua pá e picareta".

Gribier olhou para ele estupefato.

"É você, camponês"?

"E amanhã de manhã você vai encontrar o seu cartão com o porteiro do cemitério".

E deitou a pá e o colchão no chão.

"Qual é o significado disso"?, perguntou Gribier.

"O significado disso é que você largou seu cartão do seu bolso, que eu o encontrei no chão depois que você se foi, que eu enterrei o cadáver, que eu enchi a sepultura, que eu fiz o seu trabalho, que o porteiro lhe devolverá seu cartão e que você não terá que pagar quinze francos. Aí está, recruta".

"Obrigado, morador"!, exclamou Gribier, radiante. "Da próxima vez vou pagar as bebidas".

CAPÍTULO VIII

UM INTERROGATÓRIO BEM-SUCEDIDO

Uma hora depois, na escuridão da noite, dois homens e uma criança apresentaram-se no n.º 62 da Rue Petit-Picpus. O mais velho dos homens levantou o batedor e arrebentou.

Eles eram Fauchelevent, Jean Valjean e Cosette.

Os dois velhos tinham ido buscar Cosette à fruteira na Rue du Chemin-Vert, onde Fauchelevent a tinha depositado no dia anterior. Cosette passara essas vinte e quatro horas tremendo em silêncio e sem entender nada. Ela tremeu a tal ponto que chorou. Não tinha comido nem dormido. O digno vendedor de frutas lhe fizera uma centena de perguntas, sem obter outra resposta senão um olhar melancólico e invariável. Cosette não traiu nada do que viu e ouviu nos últimos dois dias. Ela adivinhou que eles estavam passando por uma crise. Ela estava profundamente consciente de que era necessário "ser bom". Quem nunca experimentou o poder soberano daquelas duas palavras, pronunciadas com um certo acento no ouvido de um pequeno ser aterrorizado: *Não diga nada!* O medo é mudo. Além disso, ninguém guarda um segredo como uma criança.

Mas quando, ao fim destas lúgubres vinte e quatro horas, voltou a contemplar Jean Valjean, deu vazão a tal grito de alegria, que qualquer pessoa ponderada que tivesse acaso ouvido aquele grito, teria adivinhado que ele saía de um abismo.

Fauchelevent pertencia ao convento e conhecia as palavras-passe. Todas as portas se abriram.

Assim foi resolvido o duplo e alarmante problema de como sair e como entrar.

O porteiro, que recebera as suas instruções, abriu a porta do pequeno criado que ligava o pátio ao jardim, e que ainda podia ser vista da rua há vinte anos, no muro ao fundo do pátio, que dava para a entrada da carruagem.

O porteiro admitiu os três por esta porta, e a partir daí chegaram ao salão interno e reservado onde Fauchelevent, no dia anterior, recebera suas ordens da prioresa.

A prioresa, rosário na mão, esperava-os. Uma mãe vocal, com o véu abaixado, estava ao seu lado.

Uma discreta vela acesa, pode-se quase dizer, fez um show de iluminação do salão.

A prioresa passou Jean Valjean em revisão. Não há nada que se assemelhe a um olhar abatido.

Então ela o questionou: —

"Você é o irmão"?

"Sim, reverenda mãe", respondeu Fauchel.

"Qual é o seu nome"?

Fauchelevent respondeu:—

"Ultimate Fauchelevent".

Ele realmente tinha tido um irmão chamado Ultime, que estava morto.

"De onde você vem"?

Fauchelevent respondeu:—

"De Picquigny, perto de Amiens".

"Qual é a sua idade"?

Fauchelevent respondeu:—

"Cinquenta".

"Qual é a sua profissão"?

Fauchelevent respondeu:—

"Jardineiro".

"Você é um bom cristão"?

Fauchelevent respondeu:—

"Todos estão na família".

"Esta é a sua menina"?

Fauchelevent respondeu:—

"Sim, reverenda mãe".

"Você é o pai dela"?

Fauchelevent respondeu:—

"O avô dela".

A mãe vocal disse à prioresa em voz baixa

"Ele responde bem".

Jean Valjean não proferiu uma única palavra.

A prioresa olhou atentamente para Cosette, e disse meio em voz alta para a mãe vocal:

"Ela vai crescer feia".

As duas mães consultaram-se por alguns instantes em tons muito baixos no canto do salão, depois a prioresa virou-se e disse:

"Pai Fauvent, você vai ter outra rótula com um sino. Dois serão necessários agora".

No dia seguinte, portanto, dois sinos foram audíveis no jardim, e as freiras não resistiram à tentação de levantar o canto de seus véus. No extremo do jardim, sob as árvores, dois homens, Fauvent e outro homem, eram visíveis enquanto cavavam lado a lado. Um evento enorme. O silêncio foi quebrado ao ponto de dizerem uns aos outros: "Ele é um jardineiro assistente".

As mães vocais acrescentaram: "Ele é irmão do padre Fauvent".

Jean Valjean foi, de facto, instalado regularmente; tinha a rótula de campainha; doravante, era oficial. Chamava-se Ultime Fauchelevent.

A causa determinante mais poderosa de sua admissão tinha sido a observação da prioresa sobre Cosette: "Ela vai crescer feia".

A prioresa, que prognosticadora pronunciada, imediatamente levou uma fantasia para Cosette e deu-lhe um lugar na escola como aluna de caridade.

Não há nada que não seja estritamente lógico sobre isso.

É em vão que os espelhos são banidos do convento, as mulheres têm consciência dos seus rostos; Ora, as raparigas conscientes da sua beleza não se tornam facilmente freiras; sendo a vocação voluntária na proporção inversa à sua boa aparência, espera-se mais do feio do que do bonito. Daí um gosto vivo por meninas simples.

Toda esta aventura aumentou a importância do bom e velho Fauchelevent; obteve um triplo sucesso; aos olhos de Jean Valjean, a quem salvara e abrigara; nas do coveiro Gribier, que disse a si mesmo: "Poupou-me essa multa"; com o convento, que, sendo habilitado, graças a ele, a reter o caixão da Mãe Crucificação sob o altar, escapou a César e satisfez a Deus. Havia um caixão contendo um corpo no Petit-Picpus, e um caixão sem corpo no cemitério de Vaugirard, a ordem pública sem dúvida tinha sido profundamente perturbada por isso, mas ninguém estava ciente disso.

Quanto ao convento, a sua gratidão a Fauchelevent foi muito grande. Fauchelevent tornou-se o melhor dos serviçais e o mais precioso dos jardineiros. Por ocasião da próxima visita do arcebispo, a prioresa relatou o caso à sua Graça, fazendo uma espécie de confissão ao mesmo tempo, e ainda se vangloriando de seu ato. Ao deixar o convento, o arcebispo mencionou-o com aprovação, e num sussurro a M. de Latil, confessor de Monsieur, depois Arcebispo de Reims e Cardeal. Esta admiração por Fauchelevent tornou-se generalizada, pois chegou a Roma. Vimos uma nota dirigida pelo então Papa reinante, Leão XII., a um de seus parentes, monsenhor no estabelecimento do Núncio em Paris, e que trazia, como ele, o nome de Della Genga; continha estas linhas: "Parece que há num convento em Paris um excelente jardineiro, que também é um homem santo, chamado Fauvent". Nada deste triunfo chegou a Fauchelevent na sua cabana; continuou enxertando, capinando e encobrindo seus canteiros de melão, sem suspeitar minimamente de suas excelências e de sua santidade. Também não suspeitava da sua glória, tal como um touro de Durham ou Surrey cujo retrato está publicado no *London Illustrated News*, com esta inscrição: "Touro que levou o prémio no Cattle Show".

CAPÍTULO IX

CLUSURA

Cosette continuou a segurar a língua no convento.

Era natural que Cosette se pensasse filha de Jean Valjean. Além disso, como ela não sabia nada, ela não podia dizer nada e, em qualquer caso, ela não teria dito nada. Como acabamos de observar, nada treina as crianças para o silêncio como a infelicidade. Cosette tinha sofrido tanto, que temia tudo, até falar ou respirar. Uma única palavra tantas vezes derrubara uma avalanche sobre ela. Mal tinha começado a recuperar a confiança desde que esteve com Jean Valjean. Rapidamente se habituou ao convento. Só ela se arrependeu de Catarina, mas ela não ousou dizê-lo. Uma vez, porém, ela disse a Jean Valjean: "Pai, se eu soubesse, tê-la-ia trazido comigo".

Cosette tinha sido obrigada, ao tornar-se erudita no convento, a vestir as vestes dos alunos da casa. Jean Valjean conseguiu que eles lhe restituíssem as roupas que ela deixou de lado. Este era o mesmo fato de luto que ele a fizera vestir quando abandonara a estalagem dos Thénardiers. Não foi muito difícil mesmo agora. Jean Valjean trancou essas vestes, mais as meias e os sapatos, com uma quantidade de cânfora e todos os aromáticos em que abundam conventos, numa pequena valise que encontrou meios de adquirir. Ele colocou essa valise em uma cadeira perto de sua cama, e ele sempre carregava a chave sobre sua pessoa. "Pai", perguntou-lhe Cosette um dia, "o que há naquela caixa que cheira tão bem"?

O Padre Fauchelevent recebeu outra recompensa pela sua boa ação, além da glória que acabamos de mencionar, e da qual ele nada sabia; em primeiro lugar, fê-lo feliz; depois, tinha muito menos trabalho, uma vez que era partilhado. Por fim, como gostava muito de rapé, achou a presença de M. Madeleine uma vantagem, na medida em que usava três vezes mais do que tinha feito anteriormente, e isso de uma forma infinitamente mais luxuosa, visto que M. Madeleine pagava por isso.

As freiras não adotaram o nome de Ultime, chamaram Jean Valjean *de outro Fauvent.*

Se essas santas mulheres tivessem possuído alguma coisa do olhar de Javert, elas acabariam por notar que, quando havia alguma tarefa a ser feita do lado de fora em nome do jardim, era sempre o velho Fauchelevent, o velho, o enfermo, o coxo, que ia, e nunca o outro; mas, quer os olhos constantemente fixados em Deus não saibam espiar, quer estejam, por preferência, ocupados em vigiar uns aos outros, não prestaram atenção a isso.

Além disso, foi bom para Jean Valjean que ele se manteve perto e não se mexeu. Javert assistiu ao trimestre por mais de um mês.

Este convento era para Jean Valjean como uma ilha cercada por golfos. Doravante, aquelas quatro paredes constituíam o seu mundo. Ele viu o suficiente do céu lá para permitir que ele preservasse sua serenidade, e Cosette o suficiente para permanecer feliz.

Uma vida muito doce começou para ele.

Habitava a antiga cabana no final do jardim, em companhia de Fauchelevent. Este casebre, construído de lixo velho, que ainda existia em 1845, era composto, como o leitor já sabe, por três câmaras, todas totalmente nuas e sem nada além das paredes. A principal tinha sido abandonada, à força, pois Jean Valjean opôs-se em vão, a M. Madeleine, pelo Padre Fauchelevent. As paredes desta câmara tinham como ornamento, além dos dois pregos onde pendurar a rótula e o cesto, uma nota monarquista de 93, aplicada na parede sobre a chaminé, e da qual o seguinte é um fac-símile exato:

Este espécime de papel-moeda vendeano tinha sido pregado na parede pelo jardineiro anterior, um velho Chouan, que tinha morrido no convento, e cujo lugar Fauchelevent tinha tomado.

Jean Valjean trabalhava no jardim todos os dias e tornava-se muito útil. Ele tinha sido anteriormente um podador de árvores, e ele alegremente encontrou-se um jardineiro mais uma vez. Recorde-se que conhecia todo o tipo de segredos e recibos para a agricultura. Transformou-os em vantagem. Quase todas as árvores do pomar estavam não enxertadas e selvagens. Ele os fez brotar e fazê-los produzir excelentes frutos.

Cosette tinha permissão para passar uma hora com ele todos os dias. Como as irmãs eram melancólicas e ele era gentil, a criança fazia comparações e o adorava. Na hora marcada, ela voou para a cabana. Quando entrou na humilde cabana, encheu-a de paraíso. Jean Valjean floresceu e sentiu sua felicidade aumentar com a felicidade que ele proporcionou a Cosette. A alegria que inspiramos tem esta propriedade encantadora, que, longe de crescer escassa, como todas as reflexões, nos retorna mais radiante do que nunca. Nas horas de recreação, Jean Valjean a observava correndo e brincando ao longe, e distinguia sua risada da dos demais.

Pois Cosette riu agora.

O rosto de Cosette até tinha sofrido uma mudança, até certo ponto. A melancolia tinha desaparecido dela. Um sorriso é o mesmo que sol; bane o inverno do semblante humano.

Fim do recreio, quando Cosette entrou novamente na casa, Jean Valjean olhou para as janelas de sua sala de aula e, à noite, levantou-se para olhar para as janelas de seu dormitório.

Além disso, Deus tem os seus próprios caminhos; o convento contribuiu, como Cosette, para manter e completar a obra do Bispo em Jean Valjean. É certo que a virtude se junta ao orgulho de um lado. Uma ponte construída pelo diabo existe lá. Jean Valjean estivera, inconscientemente, talvez, toleravelmente perto daquele lado e daquela ponte, quando a Providência lançou a sua sorte no convento do Petit-Picpus; enquanto se comparava apenas ao Bispo, considerava-se indigno e mantinha-se humilde; mas, há algum tempo, ele vinha se comparando aos homens em geral, e o orgulho começava a brotar. Quem sabe? Poderia ter acabado por regressar muito gradualmente ao ódio.

O convento parou-o nesse caminho descendente.

Este era o segundo lugar de cativeiro que ele tinha visto. Na sua juventude, naquilo que tinha sido para ele o início da sua vida, e mais tarde, muito recentemente de novo, tinha contemplado outro: um lugar terrível, um lugar terrível, cujas gravidades lhe tinham sempre aparecido a iniquidade da justiça e o crime da lei. Agora, depois das galés, viu o claustro; e quando ele meditava como ele tinha feito parte das galés, e que ele agora, por assim dizer, era um espectador do claustro, ele confrontou os dois em sua própria mente com ansiedade.

Às vezes cruzava os braços e apoiava-se na enxada, e lentamente descia as espirais intermináveis de devaneio.

Recordou os seus antigos companheiros: como eram miseráveis; levantaram-se de madrugada e labutaram até à noite; dificilmente lhes era permitido dormir; deitavam-se em camas de acampamento, onde nada era tolerado senão colchões de dois centímetros de espessura, em quartos que eram aquecidos apenas nos meses mais rigorosos do ano; estavam vestidos com terríveis blusas vermelhas; Foi-lhes permitido, como um grande favor, calças de linho no tempo mais quente, e uma blusa de lã Carter nas costas quando estava muito frio; não bebiam vinho e não comiam carne, exceto quando iam em "serviço de fadiga". Viviam sem nome, designados apenas por números, e convertiam-se, de certa forma, em cifras, com olhos abatidos, com vozes baixas, com cabeças tosquiadas, debaixo do cuzinho e em desgraça.

Então sua mente voltou para os seres que ele tinha sob seus olhos.

Estes seres também viviam com cabeças tosquiadas, com olhos abatidos, com vozes baixas, não em desgraça, mas em meio às zombarias do mundo, não com as costas machucadas com o, mas com os ombros dilacerados com sua disciplina. Seus nomes, também, haviam desaparecido entre os homens; já não existiam, a não ser sob denominações austeras. Nunca comeram carne e nunca beberam vinho; muitas vezes permaneciam até à noite sem comer; vestiam-se, não com uma blusa vermelha, mas com uma mortalha preta, de lã, pesada no verão e fina no inverno, sem o poder de acrescentar ou subtrair nada; sem ter mesmo, de acordo com a estação, o recurso da roupa de linho ou do manto de lã; e durante seis meses no ano usaram serge chemises que lhes deu febre. Habitavam, não em salas aquecidas apenas durante o frio rigoroso, mas em celas onde nunca se acendeu fogo; dormiam, não em colchões de dois centímetros de espessura, mas em palha. E, finalmente, nem sequer lhes foi permitido dormir; Todas as noites, depois de um dia de labuta, eram obrigados, no cansaço do primeiro sono, no momento em que adormeciam bem e começavam a aquecer, a despertar-se, a levantar-se e a ir rezar numa capela gelada e sombria, com os joelhos sobre as pedras.

Em certos dias, cada um desses seres, por sua vez, tinha que permanecer por doze horas sucessivas em uma postura ajoelhada, ou prostrada, com o rosto sobre a calçada, e os braços estendidos na forma de uma cruz.

Os outros eram homens; eram mulheres.

O que tinham feito aqueles homens? Roubaram, violaram, pilharam, assassinaram, assassinaram. Eram bandidos, falsificadores, envenenadores, incendiários, assassinos, parricidas. O que fizeram essas mulheres? Não tinham feito nada.

Por um lado, roubo de estrada, fraude, engano, violência, sensualidade, homicídio, todo tipo de sacrilégio, toda variedade de crime; por outro, uma coisa só, a inocência.

Inocência perfeita, quase arrebatada no céu numa misteriosa assunção, ligada à terra pela virtude, já possuindo algo do céu através da santidade.

Por um lado, confidências sobre crimes, que são trocadas em sussurros; por outro, a confissão de faltas feita em voz alta. E que crimes! E que defeitos!

Por um lado, miasmas; por outro, um perfume inefável. Por um lado, uma praga moral, guardada da vista, aprisionada sob o alcance do canhão, e literalmente devorando suas vítimas atingidas pela peste; por outro, a chama casta de todas as almas na mesma lareira. Lá, escuridão; aqui, a sombra; mas uma sombra cheia de brilhos de luz, e de brilhos cheios de brilho.

Dois redutos da escravidão; mas no primeiro, libertação possível, um limite legal sempre à vista, e depois, fuga. No segundo, a perpetuidade; a única esperança, no extremo longínquo do futuro, essa luz ténue da liberdade a que os homens chamam morte.

No primeiro, os homens são amarrados apenas com correntes; no outro, acorrentado pela fé.

O que resultou do primeiro? Uma maldição imensa, o ranger de dentes, o ódio, a crueldade desesperada, um grito de raiva contra a sociedade humana, um sarcasmo contra o céu.

Que resultados resultaram do segundo? Bênçãos e amor.

E nesses dois lugares, tão parecidos, mas tão desiguais, essas duas espécies de seres que eram tão diferentes, estavam passando pelo mesmo trabalho, a expiação.

Jean Valjean compreendeu bem a expiação do primeiro; essa expiação pessoal, a expiação para si mesmo. Mas ele não compreendeu o destes últimos, o das criaturas sem censura e sem manchas, e tremeu quando se perguntou: A expiação de quê? Que expiação?

Uma voz dentro da sua consciência respondeu: "A mais divina das generosidades humanas, a expiação pelos outros".

Aqui toda a teoria pessoal é retida; somos apenas o narrador; colocamo-nos no ponto de vista de Jean Valjean e traduzimos as suas impressões.

Diante dos seus olhos tinha o sublime cume da abnegação, o mais alto tom de virtude possível; a inocência que perdoa aos homens as suas faltas e que expia em seu lugar; servidão submetida, tortura aceita, castigo reclamado pelas almas que não pecaram, para poupá-la às almas que caíram; o amor da humanidade engolido pelo amor de Deus, mas mesmo aí preservando o seu carácter distinto e mediador; seres doces e débeis possuindo a miséria dos castigados e o sorriso dos que são recompensados.

E lembrou-se de que tinha ousado murmurar!

Muitas vezes, no meio da noite, ele se levantava para ouvir o canto grato daquelas criaturas inocentes pesadas de gravidade, e o sangue corria frio em suas veias ao pensar que aqueles que eram justamente castigados erguiam suas vozes para o céu apenas em blasfêmia, e que ele, desgraçado que era, havia balançado o punho contra Deus.

Havia uma coisa marcante que o levava a meditar profundamente, como um sussurro de advertência da própria Providência: o escalonamento daquele muro, a passagem daquelas barreiras, a aventura aceita mesmo correndo o risco de morte, a subida dolorosa e difícil, todos aqueles esforços até, que ele fizera para escapar daquele outro lugar de expiação, fizera-o para entrar neste. Seria este um símbolo do seu destino? Esta casa era igualmente uma prisão e tinha uma semelhança melancólica com aquela outra para onde fugira, mas nunca tinha concebido uma ideia de algo semelhante.

Mais uma vez ele viu grades, parafusos, barras de ferro – para proteger quem? Anjos.

Estas altas muralhas que ele tinha visto em torno de tigres, ele agora contemplava mais uma vez em torno de cordeiros.

Este era um lugar de expiação, e não de castigo; e, no entanto, era ainda mais austera, mais sombria e mais impiedosa do que a outra.

Estas virgens eram ainda mais sobrecarregadas do que os condenados. Um vento frio e duro, aquele vento que tinha arrefecido a sua juventude, atravessou a grade barrada e fechada dos abutres; uma brisa ainda mais dura e mordaz soprava na gaiola dessas pombas.

Porquê?

Quando pensou nestas coisas, tudo o que havia dentro de si perdeu-se em espanto perante este mistério de sublimidade.

Nestas meditações, o seu orgulho desapareceu. Ele examinou seu próprio coração de todas as maneiras; Sentiu a sua mesquinhez, e muitas vezes chorou. Tudo o que entrara na sua vida nos últimos seis meses o levara de volta às santas injunções do Bispo; Cosette através do amor, o convento através da humildade.

Às vezes, no crepúsculo, numa hora em que o jardim estava deserto, podia ser visto de joelhos no meio da caminhada que contornava a capela, em frente à janela através da qual tinha olhado na noite da sua chegada, e virava-se para o local onde, como sabia, A irmã estava fazendo reparação, prostrada em oração. Assim, ele orou enquanto se ajoelhava diante da irmã.

Parecia que ele não ousava ajoelhar-se diretamente diante de Deus.

Tudo o que o rodeava, aquele jardim tranquilo, aquelas flores perfumadas, aquelas crianças que proferiam gritos alegres, aquelas mulheres graves e simples, aquele claustro silencioso, lentamente o permeava, e pouco a pouco, a sua alma foi se compondo de silêncio como o claustro, de perfume como as flores, de simplicidade como as mulheres, de alegria como as crianças. E depois refletiu que tinham sido duas casas de Deus que o receberam sucessivamente em dois momentos críticos da sua vida: o primeiro, quando todas as portas se fecharam e quando a sociedade humana o rejeitou; a segunda, num momento em que a sociedade humana tinha voltado a persegui-lo, e em que as galés voltavam a bocejar; e que, não fosse o primeiro, teria recaído no crime, e se não fosse o segundo, no tormento.

Todo o seu coração se derreteu em gratidão, e ele amou cada vez mais.

Muitos anos se passaram assim; Cosette estava crescendo.

[O FINAL DO VOLUME II "COSETTE"]

www.ingramcontent.com/pod-product-compliance
Ingram Content Group UK Ltd.
Pitfield, Milton Keynes, MK11 3LW, UK
UKHW030839180225
455237UK00005B/26